ŌUR

THE HISTORY OF GLASS

THE HISTORY OF GLASS

General Editors Dan Klein and Ward Lloyd
Foreword by Robert Charleston

LITTLE, BROWN AND COMPANY

A LITTLE BROWN BOOK

This edition published in 2000 by
Little, Brown and Company (UK)
Brettenham House, Lancaster Place
London WC2E 7EN

First published in 1984 by Orbis Publishing Limited
Reprinted 1989 and 1992 by MacDonald & Co (Publishers) Ltd
under the Black Cat imprint.
Reprinted under Black Cat imprint by Little, Brown and Company in 1993.

© Little, Brown and Company (UK) 1992

ISBN 1-85605-544-2

Printed in The Czech Republic
50029/5

CONTENTS

FOREWORD

The writing of glass history has a full century of practice behind it, yet it is nearly forty years since a comprehensive work, taking the story from antiquity to modern times, has been written in English. W. B. Honey, in his *Glass: a Handbook for the study of Glass Vessels of all Periods and Countries and a Guide to the Museum Collection* (1946) was a worthy successor to Alexander Nesbitt, who in his *Descriptive Catalogue of the Glass Vessels in the South Kensington Museum* (1878), basing himself on the same collection as it then was, wrote an introduction to the world history of glass which has been laid under contribution ever since. Nesbitt had also compiled (in 1871) a catalogue of the Slade Collection, which formed the major part of the British Museum's glass collection outside its Antiquities Departments. Books based on specific museum collections are inevitably circumscribed by the limitations of those collections, extensive though they may be. In 1907, however, Edward Dillon produced, as a contribution to the Connoisseur's Library, a volume which tackled the whole history of glass with an insight into the nature of the material and its working which far surpassed anything that had gone before. The inter-war period was dominated by Robert Schmidt's *Das Glas*, first published in 1912 but reissued in 1922, a book which enormously increased knowledge of German – and to a less degree Venetian – glass, while at the same time dealing effectively, if more superficially, with the glass of other regions.

Since the Second World War there has been a notable quickening of interest in glass. The creation of the Corning Museum of Glass in 1951, and the annual appearance since 1959 of its *Journal of Glass Studies*, have created an international focus for the deepening study of glass history. Museums devoted specifically to glass have followed, at St Helens, Lancashire (The Pilking-ton Museum); at Växjö in Småland, Sweden, centre of the country's glass industry; at Frauenau in the Bayerische Wald; and at Riihimäki in Finland. These have joined older existing museums devoted exclusively to glass, such as the Museo Vetrario in Murano; or museums where the glass collections dominate, such as the Musée Curtius at Liège. To these concentrations of glass material may be added the collections annexed to many old-established glasshouses, such as Baccarat in France, or Stevens & Williams in England: these provide a condensed view of the productions of the individual firms in the course of their long lives.

To this vastly increased availability of historic glass may be added the inception of an international association for the history of glass, begun at Liège in 1958 under the title 'Journées Internationales du Verre' and thereafter meeting more or less triennially. Its *Annales* have provided an international forum for glass studies second only to the *Journal of Glass Studies* itself. The accelerating interest in the subject has in turn led to the organization of a number of important exhibitions by individual museums (such as the 'Masterpieces of Glass Exhibition' at the British Museum in 1968), and the production of an impressive number of catalogues of museum collections of glass.

All these initiatives in the glass field have generated a considerable body of literature on the subject, and provided in a measure unknown to our predecessors the materials for an ever-deeper study of the history of glass. What has hitherto been lacking, however, has been a general work like this one which would serve as a guide to the whole subject in its enormous sweep. The forty years since the appearance of Honey's work also deserve a proportionate treatment, and this 'cutting edge' of the art receives its due share of attention in the present book.

Robert J. Charleston

Venetian greyish glass goblet with enamelled and gilt decoration, sixteenth century.
Height: 22cm (8⅝in)
The National Trust, Waddesdon Manor, Buckinghamshire.

CHAPTER ONE

THE ORIGINS AND EARLY HISTORY OF GLASS

A Roman cage-cup, or diatretum, *made in the fourth century AD. Such vessels are among the most outstanding glass products of their age, and show the high degree of technical skill with which that material was being worked at this time: it is thought that they were made from a single blown-glass blank in which the network of circles surrounding the body was produced by an undercutting technique. Round the rim is a Latin inscription of raised glass letters formed in the same way.*
Height: 12 cm (5in)

Glass is a remarkable substance, made from the simplest raw materials. It can be coloured or colourless, monochrome or polychrome, transparent, translucent or opaque. It is lightweight, impermeable to liquids, readily cleaned and reused, durable yet fragile, and often very beautiful. Glass can be decorated in multiple ways and its optical properties are exceptional. In all its myriad forms—as tableware, containers, in architecture and design—glass represents a major achievement in the history of technological developments.

Since the Bronze Age, about 3000 BC, glass has been used for making various kinds of objects. It was first made from a mixture of silica (from sand), lime and an alkali such as soda or potash, and these remained the basic ingredients of glass until the development of lead glass in the seventeenth century. When heated, the mixture becomes soft and malleable, and can be formed by various techniques into a vast array of shapes and sizes. The homogeneous mass thus formed by melting then cools to create glass, but in contrast to most materials formed in this way (metals, for instance), glass lacks the crystalline structure normally associated with solids, and instead retains the random molecular structure of a liquid. In effect, as glass cools, it progressively stiffens until rigid, but does so without setting up a network of interlocking crystals customarily associated with that process. This is why glass shatters so easily when dealt a sudden blow, why glass deteriorates over time (a process call devitrification), especially when exposed to moisture, and why glassware must be slowly annealed (reheated and uniformly cooled) after manufacture to release internal stresses induced by uneven cooling.

Another unusual feature of glass is the manner in which its viscosity changes as it turns from a cold, rigid solid into a hot, ductile liquid. Unlike metals which flow or 'freeze' at specific temperatures, glass progressively softens as the temperature rises, going through varying stages of malleability, until it flows like a thick syrup. Each stage of malleability allows the glass to be manipulated into various forms, by different techniques, and if suddenly cooled the object retains the shape achieved at that point. Glass is thus amenable to a greater number of heat-forming techniques than most other materials.

Chemically, glass is a generic term for a substance manufactured from an endless number of recipes. Although most glassware contains the same basic ingredients, the term glass does not refer to a specific chemical compound, since different types of glass have a different chemical composition and exhibit different chemical and physical properties. As a result, glass has the widest applications in modern times, both in industry and the home. While some types of glass are most suitable for window-panes or services of cut 'crystal', others are designed to be spun into fibres or formed into the heat shields of spacecraft.

Ancient Techniques

In antiquity, silica (silicon dioxide or SiO_2) was the major constituent of glass, with soda added as a flux to facilitate the melting of the batch, and lime as a stabilizer making the glass less vulnerable to the adverse effects of water. To this primary mixture chemical compounds (metallic oxides) might be added to give the glass colour or remove it, or to make the glass opaque. Four major manufacturing methods (with many variations, both major and minor) were

These small, rod-formed head pendants and beads dating from the late sixth to late third century BC are attributed to Phoenician craftsmen who traded them throughout the Mediterranean area. Heights: 2.5–5.8 cm (1–2¼ in)

standard. These were rod- and core-forming; casting with open and closed moulds; free blowing; and blowing into moulds and forms of various kinds. These techniques have been deduced from physical examination and scientific analysis of ancient pieces, analogy to contemporary practices, and modern attempts to reproduce glassware in the ancient manner. Despite such studies, however, a good deal remains to be learned about the actual workings of ancient glass factories and about specific glass-making methods. Tableware was reproduced in numerous centres and cultures over many centuries, and so it is unlikely that there were uniform procedures or a common development. Indeed, most recent research has revealed an unexpectedly rich variety of techniques, tools, and practices in diverse times and places.

Rod- and core-forming, techniques first developed in the Bronze Age, involved building up a thick core of material round a metal rod into the desired shape of the vessel, usually a small unguent bottle of some sort. The core, a combination of clay and sand (but not sand alone) with an organic binder such as dung, was then covered by hot glass, either by dipping it into a crucible or, more probably, by repeatedly trailing glass over it. The outside of the vessel was

then rolled, or 'marvered', on a flat stone surface, to make it smooth. Decoration in the form of trails or blobs was applied and often combed into feather or festoon patterns, before it, too, was marvered into the surface. Once the bottle was annealed, the metal rod could be removed and the core scraped out, leaving a rough, pitted, and usually reddish interior. Handles, lugs and bases were either applied separately or drawn out from the body while the glass was hot. Purely rod-formed objects, such as a group of head pendants normally ascribed to Phoenician craftsmen, were made in much the same manner except that they dispensed with a core and were formed directly on a metal rod. Presumably the rod was covered with a very thin layer of some material which acted as a separating agent.

Casting with moulds was another technique employed from the Bronze Age until late Roman times. A great many casting methods were used to produce articles ranging from tableware and containers to beads, jewellery, inlays, plaques and window-panes, and these methods applied knowledge gained in the ancient metal, ceramic, and faience industries. (Egyptian faience was a glass-like substance made principally from powdered quartz.) At its simplest, casting might involve the forcing of hot glass into an open mould to create beads, such as those favoured by Mycenaean warriors. More complex casting procedures required two or more interlocking moulds, either using a *cire perdue* (lost wax) technique or, more commonly, the progressive filling of the space between an inner and outer mould with hot glass until the space was full. For monochrome cast vessels this could be achieved either by forcing hot glass (in a manner not now fully understood) into the hollow space between the moulds, or by filling the space with powdered glass or segments of glass rods before placing the moulds in the kiln. This latter technique was undoubtedly used for certain mosaic-glass vessels. These were made of many small discs of glass thinly cut from long, preformed canes. The discs were placed side-by-side around a mould made in the desired shape of the vessel, generally a plate, dish, or bowl. Next, an outer mould was inserted on top of the discs to hold them in place while the heat of the kiln fused them together. The glass was then annealed, the moulds removed and the vessel finished by rotary polishing using lathes and abrasives. Rims, handles and base rings were either cast as part of the vessel or added later.

An alternative casting method, and one preferred by the Roman industry of the Augustan Age, involved the sagging of a glass blank over or in a 'former' mould. In this procedure a circular blank of the same size as the

desired vessel was made, either by crucible pouring or, in the case of mosaic wares, by fusing together sections or lengths of preformed polychrome canes. Once cooled, the blank was placed on, in, or over a single mould and heated in the kiln until it sagged under its own weight and achieved the appropriate shape. Once the vessel had been annealed, it could be lifted from the former and finished by rotary polishing. Since only one surface had been in contact with the mould, the time required for polishing was reduced by half.

The technique of free-blowing, still used today, was invented in the latter half of the first century BC, probably in the Syro-Palestinian region, and was quickly exploited by the burgeoning Roman industry under the Julio-Claudian emperors. It ultimately led to the discontinuance of most core and casting procedures, and even caused the demise of certain prominent ceramic industries, because it enabled glass-makers to produce vast quantities of inexpensive, desirable wares for the daily use of all classes of Roman imperial society. The technique itself was relatively straightforward and was quickly transmitted to workshops throughout the provinces of the Roman Empire. It simply required the blower to gather a gob of hot glass on the end of a hollow metal tube, or blowpipe, and to inflate it to form a bubble, or 'paraison'. As in modern practice, the paraison was again inflated, then shaped and cooled, often in an open, cup-shaped mould, rolled on the blower's bench, inflated further, shaped by wooden paddles and pincers or cut with tools (as dictated by experience) until the desired shape was achieved. Throughout the process the vessel was rotated to prevent sagging, and reheated in a kiln when necessary. For additional finishing and decorating, the vessel (while still hot) was knocked-off the blowpipe and its underside attached to a solid metal rod, called a pontil. The rim was then formed, and decoration, handles, base-rings and so forth might be added. The

vessel was then annealed. (A contemporary example of a Roman glass-blower at work in front of a small furnace is shown on the discus of a terracotta lamp which was found at Asseria in Yugoslavia.)

The invention of glass blowing led to the realization that the paraison could be inflated entirely or partially inside a hinged mould, which would impart both shape and decoration to the finished vessel. Such moulds, manufactured from wood, ceramic, or even metal, were especially popular in the first and second centuries AD, for drinking cups and beakers with scenes of the amphitheatre and circus, often with Greek and Latin inscriptions, or for containers in the form of human heads. Experiments with mould blowing led to the development of Roman prismatic or square bottles, the forerunners of all subsequent glass

Above: The rosette-shaped beads of this Mycenaean necklace were made by casting into stone moulds, using translucent blue glass (now weathered white). They are linked with faience spacers. Length: 28 cm (11in) (Toledo Museum of Art, Toledo, Ohio)

Above: The scene depicted in this drawing of the discus of a Roman lamp from Asseria, Yugoslavia, is of a Roman glass-blower before a small furnace which appears to be similar to the one found at Nora in Sardinia (above left).

Left: Two views of the Lycurgus Cup (fourth century AD), a type of cage-cup and the culmination of Roman achievement in glass cutting. It is also important technically because of its colouring: the presence of minute amounts of gold and silver in the glass causes it to change colour from green in reflected light to magenta in transmitted light. Height: 16.5cm (6½ in) (British Museum, London)

containers made by a comparable process. These bottles were blown into body moulds with three to thirteen (but usually four) sides, with a bottom piece customarily bearing an inscription or geometric design.

A variation on the mould-blowing process involved further inflating the vessel once it had been lifted from the mould, causing the shape and decoration to become less pronounced, or twisted in a uniform manner by the rotation of the vessel on the pipe. Such expanded, mould-blown wares were particularly common in the late Roman and early Byzantine periods, when glass-makers blew vessels into wire forms or matrices, then further inflated them, to produce patterns of indistinct ridges and grooves or other geometric designs.

The colours of ancient glass depended both on the chemical composition of the batch and on the manufacturing process, in particular the oxidation or reduction state of the furnace and of the glass while hot. Most vessels fall into one of three main categories: naturally coloured, colourless (decolourized) or intentionally coloured. The bluish-green, light green or greenish-yellow colour of most ancient pieces is due to iron oxides and other impurities being present in the ingredients of the batch. Roman cinerary urns are typical examples of naturally coloured vessels, while the shade of cast Hellenistic bowls, progressing from a distinct golden-brown to dark olive or greenish-yellow, is the result of the oxidation or reduction conditions of the glass prior to and during manufacture. The addition of manganese or antimony neutralized the effects of the iron impurities, resulting in a clear, colourless glass. Since such glass closely resembled rock crystal, a commodity prized by most ancient cultures, colourless vessels

with faceted and cut designs were especially popular throughout antiquity.

Intentionally coloured glassware, often in strong hues, both translucent and opaque, was caused by the addition of metallic oxides originally discovered by trial and error but perfected by every major ancient industry. Copper, for instance, produced blue, green or opaque red glass, depending on the conditions of the furnace. Manganese under the right circumstances yielded a purple glass and cobalt an attractive dark blue. Perhaps the most sophisticated use of such additives was achieved by the Roman industry of the fourth century AD, when producing dichroic (two-coloured) glass. The recipes called for the addition of powdered gold and silver which caused the glass to show a different colour depending on whether light was reflected from its surface or transmitted through

it. The Rothschild Lycurgus Cup, presently housed in the British Museum, is the most celebrated example of such a technique. The cup is a striking jade-green colour in reflected light and a vivid magenta in transmitted light. Among translucent colours, royal blue, purple, yellow and several greens were common; and among opaque colours, red, white, yellow, light blue, turquoise and peacock blue, orange, diverse greens and even 'flesh-colour' were known. Frequently the most desirable colours resembled natural stones such as lapis lazuli and agate or synthetic materials like faience and enamels. Indeed, many of the first uses of glass were as substitutes for other substances, and in several ancient languages glass is actually referred to as 'man-made stone'.

The iridescent gold and silver surfaces now associated with so much ancient glass are the

Below: These late Roman/Coptic vessels excavated at Karanis, Egypt, are, from left to right, a small conical lamp, a shallow bowl, a flask and an oval dish. The colouration, pale green and light yellow, is a result of iron and other impurities in the sand from which they were made. Their extremely good condition is owing to the dry Egyptian climate. Height of flask: 23.4cm (9³/₁₆ in) (Toledo Museum of Art, Toledo, Ohio)

result of weathering and devitrification and were never intentional. This rainbow-like effect occurs when thin layers of the alkali in the glass are slaked out over time by moisture and chemical agents, especially when the glass has lain in the earth for many years. Eventually the surface becomes severely pitted, and the object corrodes and disintegrates. Only vessels preserved in exceedingly dry climates such as that of Egypt have escaped the deleterious effects of such weathering.

The Late Bronze Age

Although the place and time of the discovery of glass is uncertain, the earliest known industry producing articles of glass was active in the Bronze Age by the middle of the third millennium BC. This industry, first founded in western Asia, probably in the Mitannian or Hurrian region of Mesopotamia, was the natural outgrowth of experimentation with vitreous glazes used to embellish pottery, tiles and other objects, or with faience. The earliest archaeologically datable objects are beads, seals, inlays and plaques. Vessels appeared later, probably by the close of the sixteenth century BC. Shortly afterwards, knowledge of the manufacture of glass spread quickly to northern Syria, Cyprus, Egypt and the Aegean, where the palace-dominated civilizations of the Late Bronze Age used glass as a semi-precious material.

Little is known about the first vessels manufactured in western Asia, owing to their poor state of preservation, but all surviving pieces represent small unguent bottles or drinking cups made in a core or cast-mosaic technique. Shapes often resemble contemporary pottery forms, such as the footed 'bilbil' jug found at Hala Sultan Teeke near Larnaka in Cyprus and now in the British Museum. The jug is attributed to a Syrian or Cypriot workshop operating in the first half of the fourteenth century BC. Contemporary with such core pieces are others known from Marlik in Iran and Tell al Rimah in Iraq which were built up in geometric patterns of short, circular cane sections in bright colours. A deep mosaic goblet with a knobbed base from the latter site has segments of opaque blue, yellow, green and white laid in zigzag bands over the body of the vessel.

Far better known are the handsome products of the prolific Egyptian industry of the Bronze Age, which produced vessels and a vast array of other objects that display the sophisticated level of technology achieved by artisans of this early epoch. Vessels, often recovered in pristine condition, are distinguished by such typically

Egyptian shapes as the palm-column flask and wide-mouthed jar (*krateriskos*), and by opaque and translucent colours closely imitating Egyptian faience. All were made on a core. Such wares were once thought to represent the first examples of ancient glass vessels, but are now known to date from the fifteenth to the thirteenth century BC, and are mainly attributed to the Eighteenth and Nineteenth Dynasties. The factories producing them, including the one at el Amarna excavated by Sir Flinders Petrie in 1894, were established after the expulsion of the Hyksos in the mid-sixteenth century BC and the subsequent formation of the New Kingdom

Below: Early core-made bottles manufactured in western Asia, like this Mesopotamian example from a Kassite grave at Ur (c. 1300 BC), are among the first vessels to be made of glass. Often in shape they resemble contemporary pottery forms. Height: 11.3cm (4½in) (British Museum, London)

Above: Dating from the fifteenth to thirteenth centuries BC, these core-made unguent jars are among the many pieces fashioned in Egypt under the Eighteenth and Nineteenth Dynasties. Shapes are characteristically Egyptian; the decoration consists of brilliantly coloured trails that were combed and marvered on the vessels. Height of vase: 10cm (3¹⁵⁄₁₆in) Height of flask: 11cm (4³⁄₈in) (Toledo Museum of Art, Toledo, Ohio)

Related to items produced in Egypt are others discovered on archaeological sites on Cyprus and Crete and in southern Greece, Anatolia and the Syro-Palestinian area. Although many of these pieces, especially core-formed containers, were imported from Egypt, others are sufficiently different in shape, decorative patterns and colouration to suggest regional production. This is particularly evident in a series of bottles in the form of pomegranates, which are found almost exclusively on Cyprus, and in a uniform group of blue plaques depicting the near-eastern goddess Astarte, mainly known from Syrian and Palestinian excavations. There was another active glass industry in southern Iran, manufacturing white and blue spiralling rods which once ornamented the doorways of the Elamite ziggurat at Choga Zambil near Susa. In the Peloponnese, Mycenaean artisans cast hundreds of blue glass beads and pendants in open stone moulds, for use as personal adornments, in the form of appliqués for garments and headgear. The glass itself so closely resembles objects made in Mesopotamia and Syria that it may be that the Mycenaeans imported quantities of raw glass, just as they did ingots of copper and bronze, for use by their own craftsmen.

The Bronze Age industry of the eastern Mediterranean flourished at most of the points of high civilization between the early fifteenth and thirteenth centuries BC. While knowledge of glass-making spread widely at this time, glass was still a rare and costly material, used often with precious metals, ivory and other luxury goods, and sharing with them a comparable value.

In most instances, factories seem to have been based at major urban centres, where production fell under royal or aristocratic patronage. The size of these workshops was small, output was correspondingly limited, and the glass-makers formed an élite corps of workers devoted to an esoteric craft. Although these men commanded a sophisticated range of expertise, much of it borrowed from other well-developed technologies such as the ceramics, metal and lapidary industries, the process was as much imbued with magic and mystique as it was with technical facility. Certain Mesopotamian cuneiform tablets with allusions to the Bronze Age contain as many references to mysteries surrounding the making of glass as they do to accurate recipes and actual procedures.

Around 1200 BC most of the leading centres of the Late Bronze Age came under attack and collapsed, owing to war and famine. The Minoan and Mycenaean societies in southern Greece and on Crete and Cyprus vanished altogether, as did the powerful Hittite Kingdom in Anatolia. The

under such energetic rulers as Thutmose III or, later, Ramses II. In fact, it has been argued that the military campaigns of Thutmose into Palestine and Syria after 1481 BC caused Asiatic glass-workers to migrate to Egypt and found the Egyptian industry. At least three surviving vessels carry the cartouche of that pharoah, and demonstrate that the factories were in operation before his death in 1450.

Other glass objects manufactured by the same shops were many and varied; they include beads, scarabs, amulets, plaques, furniture knobs and inlays. More noteworthy are cast figurines, such as one depicting the young pharoah Tutankhamen which was found among the spectacular grave-goods of his tomb. Other glass objects found in his tomb were his headrest and most of the inlays embellishing the great throne and the first, second and third coffins.

coastal districts of Palestine, according to the Bible, were ravaged by invading Philistines, and sea peoples of uncertain origin massed in Libya and along the coast of Africa to attack Egypt, first in 1220, then again in 1189 and 1186 BC. Following the eclipse of these states, a Dark Age spread across the eastern Mediterranean and western Asia. Accompanying it was a general decline in the level of culture which seriously disrupted commerce and manufacturing, especially industries producing luxury articles. Few archaeological sites spanning the years between 1200 and 1000 BC yield glass of any sort.

Iron Age Revival

In the tenth century BC the eastern Mediterranean began to emerge from the Dark Age, and over the next three hundred years new peoples and kingdoms rose to prominence. Among them were the Phrygians of Anatolia, the Greeks in the Aegean, and the Phoenicians along the Palestinian littoral, while in the Tigris-Euphrates Valley a formidable empire under the Assyrians came to the fore as the dominant power in western Asia. At the same time, largely owing to the colonizing and commercial ventures of Greeks and Phoenicians, Italy and the western Mediterranean for the first time entered the mainstream of the ancient civilized world. Accompanying this political renascence was a vigorous revival of the arts and crafts, glass-making included. In terms of vessel manufacture the revival first occurred in Mesopotamia, and somewhat later in Syria, where artisans again produced core-made bottles. The shapes differed from their Bronze Age predecessors, but the technology and many of the colours (now weathered to an undistinguished grey) remained much the same. Examples from Ur, Samarra, Babylon, Nippur and Nimrud, predominantly from the eighth century BC, are known. The Syrian or Phoenician production, attributed principally to the late eighth and seventh centuries, led in turn to the establishment in the subsequent century of factories manufacturing core-formed bottles in Greek ceramic shapes, an innovation which was to be of the greatest significance for glass-making from the sixth to the second century BC.

Glass-makers operating in Assyria or, more probably, along the Phoenician coast, not only produced containers for scents and unguents, but exquisite carved ivory plaques and panels ornamented with many-coloured glass inlays. This same industry also seems to have introduced cast monochromatic tableware, usually in pale green (possibly incompletely decolourized), but also colourless and deliberately coloured. Hemispherical drinking bowls were especially popular, and more than a hundred examples appeared in the excavations of the Assyrian capital at Nimrud, destroyed in 612 BC. Although most of these vessels are plain, a few are engraved with figures, gilded and painted, or decorated with small glass inlays akin to those on Phoenician ivories. Of similar date are thick-walled, light to dark green flasks of variable size and form, all cast as blanks and finished by cutting, grinding, and polishing once the glass was cold. The most famous example, also found in the ruins of Nimrud and now in the British Museum, is the so-called Sargon Vase,

Below: The Sargon Vase, an alabastron which bears an inscription naming Sargon II, King of Assyria (722-705 BC), was made by casting a blank which was then finished by cutting, grinding and polishing. Height: 8cm (3in) (British Museum, London)

which carries an inscription naming Sargon II (fl. 722-705 BC), the enterprising king of Assyria. Comparable bowls and flasks have been found throughout the Mediterranean area, from Aliseda in Spain to a few vessels from Italy, a bowl from Crete and others from Cyprus, and many fragments from Nubia, but most specimens are from Assyrian or Palestinian sites. Although these diverse sites make it difficult to ascribe the glass either to Assyrian or Phoenician sources, the finds from Italy and Spain suggest strongly that Phoenicians were the traders in glass, if not the manufacturers. Possibly the most convincing evidence rests with an intact blue bowl and a fragmentary colourless example discovered among the spectacular gold, silver, bronze, ivory and amber grave goods of the Tomba Bernardini at Palestrina in central Italy. Recent reassessment of the tomb has led specialists to conclude that the bulk of the objects are of Phoenician origin.

Elsewhere, there is evidence for still other Iron Age glass industries. These include a mosaic workshop manufacturing cups of variegated glass, as illustrated by two fine beakers excavated at Hasanlu in north-western Iran; a shop producing small saucer-shaped cosmetic palettes discovered mainly in Palestine; and another manufacturing cast and polished colourless

bowls with handsomely cut petal designs radiating outwards from the centre of the base. The only known example of this last group, recovered from Tumulus P at Gordion in Phrygia, dates from the ninth century. This omphalos bowl is the precursor of others which were popular mainly between the fifth and first centuries BC, whose shapes and cut decoration closely imitate silver and bronze prototypes, but whose fabrics resemble rock crystal.

Probably because artisans from the eastern Mediterranean migrated westwards, knowledge of glass-making also spread to the emerging Iron Age cultures of Yugoslavia, southern Austria and Italy. By the close of the seventh century BC the Halstatt peoples inhabiting the southern watersheds of the Alps were using glass beads, leech-shaped brooch-runners on metal rods and small cups with marvered zigzag trails. These articles are unique to the region and were presumably manufactured by an Italo-Alpine workshop. Also of this period are a series of beads and brooch-runners and a uniform group of core-formed bottles which were found solely on Etruscan sites in central Italy. The vessels are mostly small pitchers (*oinochoai*), either blue, yellow or brown, with pincered spikes pulled outwards from the body in irregular rows. Undoubtedly, these

Above: Typical of the pre-Hellenistic and Hellenistic periods are these core-formed unguent bottles dating from the sixth to the early first centuries BC. They were made in great numbers and sold with perfumes and ointments inside them throughout the Mediterranean region. Their shapes, which copied those of contemporary Greek ceramic vases, included the amphora (far right), the oinochoe (second from right), alabastron (far left) and an unusual stamnos (third from left). Heights: 8.9cm (3½in)– 19.7cm (7¾in) (Toledo Museum of Art, Toledo, Ohio)

Left: The Achaemenid Persians of the fifth century BC developed a flourishing glass industry producing cast and cut bowls in colourless or greenish glass like this one, that imitated contemporary fashions in silver and bronze, which were then in vogue both inside and outside the Persian Empire. Diameter: 17.2cm (6 25/32in) (Toledo Museum of Art, Toledo, Ohio)

items were all the products of an indigenous Etruscan industry operating between the early seventh and fifth centuries BC.

Between the sixth and fourth centuries BC most of the trends and traditions of the early Iron Age continued. Successive industries, some transient, others more enduring, made table- and storage-wares and other assorted objects such as jewellery, beads, pendants, seals, and inlays. Glass was still a rare and relatively costly commodity, a substitute or alternative for other artificial and natural materials. Although the number of glass-making centres increased, the number of items produced remained quite small. Manufacturing techniques relied principally on core- and rod-forming or on casting in open and closed moulds, and the mosaic technique all but disappeared. Perhaps the principal innovation of the period was the increasing use of thick, colourless blanks, which were cast in moulds and then ground, polished and cut to produce vessels of superb quality.

Hallmarks of the age, however, are a series of core-made unguent bottles with forms that copied, often quite closely, the pre-eminent shapes of contemporary Greek ceramic vases. From the middle of the sixth century until Hellenistic times, tens of thousands of these diminutive vessels for containing toilet preparations such as perfumes and ointments were sold in communities along the shores of the entire Mediterranean Basin, wherever Greek or Phoenician merchants traded or settled. These bottles were also common among the Etruscans in Italy and the Carthaginians of North Africa, and cemeteries around the Black Sea are as likely to contain them as necropolises in Sardinia or the Balearic Islands. Whether they were sought after primarily for their

contents or for their intrinsic value as receptacles is not known, but the fact that most preserved examples come from graves, where they were discarded once emptied, strongly suggests that their contents were perhaps more treasured than the containers. Indeed, the unusually large number of surviving specimens results from the use of perfumes and oils during ancient funeral rites.

These bottles can be divided into three main classes, based on successive changes in their shape, decoration, and geographic distribution. The earliest group, which is also numerically the largest and most homogeneous, dates from the mid-sixth to the fourth century BC, and appears to have been manufactured on the Greek island of Rhodes, where early Iron Age cored vessels akin to certain Mesopotamian bottles may have inspired a new industry. The second group began to be produced during the fourth century, probably at several centres in the eastern Mediterranean as well as in central Italy, and continued to be made until the beginning of the Hellenistic period. At that time, roughly from the third to the first century BC, a third group of factories, possibly based along the Syro-Palestinian coast but also elsewhere, produced yet another series of these attractive multi-coloured bottles.

Analogous in mode of manufacture are a separate but highly distinctive group of cylindrical and rectangular containers which were employed to hold kohl, a black cosmetic powder used to darken the edges of the eyes. These kohl-tubes were made on rods and adorned with marvered trails and blobs of polychrome glass. One group is associated with eastern Mediterranean sites and another, larger series is confined to north-western Iran where such containers must have been produced. Both types, when discovered in dated contexts, belong to the fifth or fourth centuries AD.

Also manufactured on metal rods are a far more extensive series of beads and head pendants customarily attributed to factories in Phoenicia or the Punic colony at Carthage, but probably made at several places in the Mediterranean area. These colourful items mostly depict male heads adorned with sausage curls, full beards and golden earrings, but some take the form of demonic masks, satyrs, rams' heads and birds. Associated with them are cylindrical beads decorated with faces or apotropaic eyes. All are ascribed to between the late sixth and the late third century BC.

Among tableware of the period, the one notable development occurred in Iran, where the formidable Persians, first allied with the Babylonians and Medes, overthrew the Assyrians and established their own empire. Within the confines of their territory a new glass industry flourished, producing cast and cut bowls in flawless, colourless or greenish glass, which in shape and design mirrored contemporary fashions in silver and bronze. Although most excavated examples have been recovered from Ionia and the Aegean, suggesting factories in the western provinces of the Persian Empire, others are known from Persepolis and Nippur in the heart of the Persian domains. According to the Greek playwright Aristophanes (in *Acharnians*, 73-75; c.425 BC), such vessels were provided for the Athenian ambassadors dining at the Median capital of Ecbatana. Whatever their provenance, these elegant cut bowls were in vogue both inside and outside the Persian Empire during the course of the fifth and fourth centuries.

The Hellenistic Age

In the middle of the fourth century BC, Macedonia, north of Greece, suddenly rose to prominence as a major military power under the adroit leadership of Philip II. After Philip's assassination in 337 BC, the crown passed to his son Alexander the Great. Between his accession and premature death in 323, Alexander succeeded in toppling the Persians and in establishing his own empire which embraced most of the civilized world. Upon his death, however, this short-lived empire was divided among his generals who founded separate 'Hellenistic' kingdoms. Chief among them were Egypt under the Ptolemaic Dynasty, Syria and Mesopotamia under the Seleucid monarchy, and Macedon and Greece under the Antigonids. Lesser principalities included Pergamon in Ionia

and the island of Rhodes. In the West, the importance of the Etruscans in central Italy and the Greeks in Magna Graecia waned under the attacks of the Carthaginians and later of the Romans who, by 201 BC, had singlehandedly conquered the entire western Mediterranean. During the next two centuries the Romans continued their expansion at the expense of the Hellenistic kingdoms in the East, and by 30 BC the entire Mediterranean Basin was united under the emperor Augustus into an *orbis Romanum*.

This era not only saw the consolidation of political power and the creation for the first time of a common culture among the diverse peoples of the ancient world, but it also witnessed a remarkable rise in long-distance trade and the creation, often under royal patronage, of industries producing luxury and everyday goods for a mass market. In such a politically and economically advantageous atmosphere glass-making prospered, and glass progressively came into its own as a commodity destined for use by an ever-larger spectrum of society. Although glass retained its identification with affluence, even in the Augustan Age, it achieved for the first time wide currency throughout the Mediterranean area.

In addition to small core-formed bottles, Hellenistic glass-makers produced tableware

Below: This cast sandwich gold-glass bowl found in a tomb at Canosa, Apulia in southern Italy, is one of several types of tablewares made by the earliest Hellenistic glass industry of the late third or second century BC. It is formed from two cast colourless bowls carefully ground and polished so that one fits perfectly inside the other. The gold leaf pattern is applied between the two bowls. Diameter: 19.3cm (7⅝in) (British Museum, London)

This exceptional footed bowl of the second century BC represents one of the largest shapes produced by Hellenistic glass-makers. Of natural pale green glass, it was cast, then ground and polished on a lathe. Height: 17.7cm (7in) (Toledo Museum of Art, Toledo, Ohio)

and other objects, mostly in colourless and brilliantly coloured monochrome glass. They were cast in or over moulds, and lathes and cutting wheels fed with abrasives provided the means to polish and to decorate them. At the same time the intricate sandwich gold-glass method was perfected, and the mosaic technique was revived in order to produce ostentatiously multicoloured vessels displaying a diversity of cane configurations and colour combinations. The interplay in form and design between glassware, ceramics and metal continued to be important, often with remarkable results. Centres of production included Rhodes, possibly Ionia and Cyprus, Alexandria, capital of Ptolemaic Egypt, Sidon and other cities along the Syro-Palestinian littoral, and eventually Rome and Roman Italy.

The earliest identifiable group of Hellenistic tablewares is known principally from cities such as Canusium (Canosa di Puglia) in southern Italy and from other Greek settlements in

Magna Graecia. These vessels form the first concerted effort in antiquity to create entire services of glassware, with both serving and drinking vessels. The most common shapes are broad plates with flaring or upright rims, shallow dishes, hemispherical bowls, footed bowls, *skyphoi* (drinking cups) and handled cups, some in decolourized, royal blue or purple glass, and others in composite mosaic glass, generally with small segments of sandwich gold-glass. Also present are elegant lace-mosaic (*reticelli*) bowls and stunning examples of gold-glass vessels with painstakingly cut patterns of gold-leaf laminated between two blanks of colourless glass. The source of these elegant cast and cut wares is usually considered to be Alexandria, but excavated objects have been found that suggest a possible factory in southern Italy. They belong to the early to mid-second century BC, the earliest prototypes possibly having been produced late in the third century.

The second prominent group of Hellenistic wares are deep, conical and hemispherical drinking bowls with rounded bases and pronounced bands of cut grooves around the sides. Half of the surviving specimens are decolourized; the other half are naturally coloured and vary from golden-brown to olive depending on the oxidizing conditions of the

kiln. They were manufactured at Sidon or some other town along the Syro-Palestinian coast, the industry having no doubt emerged after the seizure of the area from Egypt by the Seleucid kings in 201 BC. Their popularity must have enhanced the reputation of the region as a major centre of glass production, since the bowls were widely exported. Not surprisingly, major concentrations of examples have been found in Palestine, where excavations in Jerusalem yielded hundreds of pieces, while the small Hellenistic settlement at Tell Anafa (Upper Galilee) has produced over 6000 fragments from less than six per cent of the tell. Elsewhere in the Mediterranean they occur in Hellenistic levels at most important communities, including Dura-Europos in the Syrian desert, Ephesus and Sardis in Asia Minor, Athens and Delos in the Aegean, Carthage in North Africa, Rhegium and Morgantina in Magna Graecia, Cosa and Luni in Roman Italy, and Emporion in distant Spain. As such, these bowls constitute the first type of glass tableware to achieve truly widespread use among the prosperous citizens of the ancient world.

In addition to these wares, other types of vessel also appeared on the market during the course of the late second and first centuries. The celebrated ship which sank off the Greek coast

Cast Syro-Palestinian bowls with cut decoration were widely exported throughout the Mediterranean during the mid-second to mid-first century BC. From left to right, the ones shown are of pale blue glass, colourless glass with a slight yellow tinge and light green glass. Heights: 9.5cm (3¾in), 8.9cm (3½in), 4.5cm (1¾in) (Toledo Museum of Art, Toledo, Ohio)

near Antikythera between 80 and 50 BC carried not only sculpture but also a small cargo of glass vessels. Some resemble the earlier Canosa-type glasses, while others represent the emergence of new styles. Among the latter, the most striking are eight cups on high base-rings in composite, lace and striped mosaic patterns and a unique greenish bowl with elaborate cutting. Other styles were also devised, including conical or hemispherical bowls made from composite mosaic canes; shallow mosaic dishes with outsplayed rims; and tall, handsome perfume flasks (*alabastra*) with removable stoppers, in wavy bands of blue, green, white and sandwich-gold glass. These wares date from between the mid-second and mid-first centuries BC and testify to an increasingly diversified industry, presumably located at several centres and manufacturing an ever-growing quantity and variety of vessels and objects.

At the beginning of the Hellenistic Age glass had been considered so precious that the Macedonian kings embellished magnificent ceremonial shields with glass inlays set amidst carved ivory figures and embossed gold and silver trappings. By 50 BC, at the close of the period, glass was much more commonplace, as it is to be found on almost all Hellenistic sites, even in fairly ordinary contexts and sometimes in unexpectedly large quantities.

The Age of Augustus

Octavian, later Augustus Caesar, brought the Hellenistic epoch to a formal end in 30 BC, when he defeated Mark Anthony and Cleopatra VII and incorporated Egypt, the last independent kingdom of the eastern Mediterranean, into the Roman Empire. The Empire now embraced the entire Mediterranean Basin and extended northwards into central and western Europe as well. Once Augustus had established peace and his authority, the Empire for the next several centuries fostered a remarkably homogeneous material culture and promoted the rapid development of large-scale commerce and manufacturing. Simultaneously, it allowed the uninhibited movement of peoples, products, and technical expertise everywhere within its borders. For glass and glass-making, these conditions inaugurated a new age, one that profoundly altered the character of this now venerable but still fairly limited industry.

In large measure, this transformation was initially due to the establishment for the first time of important glassworks at Rome and elsewhere in Roman Italy. Since there is no evidence that the Romans maintained such workshops before the late first century BC, these factories must have been innovations of their

Above: This cast mosaic bowl (second century BC) was made in the eastern Mediterranean from long polychrome glass canes cut into thin slices that were laid around a mould and fused in a kiln. Height: 7cm (2¾in) (Toledo Museum of Art, Toledo, Ohio)

Above right: Perhaps the most popular form of glass vessel in the Augustan Age was the ribbed bowl, such as this golden-brown example. Diameter: 18cm (7¹/₁₆in) (Toledo Museum of Art, Toledo, Ohio)

Right: These cast mosaic vessels, respectively using striped, colour-band and gold-band techniques, were produced in Roman Italy in the late first century BC. Height of tall bottle: 14.1cm (5½in) (Toledo Museum of Art, Toledo, Ohio)

virtually no glass before the Augustan period. Then, quite suddenly, the same types of wares appear in quantity on all Italian and Sicilian sites, whether large or small, rich or poor, urban or rural, and also in France, Switzerland, Austria, Germany and Spain, since they were exported to Augustan legionary camps. According to the ancient geographer Strabo, writing under Augustus, this industry was both inventive and productive, experimenting with colour technology and making vessels so cheaply that they cost only 'a copper coin'.

The tableware produced by the Romano-Italian factories is highly distinctive and can be

day, quite possibly founded by glass-makers from the eastern Mediterranean. In fact, excavations in Rome and Romano-Italian colonies and municipalities such as Luni in Liguria or Cosa in Etruria indicate that the Romans were largely unacquainted with glass before the Augustan Age. Whether this was owing to their celebrated distaste for *luxuria*, or their relative poverty and isolation during much of the Republic (509-30 BC), is not known, but the fact remains that Roman sites in Italy yield

easily recognized, even from tiny fragments. These fragments are brilliantly coloured, and either translucent or opaque, or polychromatic and employing sections and lengths of mosaic glass canes. They were all cast, some in two-part moulds, but a great many were sagged over or in simple former moulds, which would facilitate production. Some types bear close relationship to glass found in the eastern Mediterranean, either of the same date or belonging to the earlier Hellenistic period; but most are inventions

Left: These cast vessels (late first century BC/ early first century AD) in mosaic glass and monochrome blue glass were made by the Roman industry in shapes that copied the angular forms of Arretine pottery. Diameter of plate: 15.3cm (6in) (Toledo Museum of Art, Toledo, Ohio)

Right: The Portland Vase, in the shape of a ceramic amphora (lowest portion now missing), is the most famous example of Roman cameo glass. It is made of cobalt-blue glass overlaid with a layer of opaque white glass which was cut away by a lapidary to create in handsome cameo relief what is thought to represent the classical myth of Peleus and Thetis. Height: 24.5cm (9½ in) (British Museum, London)

of a new age and are characterized by a new repertoire of shapes, colour combinations and patterns, and decorative devices. They also occur in substantially larger numbers, and are found almost exclusively in Italy and the western Mediterranean.

Actual types include ribbed and plain 'linear-cut' bowls, generally in dark blue, purple, or yellow to golden-brown, but occasionally in opaque colours like light blue or white. The ribbed bowls also appear commonly in marbled mosaic glass, usually blue, purple, or brown streaked with opaque white or yellow, or in their last phases in natural bluish-green or light green. Both types of bowl occur on Syro-Palestinian, Cypriot and Aegean sites of this period, and it has been suggested that they were manufactured in both parts of the Empire and represent a revealing link between the industries of the two regions. Among mosaic wares, the most attractive are bowls, box-like receptacles called *pyxides*, and bottles made of 'lace' (*reticelli*), striped, colour-band or gold-band canes. Although most of these styles were anticipated during the Hellenistic Age, the forms, colours and basic designs of the Roman pieces are wholly original. Equally Roman in character are a notable series of plates, dishes, bowls, *pyxides*, and small *patellae*, or cups, in shapes that imitated ceramics made in Arretium in Etruria. Although some of these vessels were cast in composite mosaic glass, most were made in striking translucent royal blue, emerald green or peacock blue glass, or opaque red, white, light blue or jade green colours. Since the Arretine

production, with its crisp, angular profiles and fine red glaze, was manufactured during the Augustan and Julio-Claudian periods between c.30 BC and AD 50, the glass must also date from this time.

Surprisingly, almost none of the early Roman glass is blown. It was once thought that it was the invention and dissemination of the technique of blowing glass that was responsible for the creation of the Italian industry, but the finds at Rome and elsewhere in Italy amply demonstrate that what first introduced the Romans to the virtues of glass were cast wares. Indeed, many of the earliest blown vessels—coloured unguent bottles and small bowls with pinched ribs and trailed decoration—imitate their cast counterparts both in colouration and decoration.

Nonetheless, the invention and diffusion of glass-blowing did ultimately revolutionize the industry under the Julio-Claudians, if only because this technological advance enabled artisans to produce countless numbers of identical articles with relative ease and speed. By the second quarter of the first century AD blown glass largely supplanted cast wares, and glass itself became as ubiquitous as pottery throughout the Empire. According to Pliny the Elder, active during the mid-century, glassworks had by then already spread to Gaul and Spain, where provincial shops undoubtedly specialized in blown products.

The actual invention of the blowpipe and related technology must have taken place somewhere in the Syro-Palestinian region which for so long had practised the art of glass-making.

A dumping site in the Jewish Quarter of the Old City of Jerusalem, for instance, yielded 'wasters' from a workshop manufacturing, among other things, small blown bottles. These remains were sealed beneath a pavement laid in about 40 BC. Upon close examination, however, it is obvious that the bottles were not made with a proper blowpipe but from a hollow tube of glass, pinched shut at one end and inflated through the other to form the vessel. Such tube-blown wares presumably predated the discovery of normal pipe blowing, but clearly indicate that the invention of the blowpipe itself was close at hand.

Among the decorated blown vessels of the Augustan Age (or shortly thereafter), the most spectacular are cameo or cased glasses. These vessels, usually jugs, drinking cups or *skyphoi*, amphoras like the Portland Vase (in the British Museum) or bottles (such as one in the Kofler-Truniger Collection) were produced by superimposing a layer of opaque white glass over a core of dark blue, purple or even green glass. The vessel was then delivered to a gem-cutter who meticulously cut and carved away the white to create in relief handsome scenes illustrating Egyptian motifs, classical myths and rites of the Greek god Dionysius. Although it has often been argued that these precious pieces were executed in Alexandria, where there existed an age-old lapidary tradition, an Italian provenance seems more reasonable, since not only are many of the known examples from Italian soil, chiefly from Pompeii, but the carving closely resembles the classicizing style favoured by Augustus; moreover, the amphora shape is identical to Italian rather than to Greek pottery amphoras.

The Julio-Claudian and Flavian Periods

Under the immediate successors of Augustus, the Roman industry flourished as never before. Most of the trends of previous decades continued, but glass-blowing soon replaced the more laborious and costly casting and heat-forming techniques. Mosaic production, in particular, declined and had probably all but ceased by the second quarter of the first century AD. Although cast monochrome vessels continued to be made, they too were largely displaced by the mid-century by blown glass. The single important technical advance was the invention of mould-blowing, a phenomenon that occurred around AD 25 and led directly to the production of light-coloured cups and beakers, some decorated with Greek and Latin drinking slogans, others with their makers'

names, and still others displaying lively scenes from the Roman race-track and amphitheatre. In respect to colour, the fashion for polychromy or even garish translucent and opaque hues waned steadily as naturally coloured bluish-green and light green glass captured the market for utilitarian table- and storagewares, while fine colourless glass became prized for better-quality vessels.

During this period focal points of production spread further afield, both in the western and eastern Mediterranean, as a result of peripatetic craftsmen who carried their skills wherever there was a demand for glass and a ready supply of fuel and raw materials. By the mid-century glass had become as common as pottery to the Romans, with every province enjoying the influx of plain and decorated wares, many of which were made at regional factories. Indeed, the rapidity with which glass changed from a relatively luxurious commodity to an exceedingly ordinary one is mirrored in the comment of Trimalchio, Petronius' fictitious wealthy Roman in the *Satyricon*. In his famed dinner speech Trimalchio laments that he would prefer glass to gold or silver vessels had not glass of late become so cheap and common.

Among blown decorated wares of the first half of the first century the most popular were simple cups with bands of deeply cut grooves, 'splashed' vessels adorned with applied blobs of multi-coloured glass, and vessels painted with floral and animal scenes. Undecorated glass often comprised entire table settings such as a group of matched plates, bowls and cups recovered from the ruins of a shop destroyed in about AD 40 at Cosa in Italy. Blown tablewares similar to these were made throughout the Empire from the first century until the end of the Roman

epoch, with minimal stylistic change. Quite often glass supplanted ceramic and metal vessels whose shapes and functions it copied.

In the second half of the first century, under the Flavian emperors, the finer grades of glass were all intentionally decolourized. Not only did colourless glass introduce the average Roman to the novelty of transparency, but it enabled glass-cutters to exploit the unique optical properties of glass by faceting and engraving the surfaces of vessels. Shortly after AD 50 faceted beakers and bottles began to appear in the markets of Italy and the western provinces, and at the same time other factories introduced large circular and oval plates, dishes and small bowls, which were cast in colourless glass and adroitly polished. Such vessels had unusually broad rims with overhanging edges and were set on high base-rings. When decorated with facets, the effect was stunning, as is shown by the plates found in pristine condition near the Dead Sea (Israel) at the Cave of the Letters. Many other examples of this type have been found on

Above: This free-blown dark green translucent glass beaker (first century AD) is enamel-painted with colourful birds, ivy leaves and vine tendrils. Height: 6.5cm (2½ in) (Museo Civico, Locarno)

Right: Cast and blown faceted vessels like this beaker began to be made after 50 AD, as the taste for colourless glass superseded that for brightly coloured wares. Similar beakers are found throughout the Roman Empire; many were acquired by the Germanic tribes in the Baltic regions. (This one is from Cambridgeshire, England.) Height: 11.9cm (4¹¹/₁₆ in) (British Museum, London)

archaeological sites in Italy and in the western and eastern provinces. They began to be produced in the last quarter of the first century and continued to be popular well into the next century.

The most common mould-blown wares of the first century were light-coloured drinking vessels, mostly cups, small bowls and conical beakers, which can be divided into half a dozen distinctive types forming allied groups. They first appeared in about AD 25, both in Italy and the Syro-Palestinian region, and continued to be produced until the end of the century or shortly afterwards, when the manufacture of figural mould-blown products declined significantly. These groups all share many similar features, including a basic repertoire of shapes, sizes, colours and decorative components which clearly indicate that they are related in some fashion. Such affinities could represent the output of a single major centre, producing several different types simultaneously or successively, with individual types retaining or rejecting elements from their predecessors while passing along other features to the next generation of glasses. Alternatively, these common factors might represent intentional or inadvertent copying by several rival but roughly contemporary glassworks of the first century. Whatever may be the case, these vessels contribute to the amazing diversity of wares so characteristic of the Roman industry in its initial stages of development.

Perhaps the earliest of these types is a uniform series of cups and bowls which bear Greek inscriptions, either drinking slogans ('your good health') and complimentary greetings ('success to you'), or the names of glass-makers such as Ennion, Jason, or Meges, usually as part of the formula 'Ennion made me' or 'Ennion of Sidon'. Since these vessels are found in Italy as well as along the Syro-Palestinian coast, modern commentators have often suggested that they were produced in factories transferred by craftsmen from Sidon and the eastern Mediterranean to Italy early in the first century. These same workshops are also thought to have been responsible for manufacturing many diminutive jars, jugs and *pyxides*, often roughly hexagonal in shape, which carry various emblems and objects (whose significance is no longer understood) on each of their six sides. Like the drinking cups, they too are found in both halves of the Roman world.

Another series of cups and bowls of the same period was discovered almost exclusively in the excavation of Roman legionary encampments of the western Mediterranean. These vessels depict scenes of gladiators, charioteers and athletes locked in fierce competitions, and some of them have an upper register naming the most popular sports heroes of the time, such as the gladiators Petraites and Columbus, known from Latin literature as fighting during the reign of the emperor Nero.

In the latter part of the century these types fell from favour and were replaced by other mould-blown wares, including a prominent group of tall conical beakers with staggered rows of almond-shaped bosses protruding from their sides. Such vessels were found in profusion at Pompeii and Herculaneum, destroyed by the eruption of Mount Vesuvius in AD 79, and at numerous other sites throughout the Mediterranean area. A number of conical beakers were more complicated in design, with scenes inspired by Graeco-Roman religious lore. These 'myth beakers' typically display four different gods or Seasons (*Horoi*) set beneath leafy garlands suspended from columns or placed within architectural niches.

By AD 40 artisans experimenting with mould-blowing methods had invented the Roman 'prismatic bottle', which stands as the precursor of all subsequent glass bottles. These utilitarian bottles, usually of bluish-green or light green glass, proved highly successful because they were a more effective way of

Above: This colourless glass plate decorated with facets is one of an extensive series of comparable vessels made by the Roman glass industry of the early second century AD. It was recovered in immaculate condition in the Cave of the Letters near the Dead Sea, where Jewish participants in the Bar Kockba rebellion had sought refuge.
Diameter: 30cm (11¾in)
(Shrine of the Book, Israel Museum, Jerusalem)

This Roman mould-blown beaker dating from the late first century AD is one of a score of similar vessels known as 'myth beakers'. This specimen depicts the figures of Poseidon, Autumn, Dionysus and Summer, set beneath garlands of leaves suspended from Ionic column capitals.
Height: 12.4cm (4⅞in)

storing quantities of liquid than the traditional ceramic containers. They also fully exploited the qualities of blown glass: unlike other materials, it was impervious to oil and liquids, and could be easily cleaned and reused. Above all, it was transparent, permitting the owner to inspect the bottle's contents, and this advantage made glass eminently suitable for the storage, preservation, display and merchandising of all kinds of commodities. While most Roman examples are blown into four-sided square or rectangular moulds, some have as few as three or as many as thirteen sides. Still others were inflated into cylindrical moulds, mostly plain but occasionally imparting the shape of a wooden cask. Quite often their bases carry a moulded geometric pattern or a Greek and Latin inscription, usually identifying the maker ('Frontinus', 'Sentia Secunda', or 'From the Factory of Titienus Yacinthus'). The earliest prismatic bottles remained popular well into the second century.

Glass was also used for making beads and bangles of all kinds, insets for jewellery, stirring rods and applicators, and simple markers for various games enjoyed by the Romans. Especially popular was a board game not unlike chess or draughts which required small disc-shaped pieces. These discs were commonly made of opaque white and 'black' glass.

During the course of the first century, glass for the first time began to appear prominently in architecture. The first window-panes, mostly made by casting, were mounted in wooden or metal frames, and occurred at Rome in the Augustan Age where, for example, they were used to glaze windows or screens at the *Atrium Vestae*, the headquarters of the six Vestal Virgins. By the mid-century, at communities such as Pompeii and Herculaneum, glass panes were employed selectively in private dwellings or regularly in bath houses which specifically required them in order to retain heat while admitting light to major rooms. Coloured sheet glass was also the principal source of tiny *tesserae* needed for mosaics to decorate the walls and vaulted ceilings of public buildings and the floors and fountain houses of private homes. Still other artists skilfully cut coloured sheet glass into various shapes which they then pieced together to create large figural panels that were affixed to walls, often providing virtuoso displays of colour. Such work continued to be in demand throughout the imperial epoch, as is shown by the survival of a panel with Christian motifs that is thought to have come from Roman Egypt. This panel, which has been ascribed to the fourth century AD, would have been the upper part of a wall mosaic.

The Second and Third Centuries AD

During the second and third centuries the Roman Empire experienced dramatic vicissitudes, both politically and economically. At first, under the inspired leadership of such energetic rulers as Trajan, Hadrian and Marcus Aurelius, the Empire achieved its greatest territorial growth and material prosperity. Stability fostered a brilliant civic life in Italy and throughout the provinces, while security ensured the uninterrupted expansion of manufacturing and trade. By contrast, the second half of this period witnessed a dramatic reversal of fortunes as interminable civil wars, foreign invasions, and a succession of over thirty, mostly ineffectual, emperors in a period of fifty years led to almost total anarchy and the complete collapse of the state. For much of the third century, in fact, independent kingdoms were established in various sections of the Roman world.

Precisely how these external factors affected the glass industry is now difficult to judge. From the archaeological record, however, it is evident that the fashions established late in the first century continued uninterrupted in succeeding decades. Most of the blown and mould-blown styles devised under the Flavians persisted well into the second century. On the other hand, the novelty of owning glass had disappeared as glassware became affordable to all but the poorest stratum of Roman imperial society, and the proportion of handsomely decorated wares of the period seems to have declined substantially in relation to the vast quantity of ordinary, unembellished table- and storagewares. Although the range and number of shapes and

Left: Thought to have come from Roman Egypt and to date from the fourth century AD, these fragments of an 'opus sectile' panel were the upper part of a wall mosaic with Christian subject-matter.
Length: 79.5cm (31¼in)
(Galerie Nefer, Zurich)

Below left: This Romano-German blown lidded jar from the late first or second century AD was used as a cinerary urn.
Height: 32cm (12½in)
(Toledo Museum of Art, Toledo, Ohio)

Far left: This Romano-Syrian double-headed flask from the second or third century AD was blown in a two-part mould.
Height: 16cm (6¼in)

Left: A blue blown beaker with painted and gilded decoration. Dating from the third century AD, it was probably made in Egypt and exported to the Sudan.
(Khartoum Museum, Khartoum, Sudan)

Below: Probably made in the Cologne area, this Germano-Roman shell-shaped dish from the second or third century AD was mould-blown from cobalt-blue glass when it was rare for glass to be purposely coloured.
Diameter:
15.8cm (6¼in)
(Toledo Museum of Art, Toledo, Ohio)

types grew and changed, everyday domestic goods predominated, mostly plates, dishes, bowls, beakers, cups, bottles, jars and jugs, with an occasional lamp, inkwell, ladle or spoon. Most are of naturally coloured glass, while some are of decolourized glass. Although various market trends influenced glass-makers in all parts of the Empire equally, visible regional differences increasingly characterized the routine work of individual factories. For example, a group of huge lidded jars used as cinerary urns to house the ashes of the dead was produced widely throughout Italy and Illyria, North Africa, and central and western Europe, and with few exceptions each region developed its own distinctive style of urn.

Although there was continuity in glass types throughout the first half of the second century, new forms of decorated vessels began to emerge at this time. Imperial glass-makers introduced a lively group of distinctive mould-blown head-flasks, which were flasks with the bowl in the form of a human head and a neck rising from its centre. Some of these represented images of the gods, others depicted Negroes or grotesques. More common was a varied array of jars, jugs, bottles and sprinkler-flasks blown into patterned moulds which imparted intricate geometric designs. Many of these objects were further inflated once the vessel was removed from the mould. Such wares have been found everywhere within the Roman world, but are especially numerous in the eastern Mediterranean. Considerably more unusual is a dish in the shape of a shell, blown from cobalt-blue glass and probably manufactured at one of the celebrated glass-houses in or around Cologne in Roman Germany. Such a deliberately coloured piece was rare indeed.

Two new decorative styles of free-blown glass emerged in the second century, both at approximately the same time in the eastern and western parts of the Empire, thereby confirming the continuing interdependency of glass-makers throughout the Roman world. Factories at Cologne and elsewhere in the West, and others operating in the Near East, all chose to adorn colourless or lightly coloured vessels with applied glass threads or coils, loosely resembling birds, flowers or, more frequently, snakes or serpents. These so-called 'snake-thread' wares made some use of opaque white, yellow and blue threads, but more frequently employed colourless threads on a vessel of the same metal (the material from which glass is made). Shapes are often highly unorthodox, and include saucepans and tall goblets; and many have flared base-rings with a pronounced beaded stem.

Another decorative device which gained wide acceptance in the second and third centuries involved the abrading or engraving of geometric designs and figural motifs, sometimes accompanied by Greek or Latin inscriptions, on the surfaces of decolourized vessels. It appears that flint engraving tools (burins) and copper wheels fed with abrasives were used to execute the cutting. Especially popular were patterns consisting of shallow, circular and oval faceting, cross-hatching, interlocking circles and complex combinations of geometric configurations. More ambitious are figural scenes illustrating Graeco-Roman mythology, and even cityscapes such as those found on 'Populonia bottles' on which the Italian harbour town of Puteoli is depicted. Such cut wares are found on archaeological sites everywhere in the Empire and show that numerous workshops specialized in the abrading and engraving of glass vessels.

The Fourth Century AD

In the final decades of the third century the Roman state was rescued from disaster by the strong-willed leadership of Diocletian and then by that of Constantine the Great and his immediate heirs. For about a hundred years the devastation wrought by internal rebellion and external attack was stemmed, and relative stability was again restored to the Empire and its government. These successes, however, did not signal a return to the social and economic conditions prevalent in earlier generations, but instead reflected a gradual yet thorough transformation of Roman society. Not only did late imperial political institutions undergo fundamental change, but so too did the sociological climate of the Empire. Nothing reflects this situation better than the acceptance

of Christianity as the principal religion of the Romans. Even the official capital of the state was transferred from Rome to Constantinople, Constantine's newly founded metropolis.

As would be expected, the arts and crafts of the fourth century also experienced tremendous change, and for glass and glass-making a new age was inaugurated. Although the major centres of production survived the political and economic turmoil of the third century and continued to manufacture glass in abundance, there was a dramatic shift away from the decorative styles, basic shapes and preferred colours of the early Empire. For the most part, ordinary table- and

*Far right: The Worringen Beaker, found at Worringen, near Cologne, dates from the early fourth century AD. Made of colourless glass, it is notable for its wheel-engraving which illustrates, with straight superficial strokes, a pagan myth concerning Venus and Cupid.
Height: 20.3cm (8in)
(Toledo Museum of Art, Toledo, Ohio)*

*Left: This thinly blown Roman bottle from the Syro-Palestinian region, decorated with internal hollow tubes and a spiralling thread, was one of the new glass shapes favoured by glass-blowers during the fourth and subsequent centuries.
Height 20.3cm (8in)
(Toledo Museum of Art, Toledo, Ohio)*

*Right: A gold-glass medallion probably from the Christian catacombs at Rome dates from the fourth century AD. The gold-leaf laminated between two layers of almost colourless glass depicts Christ with St Peter and St Paul. The Latin inscription reads 'The Lord gives the Law'.
Longest dimension: 12.4cm (4⅞in)
(Toledo Museum of Art, Toledo, Ohio)*

storagewares were now thinly blown vessels in shades of pale yet distinct yellow, green, olive and brown, and, less commonly, colourless or bluish-green metals. The range of principal shapes also underwent fundamental change, and the total number and overall diversity of forms diminished. Among the new shapes to appear at this time were small, stemmed cups and hanging glass lamps, both hallmarks of this and succeeding centuries. The same is true of an assortment of tall flasks, jars and jugs with exceedingly long necks and pronounced funnel- or bowl-shaped rims. Decoration on these household items was rare and usually limited to spiralling threads or random blobs, either in the same colour as the vessel or in contrasting royal-blue or turquoise-blue glass. Domestic wares such as these are well documented from sites in Italy, North Africa and the eastern Mediterranean, demonstrating that important trends were still widely disseminated in and around the Mediterranean Basin. Farther north, in central and western Europe, the absence of these styles portends the increasing isolation of that region from the rest of the ancient world.

Despite the marked international flavour of ordinary glass in the fourth century, there also emerged disparate regional styles of design and ornamentation, and the finer, decorated wares

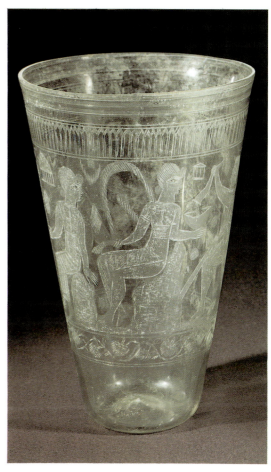

offer concrete evidence that some workshops were manufacturing articles of extraordinary quality and beauty. Several factories of the Late Empire were responsible for some of the most sophisticated examples of the ancient glass-maker's art.

For instance, during the fourth century, artisans in Rome revived the gold-glass technique for the production of a remarkable group of medallions set at the bottom of bowls and other vessels. Portraits, mythological scenes, genre subjects, and Jewish and Christian motifs above all were meticulously etched in gold leaf, often with added painted detail, then encased between two layers of colourless glass. The medallions with Christian themes were mostly preserved in the catacombs outside the walls of Rome after they had purposely been broken away from vessels and subsequently used to mark individual burials.

At Cologne in Roman Germany and else-where in the Empire, other workshops adhered to the traditions of the third century and fabricated colourless vessels which then were handed over to glass-cutters who engraved and abraded some of the most notable cut pieces known from antiquity. Different shops special-ized in different subject-matter and cutting methods. For example, the important Worringen

Beaker, now in the Toledo Museum of Art, made use of straight, superficial strokes to illustrate a pagan myth concerning Venus and Cupid. A smaller beaker, also from Roman Germany, employed broad abraded hollows to depict the Old and New Testament stories of Moses striking the rock and Christ raising Lazarus from the dead. By contrast, a workshop in Anatolia produced inscribed glass vessels on which the Greek letters were formed by double parallel lines with short, horizontal strokes as serifs.

Without doubt, the most spectacular masterpieces of this age are a series of vessels, mostly deep bowls, called cage-cups or *diatreta*. Although they are often associated with the factories of Roman Germany, their repeated mention in the *Corpus Juris Civilis*, the great sixth-century compendium of Roman civil law, suggests that they may well have been made in several places. The technique of making them called for the casting or blowing of a thick-walled blank, usually in colourless glass or bands of several colours. The blanks were then laboriously cut away to create an open-work pattern attached to a background wall with the minimum number of bridges. Most cage-cups, such as those found in and around Cologne, have a network of interlocking circles around the body and a Greek or Latin inscription at the rim. Others, more brilliantly conceived, display figural scenes such as the legend of Lycurgus, the ill-fated king of Thracian Edoni who was strangled by vines after taunting the god Dionysius and his followers. The use of a dichroic glass in this particular *diatretum* only enhances the almost magical skill implicit in the cutting. Both in conception and execution, this cup marks the apogee of glass-making in the ancient world.

The Fifth to the Seventh Centuries AD

In the fifth century the restored unity of the Roman Empire finally collapsed; by AD 476 the continual invasions and migrations of Germanic tribes ended imperial rule in the West and led to the creation of separate states in Germany, Gaul, Britain, Spain, North Africa and Italy, all under the domination of Germanic overlords. The power of the central authority, resident in Constantinople and other cities of the East, was curtailed except in the provinces of the eastern Mediterranean, where stable conditions persisted until the Arab conquest of the seventh and eighth centuries. In the East, Roman imperial culture continued to evolve with little outside interference, and imperceptibly formed what is

Left: During the fourth and fifth centuries, overall standards of glass production declined in the eastern Mediterranean, but experimentation with trailing led to the creation in Roman Syria of such imaginative vessels as this pale bluish-green flask with applied undulating coils and a basket handle.
Height: 19.3cm (7½in)
(Koffler-Truniger Collection, Lucerne)

Above: These late Roman mould-blown flasks are (left) a light yellow grape flask, (right) a light green sprinkler flask, and (centre) a colourless expanded mould-blown flask.
Heights: 7–9.5cm (2¾–3¾in)
(Toledo Museum of Art, Toledo, Ohio)

now called early Byzantine society.

The effect of the Germanic invasions on Roman arts and crafts in the western Mediterranean was felt differently in the different regions. Economic activity in Italy and Africa remained vigorous, at least initially, but in the provinces north of the Alps such industries as glass-making suffered a fatal blow, and major centres of production ceased to function altogether. In the eastern Mediterranean (as well as in Italy and North Africa) the traditions of the fourth century endured, and evolved steadily during the next two to three hundred years. Nonetheless, artefacts, which include ordinary household articles such as glass lamps, stemmed cups and long-necked flasks, also indicate that overall standards of production declined, and that decorated wares progressively became less diverse and widespread. Thinly blown or mould-blown vessels predominated, along with pale colours, and decoration was largely limited to trails and blobs of glass. Among Syro-Palestinian glass-makers of the fourth and succeeding centuries, experimentation with trailing led to the creation of imaginative if whimsical vessels such as multiple flasks with elaborate basket handles. More severe yet elegant in appearance are oval and circular plates, bowls, collared flasks and decorated lamps from Coptic

Egypt. These highly distinctive and beautifully preserved domestic wares were manufactured in or in the vicinity of the Fayoum by a local industry.

One of the last types of mould-blown or expanded mould-blown glass vessel to have been made in the workshops of Roman Germany was a greenish bowl with a rounded bottom and offset rim. This bowl is thought to date from the late fourth or early fifth century, and belongs to the period just before the end of the Roman tradition and the development of far simpler Frankish styles of glassware. In the East mould-blown articles continued to be made by Syro-Palestinian craftsmen until the seventh century. Farther east, outside the borders of the Byzantine world, the Sassanian Persians specialized in thick-walled beakers, bowls and lamps embellished with pronounced faceting. Their techniques and shapes are linked to those which were to distinguish glass made in the Islamic world. Indeed, after AD 632, the armies of Islam progressively conquered Syria, Palestine, Egypt and the coast of north Africa, ending Byzantine rule and irreversibly transforming the cultures of those areas. Following the Arab victories a purely Islamic decorative style emerged in the arts, and signalled the end of the ancient traditions of glass-making.

CHAPTER TWO

FROM THE DARK AGES TO THE FALL OF CONSTANTINOPLE

Among the finest glass-ware of the sixth and seventh centuries was the cut glass produced by the Sassanid Persians, who made pieces decorated with wheel-cut facets like this vase with a predominantly honeycomb design.
Height: 20.3cm (8in) (Corning Museum of Glass, Corning, New York)

In the wake of the barbarian invasions of Europe during the fourth and fifth centuries AD, the influence of the Roman Empire waned, and the luxury, technical efficiency and classical standards of its culture rapidly disappeared. The beleaguered continent entered a new phase in its history, a phase lasting some 500 years which has come to be known as the Dark Ages. Nevertheless, although standards of glass-making declined, the profound imprint of centuries of Roman rule could not be entirely eradicated from European soil, and the influence of its glass-makers was still evident in the styles adopted by the glass-makers of the new era. In the northern countries glass-making moved away from the centres of population into the forests, and developed different regional styles, while in southern and eastern Europe, and also in the countries of the Near East, glass remained closer to the Roman tradition.

The Byzantine culture of the Eastern Empire, which lasted from the fourth century until the fall of Constantinople in 1453, remained the centre of both Greek and Roman civilization, and its glass-makers were most noted for their use of rich glass mosaic decoration on buildings, and for enamelling and gilding on glassware which was used with much skill in the eleventh and twelfth centuries. In Kievan Russia glass was used for windows, tableware and jewellery until the Mongolian conquest in the early twelfth century, and from the twelfth to the mid-fifteenth centuries glass increasingly became an object of everyday use in the Central Balkans.

Even farther east, the Islamic Empire, which spread from the Arabic Peninsula after 632 AD to encompass North Africa and Spain in the west, and Mesopotamia, Syria and Persia in the east, evolved its own distinct style of glass-making. This style was distinguished by its skilfully cut and engraved products, lustre-painted glass, and spectacular enamelled and gilded glasses which were made in Syria in the thirteenth and fourteenth centuries.

It was not until the Renaissance that materials and techniques improved sufficiently for objects of great delicacy and finesse to be made from good-quality clear metal, especially in Italy. By the mid-fifteenth century Venice had become the predominant glass-making centre, not only in Europe but throughout the world.

The Development of the European Glasshouse

After the breakdown of the Roman Empire, two distinct glass-making traditions began to emerge in western Europe, one in the north and one in the south. In the south, glass-making, centred chiefly in Italy, was concentrated mainly in the towns, while in the north, including Germany, Bohemia, Belgium, France and Britain, the great forests provided the fuel for the furnaces of what became mainly a rural occupation. (There were exceptions in the south, however, for example in the forested areas of Tuscany and Spain, and Altare, near Genoa, which was set among richly forested hills.)

Different types of furnace were favoured by the European glass-makers of the different regions. Whereas some of the Roman glass furnaces had probably been two-tiered structures comprising a stoke-hole situated below a melting chamber, and while tank furnaces (in which the furnace itself served as the receptacle for the melted glass) were in use in Palestine between the fourth and seventh centuries, and in other parts of the eastern Mediterranean in the late Roman or medieval periods, the glass-makers in southern Europe favoured a round, beehive-shaped furnace divided into three tiers. These comprised a stoke-hole at the bottom, a middle chamber with 'glory holes' to give access to the pots of melted glass, and an upper chamber for annealing (slowly cooling) the finished products. Foundations of a circular furnace dating from the seventh or eighth century were found on the Venetian island of Torcello and at a late fourteenth- or early fifteenth-century site at Monte Lecco in the Apennines. Three-tiered furnaces were not always circular in plan, however: a rectangular eleventh- or twelfth-century furnace was found at Corinth.

In the glasshouses of northern Europe, furnaces were usually rectangular in plan with various compartments adjacent to, and on the same level as, the main melting chamber. The chambers shared either a common fire channel through the structure, or linnet holes which transmitted heat from the main furnace to the subsidiary kilns. Rectangular furnaces were not always the rule, however: a late Saxon glass-making site at Glastonbury in England appears to have been oval in plan, and oval as well as rectangular ground-plans have been found on medieval sites in Czechoslovakia. A twelfth- or thirteenth-century book attributed to a certain Eraclius describes a main furnace flanked by a fritting chamber (where the ingredients were first fused) and a third compartment for pot-firing. A different plan again is shown in a fifteenth-century miniature of a forest glasshouse, probably in Bohemia, where a smaller annealing furnace was attached to the main furnace; and examples of this arrangement have also been found in Sweden and the Baltic.

Little is known of the equipment used by glass-makers of the Dark Ages and medieval period. Blowing irons of the fourth century found at Mérida, in south-western Spain, were made up of several thicknesses of iron welded together and featuring slightly expanded wedge-shaped ends, one tube being at least 43cm (17in) long. In medieval times and later in northern Europe, a wooden handle half the length of the blowing iron was used for insulation against heat. The German monk Theophilus Presbyter (1110-40), in writings on contemporary glass-making in his book *Treatise on Divers Arts* recommended 'an iron [blow] pipe, two cubits long and as thick as your thumb, two pairs of tongs each hammered out of a single piece of iron, two long-handled iron ladles, and such other wooden and iron tools as you want'.

During medieval times, glass-making was a seasonal occupation. Venetian glass-factories worked from January to August, and glasshouses in the Spessart Forest in Germany made glass from Easter until Martinmas in November. English glass-makers in the Weald shut down their furnaces for two or three months in the summer, probably to fit in with the farming cycle. Northern glass-makers used sands from Lorraine, Silesia and northern Bohemia for silica, as well as rocks such as basalt, granite, obsidian and felspar. In southern Britain, Wealden glass-makers used local outcrops of sand at Hambledon Common and Lodsworth Common. In early medieval times, sources for enamel

This bottle, blown in the shape of a bunch of grapes, which was found in the cemetery of Dunes at Poitiers, dates from the fourth century and anticipates Frankish styles of glassware. (Musée des Antiquités Nationales, St Germain-en-Laye)

or specialized glasses were scarce, and enamellers probably used *tesserae* from Roman mosaics for their raw material. Glass beads were also widely used from at least the fourteenth century.

Frankish Glassware

After the Roman armies left Europe, the region including Germany, Belgium and Gaul (France) came under the domination of Germanic tribes known generically as the Franks. The departure of the Romans resulted in the disappearance of many of the more sophisticated aspects of glass manufacture, including enamelling, gilding, cutting and engraving, all decorative techniques usually practised in workshops separate from the glasshouse. These techniques were replaced by a new style of glassware, known variously as Frankish, Merovingian or Teutonic. This glass was blown and, like Roman glass, was a soda-lime product, but decoration now consisted of simple techniques that could be carried out at the furnace by the glass-maker. The new style, used mainly for drinking vessels, flourished between the fifth and seventh centuries, and examples of it have been found throughout central Europe, although it was only available to the rich and not made in great quantities. Most discoveries have been made in Belgium and the Rhineland, indicating that these were the main centres of production.

Common techniques included mould-blown decoration using simple corrugated moulds. Decoration was sometimes made 'wrythen', that is, made diagonally ribbed by a quick twist of the paraison by the glass-maker upon withdrawal of the vessel from the mould. Trailed, threaded decoration continued to be popular, and was brought to a high level of expertise by the Franks, in some cases outstripping that of their Roman predecessors. The threading on cone-beakers was particularly fine, and looped and feathered decoration, usually marvered smooth into the surface of the glass (often in contrasting opaque white) was used on bowls, cups and bottles of Rhenish or Gaulish origin. Thick trellis trailing is also found on objects such as jars and drinking horns from this period. Blobbed decoration, where hot drops of glass were applied to the body of the vessel, was an early precursor to the numerous *Nuppenbecher* (drop beakers) made in the later medieval period.

The new style of glassware introduced a new range of glass shapes, many reflecting the German custom of never placing a drinking glass on the table. Since German hospitality demanded that an empty glass be taken from a guest's hand and refilled, Frankish glasses had no proper base to enable the glass to be stood upright,

The cone-beaker was one of the earliest types of glass vessel the Franks produced, and this one, known as the Kempston cone-beaker, with its elegant conical shape and precise trailing, shows the exquisite results that could be obtained from the simplest techniques. Height: 26.2cm (10⁵/₁₆ in) (British Museum, London)

although occasionally a vestigial foot of little practical use would be added as decoration. Roman styles which were copied included horns, cone-beakers and palm cups, with only minor changes in shape and decoration. Squat jars, jugs, bag-shaped beakers and pouch-bottles were also produced, and so were beautifully formed bell-beakers with concave sides and rounded bases, occasionally finished with a button finial.

Cone-beakers (*Spitzbecher*) seem to have been among the earliest types of glassware produced after the Germanic invasions. Almost colourless examples of these cone-shaped drinking vessels were made in northern France and Belgium, and colourless beakers probably dating from the early fifth century also occurred in England, but early forms were also made in light olive-green and amber colours, retaining a pontil-mark and pushed-in tip. One of the most beautiful

V enerat occidus mundi de finib hostis
L uxuria extincte tam dudu prodiga fame
D e libura comas oculis uaga languida uoce

Left: This ninth- or tenth- century manuscript illustration shows the use of cone-beakers and horns as drinking vessels. (Bibliothèque Royale de Belgique, Brussels)

Below: Drinking horns like this one from Italy, dating from the late sixth or early seventh century, were blown as cones and bent into a curve while still hot (note the folds along the inner curve). The thin opaque white trails spiral round the body of the vessel, while the thicker blue trails have been scalloped by combing. The rim has been left rough and faintly pincer-marked. Length across: 23cm (9in) (British Museum, London)

examples of these is the Kempston cone-beaker in the British Museum, dating from the second half of the fifth century (and so named from the place in England where it was found). It is a long, slender cone with everted rim, made of thin, blown, light green glass, decorated with exquisite trailing which is almost mechanical in its precision, horizontal below the rim and vertically looped from the base. Kempston-type beakers date from the mid-fifth century to the mid-sixth century and later. Their production centre (or centres) remains uncertain; they may have been made in Belgium and exported to England and the Rhineland, or made in the middle Rhine or Meuse areas. A thicker type of cone-beaker was also made, and has been found in places that suggest that it was produced mainly for export to Scandinavia.

Glass drinking horns (blown as cone-beakers and bent while hot) were produced in the Rhine and Meuse valleys between the third and early seventh centuries, and in Italy in the late sixth and early seventh centuries. In Italy they were made by glass-blowers of Italian or more eastern origin for the newly arrived Langobards, and surpassed other products in quality, brilliance, colour and the deftness of the two-way feathered decoration. In general, drinking horns were of the light green, olive-green, and brown tints customary in post-Roman glass. Decoration, often in brightly contrasting colours, might include two suspension loops, or trailing either looped, twisted, pinched into a diamond pattern or combed into a feathered pattern, or two-way feathering (the latter usually confined to glasses south of the Alps) and blobbed decoration. A few horns were perforated at the tip, perhaps for a metal mount, or even for drinking, the thumb closing the aperture between draughts. A large

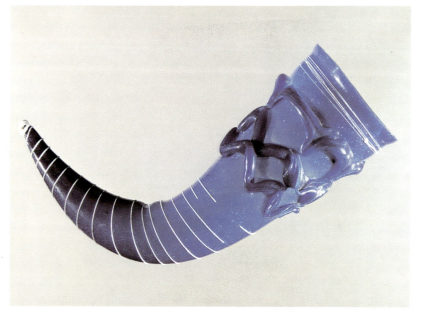

proportion of horns had rough, unworked rims, a common feature on late Roman vessels, and odd considering the small amount of skill which would been been needed to smooth them off at the furnace. It has been suggested that they were used as static liquid containers rather than drinking vessels, in the same way that natural horns were used during the Frankish period to contain ink.

One decorative technique used only occasionally in Roman times was developed and brought to a high level of perfection by the Frankish glass-makers. This was the hollow 'claw' decoration, in which trunk-like projections were applied to and then blown from the body of a conical beaker, usually in two offset rows. These claw-beakers, or *Rüsselbecher* (*Rüssel*=trunk or proboscis), were made in amber, green or blue glass and sometimes

origin in Roman times. It was made in Syria, Gaul and the Rhineland in the fourth century. This vessel had between three and five tubes grouped round a constricted waist, which divided the globular body from the upper part of the container, or neck, and the wide-mouthed rim. The few Frankish examples to have been found have vertical necks (unlike later examples in which the neck is tilted at an angle to the body), and were used for slow pouring or dripping. The name *Kuttrolf* comes from the Latin word *gutta*, a drop, or *gutturnium*, a vessel that dispensed its contents drop by drop; and the Middle High German word *guttern* also means 'to drip'. The alternative German name for the *Kuttrolf* was *Angster* from the Latin *angustum*, narrow.) It was made from a single paraison in which the neck or waist was reheated before the air was drawn out of the vessel by sucking, thus

Left: The Franks developed the technique of claw decoration into a fine art. This claw-beaker has two rows of claws, five in each row, each claw decorated with a nicked vertical trail. Height: 19cm (7½in) (British Museum, London)

Below: The Kuttrolf was a rare Frankish vessel with narrow tubes enabling liquid within it to be poured out drop by drop. Height: 19 cm (7½in) (Kunstmuseum, Düsseldorf)

decorated with brightly coloured contrasting trailing. Early types were usually smaller than later forms. Once their basic shape had been blown, it received any trailed decoration it was to have and was then left to cool while still attached to the blowing iron. When the glass was cool enough to resist inflation, a hot blob of glass would be dropped on its surface where each claw was to be sited. The glass would then be reblown in order that the areas touched by the hot blobs melted and blew out farther than the walls of the vessel. The inflated blobs would then be caught up and drawn out and down to form claws, and their tips pressed to the body of the vessel. The paraison was then transferred to a solid iron pontil rod so that the rim could be finished, and notched vertical ribbons of glass might be added to the claws for further decoration. The beakers usually tapered downward to a small circular foot. *Rüsselbecher* reached their highest point of development in the late fifth or early sixth centuries and continued to be made at least until the early part of the eighth century; they are the finest achievement of the Teutonic glass industry. They were produced in the Seine-Rhine area, and exported to other countries including England and Scandinavia.

Much rarer than the *Rüsselbecher* was the curious and complex *Kuttrolf*, which also had its

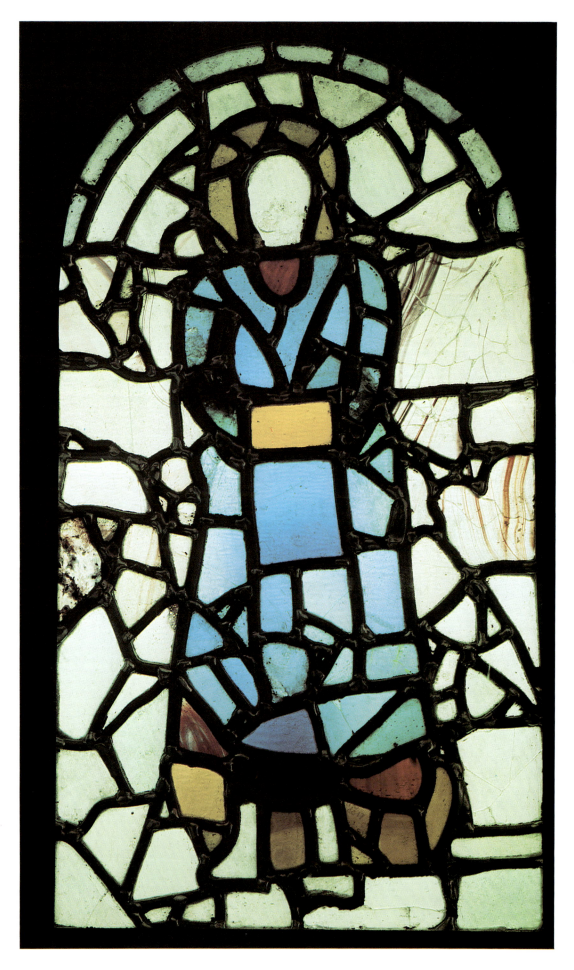

Excavations at Jarrow in the North of England have yielded much information about the glass of the Carolingian period. This is a reconstruction of a small panel found in the Riverside Guest House of St Bede's Monastery at Jarrow, and dates from 685-800AD.
Height: 32cm (12½in)
(The Bede Monastery Museum, Jarrow Hall)

creating a vacuum which caused the collapse of the softened part of the vessel. This was then composed of between three and five thin intertwined tubes. The *Kuttrolf* occurs in one form or another from Roman times to the twentieth century, in the Middle East as well as in Europe.

The Carolingian Period

Very little western European glass survives from the mid-seventh to the twelfth centuries. The Carolingian Renaissance, which began in the late eighth century, made notable achievements in the intellectual, artistic and musical fields, but glass-making was not among them. Although the making of glass vessels did not cease altogether, the industry existed only for the production of everyday items. The use of glass chalices was prohibited by the Christian Church in 803, at the Council of Reims in 813, by Pope Leo IV (847-855), and by the Council of Tribur in 895, although glass was used to make reliquaries sealed with wax and impressed with a seal, and small oil-dishes for church lamps.

Although the Carolingian period, which lasted until the mid-tenth century, was not a brilliant one for vessel making, it provided an important foundation for stained-glass-window techniques which reached their artistic peak in later medieval times. The cylinder, or broad, glass method was the main technique used for making window glass in western Europe, as it had been in Roman times. Cylinder glass was made by blowing a mass of molten glass, or gather, into a cylindrical shape which, once annealed (reheated and cooled), was slit along its length with a red-hot iron or shears. It was then reheated and flattened before being cut to size. Panes were usually set in metal or wooden frames and probably held in place by mortar, sometimes with metal angle crosses or knobs.

Since the Church forbade the use of glass vessels for ritualistic purposes but encouraged the use of glass for windows, the monasteries, which had become the new centres of wealth and culture, began to concentrate more on glass for their abbey windows. In north-western Europe several monastic records of the ninth and tenth centuries mention a 'Fra Vitrearius' as a member of the religious community, who would have been in charge of the monastery's glass. France was the main centre of production, and the founder of the monasteries of Monkwearmouth and Jarrow in Northumbria, England, had to send for French glass-makers to set up glasshouses there in AD 676. (Wilfrid, Archbishop of York, and Wilfrid, Bishop of Worcester, were reputed to have glazed their

churches shortly afterwards.) The glass-makers from Gaul produced both vessel and window glass, and were supposed to have taught the English their craft, although by 758 the Abbot of Jarrow was sending an urgent request for glass-makers to Archbishop Lullus of Mainz in the Rhineland, claiming that 'we are ignorant and helpless in that art'.

Excavations at Monkwearmouth and Jarrow have yielded much information about the glass made at this time. Both sites produced thin soda-lime window glass, plain and coloured, generally similar in type though with minor variations. Pale blue, olive-green, amber, yellow-brown, red and green-blue glass was found at both sites, and Monkwearmouth also produced emerald-green and dark cobalt-blue colours, and Jarrow *millefiori* glass (slices of coloured glass rods fused together). The panes were cut in triangular, rectangular and other shapes, and were originally set in leaded frames. (Window glass of similar date has also been found at Escomb Church and St Wystan's Church in Repton, Derbyshire.)

During the two centuries following the death of Charlemagne in 814, his empire, which encompassed France, the Netherlands, Germany and beyond, was invaded from the north and west by the Northmen, from the south by the Muslims and from the east by the Magyars. After the invaders were either driven back or settled in their new territory, there was a renewal of cultural life in western Europe, notably in England under Alfred (871-901) and in Spain, where the brilliant civilization of the Saracens made the Moors the most cultured people of the whole region.

After the Muslim invasion of the early eighth century, southern Spain developed a separate glass-making tradition from the rest of the country, and glass from Persia, Mesopotamia and Egypt was probably imported by the Spanish caliphs. However, native glass-blowers seem to have been working in Andalusia by the

This shallow rectangular dish of dark blue glass, moulded with a fish in bas-relief, was made in Spain during the Visigothic period. (Macaya Collection, Barcelona)

One of the most popular types of drinking vessel in medieval times in northern Europe seems to have been the Krautstrunk *(cabbage stalk), which was decorated with applied blobs of glass, or prunts. It was often used as a reliquary, like this one, which has the seal of the Bishop of Brixen, Tyrol, impressed in the wax.*
Height: 9.2cm (3⅝in)
(Kunstmuseum, Düsseldorf)

eleventh century. Even during the three centuries of Visigothic rule following the conquest of Spain by the Suebi and Vandals in the fifth century, glass-makers had continued in a small way to produce articles in the Roman style, but with fewer shapes and decoration which was confined to simple furnace work. In 636 Saint Isidore, Bishop of Seville, had even included a chapter on glass manufacture in Spain, Italy and Gaul in his *Etimoligías.*

The ninth and tenth centuries in Europe were dominated by political scandals, and the ensuing chaos greatly reduced the glass-making industry, which produced only utility objects such as lamps, urinals, phials, distillery and medical vessels of crude glass for a purely local market. The sees, monasteries and abbeys were potentially the industry's wealthiest customers, but the Church's prohibition of glass chalices was to continue, robbing glassware of its prestige and leading to its closer association with commoner materials like wood, pottery and tin. It was not until the Italian Renaissance that western glass-makers were able to develop their largely stagnant industry beyond the production of purely functional items.

Medieval Europe

After about AD 1000 there was a significant change in the composition of European glassware. The northern glass-makers abandoned marine plant ash from the Mediterranean countries which they had used as a source of alkali (in the form of soda), and came to rely instead on local supplies of potash, derived from the ashes of bracken, beechwood and other woodland plants. They found that potash had the same effect as soda in a glass mix, acting as a

flux to lower the melting temperature of the silica or sand. The products made from the new potash formula were simple utilitarian objects such as urinals, apothecary flasks and beakers with moulded and applied decoration. They appeared in a wide range of natural green and amber tints, caused mainly by iron impurities in the raw materials, and were known collectively as forest glass or *Waldglas. Waldglas* was made in the forests of northern and western Europe, including France (where it was known as *verre de fougère*), Germany and Bohemia until as late as the seventeenth century.

Unfortunately, potash glass is prone to weathering, and much that came from the forest glasshouses of this period has been lost through deterioration in the ground. Evidence that glass vessels were made in western Europe during the medieval period comes not only from excavated fragments but also from documents and illustrated manuscripts, which give a sparse but general picture of the development of glass vessels from the eleventh to the fifteenth centuries.

From the twelfth century onwards, the most common vessels in use, even in rich households, seem to have been cups, decanters, lamp glasses and urinals. The almost total absence of glass remains on medieval village sites, at least before the fifteenth century, indicates either that glass was not used very far down the social scale, or that much potash glass has simply perished through weathering, or perhaps been ignored by excavators in the past.

Information about glass in medieval England and France is slowly being accumulated, but comparatively little is known about the forest glasshouses of Germany, Bohemia and the southern Netherlands, and only very rarely can the productions of a particular locality be identified. The constant need for fresh sources of wood fuel kept the forest glass-makers regularly on the move, and the great variety in the colouring and quality of the products of even a single glass factory was caused by the differences in quality of the raw materials used.

Theophilus, in his *Treatise*, stated that vessel glass was relatively rare in twelfth-century Europe, although he did describe how long-necked bottles were made: the glass-maker would swing the paraison round his head while holding a thumb over the mouthpiece of the blowing iron. Lamp glasses certainly date from this period, and fragments of green glass urinals, broad-brimmed and bag-shaped, are the most common finds on sites of the thirteenth to the fifteenth centuries. In the thirteenth century, Louis IX of France used tall-stemmed plain vessels in green glass, and fourteenth-century French inventories list glass objects such as pots, stemmed drinking glasses, pitchers, bottles, tumblers, flagons, cups and plates. A document of 1338 gives a list of glasses sent as dues by a French glass-maker of Chambarand (Isère) to his ruler, including porringers, plates, ewers, pots, a large nef (ornamental ship), salt-cellars, casks, lamps, candelabra, urinals and a chess set.

The first hint of the existence of a native glass industry in England dates from the twelfth century, when Henry Daniel, a *vitrearius* (glass-maker) is documented as having been made Prior of the monastery of St Benet's at Holme, Norfolk, by King Stephen (1135-54). In the following century glass-makers from France began to settle in the Weald; one 'Laurence Vitrearius', probably from Normandy, was granted twenty acres of land near Chiddingfold in the Weald of Surrey, in a deed dating from 1240 or earlier. They were joined by English craftsmen, and the Weald of Sussex and Surrey became the most important glass-making centre in medieval England, and remained so up to the prohibition of wood-firing for glass-making in the seventeenth century. Glass-making was also carried out at the Abbey of Vale Royal in Cheshire (1284-c. 1309); records show that glass was being purchased from Shropshire and Staffordshire in the middle of the fourteenth century; and Salisbury Cathedral had its own 'glashous' in the fifteenth century. The most common objects made in England included glass lamps for both secular and ecclesiastical use; broad, horizontal-rimmed urinals with either a tubular or conical neck; green glass bottles up to 23cm (9 in) high with a long, tapering, often ribbed neck, spreading rim and concave base; items that may have been 'linen-smoothers', shaped like a mushroom cap; and a variety of

Left: This French stemmed goblet dating from the fourteenth century was found during the demolition of a church in Rouen, and matches those described in medieval French inventories.
Height: 18cm (7in)
(Musée des Antiquités, Rouen)

Below: The most common glass objects made in England during the medieval period included lamps for both secular and ecclesiastical use like this thirteenth-century hanging lamp excavated at Winchester, which would have contained oil and been suspended from the ceiling.
Height: 17cm (6¾in)
(City Museum, Winchester)

In spite of the dark gaps of missing glass, a head of Christ is suggested by this reconstruction of glass fragments unearthed at Lorsch Abbey in Germany in 1932. The pieces are thought to date from the ninth or tenth century. (Darmstadt Museum, Darmstadt)

chemical equipment. Fragments of tubing, alembics, cucurbits and receivers, presumably intended for monastic pharmacies or laboratories, have also been found.

Fine glassware found in northern Europe during the medieval period was almost always of foreign origin. Enamelled and gilt glasses came from the Near East and Byzantium, and glasses of Italian origin were also imported, the most outstanding examples of which were in an almost colourless metal decorated with applied threading in blue or manganese purple. Vessels either in, or decorated with, opaque red glass could have been made in England or imported (opaque red glass was also made in Italy and Corinth). Good-quality green glasses (as distinct from the humbler forest glassware) have been found in many parts of Europe, notably England, France, Belgium and the Netherlands, and include tall-stemmed goblets, often with ribbed decoration, which may also have been Italian imports. By the fifteenth century, stemmed glasses apparently lost favour in the north, and were replaced by plain-bottomed or base-ring goblets; and there was a general increase in the use of all kinds of glass. Rough copies of Venetian imports were attempted, and after 1450 prunted vessels became more common, particularly in the Netherlands and Germany.

The manufacture of window glass was much more important at this time than vessel-glass making in western Europe. The chief centres of production were Burgundy, Lorraine and the Rhineland, which specialized in cylinder glass (see page 45), and Normandy which specialized in crown glass from the thirteenth century. Crown glass was made by blowing a bubble of hot glass, attaching an iron rod (called a pontil) to the side opposite the blowing iron which was then broken off, and spinning the rod until the open-ended glass bubble 'flashed' open by centrifugal force, into a large flat disc called a 'crown' or 'table'. Once annealed, the crown would usually be cut up into small panels, one of which would have the 'bulls-eye' or 'bullion', the rough centrepiece where the pontil had been attached. Churches were the first buildings to be glazed (not necessarily with stained glass), and by the twelfth century window glass was in use for royal residences, and for other buildings a century later. By the beginning of the sixteenth century window glass must have been quite usual in most houses of any pretension, including town dwelling-houses.

The techniques for making stained-glass windows appear to have been well established in Europe by the twelfth century, when the glass industry was increasingly dominated by the production of such windows for cathedrals and churches, and glaziers' workshops were set up in cathedral cities. After the seventh century, examples of stained-glass windows were rare. The earliest after that time are those of Augsburg Cathedral, c. 1065, and twelfth-century examples in St Denis in Paris; but the finest are in the French Gothic churches of Notre Dame in Paris, Chartres, Sens and Noyon, and Canterbury Cathedral in England. Coloured glass was imported to England from Normandy, Burgundy, the Rhineland and elsewhere, and there is a close relationship between English and French stained glass of this period. French glass-makers excelled in the art, and from the thirteenth to the sixteenth centuries stained-glass artists from France, Flanders and Germany took their skills to other countries.

Methods of making stained glass have remained virtually unchanged until relatively recently. Besides using glass of a solid colour, stained-glass artists developed the art of 'flashing' colour in a thin layer on to a thicker layer of clear, colourless glass, so as to allow more light through it. Brilliant reds and blues were characteristic of the Gothic period. To make a leaded window, a cartoon of the design would first be drawn on a white background with the different colours specified, and glass cut to the shapes indicated. A notched grozing iron

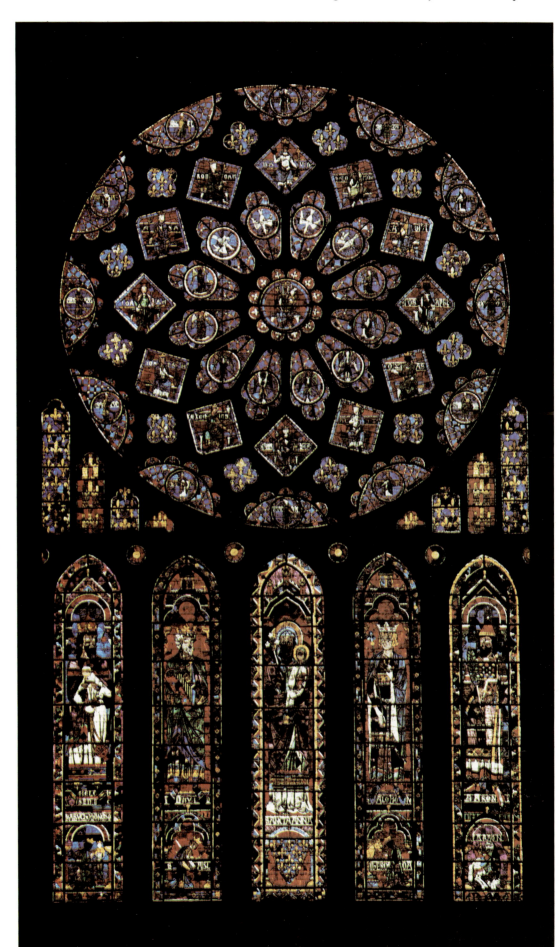

The North Rose Window at Chartres Cathedral is among the most celebrated stained glass of the Gothic period. French glass-makers dominated the stained-glass industry at this time, and took their skills to other European countries.

(a tool for snipping glass) was used to do this, leaving a characteristic rough or 'grozed' edge on the glass. Details would be painted on the glass with black enamels, and fired in a kiln. Finally the glass pieces would be joined together with grooved lead strips (calms) soldered together, each finished panel being secured by copper ties to iron bars set in the masonry of the windows. Another technique, called 'grisaille', was to make a window in mainly clear, colourless glass and to paint it with foliage in brownish-black enamels. By the fourteenth century stained-glass designs had become noticeably more naturalistic and sophisticated, and new colours such as violet, deep green and brown were introduced. The art of staining glass different shades of yellow, by firing the surface with a derivative of silver sulphide, was also developed, reminiscent of the technique for Islamic lustre-painted glass, described on pages 60-1.

Little is known about the glass-making of southern Europe in the medieval period, but it is evident that good-quality glass had been developed by the thirteenth century at the latest. The glass furnace remains discovered on the island of Torcello in the Venetian lagoon, together with glass mosaic *tesserae* and numerous fragments of stemmed goblets and bottles, indicate that there may have been some continuity of the craft in Venice through the Dark Ages, and certainly some form of glass-making was in progress in Venice by at least the end of the tenth century. Between the twelfth and fourteenth centuries the Venetians were to lay the foundations for a glass industry which by the 1500s dominated all Europe and the eastern Mediterranean.

Throughout the Middle Ages Venice had a highly complex commercial network and merchant fleet, which enabled the city to reach out to the Near East and the Black Sea, as well as to all the Mediterranean countries and north-western Europe. By the thirteenth century Venice had established its importance as a glass producer, and exported high-quality glassware which was made to satisfy the different tastes of its customers. Documents show that Venice was exporting glassware to Germany (1282), Flanders (1394) and England (1399). In order to maintain and improve the quality of their product, the Venetian authorities controlled the importation of the basic ingredients. The high cost of these ingredients, which included barilla, a marine plant growing in salt marshes, from which soda ash was made, contributed to the expensiveness of Venice's glass.

By 1268 Venetian glass-makers had formed their own guild, and in 1271 the authorities issued a document known as the glass-makers'

The shrine of stained glass at Sainte-Chapelle in Paris was built by Louis IX (1214-1270) to contain relics which he had acquired from Baldwin II, Emperor of Constantinople from 1228 to 1273.

Capitolare which laid down strict rules for guild members and prohibited imports. The only products it mentioned were glass weights, beakers and bottles with a blue band round the neck and the stamp of Venice, but glass medallions made in Venice at this time have been found, mostly coloured red and blue, moulded in relief and depicting religious subjects. In 1292 fire risks and the need for greater control led the Grand Council of Venice to decree the removal of the glass industry to the islands of Murano to the north of the city, and they have remained its production centre ever since.

By the early fourteenth century glass production was widespread in northern and central Italy, and archaeological evidence has shown that glass, particularly prunted beakers and colourless goblets, bottles and bowls, was in common use in northern Italian towns. Farther south, both glass and glass factories were less common, and even in Sicily where three factories operated, glass was still something of a luxury, although there is some evidence that glass was more widely used in southern coastal towns. Venetian glass was also manufactured at Crete, probably at Candia, in the 1430s, and possibly also at Corfu, when both centres were under Venetian rule. Venice's most important rival was Altare, near Genoa, which was operating a glass factory by 1282. By the fifteenth century the Altarists had developed a highly organized industry and were exporting their wares to France and beyond; and it was the Altarists as well as the Venetians who were instrumental in establishing Italian glass-making north of the Alps from the late sixteenth century.

Byzantine Glass

In AD 330 the emperor Constantine (who ruled between 324 and 337) transferred the capital of the Christian Roman Empire to the site of ancient Byzantium, calling it Constantinople. This act laid the foundation for the Roman Empire in its medieval form, and its supremacy was to last for more than a thousand years. The empire was soon divided into east and west, and this division became permanent after the accession in 395 of Honorius in the west and his brother Arcadius in the east. After the fifth century the authority of the western emperors barely extended beyond Italy, and the crowning of Charlemagne as emperor of the Western Empire in 800 ended even the theoretical primacy of Byzantium over Europe. The Eastern Empire, however, named after Byzantium and centred on the Balkan Peninsula and Asia Minor, exerted influence over the entire eastern half of the Mediterranean, although it was subject to important changes of boundary throughout its long history.

The most glorious period of Byzantine art and architecture was during the reign of Justinian I and Theodora (527-65), and a further period of splendour and power occurred during the Macedonian dynasty (867-1025) founded by Basil I, when Russia became an outpost of Byzantine culture. With the rule of Zoë and Theodora (1042) a long period of anarchy and decline began, and in 1204 the Crusaders and the Venetians sacked Constantinople and set up a new empire of separate states. In 1261 the empire was reconstructed under the Paleologus dynasty, and there was an impressive late flowering of Byzantine art, but this in turn was eventually eclipsed when the empire, attacked from all sides, lost territories and finally collapsed in 1453, when Constantinople fell to the Ottoman Turks under the Sultan Mohammed II.

Little is known of glass-making during the time of the early Byzantine Empire, but its rulers

These transparent mould-blown vessels were made in Jerusalem between AD 578 and 636, and probably used as containers for holy oil and sold to pilgrims coming to the city. The jug is decorated with Christian symbols, the bottle with Jewish symbols. Heights: 19.7cm (7¾in) and 8.4cm (3⁵⁄₁₆in) (Toledo Museum of Art, Toledo, Ohio)

appeared actively to encourage the art. The emperor Constantine exempted *vitriarii* (glass-makers) and *diatretarii* (glass-decorators) from all public levies in 337, and a hundred years later Theodosius II freed them from personal taxation. Bishop Menas (551-65) summoned Jewish glass-makers to the capital, and it was probably they who brought the gold sandwich glass technique (whereby gold leaf was sand-wiched between two layers of glass) with them from Palestine, then part of the empire. Mould-blown glasses decorated with Jewish and Christian symbols were made in Jerusalem between 578 and the end of the Byzantine period there in 636. They were small bottles and jugs with distinctive squat hexagonal or octagonal bodies, probably used as containers of *eulogia* (holy oil) and sold to pilgrims in Jerusalem or used in burials. About eighty of these vessels survive, most of them of brown glass, others of blue-green, olive-green or almost black glass. Some of them have handles, usually made from a tube of glass, a comparatively rare glass-making technique that provided a strong yet light construction. Decoration was in intaglio (hollow relief), probably shaped by metal moulds. The Christian symbols included three types of crosses and lozenges, while the Jewish motifs were the seven-branched candelabrum or *menorah*, the *shofar* (ram's horn), the incense shovel, the *lulav* (palm branch), gables, façades and columns, amphoras, and stylized date palms and other trees.

By the end of the tenth century Byzantine culture had become the dominant influence in Kievan Russia. Enamelled jewellery in vivid colours and comparatively free styles, similar to Byzantine products elsewhere, was being made, and enamel and glass-making workshops dating from around the eleventh century have been excavated at Kiev. Both window and vessel glass from this period have also been discovered in Russia, notably in Belgorod, near Kiev, Staryi Galich and Vyshgorod. Among the vessels found were thin-walled goblets of white glass, wine-glasses and beakers in green glass decorated with heavy pincered threading, pilgrim flasks, a type of small beaker or cup called a *stopka*, and tulip-shaped goblets decorated with coloured or opaque white threading. Coloured glass was used to make tableware, mosaics, bracelets, rings and beads in quantity. Twelfth-century glass found at Novogrudok 300 km (200 miles) north-west of Kiev included blue, violet, white, colourless and double-layered glasses, some decorated with gilding and white and red enamelling. In the early twelfth century the Mongolian conquest of Kievan Russia dealt a crushing blow to the glass industry. The main

centres were destroyed and the craftsmen either went to live under the Tartars or dispersed into the villages and countryside. Glass-making continued in a small way in western and south-western Russia, but did not re-emerge in any substantial form until the seventeenth century.

In the central Balkans to the west of Constantinople (Serbia and Macedonia), glass of the ninth to the twelfth centuries was mostly jewellery, and included bracelets, beads, buttons and pendants-amulets, and glass was also used as a substitute for precious stones. A number of the glass bracelets found in this region were imported from other parts of the empire, some showing Byzantine influence coming from Russia, but many were probably made locally, by craftsmen who probably learned their skills from contact with Byzantine glass-makers. From the twelfth to the mid-fifteenth centuries, glass increasingly became an object of everyday use in the central Balkans. From the fourteenth century, glass chalices were employed by the clergy, and other vessels in thin, colourless glass were in common use, decorated with prunts (blobs of glass), threading and moulded ribbing, and having deep kicked (indented) bases, smooth coiled base-rings or pinched motifs round the base.

This fourteenth-century prunted beaker from the Balkans is a rare complete example of a type of prunted vessel in common use in the region at this period.
Height: 8cm (3 1/8 in)
(Zavičajni Muzej, Trebinje, Yugoslavia)

Another glass-making centre on Byzantine territory was at Corinth. Here, glasses were made at two factories in a strongly Islamic style. Founded early in the eleventh century by Greeks from Egypt, the glassworks at Corinth continued production until at least 1147 (when the Normans captured the town and took craftsmen from Greece to the West). The products of the factories included pale blue bottles with moulded ribbing, blue and green bottles with bulges on the necks, beakers with prunted and ribbed decoration in pale blue and colourless glass, goblets, cups with moulded and trailed decoration, and possibly flasks and bracelets with enamelled and gilt decoration.

The influence of the Corinthian glass-workers spread across the Adriatic to Apulia in southern Italy, and perhaps through the Balkans to central Europe. Fragments of glass from the late twelfth or thirteenth centuries which have been found on several sites in northern Apulia, then ruled by the Norman kingdom of Sicily, parallel the Corinthian products, suggesting that Corinthian glass-makers may have settled there and continued to produce similar glass for a century or more. Fragments of prunted goblets from the fourteenth and early fifteenth centuries found in the central Balkans, in Yugoslavia, also suggest Corinthian influence, such as glasses found in

Above: This thick-walled bowl with ground discs in high relief, made in the twelfth or thirteenth century and mounted as a cup, was considered sufficiently precious to enter the treasuries of Byzantium and from there to be carried off by the Venetian Crusaders in 1204 to the Treasury of St Mark's in Venice.
(Treasury of St Mark's, Venice)

Left: Very similar to the cup shown above, this bowl cut with concave bosses resembling facets probably dates from the sixth or seventh century, and was made in north-western Persia or northern Mesopotamia. Diameter (top): 8.1cm (3³/₁₆ in)
(Corning Museum of Glass, Corning, New York)

graves and elsewhere in Bosnia and Herzegovina (dating from the fourteenth and first half of the fifteenth century) which were of a fine transparent metal with a yellow-brown tinge, decorated with rounded prunts, moulded ribbing and blue glass trails. Yugoslav traders from Dubrovnik often visited southern Italy after 1358, and Apulian craftsmen worked in Dubrovnik, not infrequently becoming citizens. However, it has been argued that glass of this period made in the central Balkans was of German rather than Italian design, and that some of it was perhaps made in Venice to suit Bosnian rather than Venetian taste, and some of it in Germany, Dubrovnik and Serbia, or even locally.

When Constantinople was captured and plundered during the Fourth Crusade in 1204, the Venetians took glass from the treasuries of the city and deposited it in the Treasury of St Mark's in Venice, where it remains today. These Constantinople pieces are more likely to be of Islamic than Byzantine origin, however, and therefore throw little light on the nature of glass made in Constantinople (although Oriental influence was probably as strong on Byzantine glass as it was on its textiles). For instance, a group of thick-walled bowls and cups decorated with faceting or bosses cut in deep relief probably came from Persia or Mesopotamia, and was already several centuries old when taken to Venice. The cup-shaped Charlemagne Reliquary of the Cathedral Treasury at Halberstadt (now in East Germay) was decorated in the same style as these earlier glasses, its silver-mount—which dates from much later—being inscribed with the words 'Sanctus Carolus Rex'.

A Byzantine or Russian provenance has been claimed for another group of thick-walled vessels decorated with high relief (*Hochschnitt*), and intaglio (*Tiefschnitt*) cutting. They are known collectively as Hedwig glasses, since they came to be associated with a miracle ascribed to St Hedwig (1174-1243), patron saint of Silesia. According to the story St Hedwig's husband, Duke Heinrich I, decided to check on the water which she had been drinking as part of her programme of self-denial, thinking it could be causing her ill health. He lifted up her beaker and tested its contents, and 'discovered in his mouth the taste of delicious wine which came from nothing but mere water...' After Hedwig's canonization in 1267, a number of glasses became associated with this miracle, all in smoky-brown or green-tinted glass cut with stylized motifs such as a lion, eagle and griffin, and palm leaf, crescent and star patterns. They have been found as far afield as western Germany, Cracow in Poland and Novogrudok

Left: The ninth-century Charlemagne Reliquary of the Cathedral Treasury, Halberstadt, is mounted in silver-gilt and inscribed 'Sanctus Carolus Rex'. (Cathedral Treasury, Halberstadt)

Below: A number of glasses like this one came to be associated with the Legend of St Hedwig (d. 1243), patron saint of Silesia. All of them are of the same shape and have the same style of deeply cut decoration. Their date and place of origin are uncertain; this one is probably Egyptian, dating from the eleventh or twelfth century. Height: 8.6cm (3³⁄₈in) (Corning Museum of Glass, Corning, New York)

in Russia. The two with the best claim to a connection with the saint are in the Museum of Silesian Antiquities at Breslau (Wroclaw) in Silesia, and the cathedral of Cracow in Poland. Some have been mounted in metal as chalices. Although none of them actually been found farther east, the deep cutting could also suggest a Persian or Egyptian source. Their true origin remains a mystery.

Enamelling and gilding on coloured glasses was practised with great skill in the Eastern Empire in the eleventh and twelfth centuries, and is exemplified by a dark wine-red Byzantine glass now in the Treasury of St Mark's. It is enamelled in pinkish-white, black, red, blue, bluish-green and yellow, and its chief ornamentation consists of seven round medallions depicting mythological scenes punctuated with heads in profile. It is similar in style and technique to a bowl in the Römisch Germanisches Museum, Cologne, which has four medallions containing scenes from the Old Testament (suggesting the work of a Jewish glass-maker), the intervening spaces having portraits of four young men.

Glass of this type was also found at Corinth and Cyprus, and further evidence of enamel techniques is supplied by Theophilus Presbyter, who specifically describes enamelling as done by the Greeks (those, that is, in the Byzantine dominions). After describing gilding and silvering glass, he writes:

> Then they take the white, red and green glass, which are used for enamels, and carefully grind each one separately with water on a porphyry stone. With them, they paint small flowers and scrolls and other small things they want, in varied work, between the circles and scrolls, and a border around the rim. This, being moderately thick, they fire in a furnace...

In contrast to our lack of knowledge of vessel glass-making in Byzantine times, we do know about the development of mosaic, an ancient Roman decorative technique which was brought to a high degree of perfection by Byzantine artists and craftsmen. Since the fifteenth century BC glass had been used to embellish architecture, and the rich interiors of Imperial Rome no doubt provided great scope for surface decoration by glass-makers. *Tesserae*—small pieces of glass used for mosaics—were probably made in Rome as well as Alexandria. The Byzantines adopted and developed the Roman taste for rich glass mosaic decoration on walls, floors and ceilings, and used square or rectangular *tesserae* embedded in cement for decorating domes, half-domes and other surfaces in Byzantine churches,

The great skill with which enamelling and gilding was carried out in the Eastern Empire during the eleventh and twelfth centuries is exemplified by this dark wine-red translucent glass bowl, decorated with mythological scenes in round medallions with borders of flowers, and heads in profile.
Height: 8cm (3⅛in)
(Treasury of St Mark's, Venice)

in designs which were a tangible evocation of the celestial order. Christ as ruler of the Universe (the Pantocrator) would fill the centre of a dome, and other holy personages occupied lower spaces in descending order of importance, their poses and gestures stylized against shimmering gold backgrounds.

In Kievan Russia coloured mosaics and glazed tiles were used as floor and wall coverings during the eleventh and twelfth centuries, and there are examples in Sophia Cathedral, Kiev, and Blagovechenskii Cathedral, Chernigov. Unfortunately much mosaic work in Constantinople itself was destroyed, and one has to look outside the capital, in such places as Ravenna in Italy, and Salonica, Nicaea and Daphni in Greece, for substantial examples of this technique. The church of Hagia Sophia (Holy Wisdom) in Constantinople, now a museum of Byzantine

art, has magnificent figure mosaics. Built between 523-37 by the emperor Justinian, it is the supreme masterpiece of Byzantine architecture in which Roman methods of building were modified and enriched by new aesthetic ideas, and executed in striking decorative techniques and colourful materials.

Byzantine glass-makers seem to have favoured the crown method of making window glass, in use in the Near East by the fourth century AD. Late Roman and early Byzantine examples found at Jerash and Samaria were mounted in pairs, or in greater numbers, in plaster frames. They were complete crowns about 18 cm (7 in) to 25 cm (10 in) across, with folded or rounded rims and bullion centres pushed out into rounded, flattened or slightly kicked shapes.

From the end of the twelfth century, window glass was in use in the Central Balkans, the most

The Roman technique of using glass mosaic for surface decoration was developed further by Byzantine artists, who used tesserae embedded in cement for the rich embellishment of domes and half-domes in churches such as this one in the Arian Baptistry in Ravenna, dating from the fifth century. The figures of the apostles surround the depiction of the baptism of Christ in the centre of the dome.

outstanding example being the stained-glass window in the dome of the Church of the Blessed Virgin in the monastery at Studenica (Serbia), built in the 1190s. Its fantastic animals, birds and rosettes are Byzantine in style, the glass panes being inserted in lead plates in the window. The use of crown glass in church windows was widespread in the Central Balkans by the fourteenth and fifteenth centuries.

Crown glass was made at Corinth by the eleventh century, and it was perhaps the Corinthian manufacturers who took the technique to Venice, and from there to France and Britain. Small complete crown panels, known as *rui* or *rulli*, were used by the Venetians for glazing until the seventeenth century, and crown glass was used by glass-makers near Rouen in Normandy from the thirteenth century. It is commonly claimed that Byzantine glass-makers influenced the development of glass in Venice, the city that was eventually to become the focal point for the renaissance of glass-making in western Europe. Certainly the influence of Byzantium can be seen in much of Venice's art and architecture, although the freedom and grace which was to characterize Venetian glass were very different from the stiff, stylized classicism so favoured by the Byzantines. In the first half of the fourteenth century not only were Muranese glass-makers working periodically in the Eastern Empire, on the island of Crete and in Constantinople, but Byzantine glass-makers of Corinth had probably set up their factories in southern Italy, indicating an exchange of skills and styles. However, it is not certain how the Venetians acquired the skills which flowered so dramatically during the West's Renaissance: the Byzantine connection is just one possibility.

Islamic Glass and Glass in the Far East

In the century after the death of the prophet Mohammed in AD 632, his Arab followers, the caliphs, spread his teachings through Egpyt and North Africa, as far east as Sassanid Persia and as far west as Spain. The Muslims brought a scant artistic heritage with them from the Arabic peninsula, but absorbed the cultures they encountered—Roman, Byzantine, Coptic and Sassanid—and developed a unique style of their own. With the rapid expansion of Islamic power they created a civilization comparable to the preceding era of Graeco-Roman culture.

Before the Arab conquests of Mesopotamia and Persia (now Iraq and Iran), there was already, under the Sassanian emperors (c. AD 226-642), a flourishing glass industry in the

region, catering for the luxury market. Glass-makers used mould-blowing, wheel-cutting and stamped and applied decoration for their products, which were usually in almost colourless glass (although some coloured glass was used). Among the Persian craftsmen's finest products were cut-glass items with linear and facet cutting in quincunx or honeycomb designs. In quincunx formation, circular facets were placed in an overall geometric pattern where a central facet would have six other facets placed round it. Small hemispherical bowls in thick, colourless glass decorated in this manner were exported to the East and West, some even reaching Japan. This thriving industry was badly affected by the Arab invasions, and it was to take a hundred years for a distinctly Islamic decorative style to emerge. Under the Umayyad dynasty based in Syria (661-750) only utility glass was made, but decorative glass-making skills were developed once more under the Abbasid dynasty (750-1258), which chose Baghdad in Mesopotamia for its capital. By the eighth century, after the political unification of western Asia and the southern Mediterranean lands had been achieved under one ruler, a definite Islamic flavour could be discerned in glass as well as other products. It was in Mesopotamia that a recognizably Islamic art originated, and by the ninth century Mesopotamian glassware was famous once more, Baghdad and Basra becoming particularly noted for their cut-glass wares.

It was probably the Abbasid Caliphs, who ruled from their residence at Samarra on the

This light yellow linear-cut bowl from Persia has bird and arabesque decoration. It dates from the ninth or tenth century.
Height: 8cm (3¹/₈ in)

Tigris some 80 km (50 miles) north of Baghdad from 833 to 883, from whom the new impetus for the glass industry came. Glass excavated at Samarra has shown that products with mould-blown, facet, relief and linear-cut decoration were made there. The 'bevelled' style of cutting, used by carvers and moulders in Samarra on stucco and wood decoration, was also used to decorate glass. This new style of cutting, in which the composition was defined by outlines cut on a slant, was to spread from Mesopotamia to Persia, Egypt and North Africa. Other new techniques included the use of pincers to apply a decorative motif or inscription to the wall of a vessel, and fusing together two layers of glass, as in cameo work.

From Syria, Islam inherited glass-workers noted for their manipulative skills. The Syrian glass industry had operated continuously from Roman times, producing vessels with combed, feathered and other applied decoration, as well as cut glass. Immediately after coming under the banner of Islam only everyday articles of glass were made, but later on they introduced new decorative techniques.

The Muslim invasion of Spain in the early eighth century, and the subsequent domination of southern Spain by the Spanish caliphs,

Probably from Persia, this Islamic relief-cut bottle of the ninth or tenth century depicts two running mouflon goats with curled horns confronting each other on either side of a central motif of S-shaped scrolls which probably represents the Tree of Life. Height: 16.6cm (6½in) (Corning Museum of Glass, Corning, New York)

resulted in a strong Moorish-Islamic influence on local glassware, a tradition which was to remain virtually unchanged until modern times. Although glass was also imported from the Near East, by the eleventh century it was being made in Andalucia, and in Malaga, Almería and Murcia by the thirteenth century at the latest. Although this glass had strong Islamic overtones, it remained unmistakably Spanish.

An important Islamic innovation was the technique of lustre painting, first practised in Egypt in the late Byzantine or early Islamic period, and also in Persia in the ninth century. A similar method was developed in Mesopotamia for white, tin-glazed pottery. Neither cold painting nor enamelling, lustre painting involved the firing-on of a film of pigment to the glass. It is not certain which exact method the glass-makers used, but it seems most likely that metallic compounds such as silver, copper or gold oxides dissolved in acid were painted on the cold glass surface with an oily medium, and then fired in a reducing (smoky) furnace atmosphere where the carbon monoxide would bring out the metallic lustre. A silver and sulphur compound, sometimes mixed with copper, was the simplest form of lustre. Gold would make a reddish colour and silver alone a yellow colour. Lustre

Egypt's most important contribution to the art of glass in Islamic times was the development of the technique of lustre painting, which spread to other parts of the Islamic world. This vase is an example of a lustre-painted vessel from Persia, and dates from the eighth or ninth century. Height: 14cm (5½in)

decoration on glass is almost imperceptible to the touch. It is usually reddish-brown in colour, but, more rarely, polychrome decoration was used, and it is evident from numerous excavated fragments from Fustat (the Islamic capital in Egypt between 642 and 969) that a wide variety of effects could be achieved by the technique. One complete Fustat vessel has been dated to 770-800 from an inscription. This attractive form of decoration was used for only a comparatively short time, perhaps because the glass-makers found that they were not in complete control of the colour or tone produced, and by the twelfth century they had adopted the more dependable techniques of enamelling and gilding.

Persia re-emerged as a primary producer of fine glassware under the Samanid dynasty (AD 819-1004). Cut and engraved glass was again one of the major products, with oval facet-cutting and geometric designs continuing to be used, and also linear-cut decoration as a lighter form of embellishment on vessels such as jugs and ewers. The hardstone engravers of Persia and Mesopotamia probably inspired another distinctive form of cut-glass decoration (used in both these countries and Egypt), in which the surface of the glass was ground down, leaving the decoration in relief on wafer-thin vessel walls. Persian glass-makers also used most of the other techniques known in the early Islamic period, including mould-blowing, casting, stamped and pincered work, lustre painting and applied work, but not enamelled or gilded decoration.

With so much emphasis on abrasive decorative techniques it is hardly surprising that a rare revival of the Roman art of cameo-cut glass should occur in Persia, Egypt and Mesopotamia during the ninth and tenth centuries. Complete pieces have been found in Persia and Egypt, and a few fragments in Samarra. The overlay glass was usually in green or blue applied to an almost colourless glass body, but the products did not match the technical excellence of Roman examples. Islamic glass-makers probably abandoned the cupping method of casing used by the Romans (where a paraison made of one colour would be dipped into a previously prepared 'cup' of semi-molten glass in a contrasting colour), and instead probably put patches of colour on the paraison in the desired position, ready for subsequent engraving.

This flourishing industry was all but destroyed when, at the beginning of the thirteenth century, Genghis Khan succeeded in conquering Mongolia. He united its tribes, and from his capital at Karakorum led the Mongols in establishing his great empire. The Mongols first conquered Persia, in 1231, and then Mesopotamia, sacking Baghdad in 1258. As a result, Syria

emerged as the main glass-making centre of the Islamic Empire. Islamic glass was to reach its highest pinnacle in the spectacular enamelled and gilt products of Ayyubid and Mamluk Syria in the thirteenth and fourteenth centuries. The Syrian glass-makers may have developed the art of enamelling locally, and learned the gilding technique from Egypt. Alternatively, both techniques could have been an offshoot of the lustre-painting tradition, transplanted by craftsmen leaving Egypt at the fall of the Fatimid dynasty in 1171. The products of the Syrians became renowned in the Near East, and their enamelled and gilded glasses reached as far afield as Russia, China, Sweden and England, as well as Egypt and Mesopotamia. The only other gilded and enamelled ware of this period is the so-called 'Fustat' group made in Egypt, and said to date from between about 1270 and 1340.

This Persian twin-spouted pitcher on three short feet is of light green glass with blue glass spouts. It is decorated with applied pincered trails, one of the many techniques in use in Persia during the ninth and tenth centuries.
Height: 30cm (11⁷/₁₆in)

Right: The Roman art of cameo cutting was revived in Persia during the ninth century. This flask is of almost colourless glass with an overlay of green glass in which there is a hare carved in relief, repeated on the opposite side, and a stylized lily, also repeated, between them. The patches of iridescence have been caused by weathering. Height: 15cm (5⅞in) (British Museum, London)

Below: This Syrian pilgrim flask of almost colourless glass (c. 1250-60) is painted with elaborate enamelled motifs, including a six-lobed cartouche surrounded by gilded scrolls with terminals in the form of human and animal heads. Height: 23cm (9in) (British Museum, London)

Certain styles of Syrian decorated glass have tentatively been associated with Raqqa, Aleppo and Damascus. Although there is no proof that glass was made at Raqqa on the river Euphrates (which was then on the periphery of the Syrian sphere although actually in north-western Mesopotamia), it is highly likely that it was made there, and it is certain that both Aleppo and Damascus were well established as glass-making centres. The geographer Yāqūt (d. 1229) wrote of a desert mountain which produced a white sand used for making glass in Aleppo, and the traveller al-Qaswīnī (d. 1283) wrote:

> Among the most notable things in this city is the glass-bazaar. He who enters there will be reluctant to leave, on account of the astonishing multitude of notable and exquisite objects which he sees there, and which are exported into every other country...

Earlier examples of the Syrian product, decorated with rich, thick enamelling and figures on a relatively large scale, were probably made at the northern town of Aleppo. This was near an area where glass-workers from Armenaz, near Tyre, are supposed to have settled, the glasses being brought into the town to be decorated. Aleppo's primacy in decorative techniques was probably passed on to Damascus when the Emir al-Nāsir Yūsuf II fled before Hulagu Khan to that city in 1250, and the glass industry continued to flourish in Damascus until its sacking in 1400. A European writer who was in Syria between 1345-46 spoke of 'the street of the glass-painters' in Damascus, and in medieval European inventories, rare and exotic glasses were commonly described as 'de Damas'.

The first incidence of gilding and enamelling in Syria occurred between about 1170 and 1270 in the north of the country (possibly at Raqqa), where glasses decorated with coloured enamels and gilded inscriptions were produced. Among this group were beakers in almost colourless glass, with inscriptions most often in white, gold and turquoise-blue, frequently accompanied by dotted diamond and geometric patterns. From the mid-thirteenth century, blue and red colours began to dominate Syrian enamelled ware, and much use was also made of opaque white and gold. Enamelling was sometimes applied to both back and front surfaces of vessels in a broad elaborate style, the decoration being in perceptible relief. Motifs included animals, birds, human figures, arabesque foliage and shields. One of the finest examples of Syrian enamelling from this period is a beaker known as 'The Luck of Edenhall', which was probably brought to the West by a Crusader. (It is now in the Victoria and Albert Museum in London.)

The finest enamelled and gilded wares in the

Near East almost certainly came from Damascus. Towards the end of the thirteenth century, a Chinese influence became evident in Syrian designs, following the establishment of the Mongol dynasty in nearby Persia and Mesopotamia, and the founding of the Yüan or Mongol dynasty in China (1260-1368). A new naturalism was observable in the depiction of plant forms, especially vine ornament, and new motifs included cloud-scrolls, lotuses, peony flowers, dragons, phoenixes and tigers. The objects decorated by the enamellers and gilders included sprinklers, globes, footed bowls, beakers, long-necked bottles, and mosque lamps.

Mosque lamps, destined for the Egyptian market, were the most celebrated of Damascus wares. Between the sultans and their chief officers in the Egyptian-Syrian dominions there was much competition to build and decorate mosques and madrasehs (Muslim schools), and glass lamps were used to light their interiors. Great numbers of them were suspended from the roofs of mosques by chains, and when the roof was very high the chains would run together through an enamelled glass globe before radiating out to the handles of the lamps. Three or six chains would be used, depending on the number of handles provided on the glass. Small,

This fourteenth-century hanging lamp, probably from a mosque in Egypt, is of smoke-coloured glass enamelled with a verse from the Koran which, translated, reads: 'God is the light of the heavens and of the earth. His light is the niche wherein is the lamp.' The looped handles would have been attached to chains suspended from the roof of the mosque.
Height: 39.5cm (15½in)
(Wallace Collection, London)

undecorated mosque lamps may have been made in Syria as early as the eleventh century, the decorated product appearing in about 1280. Very few lamps date from before the beginning of the fourteenth century, and earlier examples usually had three loop handles rather than the six of later products. As the fourteenth century progressed, the decoration became steadily more perfunctory, perhaps partly because it was realized that detail on the lamps was not easily seen from the ground.

In fact, mosque lamps were not really lamps at all, but lamp-holders or lanterns. Some examples have a central tube where a candle would have been fixed, and others were probably lit by a separate lamp containing a wick floating on oil. They were of an inverted bell shape which was usually decorated with rich enamelling and gilding with the name of the sultan, dedicatory inscriptions, armorial blazons, floral designs in Chinese style, and quotations from the Koran in Neskhi script.

In addition to being decorative, mosque lamps were also symbolic, since they fulfilled the words of the Koran: 'God is the light of the Heavens and the Earth. His light is as a niche in which is a lamp, the lamp in a glass, the glass as it were a glittering star.' Some lamps have this inscription enamelled and gilded on them, as part of their

Above: This Persian perfume sprinkler, known as an Omom, shows a Chinese influence which became apparent in the Islamic glass produced towards the end of the thirteenth century. In spite of being heavily corroded, it still has the remains of the rich gold enamels with which it was painted.
Height: 20cm (7⅞in)
(Museum für Islamische Kunst, Berlin)

Right: In Japan, glass was of spiritual significance and used mainly to make beads and other small ornamental objects. These eighth-century fish-form tallies are from the Shōsō-in, a monument to the Emperor Shōmu.
Maximum length: 8.2cm (3¼in)
(Shōsō-in Treasure-house, Nara)

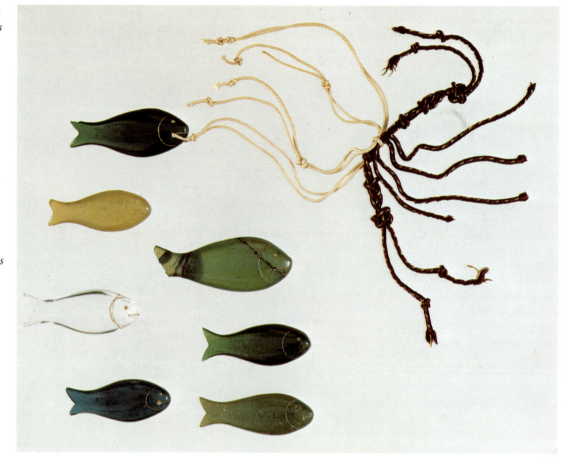

Right: These coiled, moulded or blown glass beads dating from the eighth century are among the thousands which were housed in the Shōsō-in monument in Japan.
Diameters: 0.8–2.3cm (⁵/₁₆–1in)
(Shōsō-in Treasure-house, Nara)

Below: This free-blown cut-glass bowl from the tomb of the Japanese emperor Ankan, who is thought to have died in the late sixth century, probably came from Persia, since many bowls of this type have been found there.
Height: 8.2cm (3¼in)
(Tokyo National Museum, Tokyo)

to be made at Damascus after Timur (Tamerlaine) captured the city in 1400. The glass industry gradually declined as many of its skilled craftsmen left for Samarkand, Timur's capital. After this date, little glass of any quality was produced in the Near East, although there is a slight possibility that Syrian glass-makers established a new tradition of enamelling and gilding in Transoxiana (Uzbek SSR) or Persia in the following century.

Beyond the Islamic Empire, in the Far East, there was comparatively little glass production. According to Chinese legend, the secrets of glass-making were brought to that country in AD 435 by travellers from the West. Since glass beads, amulets, pins, buckles, decorative plaques and model animals have been found in Chinese graves of as early as the late Chou period (c.1027-256 BC), this legend presumably referred to the art of blowing glass. China imported Roman glass, glasses were depicted in early Chinese paintings, and small moulded ornaments and votive objects such as Buddha figures were made in the ninth and tenth centuries, but little more is known about Chinese glass-making until the beginning of the Ch'ing period (1644-1912), when the first explicit references to it are found in Chinese literature.

In Japan, it is likely that the first glass objects were made from imported materials or melted-down Chinese glass products. From the beginnings of the glass industry in the Yayoi period (c. 250 BC - c. AD 250), it was apparent that glass was not just a material to the Japanese, but was of a spiritual significance which it was to hold for many centuries.

During the so-called Tomb period, which extended from around the mid-third to the mid-sixth century, there was a large increase in glass bead production, and new and varied types emerged. Japanese blown-glass vessels made their first appearance, and glass was also used for insets in metal ornaments and for bracelets. Cinerary urns, glass reliquaries and *cloisonné* pieces were introduced during the next two centuries. The Shōsō-in, a monument to the emperor Shōmu (d.756), housed tens of thousands of glass beads, glass pieces, insets, sash accessories and rods for scrolls, as well as *cloisonné* work. From the tenth century onwards, glass-making in Japan continued only in a very diminished form, and virtually disappeared between the fourteenth and sixteenth centuries.

In India, apart from beads and a few other small objects which appeared from the fifth century BC, there is not much evidence for glass or its manufacture until the Mughal period (1526-1857).

decoration. The majority of inscriptions, however, referred to the Mameluke sultans and their officers, their rich decoration bearing witness to the luxury of the times. Armorial bearings and blazons which were granted by the sultan to his military dignitaries, (probably referring to offices held during their careers) appear on the lamps. A cup indicated the office of Cup Bearer to the sultan, polo-sticks the Polo Master, crossbows the Arquebusier, a lozenge-shaped napkin the Master of the Wardrobe, a pen-box the State Secretary, and a sword or scimitar the Armour-Bearer.

Mosque lamps and other glass products ceased

CHAPTER THREE

THE TRADITION FROM MEDIEVAL TO RENAISSANCE

As the popularity of Venetian cristallo *increased during the first half of the sixteenth century, there was a lightening of stylistic detail in enamelled decoration to allow the ductile qualities of the glass to be appreciated. This votive lamp, or* cesendello, *which shows the Angel of the Annunciation, would have been suspended by chains and hung below a glass smoke shade.*
Height: 36.2cm (14¼in) (Metropolitan Museum of Art, New York)

During the late Middle Ages in Europe, the Church, as in so much else, was the focus of the most sophisticated achievements in glass-making, both in the stained glass of the Western and the mosaics of the Eastern Empire. The northern tradition of forest glass, or *Waldglas*, which had grown from unseen medieval and in some cases possibly older Roman roots, continued, with the manufacture of mostly commonplace vessels and utensils of rather poor-quality metal. At the same time, in southern Europe, the development in Venice of a type of thin, colourless soda glass known as *cristallo* was to contribute to the predominance of the city's glass industry over all others after the mid-fifteenth century. While early glass-making activities at Venice must have been very similar to those of other European centres, the revival of learning known as the Renaissance (emphasizing the importance of Latin and Greek classical literature) which occurred in Italy from the mid-fourteenth to the early sixteenth century, led to ideals that stimulated magnificent achievements in all the arts, including glass-making.

The Rise of Venice

A number of factors led to the rise in importance of Venice as a glass-making centre during the medieval period and to its eventual supremacy during the Renaissance. One of the most important of these was the city's geographical position, which enabled it to establish trade links with both western Europe and Byzantium and the East. For trading to be efficient, a navy became essential to protect the merchandise, and Venice was an early example of a sea power both supporting and creating commerce. At the

same time this brought the city into conflict, both with its arch-rival Genoa and with Byzantium, for superiority in the eastern Mediterranean. With the sacking of Constantinople in 1204 and the subsequent removal of its artefacts to Venice, Italy was brought into direct contact with the more sophisticated culture of the East, while contacts with the short-lived Frankish kingdoms of the eastern Mediterranean, known as 'Outremer', established during the Crusades, introduced Venice via its trading links to the enamelled glass tradition of the Syrians, mainly at Damascus and Aleppo. Enamelled glassware from these centres, now known as Syro-Frankish glass, was greatly prized in Europe, as is indicated by such glasses as the 'Luck of Edenhall' and 'Charlemagne's Beaker', which were treasured heirlooms ascribed mystical powers. It is therefore highly likely that Syrian enamelled glass had a great impact on the Venetian glass-makers: it cannot be coincidental that the foundations of the Venetian glass industry were laid during the Syrian glasshouses' peak of achievement in the thirteenth and fourteenth centuries, or that the seemingly sudden development of Venetian enamelled glass in the mid-fifteenth century should come after the extinction of the Syrian glass industry in 1400, when Timur (Tamerlane) sacked Damascus.

There are virtually no examples of Venetian glass from before the fifteenth century, with the exception of a group of beakers with enamelled decoration which have posed problems of attribution. The best-known of these is the so-called 'Aldrevandini' beaker in the British Museum, which is painted in rather a primitive hand with three German coats of arms and the inscription *Aldrevandin mefeci[t]*. Features

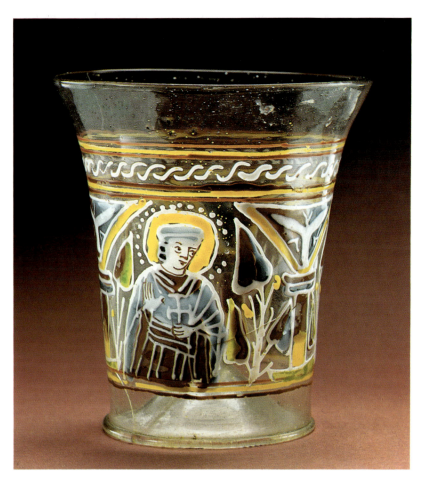

This late-thirteenth-century beaker in the Treasury at Chur Cathedral in the Swiss Alps, enamel-painted with three half-figures of saints, could have come from Venice, according to documents that have recently come to light, although it has also been attributed to a Syro-Frankish workshop. Height: 9.6cm (3¾in) (Dommuseum, Chur)

guilds, carrying water-bottles and scent flasks 'and other such graceful objects of glass'. In 1271 the glass-makers' *Capitolare* (statutes) were issued, and show the strict control exercised over the industry: the import of foreign glass was prohibited; the furnaces were only to be in production between January and August; glass was to be exported only in the late summer; foreign glass-makers were forbidden to work in Venice; the size of the furnace was stipulated; and two watches were to tend the fires throughout the night.

For the first time since the days of the Roman Empire, glass was being made in an important western urban centre. This was made possible only by the Venetian trading fleet, since all raw materials had to be imported into Venice, isolated on the lagoon. Sand was obtained from the crushed pebbles of the river Ticino, and barilla, a seaweed used for soda ash, was imported in vast quantities from Alicante. In a treaty concluded in 1277 between Doge Jacopo Contarini and Bohemund VII, Prince of Antioch, the regulation of cullet (glass fragments and broken glass for remelting), imported from the Middle East to Venice, was mentioned.

Each important aspect of the glass-making craft was separately organized. There were the makers of glass vessels, the makers of flat glass, or *rui*, the *fiolarii*, or bottle-makers, the lens-grinders, and the *contarini*, or bead-makers. Beads were made at Venice certainly from the thirteenth century and formed an important section of the industry. Bead-making itself was highly specialized, being divided into the makers of *margarite*, *perle a lume* and *paternostri*. They were used in rosaries and as decorative ornament, and also as barter with primitive peoples. From the late fifteenth century beads were often made of a combination of coloured rods fashioned over a lamp (a technique later known as *millefiori*).

In 1292 the authorities decreed that all glasshouses in Venice were to be transferred to the islands of Murano, about 5km (3 miles) away from the main city. Although most probably instigated to reduce the risk of fire, the transferal of the industry to one place must have had the effect of welding the glass-makers into a tightly knit, proud and secretive community. By the end of the sixteenth century, when Venice as a whole had a population of 170,000, Murano had 7000 inhabitants, of whom it has been estimated that about 3000 were connected with glass-making. As Venetian commerce increased and its commercial superiority in the Mediterranean was established, the authorities began to follow a policy of encouraging their own industries, particularly those of luxury goods,

such as the use of paint on both its inner and outer surfaces point to a Syrian influence, and the group has been tentatively attributed to a Syro-Frankish fourteenth-century workshop. However, in the treasury in the Cathedral at Chur in the Swiss Alps, there is another beaker painted with three half-figures of saints, and documents that have recently come to light refer to one Gregorio of Naples and Bartolommeo of Zara in Turkey as painters of beakers, and specifically mention a beaker with three figures. Whether these are early examples of Venetian work or not, it seems increasingly probable that the links with the Syro-Frankish and Byzantine glass centres were stronger than had been previously thought, and that there was a continuous tradition of enamelled decoration on glass in Venice from at least the thirteenth century, if not very much earlier.

There is definite evidence that by the thirteenth century Venetian glass was already being distributed round northern Europe by itinerant pedlars; and it is known that Richard II of England (r. 1367-1400) gave permission for Venetian merchants to sell a consignment of glass from a quayside on the Thames. The Venetian guild of glass-makers was well established by this time, and at the inauguration of a new doge in 1268 took part in the procession with other

which could be exported and thus help balance the flood of imports into the city. Through strict quality control and a continuous series of edicts, the authorities strove to encourage only the best, in glass-making as in other industries.

By the mid-fifteenth century, glass of a sophistication hitherto unknown in the West was being made at Murano. There was probably an influx of skilled craftsmen into the city after the fall of Damascus in 1400, and again in 1453 when Constantinople finally fell to the Turks (edicts against foreigners presumably being waived to absorb them). The impact of these immigrants on all branches of the arts in Italy was enormous, and undoubtedly a factor in the cultural revival known as the Renaissance. As the Turks increasingly blocked Venetian trading activities in the eastern Mediterranean, Venice sought greater ties with the West, and this coincided with the expansion of Venetian power on the Italian mainland; peace was established with Florence and Milan as a result of the growing power of the Turks.

All these events helped to create an environment stimulating to the growth of the decorative arts, and at about this time the first fine-quality, artistic glass was manufactured. Enamelling on clear coloured glass became popular, and among the glassware produced was a range of ceremonial standing cups, originally with covers, in deep blue or green glass, and distinguished by the style and subject-matter of their enamelled decoration. These cups followed ecclesiastical metalwork shapes, with strong Gothic elements such as ribbing, lobed knops and pincered flanges. Their massive vigour ignores the plasticity and ductile possibilities of the medium, not to be fully exploited until a century later, and

By the mid-fifteenth century, enamelling on clear coloured glass had become popular, and ceremonial cups like this wedding cup of blue glass, attributed to Angelo Barovier (and known as the Barovier Cup), were being made at Murano. The horseback procession divides medallions on opposite sides of the bowl portraying the bride and groom, and the other side shows women bathing at the Fountain of Love. Height: 18cm (7in) (Museo Vetrario di Murano, Murano)

Right: Enamel decoration became more refined during the 1470s, as is shown by this large Venetian chalice with conical bowl and foot (the knop has been restored with a metal frame).
(Museo del Castello Sforzesco, Milan)

Below: The painter of the enamelled frieze on this lattimo *jug might have seen Mantegna's famous engraving 'The Battle of the Sea Gods'.*
Height: 20.3cm (8in)
(Toledo Museum of Arts, Toledo, Ohio)

instead concentrates on painted decoration which is thickly applied, suggesting an unsophisticated, experimental approach. Their bowls are divided into a broad continuous frieze flanked by rich gilded and enamelled borders.

The subject-matter depicted on this group of goblets is exclusively allegorical or mythological, except for the goblet now in the Museo Civico, Bologna, which depicts two biblical scenes, the 'Flight into Egypt' and 'The Adoration'. The sources for the allegorical and mythological themes would almost certainly have come from contemporary books of drawings, prints and possibly original painting or frescoes. Renaissance influences from Florence had reached Venice via Padua, through Gentile da Fabriano, who decorated the Doge's Palace in 1423. The 'Triumph of Venus' goblet in the British Museum has a broad, slightly convex bowl of

marked irregularity, painted in (to modern eyes) a charming childlike manner with two processions accompanying the cars of Venus and Chastity. The figures are short and ungainly, with little individuality of expression, but they succeed through their sheer exuberance. The classical allusions are gauche but unmistakable—Venus sits on what could be a Gothic throne or classical chariot. The gilding that enlivens and enriches the figural scenes consists of line borders sometimes edged with lappets, and gilt scale pattern or rosettes embellished with dots of white, red or blue enamel. Another goblet probably from the same workshop and now in the Bargello, Florence, shows the 'Triumph of Justice'. The judicial car, reminiscent of a float, is decorated with classical swags and surmounted by a canopy, or baldaquin, and pulled by a lion and a panther flanked by attendant maidens in flowing dresses, presumably influenced by the chiton worn by the ancient Greeks. The goblet in the Gewerbemuseum, Cologne, is decorated with one of the richest processional scenes of the group, a marriage cortège displaying a mixture of classical and contemporary detail typical of this date: the costumes of the wedding guests are in the height of fifteenth-century fashion, while the bride is drawn in a classical chariot decorated with sphinxes, and the whole is surmounted by a proverb inscribed in early Italian.

The work of contemporary artists was influential, too. For example, the painter of the frieze of merfolk on a *lattimo* (opaque white) jug in the Toledo Museum must have seen Mantegna's famous engraving 'The Battle of the Sea Gods' at either first or second hand. Similarly, the portraits on the 'Betrothal Goblet' in the British Museum show marked similarities to those by Carpaccio, whose famous *St Ursula* cycle could have been seen in Venice. Though still of Gothic form, the goblet is decorated with greater sophistication, with portrait medallions of the betrothed flanked by putti and surmounted by a continuous wreath. The classical details of putti and wreath, elements also found on a fine *tazza*, or saucer-shaped dish (also at Toledo), point again to Mantegna's influence, possibly through artists such as Mocetto and Montagna.

The *Metamorphoses* of Ovid were also a potent source of inspiration for the fine and applied arts, and enamelled decoration on glassware shows similarities to illustrations of Ovid's work published in Venice. The celebrated 'Fairfax Cup' of about 1480, a charming small enamelled turquoise beaker, is decorated with three episodes from the story of Pyramus and Thisbe from Ovid, painted in the same style as the 'Triumph' goblets. Books of emblems and miscellaneous lore, such as *The Dream of Polyphilus* by Francesco Colonna, and the Tarot cards, were also used as sources.

Although suggested chronologies for early enamelled wares will always be tentative since so few examples have survived, it seems that by the end of the fifteenth century enamelled decoration had become more refined, as the early method of applying thick layers of enamel was

This enamelled Venetian plate of amethyst-coloured glass is decorated with a border of vines, peacocks and goldfinches in flight, surrounding a portrait that shows the influence of Piero della Francesca. Attributed to Angelo Barovier, it dates from the mid-fifteenth century.
Diameter: 25.6cm (10in)
(Museo Provinciale d'Arte, Trento)

replaced by thinner, more painterly washes. The whole process, which was extremely hazardous, is described in detail in a fifteenth-century manuscript preserved in the Convent of S. Salvatore in Bologna. The glass would have been gilded as the final stage in its making, then transferred to the annealing chamber to be slowly cooled before eventually being brought into the outside atmosphere. The glass would then be either painted in the glasshouse if it was a large concern or sent out to a decorator's studio. The enamel was affixed in powder form with an agent such as oil of lavender, and the glass was then slowly reheated by being passed through the annealing chamber and then cautiously reintroduced to the heat of the furnace or muffle kiln until the enamel melted and fused with the glass. The piece would then be returned to the annealing chamber for the slow process of being cooled. The whole lengthy process had to be controlled extremely carefully, and the possibility of breakage existed until the last moment. (The application by Maria Barovier for a licence to build a furnace in 1487 may possibly relate to a small furnace for firing outside-decorated enamelled work, as well as to the production of *millefiori* which also required low temperatures.)

At the same time as enamelled vessels were being made in translucent coloured glass, a timespan of less than a hundred years, they were also being made in an opaque white glass called *lattimo*—derived from the word *latte*, meaning milk. The opaque effect was obtained by adding an opacifying agent, oxide of tin, to the ingredients. *Lattimo* or milk glass seems to have been made for only about fifty years after 1475; after about 1525 documents cease to refer to its manufacture. Milk glass reflected a European response to the exotic: it was made to imitate Chinese porcelain, imports of which came to Venice through trade links with the Middle East. In 1561 the Doge Malipiero received a gift of Chinese porcelain from the Sultan of Egypt, and both *lattimo* and Medici porcelain reflect the beginnings of centuries of influence by, and the imitation of, Oriental works of art. Only very few pieces of *lattimo* have survived, despite the fact that a glass-master, Bernadino Ferro, was reported to the authorities for having illegally fired more than a thousand *lattimo* and other coloured pieces for the painter Mario Obizzo.

As a group, these known *lattimo* survivals, fourteen in all, are a useful study in microcosm of the broad field of fifteenth- and sixteenth-century Venetian glass, since they include all the conventional shapes. There is a standing cup of Gothic type, a simple shallow bowl, a straight-sided beaker with milled foot-rim, a pilgrim flask, a double-handled bottle and a jug.

Except for the Chinese porcelain-inspired motifs in the form of foliate decoration on two of the pieces, all the other decorative elements are representative of Venetian decoration in general. For example, the fashion for betrothal or marriage goblets (*coppa nuziale* and *coppa amatoria*) is represented by two bowls with Carpaccio-inspired male and female portraits in typical roundels, framed by gilt and dot border and with a sinuous ribbon bearing a Latin motto. Mottoes expressing sentiments such as 'ego vobis servo son' (I am at your service) were common on all kinds of glass vessels.

A unique *lattimo* piece, now in the British Museum, is the bottle or ring-handled vase painted with the portrait and badge of Henry VII of England. A green glass variant was recorded as existing at the end of the nineteenth century, but has since vanished. Both pieces were discovered in England, and examples of painted glass are recorded as appearing in an inventory of Henry VIII in 1542. It is known that in 1506 the diplomat Castiglione was sent to England to receive the Order of the Garter on behalf of the Duke of Urbino; Venetian enamelled glass would certainly have been considered a suitably princely gift in return. (In contrast, the Emperor Frederick III, on being offered gifts of glass during a visit to Venice in 1468, rejected the gifts by smashing them to the ground, thereby implying that something more durable, such as gold or silver, would have been more appreciated.)

Allegory and mythology are also represented on *lattimo*, not only by the jug at Toledo already mentioned, but by two pilgrim flasks, one of which (now in Baltimore) is decorated with scenes of Apollo and Cyparissus and Europa and the Bull, and the other (now in Leningrad) with a nymph and satyr. The sources are engravings from either Colonna's *The Dream of Polyphilus* (as on the Leningrad flask) or other artists such as Montagna, the literary source being the popular Ovid. Both flasks are painted by the same hand. Three of the surviving *lattimo* objects are painted with religious subjects. One of them, a bottle of similar shape to the Henry VII bottle, bears a coat of arms, another important aspect of Venetian decoration. Many parallels can be found between all these pieces and contemporary majolica (enamelled earthenware) decorated in the so-called *historiato* tradition.

As a result of the destruction and disappearance of the glass formerly in the Kunstgewerbe Museum, Berlin, there no longer exists a number of Venetian enamelled glasses which represented one of the high points of this art form. For example, in the comprehensive study of Renaissance Venetian glass by Robert Schmidt,

This lattimo *bowl with enamelled and gilt decoration (c. 1500) is thought to be one of a pair of marriage cups. It depicts the head of a young man in a style reminiscent of the work of the Venetian painter Vittore Carpaccio (active 1490-1523/6). The ribbon fluttering in front of him bears the legend 'Ego vobis servo son', a mixture of Latin and Italian meaning 'I am your servant'. Height: 5.9cm (2³⁄₈in) Diameter: 14.1cm (5¹⁄₂in) (Corning Museum of Glass, Corning, New York)*

Decorated with an applied blue band and vertical rows of prunts enamelled in opaque colours, on a ground engraved with birds and foliate scrolls in diamond-point, this large Venetian beaker of about 1520 is made of cristallo, *but its style is in some ways reminiscent of products from the Tyrolese glass-houses.*
Height: 22cm (8⅝in)

Die Venezianischen Emailgläser des XV und XVI Jaarhunderts (1911), there is an illustration of a beaker from the collection decorated with scenes from the legend of Jason and Medea, painted by a most competent hand.

The Renaissance ideas which affected all aspects of life soon influenced the course of glass-making in a fundamental way. The Renaissance courts of Italy and the upper classes were creating a way of life based on the ideal of the cultured courtier, later taken up by Castiglione in his famous manual on courtly matters, *Il Cortegiano* (1528), which described the highest moral aspirations of the Renaissance. An increased interest in science and natural history reflected these aspirations, and princes vied with one another to collect curiosities and examples of precious and figured semi-precious stones, in both raw and worked forms. Rock crystal, a natural quartz, was especially prized: it was held to have magical properties, and was incorporated into religious objects of veneration; only the very rich could afford to use it for domestic purposes. A substitute was eagerly sought, and by the middle of the fifteenth century the Venetian glass-makers, by using manganese as a decolourizing agent, had perfected an almost colourless soda glass in imitation of rock crystal.

This *cristallo*, as it was called, was far superior to any glass produced before, and created an insatiable demand for the products of the glasshouses using it. Its purity and thinness were a source of wonder and fascination, and *cristallo* gradually superseded the heavier, coloured glass

previously used. It is not known who invented or perfected it, but it is now thought that Angelo Barovier (d. 1460), of the famous Muranese glass-making family, played an important role in experiments to perfect *cristallo* as well as coloured glass. He had a particular interest in the technical aspects of glass-making, and has long been credited with having perfected the art of enamelling. All that is definitely known, however, is that two glass-blowers were given the exclusive right to produce the new glass in 1457. Before long, Venetian glass was considered to be the finest made anywhere in the western world, and by 1500 Venice, at the height of its prosperity and power in the Mediterranean, one of the four great cities of western Europe with a population of over 100,000, had a glass industry which was one of the major sources of its wealth.

During this period Venice was carrying out special commissions for export to clients north of the Alps. A goblet with the arms of Bohemia and Hungary, possibly the earliest datable Venetian glass with armorial decoration, was almost certainly made for Matthias Corvinus, King of Hungary, who died in 1490. Another armorial beaker, formerly in the von Hirsch Collection (now dispersed), is reminiscent of earlier simple Gothic vessels, but made of the new *cristallo* metal and (unusually) decorated with St Michael and St Catherine in typically Gothic cinquelobed panels, a third panel being painted with the arms of the Behaim family. Since Michael Behaim of Nuremberg married Katerina Lochnerin in 1495, it would seem that this small beaker is a variant of the *coppa nuziale*. The figures of the saints recall the 'Triumph' goblets, particularly in their white faces which have a mask-like quality, but at the same time they are more three-dimensional and statuesque, betokening a slightly more sophisticated hand. Armorial pilgrimage flasks have survived, probably made for the marriage of Alessandro Bentivoglio to Ippolita Sforza in 1492, and other glasses bear the arms of Louis XII of France and Anne of Brittany, who were married in 1499.

By the early sixteenth century decoration in the High Renaissance style was firmly established, and typical decorative elements included the use of grotesques and arabesques (as first used by Raphael in the Vatican) in all the applied arts. Mythical and imaginary animals such as centaurs, sphinxes, satyrs and mermen were often depicted, for example on a distinct group of enamelled wares, painted mainly in strong oranges and yellows, on which a bold type of foliate scroll also appears. Typical of the group is the Waddesdon 'centaur' goblet, the form of which is still of the chalice type but which is made of *cristallo*, evidence of its later date. The enamelling is boldly executed with scrolls springing fancifully in the background. There are still echoes of earlier influences, however, in the decorative details on the spreading foot, where a loop border is embellished with crocket finials. This type of decoration appears on a number of goblets, one of which was found at the base of the Campanile when it collapsed in 1902. Another example, in the British Museum, is of trumpet form with a spreading foot, and painted with opposing mermen entwined with dolphins arranged as a grotesque. Also in this group is a blue pilgrim flask from the same workshop, painted with a putto riding erect on a dolphin and brandishing a typical leafy scroll. The sky is flecked with yellow dashes like rain, another feature of this group, introduced no doubt to enliven the backdrop. The detail is invariably outlined in black, and the figures are made three-dimensional with abrupt shading.

Whereas only a few of the earliest monumental enamelled glasses still exist, a larger, more representative group of enamelled wares from the first half of the sixteenth century has survived, and shows a lightening of stylistic detail as the popularity of *cristallo* with its ductile qualities increased. *Cristallo* could be blown wafer-thin and, while still semi-molten, would respond to the imaginative manipulation of the glass-blower. As the century progressed, the demand for enamelled decoration, less appropriate for the delicate *cristallo*, gradually declined, except from customers in northern Europe. The Venetians seem to have continued to execute special export orders possibly into the following century, particularly for Germany, until gradually the demand was fulfilled by German glass-making centres.

It is difficult to understand the purpose of many of the wares of this period. This luxury glass, desired by the smart and rich who were the only people who could afford it, was both for display and for use, but there is no way of knowing which of the Venetian glass that survives was for what purpose, or whether it is representative of the whole output or not. One

This Venetian enamelled beaker was probably made for the marriage of Katerina Lochnerin and Michael Behaim of Nuremberg in 1495. It is decorated with three panels outlined in latti-mo, *one containing the arms and crest of the Behaim family, one with St Catherine and the head of the Emperor Maximinius, and one (shown here) of St Michael slaying Lucifer with his sword. Three flowering trees divide the panels. The use of figures of saints to indicate the names of the betrothed is most unusual: normally the arms of both parties would be depicted. Height: 11.5cm (4⅝in)*

The tazza *was one of the most popular types of luxury glass made in Venice during the Renaissance period. This one, made in about 1500, has a shallow bowl on a low spreading foot with a folded gilt ring. The enamelled medallion in its centre, depicting the winged lion of St Mark, is encircled by coloured bands and twelve gilt spiral ribs radiating from the centre towards a border of gilt scale pattern embellished with enamelled dots.*
Height: 7cm (2¾in)
Diameter: 25.5cm (10in)
(British Museum, London)

of the most popular types of glass at this period seems to have been the wide, shallow bowl, or *tazza*, which was sometimes on a stem but more often with a spreading foot supporting the bowl directly, with the rim of the foot (and sometimes the bowl as well) folded up or under to give strength to the edge. *Tazze* were possibly intended for holding fruit or sweetmeats as a table centre, and their decoration was comparatively restrained, restricted to a band of gilt scale or lappets round the rim and enamel dot borders, creating a muted but rich effect. The centre of these dishes was decorated with a roundel flanked by bands matching the rim, and filled with either further geometric decoration or vignettes, which were often of emblematic significance (such as a hind stretched out on a grassy bank or the slaying of a sea-monster), and coats of arms, implying perhaps that these are survivals of larger sets which would have included other types of wares *en suite*. The shapes are inevitably reminiscent of a range of similar items produced in metal, and show typically the use of ribs and gadroons and the division of the surface into zones.

Simple decorated pieces of table glass had been produced at Murano in the fifteenth century but none has survived, though they are recorded in contemporary paintings. Examples of wine cups

and goblets, which were obviously made in great numbers in plain *cristallo*, have survived from the sixteenth and seventeenth centuries. In terms of design, these pieces are among the most economically elegant objects made in glass, showing a perfect balance between the various parts of bowl, stem and foot. Their simplicity of line emphasizes the lightness and clarity of the material. Bowls are trumpet-shaped, with a flared or frilled lip, the cigar-shaped, hollow stem is usually separated from the bowl by a collar and is sometimes moulded with wrythen ribs, and the foot is invariably conical and folded at the rim.

As the century advanced, the influence of Mannerism in art became stronger, with emphasis on the bizarre, etiolated and fanciful, and these tendencies were reflected in the glass produced at Murano. Nipped and teased straps and scrolls worked with pincers were added to stems and sometimes up the sides of bowls; stems were shaped into a series of bulbs or moulded lion's masks, and bowls into a series of lobes. Another element in Muranese decoration was the use of gilding. Where it was not used to enrich borders on rims it was occasionally used to form the main decoration, various zones of the vessel being gilded to give a granular effect. With the point of a needle, the gilding could also be imbricated (arranged to overlap) to achieve inscriptions. These elements, along with the growing popularity of *filigrana* (filigree) glass, led to the production of the type of luxury glass for which Venice became most famous: rich yet restrained, elegant but not effete, fanciful but not flippant.

The technique of making filigree glass was first recorded in the Venetian Acts of 1527, when the brothers Filippo and Bernardo Serena applied to the authorities for a patent of monopoly to make 'glass of stripes with twists of cane'. It is later referred to by Biringuccio in his book describing current chemical knowledge, *Pirotechnia* (1540), in which he marvels at the uniformity of the threads and their geometric perfection. Without the discovery and perfecting of *lattimo* in the previous century, however, filigree glass could not have been developed. Experimentation possibly began in the fifteenth century on early *cristallo* ware, which was sometimes embellished with translucent-blue trailed threads and later with threads in *lattimo*. At some stage the technique was discovered of placing *lattimo* canes or tubes in a mould alternating with colourless lengths, then picking them up in a gather of glass and rolling them on a flat surface into an homogeneous whole in which the white threads were embedded in the clear glass. It is thought that wares decorated in this manner, *a fili*, are probably the earliest productions in filigree, a famous example being the 'Parr Pot' and another almost identical silver-gilt-mounted jug in the British Museum, both dated by the hallmarks to the late 1540s, and possibly made in England by Italian glass-makers. The technique was quickly extended to include two other, more sophisticated variations, *a retorti*, where the canes were twisted to form groups of spiral threads, and *a reticello* (*Netzglas* in German), where two sets of spiral threads were placed in opposition to form a regular fine network of crossing threads with little pockets of air trapped in each diamond which was formed by the pattern of the threads.

A number of different types of glass were still made in Venice for export at this time, and, indeed, over most of the great period of Venetian glass production. Besides the continuing demand for enamelled wares from the German Lands, which kept the enamellers busy even though the fashion for such wares in Italy had declined, there seems to have been a considerable production of wares such as rosewater sprinklers in filigree glass and lamps in the Islamic style for export to the eastern Mediterranean, despite the growing power of the Turks. In 1569 the Venetian ambassador to Constantinople was writing to the Signoria about an order made by

Above: This early seventeenth-century tazza is made of filigree glass, or glass a fili, in which opaque glass threads were embedded in clear glass in continuous spiralling lines. (Victoria and Albert Museum, London)

Left: A retorti was another variation of filigree glass, in which the canes of opaque and clear glass were twisted to form spirals, and was used on this mid-sixteenth-century covered standing cup. Height: 18.5 cm (7¼ in) (British Museum, London)

Right: 'Ice glass' was produced by plunging a semi-molten object into cold water in order to crack it and give it the appearance of ice crystals. Height: 21.5cm (8½in) (British Museum, London)

Below: This large filigree plate has a reticello pattern, a network of opaque threads with air bubbles between them. Diameter: 54cm (21¼in) (Museo Vetrario di Murano, Murano)

Natural stones such as chalcedony, a type of quartz, were widely imitated in coloured glassware. This calcedonio jug, in which several colours have been blended into each other, was made in Venice in about 1500. Height: 33.3cm (13⅛in) (British Museum, London)

Mohammed Bassa for 900 mosque lamps from Venice for a mosque being constructed under his patronage. This was a continuation of a long tradition, for soon after the extinction of the Syrian glass-making centres in 1400 Venice had begun to supply the mosques of the Middle East with enamelled lamps.

Another type of glass offered by the Venetian glass-blowers at this time was 'ice glass', which was typical of the Mannerist influence on glass-making fashions of the latter part of the sixteenth century. Having striven to achieve a crystal-clear glass, the glass-maker then obscured its clarity by plunging the glass, while still semi-molten, into cold water to produce a 'shattered' effect of crystals rather than crystal. Phillip II of Spain so admired this type of glass that he is recorded (in 1564) as owning sixty-five examples of it in various forms.

The Venetians also perfected two other types of glass, which again reflected the fascination for rare and curious natural phenomena, collections of which were proudly displayed by the rich and fashionable. Glass was made to imitate agate or chalcedony, and called *calcedonio* glass. It had most probably been perfected by the beginning of the sixteenth century, but too few examples from this early date have survived to represent an accurate corpus. What has survived is, however, often impressive in its monumentality and richness, which would have appealed to the Renaissance eye. The other type of glass perfected by the Venetians was *millefiori* (literally, a thousand flowers). It is not known whether this technique, employed in Rome in the first century AD, survived without a break and possibly returned to Italy from the Middle East, but at some stage during the burst of experimental activity towards the end of the fifteenth century, the process of grouping together random selections of canes sliced into short lengths, later known as *millefiori*, was revived and used in the making of beads. Other wares in this technique were probably curiosities rather than bona fide glasses, particularly as some of them have been preserved in costly mounts. It is thought that Maria Barovier may, in view of her application for a licence in 1487 and the reference to a small furnace, have been engaged in the making of *millefiori* as well as enamelling. In an inventory taken in 1496 of the stock of Giovanni and Maria Barovier, *millefiori* knife handles are mentioned.

Engraved decoration made with the point of a diamond was another embellishment on Venetian glass practised from the mid-sixteenth century onwards. Vicenzo di Angelo dall Gall is credited with introducing the technique, almost certainly derived from that used on metalwork,

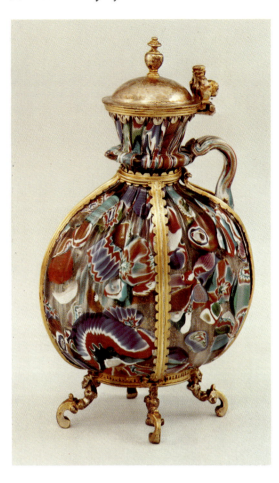

style—*à la façon de Venise*—and it is often difficult to distinguish between glassware from Venice and that from other glass centres where production was in the hand of Venetian-trained glass-blowers.

It was inevitable that the great demand for Venetian luxury glass would result on the one hand in great efforts being made to lure glass-makers to other courts in Europe, and on the other in trying to keep an increasingly jealous grip on an industry which had become such a major part of Venice's vital export trade.

In 1490 it had been laid down that reprisals would be made against glass-makers who defected or divulged the secrets of their craft, and that penalties would be inflicted on those who wished to return to Venice after working abroad. Despite these threats, workers still left Venice to offer their services elsewhere, probably first in other Italian glass-making centres such as Altare, and then beyond the Alps in the Tyrol, the German Lands, the Low Countries and even England. They took the secrets of their craft with them, including the recipes for Venetian *cristallo* and for the fashionable filigree glass in all its various forms, which included wine-glasses with filigree bowls on various plain or moulded stems, sometimes in contrasting *cristallo*, and many kinds of *tazze* and dishes, tumblers, beakers and

Left: Millefiori *was one of the techniques perfected by the Venetians during the sixteenth century. Objects made by this technique, in which coloured canes were sliced and fused together, were probably curiosities rather than practical vessels, since many of them, like this miniature ewer, are preserved in valuable silver-gilt mounts.*
Height: 12.6cm (5in)
(British Museum, London)

Below: This elaborately engraved armorial dish was one of a series made in the 1560s for the Medici Pope Pius IV, and has the papal arms in its centre.
Diameter: 27.5cm (10¹³/₁₆in)
(Toledo Museum of Art, Toledo, Ohio)

and in 1549 he is recorded as being granted a licence. A series of engraved dishes was made in the 1560s for the Medici Pope Pius IV (1559-66), probably for display on a buffet. The circular plates are divided into alternate zones of engraved decoration and gilding, sharpened with an edging of *lattimo* threads. The engraved elements are typically Mannerist in content, with elaborate winged satyrs or mermen with linked dragons' tails flanking vases, borders of fleurs-de-lis, cornucopia and ornamental scrolls. The standard of engraving is not particularly high—the detail is invariably filled in with slanting hatched strokes which render the overall effect rather crude—but the drawing and use of ornament is lively and always in proportion to the space available.

The Spread of Venetian Influence

The glass-making phenomenon that occurred at Murano soon spread throughout Europe. Glasshouses sprang up wherever the influence of the Renaissance made itself felt, answering a new and increasing demand for luxury glass. By the sixteenth century glass-making centres all over Europe were making glass in the Venetian

Right: This enamelled beaker decorated with violets was made in France in the first half of the sixteenth century in the Venetian style, probably by a Venetian glass-maker working abroad. Height: 12.8cm (5½in) (Metropolitan Museum of Art, New York)

Below: This cold-painted plate with pressed rim in colourless glass dates from the second half of the sixteenth century. It has a portrait of Felix V, the last of the anti-popes, who renounced his claims to the papacy in 1449. Diameter: 24.6cm (9¹¹/₁₆in) (Museum of Decorative Arts, Prague)

covered goblets in different combinations of filigree and clear glass.

At the same time as the developments taking place in Venice, many glass-making centres elsewhere on the Italian peninsula continued a humbler glass-making tradition more or less unchanged. For instance, although glass had been made in Florence since the fourteenth century when glass-makers from the Tuscan mountains moved into the town, it was not made in the Venetian manner until 1567, when Cosimo de Medici managed to lure a team of glass-makers from Murano. Factories were also operating in Treviso, Bologna, Ancona, and Ferrara in the north-east. However, the only rival of Venice as a centre of luxury glass-making seems to have been Altare. Not far from the important port of Genoa, Venice's great commercial rival, Altare in the Ligurian mountains came within the fiefdom of the Marquises of Montferrat, who since the twelfth century had been closely connected with the Crusader Kingdoms of Outremer through complicated marriage alliances. It has been recently put forward that Altare could have received its superior expertise from immigrant craftsmen from Syria rather than Normandy as had previously been thought. The Monferrats also had links with Byzantium and Armenia, and

it is possible that the glass industries at Altare and Venice developed simultaneously, particularly the art of enamelling.

By the end of the fifteenth century Altarist glass-makers were organized into a guild or 'university', and their statutes were formalized in 1495. It is thought that Venetians came to Altare in the fourteenth or fifteenth century, thus creating a fusion of knowledge and styles. At this time, Altarists were at work all over Europe on cathedral sites: in contrast to Venice, the Consuls of the university actively encouraged the Altarist glass-makers to go abroad, and looked upon them as a useful source of income, hiring them out but stipulating that they should not divulge the secrets of their trade, and that they must return home regularly. In this way the Altarists seem to have had as much influence as the Venetians, for whom working abroad was so

beset by threats of punishment and even poisoning.

So far it has been impossible to identify or attribute any glass to Altare, even though contemporary documents refer to glass *à la façon d'Altare* or *ad uso d'Altare*, implying that it was distinguishable from that of Venice. Since Venetians and Altarists often worked together in the same glasshouses abroad, it is highly likely that their putative different styles soon merged, and that the term *à la façon de Venise* referred to all Venetian-style luxury glass including that made in Altare. An interesting example of the spread of glass-making from Altare is the case of

such as the famous Perrot of Orléans, originally Perotto, the Saroldi who became the Sarode, and the Massari who became the Massary, did settle permanently in France. It seems that there was great rivalry between the Muranists and the Altarists in the Low Countries, the former predominating mainly at Antwerp and the latter at Liège, the two most important centres of luxury glass-making there. From here the glass-makers spread to Maastricht, Brussels, Middelburg, Haarlem and Amsterdam.

Germany, Austria and Bohemia

Since the Middle Ages, the German Lands had developed a very strong tradition of making forest glass or *Waldglas* with a distinct repertoire of forms arising out of small Gothic prunted beakers such as the *Krautstrunk* (cabbage stalk) and the *Berkemeyer*, which seem to have been in production from at least the eleventh century. Even simpler forms of vessel blown in a mould were also made, always with a strong greenish tint caused by impurities in the sand. Gradually, as the influence of Venice spread north, glass of the forest type began to improve in quality, and as glass recipes became more precise, beautiful

Left: The few surviving examples of French enamelled glasses such as this goblet were probably made by Altarists brought from Italy to France by Duke Louis Gonzaga of Nevers after 1565.
Height: 22.3cm (8¾in)
(Wallace Collection, London)

Below: This footed bowl with the arms of Louis XII of France and Ann de de Bretagne shows the Venetian influence frequently evident on the glass made in France in the sixteenth century.
Height: 21cm (8¼in)
(Musée de Cluny, Paris)

Lanzaroto Beda, or Bederio, an Altarist who was granted the right to set up a furnace in Genoa in 1441. From there he emigrated to the Genoese trading colony of Caffa on the Black Sea, where he was still working in the 1480s, no doubt exporting his products to the eastern Mediterranean, where the production of glass had declined.

By a series of marriages the Gonzagas of Mantua acquired the Marquisate of Montferrat, and in 1565 a Gonzaga became the Duke of Nevers in France. This dynastic development resulted in a large exodus of Altarists to France, where they set up glasshouses in towns and cities such as Paris (to which Venetians also went), Nantes, Rouen, Poitou and Bordeaux. There they produced window and bottle glass as well as luxury glass. As late as 1598 Buzzoni and Bertoluzzi were authorized by Henry IV to set up a glasshouse at Rouen to make 'verre de cristail, verres dorez, esmaulx etc.' (crystal, gilt and enamelled glass). The fact that enamelled glass is still specifically mentioned at this late date means that it is highly likely that the few surviving examples of French enamelled glasses were made by Altarists brought to France by Duke Louis Gonzaga of Nevers. These glass-makers were restless, and often went to other centres after a few years, although some of them,

green and turquoise-tinted glass was made, and its clarity and tone was particularly appreciated. Later, Venetian *cristallo* in its more sophisticated forms was made in the German Lands, in various mainly urban centres such as Hall-im-Tyrol, Innsbruck, Munich and Kassel, but this was a tiny proportion of the German glass output, which relied more firmly on its own traditions than did other countries.

To the Germans, the green tint enhanced the aesthetic appeal of their wines, and larger vessels than were normally made under the Venetian method were in demand for the consumption of beer. The large surface area of these made them an ideal medium for decoration with enamels, the area in which Venice can be said to have had the greatest and most long-lasting influence. There is evidence that Venice was executing enamelled ware for the Germans by the end of

the fifteenth century, and although by the middle of the sixteenth century the fashion for enamelled decoration had died out in Venice itself, it was still extremely popular north of the Alps, and enamelling studios in Venice probably continued to decorate glasses for the German market. At the same time German centres making glass in the Venetian style were being established, thus creating confusion and controversy about the provenance of certain glasses. This is particularly true of a type of tall cylindrical beaker with a short spreading folded foot called a *Stangenglas* ('pole glass'), usually decorated with the coats-of-arms of German families and mostly dating from between 1575 and 1600. The glass itself is of Venetian type, although sometimes slightly greyer than the Venetian *cristallo* of this period. The enamelling, however, is definitely in the

Above: Enamelled pilgrim's bottle made in Venice for the German market. Height: 34.7cm (13¹¹/₁₆in) (Wallace Collection, London)

Left, above: German-made distinctively shaped flask in Waldglas. Height: 17cm (6³/₄in)

Left, below: Prunted beaker made in Germany. Height: 6.2cm (2¹/₂in) (Kunstgewerbemuseum, Cologne)

These are two of a number of Stangengläser *made for the merchant family of Praun of Nuremberg, and they are decorated with the Praun coat of arms as well as fashionable figures from a Venetian book of costume. Dating from about 1598, these tall beakers are of German or possibly Venetian origin, and may have been made as marriage glasses. Heights: 39.5cm (15½in)*

Venetian tradition, used with painterly precision, as opposed to later, definitely German, decoration which is slacker and more thickly applied. The beakers also have typically Venetian decorative bands of scale pattern and other imbricated variations in gilt punctuated with enamel dots.

There were strong links between important German trading centres, such as Nuremberg, and Venice, as is illustrated by a survival of a number of *Stangengläser* made for the important merchant family of Praun of Nuremberg. This family had strong connections with Italy, where one Paul Praun carried on a silk manufacture at

Bologna, and his cabinet of curiosities was still intact at the beginning of the nineteenth century. Besides the conventional coats-of-arms, the Praun glasses are also decorated with fashionable figures, many of which are taken from a Venetian book of costume by Titiano Vecellio, and later allegorical figures such as Justice and Prudence, taken from woodcuts by Jost Amman.

Hall, in the Austrian Tyrol, was probably a source of this type of enamelled *Stangenglas*. The glassworks there were founded in 1534 by Wolfgang Vitl of Augsburg, who attracted both Altarists and Muranese glass-makers, and they produced clear crystal as well as stained glass.

The production at Hall and at the Court glasshouse founded in 1570 by the Archduke Ferdinand II of the Tyrol at Innsbruck seems to have been of soberer quality than that of Murano, the forms being heavier, fuller and more monumental. Archduke Ferdinand was personally interested in glass production, and persuaded the Venetian authorities to send a team of glass-makers to Innsbruck to set up a glasshouse attached to the Court, the emphasis being on esoteric forms of luxury glass rather than commercial production, much of it destined for the Archduke's own cabinet of curiosities at Schloss Ambras. When applying to the Venetian Signoria for glass-blowers he specifically asked for those 'with the most fantasy in them' to be chosen.

Besides enamelled wares produced at Hall, definite examples of which are difficult to identify, two other very important techniques, diamond engraving and low-fired or 'cold'-painted enamels, were employed during the latter part of the sixteenth century. At the same time, elements of the forest-glass tradition began to enter the glass-makers' vocabulary at Hall and other German centres working in the Venetian style. The form of the Venetian funnel-shaped beaker (like the one discovered at the base of the Campanile) which seems to have been popular at Hall, began to show subtle changes, gaining in height, developing a more pronounced flare at the lip, and being embellished with motifs to be found on glasses made at forest-glass centres, including rows of applied knops or prunts such as are found on the *Krautstrunk*, moulded nodules, and nipped diamonds.

From Schloss Ambras there has survived a series of covered urns or vases of classical form, bearing idiosyncratic decoration which seems to have been developed only at Innsbruck. It is diamond-point decoration of Venetian inspiration, which includes simple bands of foliate scrolls and false gadroons, combined with areas of cold-painted or low-fired enamel decoration and frequent use of the Hapsburg double-headed eagle. There are cartouches bearing profiles of soldiers reminiscent of Roman legionaries or German halberdiers, as well as birds and fruit and floral swags, all in rather primitive colours liberally heightened in gilt. The effect must have been very rich, but has unfortunately in many cases worn badly over the centuries. Versions were produced in blue-tinted glass as well as clear glass.

Elsewhere in Germany, princes and landgraves were eager to institute luxury glass-making at a local level. In 1583 Landgrave William IV of Hesse instigated a glasshouse at Kassel under the supervision of Italian masters.

Here the forms favoured were particularly close to those produced in Venice and the Low Countries, and included filigree and fanciful serpent-stemmed goblets, types seemingly not made in Austria. It was in production for a little under a year, but in that time produced 36,000 drinking glasses and 9000 window-panes. Between 1584 and 1595 a court glasshouse in Munich for Duke William V was producing, it is recorded, window and mirror glass as well as tableware, none of which can now be definitely identified.

While the production of luxury Venetian-type glass was restricted to a few urban centres in the

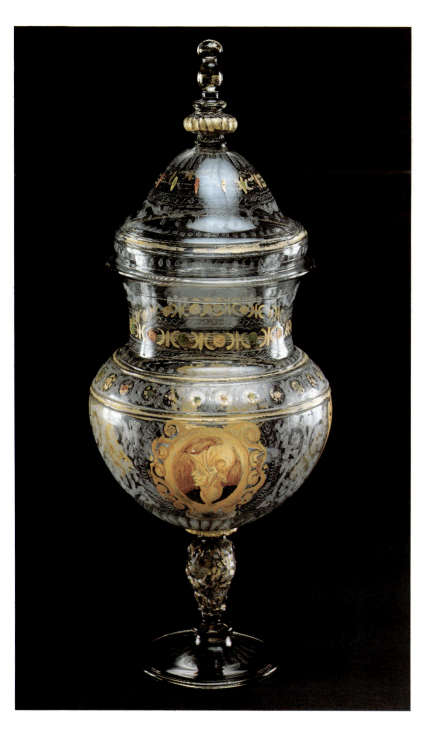

The style of decoration on this covered vase seems to have been developed only at Innsbruck, where Venetian-inspired engraving was combined with cold-painted decoration. Height without lid: 24.6cm (9¾in) (Kunsthistorisches Museum, Vienna)

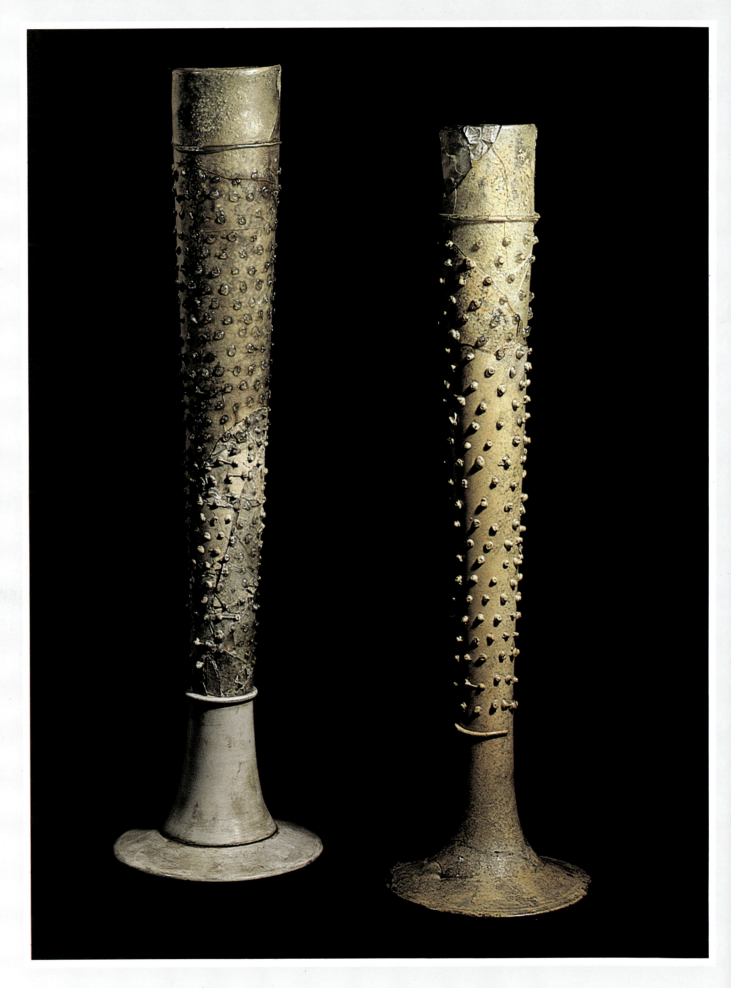

German Lands, the ordinary production of forest glass was spreading rapidly, often stimulated and influenced by Venetian-style luxury glass. One Hans Breitenbach, for instance, was granted a licence by the Duke of Saxony in 1564 to start a glasshouse in the Forest of Fehrenbach in Thuringia. He was only given permission because the inaccessibility of the site prevented the gathering of windfallen wood or the burning of charcoal for any other purpose.

In Bohemia, where glass-making had been carried on since early medieval times, there were twenty-four glasshouses by the sixteenth century. There the foundations were laid of a glass-making tradition which was to challenge and eclipse that of Venice during the following century. Bohemian glass-making was greatly stimulated by entrepreneurial landlords—families such as the Kinskys, Starkenbachs, Bouquoys and Harrachs—who encouraged teams of glass-makers under professional glass-making families such as the Preusslers and Schürers to establish several new glasshouses in the Isergebirge and Riesengebirge regions. It was, of course, to the landlord's benefit to encourage the industry on his property, so that not only would rents and a percentage of the profits accrue to him, but his woodland would at the same time also be cleared for agriculture. On the other hand, the industry expanded so rapidly that deforestation became a real threat, so much so that the Emperor Maximilian II tried, without success, to have these glass-making ventures curtailed. The Schürers founded glasshouses at Labau in 1558, at Rochlitz and Hoflenz before 1589, and the most renowned at Falkenau in 1530. Christopher Schürer is generally credited with inventing the distinctive Bohemian cobalt-blue glassware made in the late sixteenth and early seventeenth centuries. These glasshouses seem to have produced glass mainly of the Germanic type, decorated almost invariably with enamel and little influenced by current Venetian fashion, except in the use of filigree glass which continued well into the seventeenth century, often with enamel decoration superimposed. It is recorded that by the 1560s filigree glass of a quality to rival Venice was already being made in Silesia, and more cheaply too.

The sixteenth-century development of scientific thought and phenomena which grew out of medieval alchemy was particularly important for glass-making, as it resulted in another period of chemical experimentation under such patrons as the Emperor Rudolph II. This eventually led the Bohemians to produce their own type of colourless glass to rival rock crystal. Their glass, made with potash, was stronger than Venetian *cristallo*, and thus able to take the wheel-

engraved decoration developed at the Rudolphine Court at the beginning of the seventeenth century, a fashion which was to be all-important in the next century or so. Rudolph had ordered Venetian glass so that it could serve as a model for similar Bohemian production. The land-owner Petr Vok also ran a *façon-de-Venise* glasshouse on his estate at Rosenberg in southern Bohemia.

From Bohemia, glass-making families colonized other areas of Germany. The Wanderer family established glasshouses in Franconia and Thuringia (where the Glasers and Greiners were also prominent), and also appeared at Crottendorf in Saxony in the first half of the sixteenth century. The Preusslers settled near Johann Georgenstadt in 1571, and the Bohemian glass-makers under Martin Friedrich were brought to Grimnitz by the Elector Joachim Friedrich of Brandenburg in 1602.

Spain

Spain has always been geographically and culturally somewhat separate from the rest of Europe. Even so, its long Mediterranean seaboard meant that it was, as with Venice and Genoa, exposed to influences from abroad. Records dating from the end of the fifteenth

Facing page: These two flute-shaped beakers in yellow-green glass with applied prunts are typical of the style of glassware which was produced in Bohemia from the early medieval period to the sixteenth century. Height of right-hand glass: 43cm (17in) (Municipal Museum, Prague)

Left: Made in Barcelona in about 1580, this clear, colourless vase with thickly applied enamelling which gives a vivid but crude effect is of the type known as 'Barcelona green-leaf'. The shape of the vessel shows an Islamic inspiration. Height: 23.5cm (9¼in) (Hispanic Society of America, New York)

century refer several times to the reputation of Barcelona glass, as rivalling the products of Murano. This is perhaps borne out by the fact that King Ferdinand had 148 glasses sent from Barcelona to Queen Isabella to add to her collection which already numbered 260 pieces. An inventory of this collection was taken in 1503 by the Queen's lady-in-waiting, the Lady Violante de Albion, who described each piece in considerable detail. A wide range of tableware is enumerated, including plates, bowls, trays, ewers, goblets and covers, wine flasks, kegs, bottles and cruets in 'white' (which could refer to clear *cristallo*), blue, green, red or purple glass, combinations of these colours being used on one piece as well; and a form of *calcedonio* is also mentioned. A list of the decorative motifs painted on the glasses includes elements typical of the *estilo Isabel*, a fusion of Gothic, Moresque and Renaissance motifs, also found in other spheres of the decorative arts towards the end of her reign. Heraldry, human figures, animals and birds feature prominently, as do inscriptions in Gothic and Moorish letters. A few surviving examples which seem to correspond to those described in the 1503 inventory have bold and thickly applied enamelling with the details outlined in black, and the overall effect is vivid but crude.

Dating from later in the sixteenth century is a small group of glasses also attributed to Barcelona on which another style of enamelled decoration is to be found. Examples are mainly in the form of either *tazze* or curiously formed vases reminiscent of pilgrim flasks and probably of Islamic inspiration. The faintly straw-tinted glass is often completely covered in motifs in a limited palette of green, white, yellow and occasionally other colours; the human figures, birds or animals are childishly two-dimensional and surrounded by a fussy wriggling tracery of stylized green foliage punctuated with rosettes and borders of yet more foliage. Although primitive, the decoration is applied with precision and achieves the same effect as that on textiles and other contemporary wares. The group is generally known as 'Barcelona green-leaf'.

The economic policies of Charles V (r. 1516-58), grandson of Ferdinand and Isabella, encouraged the importation of foreign goods to the detriment of the home industries. Through links between Barcelona and Venice, Venetian glass began to be imported in large quantities into Spain, and is very frequently mentioned in sixteenth-century lists and inventories of the possessions of the Spanish nobility. Barcelona glass, though, managed during this time to hold its own against the Venetian imports, and still had an international reputation at the beginning of the seventeenth century. Venetian craftsmen began to settle in Spain in about the middle of the sixteenth century, no doubt in answer to a growing interest in the products of Murano. Philip II, king of Spain from 1556-98, negotiated to buy considerable quantities of Venetian glass direct, for his palace at El Pardo where he indulged his particular passion for 'ice glass'. Spain also imported much glass made in the Venetian style from the glasshouses of the Spanish Netherlands. Thus did the Venetian influence go back and forth, until by the seventeenth century even experts could not tell the produce of Murano and glass *à la façon de Venise* apart.

In addition, Spanish glass-makers went to Venice to learn the Muranese techniques. For example, Juan Rodriguez studied at Venice and

This cobalt-blue glass goblet from Barcelona, gilded and enamelled in green, rose and white, is of the type of ware described in an inventory of Queen Isabella's glass collection taken in 1503. Height: 20.3cm (8in) (Hispanic Society of America, New York)

Some Spanish glass-making centres were un-influenced by Venetian developments, and continued to produce green-tinted glass in the forest-glass tradition, like this sixteenth- or seventeenth-century vase probably from Andalusia.
Height: 14.9cm (5⅞in)
(Corning Museum of Glass, Corning, New York)

Barcelona before returning to Spain and establishing himself as a master glass-blower at Seville. He is recorded as making Venetian filigree glass, and it was through such masters as Rodriguez that the Venetian styles of the sixteenth century were taken up in Spain.

Although in some centres Venetian influence was powerful, glass centres in other parts of Spain such as Almería and Granada continued to produce a provincial type of green-tinted glass in the forest-glass tradition into the eighteenth century, and were hardly affected by Venice at all, except in the use of primitive nipped and pincered strapwork.

The Low Countries and England

For various reasons, the Low Countries—now Holland, Belgium and northern France—saw the founding of more glasshouses for the production of Venetian-style glass than almost anywhere else in Europe. The Muranese had developed strong links with Antwerp, which by the sixteenth century was the largest seaport on the Atlantic seaboard and was taking over from Venice the role of trading powerhouse of Europe. As early as the 1530s Italians were

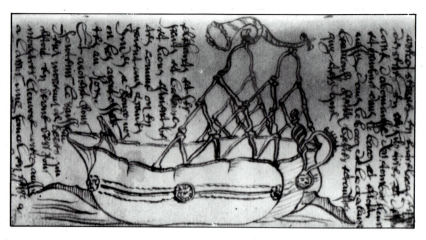

attempting to set up viable glass production there, but it was not until 1558 that the Muranese craftsman Pasquetti founded a glasshouse in Antwerp that flourished into the following century. At the same time, the impetus of Altarists in France was pushing northwards to Liège, which became the other important centre of luxury glass-making. The third important factor influencing the course of glass-making in the Low Countries was the effect of an indigenous family of glass-makers and entrepreneurs, the Colinets, who controlled numerous glasshouses in the province of Hainault, the most renowned of which were at Barbancon and Beauweltz.

A fascinating catalogue of drawings (R. Chambon Collection) illustrating the range of glasses produced in the Low Countries has survived from the middle of the sixteenth century. Besides simple bottles, flasks, wine-cups and goblets in simplest *façon-de-Venise* style, there also appear the more complicated and ambitious products associated with luxury glass, such as elaborate nefs and centrepieces (two of the pieces illustrated were offered to Charles V and Philip II of Spain on their progress through Beauweltz in 1549). There are also detailed illustrations showing one of the most popular decorative elements used at this time, the lion mask, which was either employed as a prunt to embellish applied straps (trails of glass), or as part of the mould-blown stem. The Netherlandish type of tall flute with elongated bowl, very often on lion-mask stem, was beginning to be made, as was the covered vase, in form similar to that made at Hall and Innsbruck, but seldom with diamond-point or cold-painted decoration. Ice glass and filigree were part of the repertoire of the Italians in the Netherlands, and non-Venetian filigree glass can sometimes be distinguished by silver mounts which were applied to bells, stirrup-cups and drinking horns.

The forms of luxury glass in the Netherlands remained close to their Venetian counterparts, causing confusion as to provenance, because the Netherlands had become a sort of clearing house for Italian glass-blowers by the mid-sixteenth century. They would rest there before either returning to Italy or moving to other centres throughout north-western Europe.

Luxury glass-making reached Britain from the Netherlands, and was established there on a permanent basis from 1567 onwards. As early as 1504 an Altarist, Nicolo Creno, was working among the glaziers at Norwich Cathedral, while in 1549 eight Italian glass-blowers arrived in London from Antwerp. They had actually been brought to Antwerp from Italy by a merchant, Jean de Lame, who had been authorized by

Charles V to set up a furnace in Antwerp. Why de Lame sent them on to England is not known, but after only two years they had all returned to Italy, no doubt as a result of the threats of reprisals by the Venetian authorities. It is possible that two filigree tankards which have survived—datable by the silver-gilt mounts to 1547—were made in London by them.

Up to this point glass-making in England had been more or less confined to the Weald of Surrey and Sussex where foreigners, mostly from the famous window-glass-making areas of Lorraine and Normandy, worked, supplying window glass for English churches and

Top: Illustration of a glass nef, or ship, from the mid-sixteenth-century Catalogue Tolinet *showing the range of glass then being produced in the Low Countries. (Chambon Collection, Marcinelle, Belgium)*

Above: Galley-shaped water jug of the same date as the illustration. (Museo Vetrario di Murano, Murano)

cathedrals. Up to the 1560s almost all window glass was imported, however, since there was no indigenous window-glass industry.

The arts of making window glass and glass vessels were revived in England by Jean Carré (d. 1572), a native of Arras who had been living for some years in Antwerp, where he seems to have been connected with the town's flourishing glass-making industry. Carré arrived in London in 1567 with the capital needed to set up production and firm contracts with glass-makers in Antwerp. He immediately petitioned for and was granted licences to set up two furnaces near Alfold in the Weald for the making of window glass and forest-glass utensils, and another furnace in London at the Crutched Friars for the production of crystal glass *à la façon de Venise*. He was granted a patent to produce window glass for a period of twenty-one years. Carré then brought well-known Lorrainer families such as the de Hennezells over to work at the furnace at Alfold in Surrey, while Peter and John Bungar from Normandy made crown glass at the other furnace in the Weald. Carré himself supervised the glasshouse at the Crutched Friars, where at first he employed mainly Flemish craftsmen.

After 1550 relatively large numbers of glass-makers began to move across the Channel as a result of the increasing religious troubles and persecution of the Protestants on the Continent, particularly in France where from 1562 religious civil war broke out, and in the Spanish Netherlands where in 1566 Philip II's Council of Blood was set up and Alva's troops were sent in to stamp out heresy. The Norman and Lorrainer glass-makers were proud and secretive communities who largely intermarried and prided themselves on being members of the nobility—*gentilhommes verriers*—and their temperament seems to have soon led them to embrace Calvinism. As life became more disrupted on the Continent, the sympathetic religious policy of Elizabeth I attracted streams of Huguenots to Britain. The Tudor Court welcomed the foreign craftsmen, who could produce the admired Venetian-type glass on its doorstep. Venetian glass is mentioned in inventories of Henry VIII's palace at Nonsuch, and even in backward Scotland it is recorded that the Earl of Moray gave a banquet for the Patriarch of Venice at which, in order to impress, he caused the servants to pull the cloth from the table, bringing crashing to the ground a number of crystal glasses which were then replaced with more glass of even finer quality.

By 1570 Carré had become unhappy with the results from the crystal furnace, and brought over Italians from Antwerp, including a Venetian, Jacobo Verzelini, who had been working there for twenty years. He was master of the Crutched Friars glasshouse in 1572, at the time of Carré's death, and in 1574 he persuaded the government to grant him a patent for twenty-one years to produce glass in the Venetian manner, and to forbid the import of Venetian glass from abroad. It is highly likely that such a competent master made glass in a wide range of Venetian styles, but only ten goblets can with any certainty be ascribed to his glasshouse. They all fall within the last quarter of the sixteenth century and are distinguished by single and capacious bowls with elaborate diamond-point engraving, except for one which is gilded. Were it not for the fact that they have inscriptions or names in English, they could have been made in Flanders or Hall. Thus the English glass industry received its first important stimulus with the introduction of Venetian styles. By 1592, when Verzelini retired, leaving the working of the glasshouse in the hands of his sons, glass-making in England had been revived considerably, particularly forest-glass-making to which numbers of Lorrainers were attracted, and which spread through the Weald and into Hampshire and Staffordshire. Many new factories were established, laying the foundations of a vigorous English glass-making tradition.

Jacopo Verzelini, from Venice, was brought to England by Jean Carré to improve the quality of the glass being produced at his London glasshouse. Among Verzelini's work is this blown diamond-point engraved goblet made in 1584.
Height: 16cm (6⁵⁄₁₆in)
(City Museum and Art Gallery, Birmingham)

CHAPTER FOUR

SEVENTEENTH-CENTURY GLASS

Throughout the glasshouses of Europe, the influence of Venetian glass as a pervasive international style declined in the seventeenth century, and the new era saw the rise of different national styles of glass-making. There was also a change in the nature of the glass produced, and a shift in dominance from southern Europe to the North. These changes were due to many factors, both social and historical. The rise of Protestantism and of a prosperous class of burghers in the Low Countries were as significant as the decline in power of the Papacy and the relatively minor political importance of Italy during the seventeenth century. In glass, as in so many other fields, Italy no longer enjoyed a monopoly of artistic innovation and patronage.

Previously, glass had been used as a vehicle for elaborate and fantastic works of art, often of very slight practical value and so delicate that their chances of surviving intact for long were extremely limited. Now a compromise gradually came to be worked out between the aesthetic and the practical, with the result that the objects produced were relatively robust and yet also aesthetically satisfactory, using a wider range of new decorative techniques.

The Holy Roman Empire

While the Venetian glasshouses had experimented with enamelled decoration and had also employed the diamond-point to engrave formal designs which were a part of the surface treatment of the glass vessel, it was in Germany and Holland that enamelled and engraved decorative techniques were to be more widely explored. The technique of diamond-point was to be vastly extended, and engraving as a decorative vehicle in its own right was to be fully developed. Wheel-engraving, often coupled with diamond-point, was also to be developed, not only by professional craftsmen but also by virtuoso amateurs such as Willem van Heemskerk in Holland. In the sphere of enamelling, the glasshouses of the Holy Roman Empire (which encompassed almost the whole of central Europe at that time—the Low Countries, Germany, Austria, Bohemia and Silesia) were to apply coloured decoration to plain glass forms for subjects ranging from the simple to the most sophisticated. This type of glassware, hearty and robust and enamelled in bold colours, has sometimes been dismissed as not much more than peasant art, a view which is not, however, supported by a serious examination.

The seventeenth century was not a period of great innovation in the field of shapes. Previously, pincers had been used to apply wings to the stems of glasses, and bowls had been of complex forms. The goblets of that era had been destined for a wealthy and aristocratic society whose principal drink was wine, whereas northern Europe was to supply much of its glass to a stratum of society whose staple drink was beer, and the vessels from which this was drunk were generally very plain. One type, made since medieval times, was the *Roemer*, a large bowl on a hollow prunted stem, but most of them, called *Humpen*, were large, simple cylinders up to 60cm (2ft) high set on conical or kick bases which were reinforced round the edge with a trailed band. Many *Humpen* were made with lids, slightly domed and with knop finials, but, as with most engraved goblets made with covers, nearly all today have lost them.

Enamelled *Humpen* were first made in the mid-sixteenth century. Though the earliest recorded pieces for German clients were

This Silesian enamelled Humpen of 1680 is inscribed by Christian Preussler, whose family owned the Zeilberg Glassworks in Bohemia. The decoration shows an interior view of the glassworks with the names of the apprentices below it. Height: 26cm (10¼in) (Museum of Decorative Arts, Prague)

varied from region to region, from yellowish to blackish; but some enamelling was done on opaque blue glass, notably on pistol-shaped flasks probably from Saxony or northern Bohemia, and bottles and spirit flasks of the mould-blown type.

There were several varieties of *Humpen*, including the *Passglas*, which was also cylindrical but narrower and of taller proportions. The body was generally divided into equal sections by horizontal bands of decoration, either enamelled or trailed, which served to mark the allotted portion for each drinker as the glass was circulated among the assembled company. The cylindrical bowl was set on a spreading foot with folded rim which was blown separately and annealed to the base of the bowl. The *Passglas* was also generally made with a domed cover.

Another type of *Humpen*, a purely Saxon product, was the smaller *Hofkellereiglas*, which was precisely similar in construction but designed to contain a more reasonable quantity of beer. Like that of the *Humpen*, its cylindrical shape was often only very approximate, perhaps because vessels drawn out with rod and pincers into a cylindrical form tended to belly out somewhat during the annealing and firing processes.

Beer was also drunk or served from glass jugs. These were generally pear-shaped with applied scroll or flat, strap-like handles and folded flange feet applied to the base. Often the base and top of the handle were joined by rings of trailing round the body. Jugs usually had hinged pewter covers, which were less likely to become separated from the glass and, of course, less liable to breakage. These pewter mounts frequently bear inscriptions and touch marks which can help to date the glass vessels to which they are attached.

The *Humpen* and its variations were the standard shapes to which enamelled decoration was applied throughout the seventeenth century, which was the golden age of glass enamelling in the Holy Roman Empire. Since many examples, owing to their folk nature and often commemorative function, are dated, it is not difficult to classify them into various periods. Distinguishing precisely where they were made within the wide bounds of the Empire is another problem of rather greater complexity. Earlier German glass had been made principally in the Rhineland and at Hall-in-Tyrol. The great centres of enamelling were spread across the middle of what is now West Germany, that is, through Franconia, the Fichtelgebirge which divides it from Thuringia, and across Thuringia into Saxony, Silesia and Bohemia.

An important type of *Humpen* that was produced throughout the period was the

probably made in Venice, there is a significant number of dated examples of German or Bohemian manufacture from the latter half of the century. The enamelled glassware of the sixteenth and seventeenth centuries was often elaborately decorated, and generally had certain features in common, including a border of gilding and coloured enamel beading above the subject-matter, where the individual leaves of gold can usually be distinguished, and the coloured enamel decoration was applied over it. The formal patterns used—rosettes, scale patterns and others—varied from area to area: for example, the wares of Franconia are said to have a predominance of white enamel. The trailed foot-rims of *Humpen* were also decorated, generally with enamel dashes, mostly in white. The material used for most enamelled ware was plain or clear soda glass, with tints that

Enamelled Franconian betrothal Humpen *and cover made for Michael Menborn of Nuremberg in 1615.*
Height: 41cm (16¹/₈in)

Left: This rare Saxon pistol-shaped flask, dated 1613, is made of opaque blue glass with enamelling.
Length: 34.5cm (13½ in)

Below: Reichsadlerhumpen *like this one from Bohemia depicted the double-headed Imperial Eagle, the arms across its wings representing the structure of the Holy Roman Empire.*
Height: 32cm (12½ in)

Reichsadlerhumpen (literally, Imperial Eagle beaker), the earliest example of which dates from 1571. All the pieces of this type depicted the structure of the Holy Roman Empire, its Electors (the German princes who elected the King and Emperor), and the representatives of the various professions, classes and places which it contained, set out in seven rows of four shields each, on the outspread wings of the double-headed Imperial Eagle. On the breast of the bird there was initially a crucifix, though later the Imperial orb took its place. This design, which endured until the beginning of the eighteenth century, was a remarkable expression of conservatism, since it had its source in the late fifteenth century, and the actual motif used by the glass-enamellers as their inspiration was probably derived from a woodcut published in 1511. The schematic presentation of the structure of the Empire in groups of four, the so-called Quaternion system, though delightful in its aesthetic balance and subtle in its theoretical tidiness, bore little if any relation to the actual structure of the Empire itself. Perhaps it should be regarded more as a representation of what the Holy Roman Empire ought to have been.

Another echo of the Empire is to be found in the *Churfürstenhumpen* or Electors' beakers, which depict the Holy Roman Emperor enthroned with the seven Electors of the Empire, three spiritual from Mainz, Trier and Cologne and four temporal from Brandenburg, Saxony, Bohemia and the Palatinate. During the course of the seventeenth century the number of Electors was increased by two to nine, but seven remained on the *Humpen*. This is probably because they were derived, like the *Reichsadler*, from a single iconographic source, a print by the Augsburg engraver Hans Vogel, executed in the sixteenth century well before the number of Electors began to change and fluctuate. It was later in the seventeenth century that the representation of the Electors changed: they were shown mounted

as *Ochsenkopfhumpen*, but the depiction of the mountain is not realistic. It approaches, rather, the quality of a small child's painting of a tree-covered hill with bovine features. Once again, though the production of these *Humpen* spanned about 100 years and endured well into the eighteenth century, the basic treatment hardly varied. It did not, unfortunately, improve with repetition and some of the later examples look as if the enameller did not really understand the subject, so confused has it become.

One of the most attractive types of *Humpen* is the *Jagdhumpen*, or hunting beaker. These vessels depict various hunting scenes such as

on horseback rather than in the seated arrangement derived from Vogel's depiction of them. The eight figures obviously could not be arranged running in a single frieze round a tall cylinder, and had to be placed in two rows to fit them all into the available space.

The hieratic and symbolic treatment accorded 'the State', as represented by the *Reichsadler* and the temporal and spiritual rulers portrayed on the *Churfürstenhumpen*, reflects the conservative nature of all popular art. The people who owned and used these enamelled glasses had little or no idea what their rulers actually looked like, or indeed how such a large and complex system of government really worked, so the decoration on them was intended purely to represent the popular ideal of the Holy Roman Empire, its hierarchy and rulers. The use of old iconographic sources and an unchanging depiction of these themes also served to reassure the uneducated of the stability and orderly nature of the society in which they lived.

This stereotyped and schematic treatment was not confined to these *Humpen*. For example, a strange pine-clad mountain called the *Ochsenkopf*, owing to its resemblance to an ox's head, dominates the Fichtelgebirge area between Franconia and Bohemia. This mountain frequently appears on *Humpen* known, as a result,

These three examples of German enamelled beakers are (from left to right): an Ochsenkopf flared beaker with an ox's head, chain and lock and animals' heads on a pine-covered mountain with four named rivers below; a Hofkellereihumpen painted with the arms of Saxony and Poland and the Elector's initials above it; and a small armorial Humpen inscribed LANDGRAV V HESSEN-CASSEL and dated 1634.
Heights (left to right): 13.5cm (5¼in), 23.5cm (9¼in), 12cm (4¾in)

Dated 1577, this fine Bohemian Stangenglas depicts Abraham about to sacrifice Isaac, a common subject on glass from Bohemia before and after 1600.
Height: 21.5cm (8½in)

hunters driving their quarry into a net which zigzags aesthetically over the surface of the glass. They are relatively rare compared with the other types already discussed, but, like them, the subject-matter is not contemporary, but derived from an engraving after a painting from the days of Charles V in the previous century.

Towards the end of the seventeenth century, Saxony began producing its own type of enamelled glass, called the *Hofkellereihumpen*, or Court Cellar glass. Painted with the arms of the reigning Elector, these usually had the initials of the monarch above the arms, with those of his major titles in white enamel. Also from Saxony came the *Hallorenglas*, a type of *Humpen* made for the members of the Halle Guild of Saltmakers.

Guild glasses in *Passglas* and *Humpen* shapes were made widely, with the arms of the corporation and members of the Guild practising their craft enamelled or sometimes diamond-point engraved on them. Armorials also appear, but there are far fewer genuine examples than later copies. Entire families, too, appear on enamelled *Humpen*; sometimes there were so many members that they required two rows.

The Bible was another source of material, and the range of themes taken from both the Old and New Testaments was wide. The Twelve Apostles and the Evangelists were popular subjects, as were the Magi, and the Crucifixion also appears without the *Reichsadler*. The Sacrifice of Abraham occurs on glass from Bohemia; and there is a beaker in the Victoria and Albert Museum in London, probably from Upper Franconia, which shows the Madonna and Child.

A great variety of other subjects was depicted on *Humpen*. For example, late in the seventeenth century and well into the next, *Passgläser*, most of which probably came from Altenburg in Thuringia, were decorated with playing cards. The relationship between the decoration and the object is particularly successful on these pieces. Many other pieces had purely stylized floral decoration which as time went on became of poorer and poorer quality. Spirit flasks, which were generally oblong-octagonal and blown into a mould, were decorated in this way until late in the eighteenth century.

The German-speaking world was also active in the field of glass engraving, and the early years of the century witnessed one of the highest peaks of achievement in the glass-engraver's art, when the glasshouses of Prague, and subsequently of Nuremberg, each boasted an artist who brought the skill of engraving to a remarkable height. The first of these was Caspar Lehmann, or Leman, as he signed himself. Born at Illzen near Lüneburg in about 1570, he must have been something of a prodigy because by 1588 he already held the post of *Hofdiener und Kammeredelsteinschneider* (Gem-cutter to the Imperial Court) to the court of Rudolf II in Prague. Here he was in splendid company, as the Prague workshops of the day also produced marvels of the goldsmith's, jeweller's and enameller's art. Engraving of precious stones in the late Renaissance era had attained a pitch comparable to that in the Antonine era of the Roman Empire. Indeed, such was the Prague engravers' skill that confusion still arises between their creations and the antique gems that they counterfeited. It was Lehmann who had the vision which enabled him to make the conceptual leap of realizing the enormous potential of glass as a medium for the gem-engraver's technique. He usually used plaques (because of their thickness and resulting solidity) as the vehicle for the first really virtuoso display of wheel-engraving on glass, but because he nearly always confined his work to flat surfaces (although a beaker by him does exist in Prague, signed and dated 1605), he was unable to realize the technique's fullest potential by exploring its application to shaped glass.

Perhaps Lehmann's greatest contribution to the development of engraving on glass lay not in his own work but in what he taught his leading

Left: Caspar Lehmann realized the potential of glass as a medium for engraving, and usually used plaques like this example, engraved with a portrait of Christian II, Elector of Saxony. Height: 25cm (10½in) (Corning Museum of Glass, Corning, New York)

Below: This parcel-gilt mounted goblet made in Nuremberg in the late sixteenth century was engraved in about 1630 by Schwanhardt the Elder. Height: 29.5cm (11½in)

pupil, Georg Schwanhardt, who had joined him in 1618 at the age of seventeen. In March 1609 Lehmann had been granted a concession for glass-cutting by Rudolf II. On his death in 1622, Lehmann left this to Schwanhardt, who returned to his native Nuremberg, taking with him his concession and, more importantly, his technical accomplishments. Nuremberg was a centre for the production of hollow vessels, particularly flared glasses with a single knopped stem, and Schwanhardt applied his art to these, perhaps realizing the virtue of the relationship between the patterns he wished to engrave and the curved surfaces that the glasses offered. In Nuremberg,

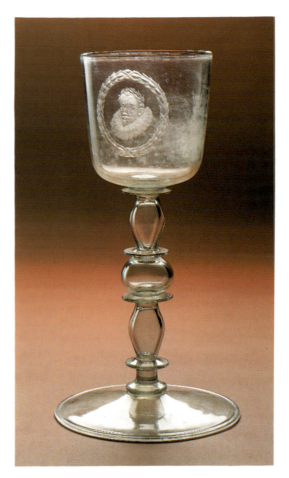

Schwanhardt made another vital contribution to the development of the glass-engraver's technique. This was the art of polishing the hollow areas scooped out by the engraver's wheel, the essence of the art of intaglio cutting. It had been available to Lehmann, for it was among the gem-engraver's range of skills, but Schwanhardt was to develop it more fully than Lehmann had done. The dull surface of wheel-engraved decoration, where the wheel had ground away the surface of the glass, was polished, and light and life were thereby restored to the engraved areas of the vessel.

With his two sons, Georg the Younger and Heinrich, and three others—Hermann Schwinger, Hans Wolfgang Schmidt and Georg Friedrich Killinger—Schwanhardt founded a flourishing but self-contained school of great glass-engravers in Nuremberg. The school achieved and maintained a high level of skill in the art, which was in many ways ahead of all but the finest Warmbrunn work of the succeeding century. The second generation of engravers in Nuremberg was of course able to display its skills on new shapes, as output at the local glasshouses evolved. Killinger's signed work is thus to be found on the multi-knopped stems made in the city in the second half of the century.

During the last quarter of the century, a new type of glass was developed in Bohemia. Experiments carried out by Michel Müller and Louis Le Vasseur d'Ossimont between 1674 and 1683 produced a material with potash instead of the traditional soda and a significant amount of chalk (carbonate of lime) which added to its stability. This crystal-clear potash-lime glass was hard and less fragile than soda glass, giving results identical to the lead glass being developed in England at the same time, and, as was quickly appreciated by the heirs of Schwanhardt and the glass-workers of Potsdam and Warmbrunn, just the vehicle for engraving since it allowed cuts of considerable depth. It was the availability of this new material that was to lead to the great flowering of glass-engraving in the Bohemian-Silesian area during the following fifty years.

Engraving was sometimes done on coloured glass, which had of course been in constant production during this period, both for wholly coloured objects and those made of both clear and coloured glass. For example, Nuremberg goblets of the late seventeenth century had a clear vari-baluster stem, that is, with balusters of

Left: This Nuremberg Pokal *from the last quarter of the seventeenth century was engraved by Georg Friedrich Killinger (1694-1726) with a portrait of Ferdinand II. Height: 22.2cm (8¾in)*

Left: From Bohemia, this cut-glass bowl of about 1690 is made of ruby glass or Rubinglas, *then recently developed by Johann Kunckel. (Museum of Decorative Arts, Prague)*

Right: Decorated in the manner of Johann Schaper, this Nuremberg Schwarzlot *bun-footed beaker (c. 1675) shows three warriors on horseback, two firing muskets and one blowing a horn, in a landscape featuring a distant fortress. Height: 9cm (3½in)*

varying sizes, and the foot and bowl sometimes in coloured glass, generally green, blue or amethyst. A legacy of Venetian technique, in pieces such as puzzle glasses (popular for convivial drinking parties), was the combination of clear glass with coloured edging on bowls, feet, spouts and handles.

The greatest achievement in the realm of coloured glass was, however, made by Johann Kunckel (1630?-1703), a chemist who had studied earlier treatises on glass and written, in 1679, a technical study of his own, *Ars Vitraria Experimentalis*. In the same year he founded a factory in Potsdam where he developed the process for making a type of red or ruby glass, *Rubinglas*, by the addition of gold chloride. This glass was of a particularly warm and attractive hue and ideally suited to being mounted in gold, silver-gilt or gilt metal. Most of the pieces attributed to Kunckel are undecorated and, in fact, mounted in these materials, and are generally luxury examples of useful objects which were purchased by the rich, frequently parts of travelling and other services in precious metals. Kunckel produced glass in other colours, too, and also attempted to make an opaque white glass to look like porcelain, but in this he was unsuccessful.

At the same time as Kunckel's breakthrough, which led to the spread of ruby glass southwards through Germany, another innovation was taking place in Nuremberg. This was the freehand decoration of glass in transparent coloured enamels, in a totally different fashion from the conventional manner of opaque enamelling on *Humpen*. This new type of decoration was initially executed in monochrome, iron-red (*Eisenrot*) or black (*Schwarzlot*) being the most usual techniques.

Sometimes the two were used together in a most felicitous combination of colours. The black paint was frequently heightened with gilding which added life and richness to the design. Not only the technique but the subject-matter was completely different from the earlier style of popular enamelling, and included mythological subjects, hunting scenes, scenes of harbours, motifs inspired by engravings by Jacques Callot of humorous dwarves, and armorial and landscape decoration.

The earliest exponents of this type of glass painting in Nuremberg were Johann Schaper (1621-70), his family and his followers Johann Faber and Abraham Helmhack. They decorated low cylindrical beakers which usually had three flattened hollow-ball feet. In many ways their choice of glass as the vehicle for their art was almost incidental: they also used faience which offered the challenge of an opaque white surface, and both glass and pottery can therefore be regarded as the incidental supports on which highly skilled enamellers exercised their art.

Left: Johann Faber of Nuremberg decorated this Schwarzlot *goblet in about 1700, in a style derived from Schaper. It shows a scene of figures netting fish from a boat and from the shore, with fishing smack and sailing boats in the distance, buildings on an island and a ruined castle in the foreground. The hollow knopped stem has an inverted baluster section, and the folded foot is decorated with a band of foliage.*
Height: 19.5cm (7³⁄₄in)

Far left: Attributed to Ignaz Preissler, this colourless glass ewer with octagonal bowl, faceted knop and flat octagonal foot is enamelled on one side with an oriental building and on the other with an oriental figure, in Schwarzlot *heightened with gilding. Height 12cm (4³⁄₄in) (British Museum, London)*

Left: Anna Roemers Vischer executed the diamond engraving on this Roemer *in 1621. It is the only known signed example of her work. Height: 15cm (6in) (Rijksmuseum, Amsterdam)*

Ignaz Preissler (b. 1670), who worked in Breslau before and after 1700, was a brilliant exponent of *Eisenrot* and *Schwarzlot* decoration. Examples of his art are to be found on Chinese blue and white porcelain as well as glass (and, after about 1715, on the new wares appearing from the Meissen factory). He, like the Nuremberg painters, portrayed the same subjects and themes on all three materials, which included landscapes, peasant scenes and mythological subjects. These artists' main concern, however, was that their chosen material should offer good smooth areas for decoration, and so as vessels the glass pieces they decorated are often unremarkable. The typical Nuremberg piece, a small cup-shaped beaker on three bun feet, is extremely plain. Beautiful though the output of these German painters' studios was, it is therefore perhaps not as glass that we should admire it.

In Holland, styles and developments taking place throughout the seventeenth century were enormously influenced by contemporary movements across the frontier in Germany. Little of significance in terms of shape was produced, and many of the standard items made there were merely pale reflections of German pieces of the day. Only in the field of engraving did Dutch glass make a positive contribution; and the extraordinary flowering of calligraphic wheel-engraving that took place there is a fascinating by-way in the history of glass. Its origins were not in the glasshouses, nor were they derived from the workshops of professional engravers such as had operated in Prague or Vienna: it was

an amateur who dominated the field. The founder of this school was Anna Roemers Vischer (1587-1651). Indicative of the sort of glass available is the fact that most of her work is to be found on glasses of the *Roemer* type. Her subjects, while heavily biased towards calligraphy, included floral motifs, insects and fruit. There does not seem to be a precise relationship between the objects she engraved and the decoration she worked on them. This is very different from the case of Willem van Heemskerk, the outstanding example of the brilliant amateur.

Van Heemskerk (1613-92) was professionally a cloth-merchant who also wrote poetry and plays, and during his long life he created a group of splendid and individual calligraphic glasses. Unlike Anna Vischer, however, he seems to have been able to indulge his amateur status, for a great deal of his engraved work is on glass of a type virtually confined to his *oeuvre*. Most of his pieces are pear-shaped bottles or jugs, generally of a robust, coloured metal which lent itself perfectly to his all-enveloping engraved decoration in which he, like Vischer, used both the wheel and the diamond-point. The calligraphy included mottoes and quotations from Holy Writ, to which he often added his signature with the date and the name of the city of Leiden where he lived and worked. However, the text, though it made perfectly good sense, was largely subordinated to the artistic spirals of the serifs which dominated the entire upper surface of the bottles; the written content was actually peripheral to the artistic element. In his life-

Right: The cylindrical bowl of this Dutch glass goblet (c. 1660) is diamond-engraved with figure subjects in a similar style to many pieces of this period which were intended for the English as well as the Dutch market. Height: 17.5cm (6⁷⁄₈in) (Victoria and Albert Museum, London)

time and for generations after his death van Heemskerk enjoyed an immense reputation. By the mid-eighteenth century there was already an active market in his work, resulting in detailed lists of his *oeuvre* which still exist today.

While Willem van Heemskerk combined wheel-engraving and diamond-point, diamond-point was used increasingly on its own during the middle years of the century. The engravers showed a preference for a thinner-bodied material, often in the Venetian tradition, such as came to the Low Countries from the glasshouses in Liège. It was usually made into goblets or flutes, with tall slender bowls set on hollow baluster knops and almost flat, folded feet. The hatched criss-cross technique used by Dutch engravers of this school was a new venture in the use of a two-dimensional treatment of glass. However, though it thus enhanced narrative powers it was not really an improvement in the art of glass engraving: the decoration did not relate to the glass as Schwanhardt's and van Heemskerk's engraving had done. The engravers used the surface of the glass as a background for what they had to say, in the same way as the glass enamellers of Germany did, but there was no real link between the decoration and the shape of the object on which it was placed.

Confusion as to provenance has surrounded

many glasses of this type, because of the overtly English nature of the subject-matter with which they were decorated, but it has to be appreciated that there were very close links between Holland and England during this period, including artistic links. Charles II's government in exile during the time of the English Commonwealth was based in Holland; his sister, Mary, was married to the Stadholder William; and their son, William III, was married to James II's daughter, Mary, before he himself became monarch of both countries. This situation was reflected particularly in the pottery industry, where Dutch people worked in England, producing wares almost indistinguishable from those made in Delft. Many of the extant glass pieces of this period are engraved with English arms and loyalist inscriptions. An outstanding example is the Royal Oak glass of 1663, engraved to

Above: The bulbous body of this rare green-tinted glass bottle (c. 1680) is engraved in diamond-point in the manner of Willem van Heemskerk, who subordinated any inscription to the overall decorative effect of calligraphic scrollwork.
Height: 28cm (11in) (Nationalmuseum, Stockholm)

commemorate the marriage of Charles II and Catherine of Braganza, and there are a number of other glasses of evidently Dutch origin with engraving of purely English interest. Similar engraving and technical detail also occurs on pieces clearly destined for the Dutch market. The names of several of the artists are known, as they, like the amateurs of the calligraphic school, signed their work. Unfortunately the names cannot be linked precisely with records of working artists in specific places.

England

It was to take most of the century for the glass industry in England to make the transition from the Venetian style of Verzelini to a truly vernacular production. At the beginning of the century the infant glass industry was depressed by the stifling hand of monopoly which discouraged any improvement or initiative. In about 1615 Sir Robert Mansell (1573-1656) was granted a patent, with associates whom he shortly afterwards discarded, and by one means or another he soon gained almost total control of the industry, which he dominated until his death. The colossal upheavals of the Civil War also had a devastating effect on glass-making and, indeed, on all forms of artistic activity, even well-established ones. It was not until after the Restoration of Charles II in 1660 that the glass industry was able to begin to develop, but even then it seems to have been controlled by one man, the Duke of Buckingham, who was more famous in other fields. Other names actually appeared on his patents and other documents concerning the manufacture of glass; for example, his patent of 1660 was obtained at the instance of John de la Cam, who was of French origin, and gave rise to his glasshouse at Greenwich. At the same time, Buckingham appears to have controlled other sections of the industry through three other glass-makers, Thomas Powlden and Martin Clifford, to whom patents were granted in 1661, and Thomas Tilson, who obtained one in 1663. They all claimed to produce 'crystal glass', the *cristallo* developed by the Venetians a century earlier.

The output of the 'monopolist' period is unfortunately very difficult to identify. Various glasses have been put forward as examples of English production of this time, but usually unconvincingly. The situation is confused not merely by the presence of the Dutch but also of the Italians throughout the English glass industry, and possibly a fair quantity of the surviving seventeenth-century glass at present classified as of Italian or Low Countries origin was in fact made in England. Without

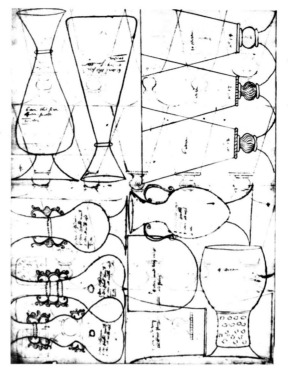

This page of drawings with instructions, dated 1669, is from the letters of John Greene (of the London retailers Greene and Measy), ordering glass from Allesio Morelli of Venice. The four vessels with handles are each inscribed '1 doz. Calsedonia, 1 doz. speckled enamel, 1 doz. all milke whit', and the beaker and the bowl are inscribed '2 doz. made very thick and strong'. (British Museum, London)

contemporary documents that actually describe or, better, depict pieces made in England during this era, however, there is no way of knowing what was really produced, and by whom. Even though there are records about the Italians involved, there is also a frustrating lack of information about what they produced. Both Mansell and Buckingham had Italians in their employ. Among Mansell's workers were Antonio Miotti and Paolo Mazzola. Miotti, who was with Mansell from 1618-23, was from a family well known in the industry, which had until then worked in Middelburg in Holland. Mazzola was active throughout the Civil War and early Commonwealth era (c. 1640-55), when he probably produced *verres ornés* (it is known that he was noted as a maker of them at another stage of his career). Whether this refers to *Flügelgläser* (winged glasses), or to glass decorated in other ways, is not clear.

Lack of information about what was actually made in England is compensated for somewhat by information about what the English clientele of the day was buying from abroad. There survives an illustrated record of the glass ordered by the London retailers Greene and Measy from Morelli in Venice. The types of glass ordered were those suited to local demand and subject to local fashions, and may therefore offer some clue as to the kind of glass local glasshouses would have produced at the time, had they been capable of so doing. (It seems unlikely, however, that if quality domestic products existed in any quantity a retailer would attempt the importation of a commodity as fragile as glassware from so far distant). The drawings made by Greene for his orders to Morelli include *Roemers*, the classic glass developed in Germany for the consumption of hock (and still made in mass-produced form today), cylindrical tumblers of a straightforward nature, covered goblets with winged or eared stems, and wine-glasses with conical bowls with flattish bases set on short stems which were knopped (or, as the order document states, 'with wrought buttons'). Glasses of these types are to be found in England and may in some cases have always been made there. However, there is no absolute means of identifying glasses of these descriptions, or even of this date, with those the English glasshouses were making.

Mirror glass, as yet not a wholly industrialized process, was another sphere to which the Duke of Buckingham extended his attentions. Like Mansell before him, he probably still used the heavy cylinder method, and the results were probably but poor imitations of contemporary Venetian products which were still imported in quantity. Like so much English glassware of this era, nothing from either Mansell's or Buckingham's output can be positively identified.

There is, however, one area of seventeenth-century English glass-making that is easy to identify and to date. Since the Middle Ages wine had been bottled in stoneware jugs of, first, Rhenish and subsequently local origin. In about 1620 similar vessels in tin-glazed earthenware were being made at Lambeth, Southwark and elsewhere. These were usually inscribed with the name of the contents, such as 'Sack' or 'Whit' (white wine) , and, frequently, the date. Shortly after the Restoration, a third form of container began to be made, a bottle of a robust brownish glass, which was of relatively little interest from an artistic point of view but possessed one great virtue: it was quite often produced with a circular seal stamped with the owner's name, initials or arms and generally a date. The clients for whom these bottles were made were publicans, wine merchants and members of the gentry, who often wanted to know the date of the contents. Evidently they were also proud of their ownership. The presence of the dates gives us an accurate knowledge of the development of the glass bottle from this time. Initially, it was the simplest shape the glass-blower could produce, but as the decades passed the bottles gradually became taller and their sides straighter, until the almost cylindrical container we know today began to appear in around 1760. No class of glassware is more accurately datable than the English sealed wine bottle. How the early sealed bottles were stored is a matter of conjecture, for their ungainly shape precluded stacking in racks and bins, which is such an essential feature of the easy storage of bottled wine today.

The English glass-makers had long wanted to rival the Venetians, but it was not until about 1675 that a new formula for glass was developed that enabled their desire to be fulfilled. This was the invention of lead glass, perhaps the most important technical step since the original discovery of glass itself. Like so many great discoveries, the same breakthrough took place almost simultaneously in two places, England and Bohemia.

In England the guiding force behind the invention was the Glass Sellers' Company, a city guild which had had a new charter from Charles II in 1664 and which controlled the entire glass trade. In 1674 the company employed George Ravenscroft (1632-83) to research into the production of a native English glass. This aim was the result both of national economic necessity and of the new spirit of enquiry which had come with the restoration of the monarchy and the foundation of the Royal Society in 1662. In that year, too, Christopher Merrett had translated into English the key Italian work on glass, Antonio Neri's *L'Arte Vetraria* of 1612, which made available for the first time the basic principles of Italian glass-making (although it was 'Italian' glass-making that was already practised in England). Only now was English

This English sealed wine bottle of 1706 has the squat body and sloping shoulders characteristic of glass bottles of the period. Height 17cm (6¾in)

This Roemer *dating from about 1680 shows the crisselling which occurred frequently in the newly developed lead glass of the period. Its ovoid bowl has vertical ribbing, its hollow stem carries raspberry prunts, and it has a high conical and folded foot.*
Height 20cm (8in)

glass-making, a fresh and different art, to emerge, but even this was not to be achieved without the help of an Italian. On 16 May 1671 Ravenscroft, working with a certain da Costa, of Italian extraction, obtained a patent to produce a 'particular sort of Christaline Glasse'. His operations were based at two glasshouses run by the Glass Sellers' Company, the Savoy glasshouse between The Strand and the river in London and what appears to have been a research establishment at Henley-on-Thames.

The glass that eventually resulted from Ravenscroft's efforts, known as 'flint glass', 'lead glass' or 'lead crystal', contained a large percentage of lead oxide. The Venetians, or at least Antonio Neri, had been aware of some of the advantages of lead in glass—it made the glass less fragile and enhanced its brilliance—but had never achieved perfect control over it in the furnace. It is not at all certain that this is what Ravenscroft was looking for, although he was undoubtedly trying to find a replacement for Venetian cullet on which the manufacture of glass in England was to some extent dependent. Initially his efforts were not entirely successful: owing to a chemical imbalance caused by the excessive use of potash in the ground English flints, the glass tended after a time to disintegrate into a minutely crackled surface which obscured its transparency and thus vitiated it totally. This defect, called crisselling (or crizzling), which was a progressive deterioration and unstoppable, also occurred frequently in glass of this period made in Potsdam and Bohemia. Fortunately, by 1676 the problem had largely been overcome, apparently by the addition of protoxide of lead, or litharge, instead of a proportion of the potash that had previously caused the trouble. This was done progressively until it reached about thirty per cent of the weight of the mixture, in order to render the whole mass more fusible as well as to avoid crisselling. The result, English lead glass or lead crystal, was the most brilliant and elastic greyish-white metal.

From the outset the importance of this new glass was recognized. It could not be blown out nearly as thinly as the Venetian *cristallo* it was to replace, but this was not necessarily a defect: its very robust nature and its inherent thickness at which it had to be worked made it a wonderful refractor of light. No previous glass material had been able to absorb and disperse light in so exciting a manner, and the splendid ring emitted by the glass when struck was also immediately admired. (This resonance, which is totally lacking in soda glass, is a most useful and wholly reliable diagnostic feature which is quite impossible to counterfeit. Although lead glass usually shows up a different colour from soda glass under ultra-violet light, it does not invariably do so, whereas the ringing test is consistently reliable for bowls, drinking glasses and other hollow vessels.) When the art of cutting glass was developed about seventy years later, this was to be the perfect material for it.

No sooner had Ravenscroft achieved a satisfactory and virtually sickness-free material than he sought and obtained permission to mark it. To this end he used a seal which he advertised as a form of guarantee, and on 29 May 1677 he registered it with the Glass Sellers' Company. This seal was in the form of a raven, a canting reference to his name. This seems to have started something of a fashion, as the practice of sealing their wares was to be adopted by many glass-makers of the day. Nine specimens of Ravenscroft's output bearing his seal are known, and not all are completely free from crisselling—proof that the defect had not been entirely remedied.

Ravenscroft did not live long enough to enjoy the benefits of his successful creation. Within a few months of his death in May 1683, the operation of the Savoy glasshouse passed to Hawley Bishopp, who had worked under him and had managed the Henley glasshouse since 1676. Bishopp had signed an agreement with the

Left: This massive goblet (c. 1690) has the elaboration typical of the Anglo-Venetian style, with its gadrooned funnel bowl and looped rope-twist stem edged with trailed flanges and large raspberry prunts on either side. The domed cover also has gadrooning and a rope-twist figure-of-eight finial with trailed flanges, and strapwork scrolls terminating in a twisted point.
Height: 52cm (20½in)
(The National Trust, Erddig Hall, Betws-y-Coed, North Wales)

Glass Sellers' Company on 22 February 1682 (1681 old style) whereby he was to produce glass for them at the Savoy glasshouse for a term of twenty years, but he does not appear to have remained there until the end of it.

The discovery and successful production of lead glass created a large and prosperous indigenous English glass industry almost overnight. Within twenty years of Ravenscroft's invention there were almost 100 glasshouses working in the material throughout the kingdom.

As the new glass could not be worked as thinly as the Venetian metal it was to supplant, the shapes in which it could be worked had perforce to be different from those previously produced. This, however, was a good thing: the impossibility of producing pieces in the Venetian style compelled the British glass-workers to establish a native style of their own. Since the robust nature of the metal did not lend itself to finely pincered wings and scrolls, a happy discipline of restraint was imposed on the objects that were

produced. This spirit of robust constraint, combined with a splendid sense of balance, was to characterize and inspire the continued stream of glassware coming out of English glasshouses over the next century.

Of course, the debt to Venice was not entirely forgotten. Ravenscroft had used gadrooning, folded rims, hollow moulded knops and fluted bodies on his early pieces, which are strongly reminiscent of *façon de Venise* glasses, but the new material in which they were made gave them a solidity and permanence never previously evident in the glass-maker's art. Although robust simplicity had become the keynote of the British glass of this period, there are one or two splendid pieces made at this time which were enriched with scrolls and pincered work on winged stems of great complexity and conceived on a scale which rendered them totally impractical. These were no doubt parade pieces, intended for display either in the houses of the great (there is such a goblet at the Yorke family house of Erddig) or in the halls of city corporations. By

Far left: The posset pot was specially designed for drinking posset, a popular beverage made from hot milk mixed with wine or ale. The thin curved spout was positioned at the base of the pot to enable the drinker to avoid the curdled milk on the surface of the posset. This one, of clear glass with moulded ribs, was made at the glasshouse of George Ravenscroft and has his raven's head seal on the spout.
Height: 8.5cm (3⅜in)
(Toledo Museum of Art, Toledo, Ohio)

The Flügelglas, *the most extravagant expression of the Venetian style, was made in northern Europe. This one is set on a stem consisting of a double-headed serpent with blue and white twist body, pincered crests and fins.*
Height: 30cm (11¾in)
(Pilkington Glass Museum, St Helens, Merseyside)

secrets and to regulate the operation of the industry. The influence of Venice had spread through the migrations of Venetian glass-workers, and much of what happened elsewhere was the story of the vicissitudes of Italian glass-makers abroad.

Artistically, the seventeenth century was not Venice's (or more properly Murano's) greatest age; the passage from late Renaissance to high baroque did not benefit the craft stylistically. The previous century had been characterized by splendid, balanced shapes, but now a fussy element seemed to develop, and objects which had their origins as functional pieces became so fanciful and complex that they were often of little practical use. The sixteenth century had produced pieces that were impractical because they were too beautiful and wonderful to use; now they were often just badly designed. The use of coloured elements also detracted from the artistic success of the products. Previously, the delicate use of winged decoration on the stems of otherwise fairly simple glasses had been a balanced arrangement, in which the applied decoration enhanced the glass to which it was attached, but by the early seventeenth century this balance seems to have been lost. Many glasses made in Venice and in places where Venetian influence predominated seem merely to have been a vehicle for displays of virtuosity on the part of the craftsman. No longer did the decorative element enhance the object to which it was applied; it rather militated against the purpose for which it was intended.

The classic and most extravagant expression of this phenomenon was the winged glass *(Flügelglas)*, which was made all over northern Europe in glasshouses that owed their existence to Venice. These glasses had an elaborate winged stem with a riot of scrolls and pincered work on the stem and finial, often in a wide spectrum of colours, which made the glasses almost impossible to use (and progressively so as their contents were consumed). They became more and more displays of fantasy and virtuosity, to be admired merely as decorations.

Paradoxically, Venetian glass-makers in Venice itself were perhaps less extravagant in their ideas and creations than their cousins and colleagues elsewhere in Europe, and attempts were made to import glass of foreign manufacture to Venice, the homeland of the art. This situation greatly disturbed the glass-workers of Murano, who petitioned the Council of Ten early in the century, talking of the damage done to their craft by the fact that 'it had been taken abroad from this our State and taught to persons who make glass in foreign parts and have even started to send it and to enamel it in some parts

the end of the century, however, a clearly British style of glass-making had been evolved, which was to lay the foundation for the enormous success of the industry during the eighteenth century.

Venice and Spain

Although developments in other countries during the seventeenth century meant that the Venetian glass industry was facing real competition for the first time, the Muranese glass-makers continued to work at their craft as before, and every effort was made to protect their trade

This early seventeenth-century Venetian latticinio vase has been mounted as a ewer with silver-gilt, enamel and jewels by Heinrich Straub of Nuremberg, who was active between 1608 and 1635. Height: 29.7cm (11 11/16 in) (Toledo Museum of Art, Toledo, Ohio)

The Galerie des Glaces (1678) at the Palace of Versailles is a magnificent testament to the French success in producing mirrors of a quality to rival those made in Venice.

and cities of the mainland'. The reaction of the Council was prompt: in 1607 it published a decree prohibiting the import of ordinary glass within the entire territory under Venetian control. The penalty was confiscation of the goods and a fine of fifty ducats for both importer and retailer. Apparently the decree had a positive effect: for a considerable number of years, to judge from public documents, the problem did not arise.

Later in the century, however, there is evidence (in the minutes of the Marigola, the chapter of Muranese glass-workers) that new problems were developing for the industry. By a decree of 1660 the owners of glass furnaces were bound to give employment to all those qualified to exercise their profession. Unfortunately there were more qualified glass-workers than there was work for them to do, so that the furnace

owners quite often paid them a salary, generally a sum not less than seventy ducats, without calling on their services for which they had ·no need. This situation was in fact given the stamp of legality by a decree of the Council of Ten in 1690, but more glass-workers were still being trained and admitted to the craft than the industry could employ or, indeed, afford. As a result of this inefficiency, the examinations by which an apprentice could become a free master of the art had to be suspended, in 1695.

Not only were the Venetians less successful than their pupils in northern Europe in terms of artistic invention, but the very material in which they worked was being superseded by the two new types of glass which had been discovered in England and Bohemia, each of which was to prove revolutionary and lead eventually to the international eclipse of the great Venetian glass industry. While the Venetian State and the glasshouses strove, unsuccessfully, to protect a shrinking market at home by banning imports and trying to stop the departure of workers to other countries, the new spirit of invention beckoned from abroad, and the declining industry was unable to offer any reward that might persuade its skilled craftsmen to stay.

This situation was highlighted by what took place in the mirror-making industry, in which Venice enjoyed a virtual monopoly until well into the second half of the century. In other countries local attempts to set up mirror-glass-making had proved abortive, and this was naturally of immense financial benefit to the Venetian State. When the French under Louis XIV and his minister Colbert set out to establish a mirror-glass industry of their own, based on Venetian expertise and manpower, there ensued a period of vicious trade war combined with industrial espionage. A prosperous French aristocracy surrounding a magnificent monarch was building palaces and châteaux with ample wall-space for large mirrors, and was anxious to contain the cost of this commodity by producing it at home. However, the French needed the technical knowledge that could come only from Venice. In spite of Venetian efforts to stop the leakage of skills, the French, with the assistance of Italian workers who had been bribed to travel to Paris, were eventually able to set up a mirror-making industry. (The credit for this is sometimes given, incorrectly, to a Frenchman, Louis-Lucas de Nehou, either because of a chauvinistic desire to give France credit for an industrial technique it had acquired elsewhere, or in an attempt to distract attention from the actual source of information and expertise.) Within a few years the French were capable of producing mirrors that were larger and finer than those that Venice had ever produced.

Venice was of course deeply committed to the export of anything vitreous but technical skills, but where the technique was obvious or easily discovered, they could not prevent it being copied. Among the major commodities that continued to be exported from the Republic were glass drops and beads, the trade in which extended through Amsterdam and Lisbon to North Africa and even as far as Angola. With these soon went the lampwork technique developed to produce them. This technique of working over a burner enabled the glass-worker to produce pieces from glass rods, and was to facilitate immensely the almost instant production of animals and figures which has continued to this day. The instantaneous nature of the process has served to give it an enduring appeal to tourists. It was to be taken up by the glass-

workers of Nuremberg, Antwerp and Nevers. In Nevers the technique was used to create little tableaux of figures—sometimes resembling traditional Neapolitan terracotta crib groups—in which opaque white glass predominated. In Venice itself, it led to the application of coloured and contorted flowers and other enrichments to chandeliers, mirror frames, candlesticks and a variety of glass for daily use, but none of it was aesthetically successful.

An amusing sideline of the Venetian industry throughout the century was an extensive output of oil-lamps of an increasingly bizarre nature. Like the bronze lamps made in Renaissance

This Spanish jug from Catalonia has a cracked-ice body pattern which shows a Venetian influence, and yet its shape is derived from a long-standing Moorish tradition.
Height: 19cm (7½in)
(Victoria and Albert Museum, London)

times, many of them were of zoomorphic shapes, the heads or tails of the beasts forming wick-holders. Other extremities—feet, ears and manes—were applied over a lamp and sometimes coloured. Since the life-expectancy of a domestic glass lamp in daily use was probably not great, these simply made pieces were no doubt conceived as charming expressions of folk art rather than as serious artistic works, although some examples are of exceptional quality.

Spain, comparatively isolated from the rest of

demanded particular shapes, such as the *porrón* and the *cántir*, spouted vessels used for the consumption of wine, while the Islamic tradition influenced the shapes of other objects such as ewers (which were also produced in other countries), a classic example of which is in the Victoria and Albert Museum in London. Made in Catalonia early in the century, it has a cracked-ice body pattern which places it firmly in the Venetian tradition and reflects a fashion found in the Low Countries as well as Murano, and yet its shape is derived from the Hispano-Moresque Manises pottery from Valencia of 150 years earlier. The rather gauche treatment of the handle and the untidy set of the spout is typical of 'provincial' products and is to be found on other ewers of the period from different parts of Spain.

The Spanish glassware of this period, while largely outside the mainstream of European developments, did retain a tradition of lamp-work that was perhaps Venice's most important contribution to its industry. The influence of Spanish glass as much as that of elsewhere in Europe was to be felt in the New World, to which massive quantities of its wares were to be shipped from Cádiz and Seville.

Above: This Venetian-style serving dish, or tazza, *from Catalonia is of transparent uncoloured glass with diamond-point engraving and cobalt-blue trailed threads in a looped-chain pattern. Diameter: 31.5cm (12³⁄₈in) (Museos de Arte, Barcelona)*

Right: There was a brief flowering of stained-glass-window making at Oxford during the first part of the century. This detail of Nineveh from the Jonah Window (1631) at Christ Church is by the German glass-painter Abraham van Linge, who lived in Oxford at this time.

Europe, was the last country to feel the effects of the developments taking place north of the Alps. The fact that its population was mainly Catholic also allied it more closely to the conservative Venetian tradition than to the more progressive ideas of the Protestant countries of the North. As a result, much of the glass made in Spain looked like the Venetian products of a few decades earlier or the less successful contemporary creations of the Muranese workshops. Some Spanish wares seem to be almost direct copies of Italian pieces. Examples are *tazze* with a blue looped-chain pattern and diamond-engraved decoration, derived almost slavishly from Murano but lacking the sophistication of form and purity of line to be found in the originals.

While a large proportion of the output, from the many glass-making centres such as Granada, Catalonia and Almeria, shows somewhat de-based Venetian shapes it also shows an ingredient peculiar to Spain, arising from the long-standing Moorish influence that had survived the expulsion of the Arabs from Granada by Ferdinand and Isabella in 1492. Even the simplest Spanish pieces are covered with a wealth of pincered, looped and trailed decoration redolent of this Moorish inheritance and echoing Islamic glass of the same period from the eastern Mediterranean. Local social conditions also

Stained glass

The political and philosophical climate of the seventeenth century was not at all favourable to the manufacture of stained glass, an art form that found itself out of tune with the era and little in demand. Whereas in the medieval church stained-glass windows were the richest decorative element and coloured the whole interior, the typical Catholic churches of the Counter-Reformation, for the most part inspired by Giacomo da Vignola's Gesù in Rome, had so few windows that those that were provided required clear glass in them in order to light sufficiently the rich ornament that covered every surface within. This phenomenon is to be seen in the architecture of Bernini and Borromini in Rome, in Hardouin-Mansart's Invalides church in Paris and in the whole *oeuvre* of Christopher Wren. The baroque tendency towards theatricality, often to be seen in ecclesiastical architecture, also militated against 'the dim religious light' that stained glass created.

Wren was not of course a Counter-Reformation architect, but he was an architect of the generation that followed the Common-wealth, and his clients, though they had turned away from excessive Puritanism, were still chary of decorative tendencies that might smack of popery. The Age of Enlightenment and of Rationalism viewed religion as something one

should enter into with one's eyes open and without any false aura such as might be induced by stained glass. What applied to Wren applied to Protestant architects throughout northern Europe and America, and during the seventeenth century the already limited output of stained glass became smaller and smaller. Only in a few places did it survive to any effect, notably in northern Switzerland and, until the Civil War was well under way, the city of Oxford in England.

Switzerland's stained-glass industry survived into the seventeenth century because, though the advent of Calvinism had resulted in the destruction of much stained glass, there were other outlets for the glass-stainer's work. The strong civic spirit of the cantons, with their prosperous mercantile class formed into guilds, led to the replacement of noble patronage, so evident elsewhere, with a corporate patronage through guilds and town halls. These offered plenty of work to designers and producers of stained glass, and afforded them a range of subjects less circumscribed than the established and relatively rigid themes of ecclesiastical art. This variety of subject was a strong stimulus to adventure and experimentation.

The first great stained-glass artist of the

Richard Greenbury was the leading exponent of stained-glass portraiture in royalist Oxford. He painted this portrait of Charles I, which is in the Hall of Magdalen college, in 1633.

Greenbury also painted this portrait of Henrietta Maria, Charles I's wife, for the Hall of Magdalen College in Oxford.

stained glass was valued for this reason by wealthy bourgeois society of this period in much the same way as book-plates were for their collections of books. In fact, glass-painters like Vischer also produced designs for heraldic book-plates.

The Swiss school of glass-painting did not long survive Vischer's death. His sons and their fellows Jakob Wannerwetsch and P. Stocklin continued his work for another few decades, but the changing political and philosophical climate effectively extinguished all demand by 1670. However, the skills of the glass-painter (*Glasmaler*) were not lost because Johann Schaper in Nuremberg, the first *Hausmaler*, or home decorator of glass, had learned his art on this larger scale and now adapted it to the making of glass vessels.

At Oxford, the brief flowering of stained-glass decoration during the first forty years of the century was due to a variety of special factors. The accession of James I once more allowed the production of stained glass for ecclesiastical purposes, an activity fostered by the anti-Puritan Archbishop Laud, and it was particularly concentrated in Oxford because of its High Church and cavalier connections. The presence there of the great German glass-painters Bernard and Abraham van Linge was another vital element. Wadham College Chapel was completed only in 1613 and thus required glass for its windows at this time, and its East Window was to prove the last great essay in stained glass for 200 years or more. Balliol, Christ Church, Lincoln and University Colleges were also adorned with the work of the two German artists. Their activities in the city were halted after the collapse of King Charles I's government in 1642, and they were forced to return to their native town of Emden.

Stained-glass portraiture also prospered in Oxford under royalist rule. Its leading exponent was Richard Greenbury who, amongst other things, produced portraits of Charles I and his consort Henrietta Maria for the Hall of Magdalen College. He was a portrait painter by profession and glass was simply another kind of support for his work, but this does not detract from the high quality of his portraits in this medium. As well as narrative and portrait windows, there was also a demand for heraldic glass and domestic stained glass of a vernacular nature, a demand that continued until almost the end of the century, when the availability of enamels reduced the craft to painting on glass rather than forming paintings from glass. The application of the new technique effectively destroyed the traditional craft, which was not to be revived for more than 200 years.

seventeenth century was Hieronymus Vischer of Basle. Born in 1562, he was already well established as an artist of renown by 1600, and during the next thirty years, until his death in February 1630, he was to produce an enormous number of designs for glass-painting. He was an admirable draughtsman, and many of his preparatory drawings for his work on glass have survived. They show that heraldic designs played a major part in the work he produced for clients all over southern Germany and north-western France, for the guilds of his own and other Swiss cities, for the patricians of Berne and for the Catholic Church. The panels he created display a tremendous fantasy, in his use of an architectural framework with lesser and greater pictorial fields subtly linked and overlapped in a late Mannerist orchestration of patterns. His human figures were usually insubstantial and lacking in personality, but the overall effect of his art was one of richly patterned decoration. Many of his clients must have had their armorial medallions done by him as decorative status symbols, and

THE EIGHTEENTH CENTURY 1700-75

The rapid social and political changes taking place throughout Europe during the eighteenth century led to increasing affluence, which generated a demand for luxury products including fine tableware and ornamented glass on a prodigious scale. During the first three quarters of the century, dozens of different glass styles were produced by the 350 or so glasshouses in the eleven main glass-producing countries. An interplay of artistic, technical, social, political and economic influences generated this abundance of output and wealth of style, and most of the glass that was produced was of high artistic and technical merit. A wide variety of attractive pieces has survived from all the major glass-making centres.

The huge demand for quality glass led to greater competition between different manufacturers, which was to result in the final eclipse of the soda-based, pre-Renaissance forest glass and of Venetian *cristallo*, developed in the fifteenth century. In their place came Ravenscroft's 'glass of lead', perfected in the last three decades of the seventeenth century, and potash-lime glass, which had been developed throughout the previous century in Germany and Bohemia. These new metals caused tremendous changes in the actual forms of the glass produced. Other influences were also at work, which were to mould and temper the art of glass-making.

Venice

At the end of the seventeenth century Venice was still the world's major glass-making centre, as it had been for 400 years. The long-standing splendour of the Serene Republic was declining, however, and Venetian glass, a fading shadow of former glories, was to be surpassed by the products of other glass-making centres before the eighteenth century was out. Nevertheless, the established trade of Venice induced many technical developments and the marketing of many new forms and styles, which reflected the great variety of glass still produced.

At least seven specific forms of Venetian glass were made in the eighteenth century and, while several of these are imitative of earlier production or foreign styles, all are worthy of note. The Muranese craftsmen's ability to evoke both past local and foreign styles stemmed from Murano's long history of development as a glass-making centre, which had enabled them gradually to learn how to manipulate virtually all glass forms. Thus the enamelling and gilding traditions of the fifteenth and sixteenth centuries had allowed for experimentation in coloured glass additions and in *semi d'or* (gold dust within the glass). The resulting freedom of expression, based on the brilliant *cristallo* metal, tempted extravagance in ornamentation.

During the early 1700s the classic baroque stem and bowl shapes which had been popular in the last few decades of the previous century continued to be the mainstay of the industry. Their decoration was mainly diamond-point and shallow wheel-engraving. Forms included stemmed wine-glasses, flutes, goblets, beakers, nests of tumblers, salts and cruets, executed in pinkish-grey *cristallo* clarified with liberal additions of manganese. Though lacking somewhat perhaps in craftsmanship and originality, these pieces, which were thin, light and cheap, had an elegant simplicity of form and remained in vogue for several decades. They are well represented in the collection of King Frederick IV of Denmark and Norway, which was purchased in Venice during the monarch's visit to the city in 1709 and is now at Rosenborg Castle in Copenhagen.

With a national tendency towards ornamentation, it was inevitable that the simple curves of baroque *cristallo* would be elaborated. This was already evident in the application of moulded lions' masks on stems in the late sixteenth and seventeenth centuries, and the symbol of Venice was used again in the eighteenth century. It was by no means the only creature depicted on wine-glass stems: cockatrices, birds and even houses followed, whereby the stem became a three-dimensional vehicle for the glass-maker's skill. Styles of vessel also became more elaborate, and tall-stemmed glasses predominated. Bowls were flared, round funnels, thinly blown and sometimes simply engraved. Feet were wide, elegant and usually folded (their rim turned under to make a double layer of glass), and the overall effect was one of graceful height and lightness. By the 1720s *cristallo* of great purity was being produced.

The Glass Room at Rosenborg Castle, Copenhagen, was designed in 1714 to house the large collection of glass acquired by King Frederick of Denmark during his visit to Venice in 1709.

Colours were added to the *cristallo*, not usually to the extent of colouring the whole body of the vessel but to add light blue or red tints to applied trailing, cresting and fringing. White opaque glass was also used in stripes on bowls and feet, and in stems and appendages. Indeed, there was an overlap between this style of applied white ornamentation—*lattimo*—and the overall white threading of *latticinio*. Originally a Roman technique, *latticinio,* the embedding of spiralling geometrical arrays of white glass canes in a clear *cristallo* ground, had been used throughout the previous two centuries in Venice. The technique was perfected by the eighteenth, but was perhaps over-elaborated. *Filigrana, retorti* (twists), *vetro di trina* (lace glass) and other techniques using threading were all employed on bowls and feet, tumblers, vases, plates and ewers throughout the first half of the century. Towards the city's decadent eclipse, coloured twists were introduced, *semi d'or* was liberally applied, and shapes became more and more elaborate.

From about 1740 onwards, there was a revival of enamelled glassware. Typically, this took the form of red pictorial line-work on white glass plates. Miotti, an old-established Murano firm, produced some excellent work from 1741 onwards. Standing cups in blue and green, echoing those of the fifteenth and sixteenth centuries, were also enamelled in polychromes with added gilding. These seem to have been popular with visitors to Venice from about 1760, and may have been deliberate forgeries of antique pieces for sale to gullible travellers. Better-quality, more original pieces seem to have been attempts to copy in glass the work of German porcelain factories.

The glass chandelier was another major eighteenth-century development. There were sixteenth- and seventeenth-century pieces, but the form was really fully developed only after 1740. In 1739 Giuseppe Briati set up a new factory in Murano, from which came the first of a feast of exuberant chandeliers called *lampadari.* These were composed almost entirely of glass, and exhibited all the old Venetian craftsmanship with every conceivable ornamentation. The basic form was that of curved, ribbed or wrythen *cristallo* branches adorned with multicoloured floral bouquets, streamers, loops, free-hanging baskets and trays. Each flower-head held a candle-nozzle, and when illuminated the effect, epitomizing the splendour and extravagance of Venetian design, still seems inspired. Venetian chandeliers became very popular throughout Europe, particularly in Bohemia, where chandeliers seem to have been a most prestigious possession. They are still highly regarded today, and form the centrepiece of many elegant halls

Above: Flowers and other polychrome decorations adorn this white glass pagoda-shaped chandelier of the mid-eighteenth century. It is typical of the exuberant styles of chandelier produced in the Murano workshop of Giuseppe Briati.
(Palazzo Rezzonico, Venice)

Left: Venetian cristallo *centrepiece on bun feet, late seventeenth–early eighteenth century. The decoration includes moulded masks.*

both public and private, although there exist many debased copies, made in the nineteenth and twentieth centuries, to deceive the uninitiated.

Since the early sixteenth century Venice had been producing mirrors, and had perfected amalgams of tin and mercury which gave greater reflectivity and permanence than the lead alloys used elsewhere. This development, coupled with the steady increase in the clarity and consistency of *cristallo*, had given Venice an apparently unassailable market position by the late seventeenth century. It was not long destined to remain unassailed, however: from the 1690s onwards the Bohemians were challenging it with potash-lime glass mirrors backed by similar mercury-based amalgams; English lead-glass varieties were appearing in the first decade of the new century; and extremely well-made French mirrors appeared soon afterwards, their manufacture becoming the major part of the French glass industry's output at this period. Venetian mirrors were still the product by which others were judged, however, and the greatest market share was held by Venice throughout much of the century. As fashions changed, so did the ornamentation applied to Venetian mirrors: in the 1740s the addition of coloured glass florets was common, while in the 1760s the faces of mirrors were engraved in a style copied from Bohemia. The range was wide, and extended from massive mounted pieces framed in elaborately carved wood surrounds to tiny hand-mirrors with *cristallo* handles and decorated with a minimum of enamel glass florets.

Glass engraving was taken up again in Venice from about 1750 onwards. This time an attempt was made to cut deeply into the *cristallo* surface so as to produce carved glass in a rock-crystal style. This was in response to the attack on the Venetian markets being made by Bohemian glass-makers, but was not really a success. Good specimens exist, some with gilding, but the style looks and feels out of place on the Venetian metal, and must have been very difficult to achieve. The *cristallo* could not be blown thickly enough to compete in solidity and depth of engraving with the German and Bohemian potash-lime metal, and the style was short-lived.

As the Venetian Republic declined, its glass industry was allowed to slip from its former pinnacle of greatness. The Doges, unable to counteract the shift away from their maritime dominance of the Mediterranean once the old route to the riches of the East had been bypassed round the Cape, were faced with a trade slump which affected all artisans, including glass-workers. Just as, politically, the decline seems to have been unavoidable, it could be argued that there was nothing the glass industry could do about its downward course. However, the competition might have been kept at bay had all the eighteenth-century production been of the highest standards of clarity, consistency and form, of which *cristallo* had long shown itself capable. These standards were unfortunately not maintained, and the Bohemians and the British were able to capture Venetian export markets. It may have been a mistake for Venice to try to emulate the design features of lead and potash-lime in such a different metal; perhaps it would have been better to have continued with baroque curves, possibly emphasized with colour, *latticinio* and enamelling, while retaining the tall, thin elegance more suited to *cristallo*. In 1798 the last Doge abdicated, and the Austrians annexed the City State.

Germany, Austria and Bohemia

The Peace of Westphalia (1649), which followed the end of the Thirty Years War, marked the beginning of rapid developments in German glass-making. Although still fragmented into several different countries and numerous tiny states, the lands of the German-speaking peoples were to be relatively stable and prosperous for the next 150 years, and the glass industry expanded, patronized by increasingly wealthy houses and displacing Venetian wares from most European markets in the first half of the eighteenth century. During the period 1680-1750 styles developed rapidly and numerous

Left: This Venetian mirror has a glass frame in which the decorative elements have been engraved with the wheel. In spite of competition from abroad, the Venetians retained the greatest share of the market in mirrors throughout much of the eighteenth century. (Museo Vetrario di Murano, Murano)

new techniques were invented, both for home consumption and for export, until English lead crystal became widespread in about 1770, replacing the German forms in popularity.

It was the discovery of a new metal in the previous century (see Chapter 4) that laid the foundation for this dominant period in German glass-making. Formerly, glass had been made since Roman times in the forests of Europe, and the greenish *Waldglas*, or forest glass, produced there was made from raw potash (from the ashes of burnt wood) and silica sands. Potash glass was quite different from Venetian soda glass, since it was more viscous and set more quickly, and was thus easier to fashion into thick-walled beakers than to draw out into thin-walled, stemmed drinking glasses. Continued experimentation with potash glass during the latter half of the seventeenth century was, however, to yield something much more exciting. By adding a secondary alkali—lime—to the batch, the German potash glass of old was transformed into a metal capable of lapidary-style engraving after the manner of rock crystal. This potash-lime glass had the same qualities as the lead glass simultaneously being developed in England. For both metals crisselling was an initial problem: this exudation of excess alkali from the glass surface, coupled with recrystallization of the glassy silicates, causes a network of tiny cracks to be formed in the glass and drops of moisture to form on its surface. Surviving pieces suggest that the 'disease' was not fully cured in German glass until about 1714. Once this had been achieved and the stability of potash-lime glass confirmed, the German glass industry rapidly exploited the new discovery.

By about 1750 there were at least nine distinct glass-making centres: Bavaria, Brandenburg, Franconia, Hesse, Nuremberg, Saxony, Thuringia, Silesia and Prague. Although styles obviously varied from place to place, many basic shapes remained the same, and glass-workers moved from one centre to another, so that it is often difficult to discover the exact origin of many pieces of similar form. With the new metal, the bulbous *Roemer* and *Humpen* styles were succeeded by shapes which were better at displaying the decorative capabilities of the new glass, although the earlier forms continued to be produced, using the old metal.

The *Roemer* was a particularly persistent form. By the beginning of the eighteenth century, this traditional German drinking vessel had been made for more than 200 years. It had developed from the squat prunted beakers called *Warzenbecher* (literally, wart beaker) of the sixteenth century as the metal improved and the furnaces gained in temperature. Typically, it had

Various types of Humpen *such as the* Passglas *continued to be made in the German-speaking countries during the eighteenth century. This* Passglas *of 1750, from Franconia or Thuringia, shows a young couple in contemporary dress. Height: 26.3cm (10³/₈in)*

During the eighteenth century the glass industry in the German-speaking countries was expanding. Beakers like the one illustrated here, enamelled with the coats of arms of guilds, were typical of the wares produced. (Museum of Decorative Arts, Prague)

Right: This colourless glass beaker, made in Silesia during the 1740s, has Tiefschnitt engraving on the bowl, which is divided into six panels with hunting subjects. Height: 12.5cm (5in)

Below: Two colourless glass goblets decorated with relief cutting (Hochschnitt). The left-hand one, by the Silesian Friedrich Winter, depicts the coat of arms of the counts of Schaffgotsch, which incorporates acanthus leaves, a lion and two eagles. The right-hand goblet, from Winter's workshop, is decorated with large flowers. Heights: 30 and 22cm (11⅞ and 8⅔ in)

a large ovoid bowl, usually plain or lightly engraved, a hollow, cylindrical stem decorated with raspberry prunts and a spreading coiled or blown foot. By 1700 *Roemers* had reached truly grand proportions, and it was not uncommon for one over 30cm (12in) tall to command a central position on a table. When large, they were communal drinking vessels, and when small they were individual wine-glasses (though even a small German wine-glass would equal an English goblet in capacity). The glass was still naturally greenish, but could be clarified with manganese, making it greyish, or deliberately tinted a deeper green or blue-green. Any engraved decoration on a *Roemer* was usually diamond-point. Most, if not all German factories made them, and both commemorative and convivial work was also done by amateur hands, sufficient numbers having survived to suggest that this was a popular pastime. Though they were eclipsed by the newer styles after about 1730, *Roemers* never completely died out, and are still made in Germany today.

The *Humpen*, another old style, had reached its final stage of development and diversification by the beginning of the eighteenth century. This type of large, communal drinking vessel was a tall, slightly incurved cylinder mounted on a squat, flared foot or a simple applied foot-ring, and usually carried elaborate decoration in either cold or fired polychrome enamels, and was often dated. *Humpen* continued to be made during the first half of the eighteenth century, throughout Germany, Silesia and Bohemia, and to carry much excellent enamelling.

These massive vessels began to fall from favour as the increasing affluence and sophistication of the public led to a demand for what was to be by about 1710 the more usual style of European drinking glass, the goblet, and it was made from the new potash-lime glass. The German style of goblet, the *Pokal*, was a grand, tall-stemmed, lidded glass with a generous, flared bowl. Its basic form was a round funnel bowl set on an inverted baluster and a large foot, and its thick walls allowed deep engraving. Each German centre developed its own glass form and engraving style, usually sufficiently characteristic to indicate the origin of a piece. Overall there is more detail, elegance and sheer brilliance displayed on the German *Pokal* of the first half of the eighteenth century than virtually any other type of drinking glass.

Nuremberg was probably the first glass-making centre to produce engraved goblets featuring the polished highlights (called *Blankschnitt*) which enhanced the sculptural effect of the engraving; and both cutting with a lapidary wheel and diamond engraving were practised

A group of Bohemian pieces–including a covered goblet, two beak and a flagon with a stopper–dating from the second quarter of the eighteenth century and all made by the Zwischengoldglas technique. In this process gilt foil engraved with figurative and plant motifs and painted with enamel colours was enclosed within a double wall of glass, then sealed with clear resin. (Museum of Decorative Arts, Prague)

there. Several glass-engravers of Nuremberg signed their pieces, including Hans Wolfgang Schmidt (fl. 1676-1710), who depicted battle scenes, ruins and hunting scenes, and Georg Friedrich Killinger (fl. 1694-1726), who used wheel engraving with some diamond-point engraving on his early work. Stems were composed of several bulbs and multiple collars, lids were made with knopped finials matching the stems, and bowls and feet were sometimes in green, amethyst and blue glass.

After about 1700 Bohemian glass-cutters started to use water power to drive their wheels. This prompted the development of really deep engraving in the style of rock crystal, and heavy cutting and scrollwork in high relief was also practised. These techniques became known as *Hochschnitt* (high-relief engraving) and *Tiefschnitt* (intaglio or deep carving). Stems and feet were also engraved and cut; the moulded 'Silesian' stem of English glass derives from the German shoulder and slanting side-cutting on an inverted baluster stem.

In Silesia, at that time part of Bohemia, engraving and cutting were probably at their best in the first quarter of the century, becoming somewhat over-elaborated thereafter, as baroque gave way to rococo styles. Among the many

Right: A covered goblet (Deckelpokal) of colourless glass with Tiefschnitt decoration, produced at Potsdam in the 1720s. Height: 31 cm (12¼ in) (Kölnisches Stadtmuseum, Cologne)

Below: Ruby and gold threads have been sealed into the stem and finial of this cut-glass covered goblet, which was made in Bohemia in the second quarter of the eighteenth century. (Museum of Decorative Arts, Prague)

known engravers, Friedrich Winter (d. 1712) and Christian Gottfried Schneider (1710-73) produced exceptional work. Rococo bowls became fashionable after 1750, and many strange forms of ambrosia cups and sweetmeats resulted. The cutting on them was excellent, and some were gilded, but the overall effect was less elegant than earlier work. Twists in white, red and gold enamel were added to stems from about 1760 onwards, like those introduced earlier in Bohemia.

Shortly after 1700, glass-workers at Lauenstein in Germany began producing similar work to Silesia, and also experimented with lead glass, but were afflicted with crisselling problems. Some Lauenstein *Pokale* have their pontil marks ground flat and carry an engraved lion motif and sometimes also a 'C' for Calenberg, the principality in which the factory was situated.

The lips of Lauenstein glasses are frequently gilded. Also in Germany, the Kassel glasshouse produced some exceptionally fine engraved *Pokale*, particularly those by Franz Gondelach (1663-1726), who worked in a baroque style involving both *Hochschnitt* and *Tiefschnitt*. Portraits and pastoral scenes were typical, and it may be that an eight-pointed star engraved on the base of the foot denotes his work.

Potsdam (Berlin) fostered two brilliant engravers, Martin Winter (d. 1702) and his pupil Gottfried Spiller (?1663-1728), who both used a similar intaglio style. Sometimes their carving would be as much as 7 mm (³⁄₁₀ in) deep in glass 10 mm (²⁄₅ in) thick, and usually depicted richly decorated mythological subjects with figures in classical poses. In 1736 the Potsdam factory was moved to Zechlin. The style of glass produced there remained similar, with possibly more emphasis on the faceted treatment of stems and upper feet domes. Such gradual elaboration typifies the chronological development of the *Pokal*. Glass made at Brandenburg also included

excellent *Pokale* in both *Hochschnitt* and *Tiefschnitt* styles, and gilding was introduced there in about 1730. Zechlin followed suit in about 1740. *Pokale* made in Saxony were tall and elegant; and it is recorded that there were nineteen independent engravers working in Dresden in 1712. Johann Christoph Kiessling (d. 1744) was court engraver at Dresden from 1717 until his death, decorating goblets mainly with hunting scenes, and Johann Georg Müller worked at Weissenfels until 1783. Saxon *Pokale* often feature a graduated prismatic-cut stem and distinctive lower bowl. Another type of *Pokal*, the *Trichterpokal*, was made in Saxony and Thuringia. This was a drawn-trumpet teared goblet, similar in style to those made in English lead glass at this time, but characteristically with a lid (*Deckelpokal*).

Zwischengoldglas was a German rediscovery of a Roman technique found on catacomb beakers. Said to have been developed in about 1725 in a Bohemian monastery, as yet untraced, the technique became popular, particularly in the mid-1730s, until the 1750s. The process involved decorating the outer surface of one glass with engraved gold leaf and then fixing a clear glass sleeve in the shape of a bottomless 'overbowl' (sometimes further faceted) over the gold-leaf work to protect it. A decorated glass disc (usually stained red) was then cut to fit the bottom, and the narrow air space between the two layers of glass was sealed top and bottom with a clear lacquer resin. The visual effect achieved by this process is outstanding even today. The technique was used on both *Pokale*

and beakers, and combined with skilled cutting of lid, stem and foot; and all was executed in the clearest potash-lime glass. Occasionally silver leaf was used, either instead of or in conjunction with gold. Ruby staining was sometimes applied to the inner glass bowl, and this effect was much used again later by Johann Josef Mildner (1763-1808) of Austria, in his beakers with medallions. The technique was revived in the late nineteenth century, resulting in a number of inferior copies. The original method was immensely popular, and became the obvious choice for commissioned ceremonial glasses, which provide us with a valuable historical record.

Another type of glass developed in Germany was *Milchglas*, an opaque white glass imitating porcelain. From the fifteenth to the seventeenth centuries, this type of glass, designed to carry coloured enamels as did contemporary porcelain, was often seen in Venetian glassware, and the evidence points to the fact that European glass-makers and Chinese porcelain manufacturers were in fierce competition with it. Apparently it was the Potsdam glass-workers who reacted most diligently to the need for *Milchglas*, and by the early years of the eighteenth century it became available. Johann Kunckel is often given the credit for the development of this opaque glass, as well as for potash-lime glass, but whether it is due to him in this case is less certain. It seems likely that many German factories followed the Potsdam example through the first half of the century: many pieces of indeterminate origin survive, enamel-painted with figures, foliage and simple pictorial scenes on beakers, travelling bottles, vases and flasks. From 1750 onwards *Milchglas* flourished in Bohemia, when it was decorated with elaborate

Left: The Zwischengold-glas *process used on Bohemian glass was often combined with other techniques, for example, enamelling and faceting of the outer layer of the glass, as in this beaker dating from c.1740. Height: 9.2cm (3⅝in)*

Below: A Bohemian jug and saucer of Milchglas. *This opaque white glass imitating porcelain, which was generally decorated with figurative and floral themes in polychrome enamels, became popular in Bohemia after 1750. (Museum of Decorative Arts, Prague)*

beginning of the eighteenth century a third of all existing British glasshouses, including those in Ireland and Scotland, where the industry was just beginning, were using the new metal. Its use encouraged the development of new styles of drinking glass, and there was also at this time an important coloured glass output, a family of brilliant enamellers and both an internal and several external engraving schools.

For the first time in British history since the Roman occupation glass utensils and vessels became available for every aspect of social life. All kinds of glass vessel appeared, not only for all the different beverages of the time but also for

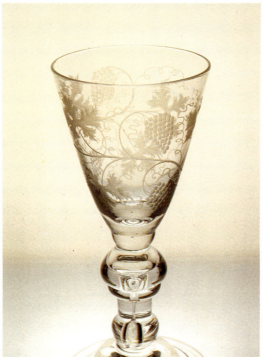

Far left: Anglo-Venetian influences are apparent in this early lead-glass goblet with vertical gadrooning on the bowl. The hollow knopped stem with raspberry prunts contains a James II four-penny piece of 1686. Height: 21cm (8¼in)

Left: An engraved fruiting vine decorates this massive English baluster dating from about 1710. The foot is domed and folded. Height: 26cm (10⅜in)

polychrome enamelled figures in contemporary dress and porcelain-style floral displays. German *Milchglas* is among the more difficult types of glass to define, because very similar pieces were also made and decorated in England, France and Spain, principally by immigrant German glass-workers.

By 1750, German glass had largely ousted the Venetian product from the central European market. Only in Italy itself did local manufacture survive the onslaught of the superior potash-lime metal. During the second half of the century, however, the Germans' supremacy was to be challenged by English lead glass, which by about 1770 had become the second new metal of the German glasshouses.

Britain

In the years after the restoration of the monarchy in 1660, there was an economic and political strengthening of Britain's position, which resulted in an environment conducive to industrial growth. In terms of glass, what had been virtual dependence on imports in 1670 was transformed by 1700 into a predominantly indigenous production with export capabilities. It was Ravenscroft's lead crystal glass that had facilitated this change (see Chapter 4), and by the

foods and condiments at the table. Much kitchen glass was also made, as was glass for the boudoir. Perhaps it was the influence of the French Lorraine glass-makers that extended the range of glass items produced in Britain, where previously 'glass' the material and 'glass' the drinking vessel had been almost synonymous.

The first completely original English glass designs were lead-crystal drinking glasses called balusters, which had stem forms derived from the architectural baluster. Before these were introduced, at the end of the seventeenth century, the Venetian influence lingered, and glasses with applied ornamentation on the stem

(wings, trails and pincered work) and bowl (ribbed, stipple and flammiform gadrooning) predominated. Glasses of the late seventeenth century are more correctly called 'Anglo-Venetian' than 'English', though they are often made of lead glass; the transformation from the ornate Renaissance style to simpler baroque lines came with the realization that the new English metal was more suitable for graceful curves than extravagance, and that such a change conferred a strength and durability that had been lacking in the Venetian style. It was not that the English product was artistically better than the Venetian or the Anglo-Venetian hybrid, but merely that it came closer to satisfying the need to balance elegance with durability.

Balusters were in vogue from about 1690 to 1725, and during this time a huge variety of different stem styles was made, the earliest being the inverted baluster of 1690. The most unusual stem developments took place between 1715 and 1725, and featured different arrangements or numbers of knops. The most common early

bowl form was a round funnel with a solid, heavy base, often lightened with a single rounded tear (an air-bubble in the shape of a tear-drop). Later bowls were drawn trumpets and bells, but the solid base remained. Feet were first folded and later domed and folded; rarely were they plain. More than twenty factories made balusters, including those centred at Southwark, Woolwich, Bristol, the Isle of Wight, Worcester, Coventry, Stourbridge, Warrington, Nottingham, Rotherham, King's Lynn and Newcastle. Their glass was so similar that pieces cannot be confidently ascribed to one centre rather than another.

The quality of the metal used was generally excellent, although a few of the early specimens are of bubbly, yellowish glass, the darker tints indicating the use of impure sands which necessitated liberal additions of glass-maker's clarifying manganese soap. Tints then diminished until pale blue-greys predominated in the later styles, signifying the use of cobalt oxide, or zaffa. The main impression given by balusters is one of uncluttered, symmetrical curves, pleasing to the eye and reassuring to the touch. One has to remember the boisterous behaviour of the era, induced by over-indulgence in food and wine, to understand that a dependably solid-stemmed goblet must have been appreciated. Goblets and large wine-glasses are the predominant surviving forms of these heavy baluster glasses. The goblets have truly magnificent proportions and represent the finest skill of the day. They were usually engraved, and a few bear simple royalist sentiments.

When George I succeeded Queen Anne in 1714, thus establishing the House of Hanover, there was a change from the classic baroque curved pedestals of the balusters to a more angular, less flowing style. Moulded pedestals, at first with four, then six, then ultimately eight flattened faces, constituted a significantly different stem feature in a style apparently derived from middle Europe and therefore called 'Silesian'. The first in the Silesian series were four-sided stems. They may be precisely dated, since they were made to celebrate the Coronation of George I, and often carry crowns and George's cypher and initials proudly moulded on their shoulders, and sometimes the words GOD·SAVE·KING·GEORGE moulded on their four sides. They therefore date from 1714. The six-sided form was soon to follow, and may be dated 1718-25. From this started the final, and usually poorest, derivative, the eight-sided stem, which continued gradually to become twisted, rounded and debased, until it ceased in about 1770. Curiously, its use was continued on candlesticks, tapers and sweetmeats in fairly crisp form throughout the century.

Not all English glasshouses made moulded pedestals their principal motif, however. Western, northern and even some Midlands glass-making cities still retained strong Jacobite loyalties and would have been unlikely to have indulged in such a Hanoverian design. Indeed, the surviving numbers, compared to the earlier balusters, suggest a less widespread provenance. It may be that only London houses catered for the new affiliation, and that it was some time

Right: A Jacobite cider goblet, c. 1760. The cup-shaped bowl is engraved with swags of apples and pears held aloft by cherubs, and the plain foot depicts heraldic roses and other flowers of Jacobite significance. The stem combines a single central knop with a multiple-spiral air-twist. Height: 25cm (9⅞ in)

Left: The production of light balusters in England coincided with the development of native glass engraving. This example, with double-knopped and multi-spiral stem, dating from c. 1750, is engraved with a heraldic rose, a Jacobite symbol. Height: 17cm (6¾ in)

Below: A collection of English sweetmeat glasses dating from about 1714 to 1750. As was common with such receptacles, these examples have moulded Silesian stems.

after it was first made that the style spread to provincial makers. The early examples of four and six-sided stems compare well with contemporary balusters in both metal colour and texture. This also suggests a provenance of the capital's glasshouses, since they had by then some thirty years' experience in using lead glass. Conversely, it is noticeable that a good many of the later eight-sided specimens are less well made and of less perfect metal. Perhaps they derived from and were made for the less exacting provincial market.

Other influences on the moulded-pedestal stem glasses of this period include further remnants of the Anglo-Venetian style, such as gadrooned bowls on some of the early wine-glasses and so-called meads, but truly English styles are evident in the forms of even the earliest of them, including the extended solid bowl base reminiscent of that found on early balusters, and again a tear-drop which often lightens the form. Feet were folded at first, then became domed and folded, as they did in the

Two English wine-glasses, c. 1720-40, having plain drawn stems with tears. The tendency for drinking vessels to become lighter and the stems plainer was accelerated by the reintroduction of the tax on glass in 1745.
Heights: 21 cm (8¼ in) and 15 cm (5¹⁵⁄₁₆ in)
(Merseyside County Museums)

balusters, while the bowl might be a round funnel or, later, a thistle, a bucket or the rococo-style double ogee particularly associated with sweetmeat glasses. Sweetmeat glasses were in fact typical of the Silesian stem style. These tall-stemmed containers were specifically designed to hold such delicacies as chopped or crystallized fruit which were served at table, perhaps as a centrepiece towards the end of a meal. There is evidence that travelling catering companies would erect pyramidal glass structures on the table up to 120 cm (4 feet) high to carry sweetmeats, the structure comprising a set of graduated *tazze*, each tier decked with a set of sweetmeat glasses, every one carrying a different delicacy. Many Silesian-stemmed *tazze* and sweetmeats were made during the mid-century, and far more of them survive than drinking glasses.

While the baluster tradition was broken in London by the 'Silesian' influence of George I, the older designs continued to be produced in the more distant provincial cities. In Newcastle, the glasshouse established by the Dagnia family in the previous century continued to make balusters, but of a lighter, more complex and graceful form than before. After about 1725 a distinctive Newcastle style appeared, typified by fine metal, air-beaded knops and thinly blown bowls and feet. The style was still derived from the baroque baluster, but now took on a height and elegance that far surpassed that of the earlier, more solid specimens. It was also superior to all previous English metals in colour and clarity. The Newcastle style spread, and began to predominate elsewhere after 1730, so that balustroids—lighter glasses derived from the baluster tradition—were being made in many glasshouses until 1760. The light baluster seems to have been made for a wider clientele than previous styles, and was made into simple dram and gin glasses as well as finer wine-glasses. While many of the glasses were clearly made for table or banquet services, others were designed for humbler use. Pictorial references show that drinking clubs used light balusters, and gin and dram glasses appear in depictions of tavern scenes. As well as light versions of the older baluster stem, stem styles include hollow angular knops, simple swelling stems, teared or plain, and multiple ball knops. Few elaborations exist; the rarer baluster formations of the heavier types are absent, and styles are generally less contrived. Bowls were usually flared and light without the earlier solid base, and feet were plain and conical, occasionally with folded rims or domes.

The earliest and best of these light balusters are called Newcastles, even though they were made in other centres too. Similar glasses with Dutch

A group of knopped and plain-stemmed air-twists. All are Jacobite glasses except the central one, which bears the word 'LIBERTY' above the white horse from the arms of Hanover, Germany, which was ruled by the British sovereign.

engraving abound, and while there is no doubt that the soft English lead glass had by then come into favour with the European engravers of fine wares, the sheer volume of engraved Dutch pieces of 1725-49 suggests that local production may have supplemented a well-established import trade from England. Engraving of English origin became common at the same time as the light baluster style was made. Glasses displaying Jacobite sympathies, with their symbols and inscriptions of loyalty to the exiled James II and, later, to 'Bonnie Prince Charlie' before his defeat at Culloden in 1746, were engraved with portraits and symbols such as the English rose with one or two buds and mottoes such as 'Redeat' ('May he return'). After 1746 the symbols used became more disguised until 1770, when the cause was lost and secrecy was abandoned. Glasses were also engraved with Williamite and Georgian Protestant motifs (such as the Orange Tree) at this time. The finest of the light balusters, however, are a series of tall, gracefully knopped armorial-engraved drinking glasses in which marriage and heraldic motifs predominate. Enamelling (usually heraldic) was also practised on Newcastle balusters.

The tax on glass reintroduced in 1745 quickly brought about a change in style and manufacture, at least at the cheaper end of the market. The tax was levied on a weight basis, so that glass producers had to make lighter pieces in order to keep a glass service at the same number of items as before. This realization brought about the final demise of baroque stems; even light balusters ceased to be made soon after the

introduction of the tax, and plain, drawn stems replaced them. These plain stems seem to have been derived from Netherlandish pieces of the late seventeenth and early eighteenth centuries, and are typified by slender toasting stems, so thin that they could easily be broken deliberately after toasting the lady of the moment. The English versions of 1740-60 range from somewhat less slender examples to more robust wines, ales and goblets. Most of them have drawn trumpet bowls rising out of stems that often contain a single tear just below the bowl, and feet were at first folded but later became plain. In the quest for lightness some glass-makers extended the tear so much that the whole stem was hollow, apparently in response to the 1745 Excise Act. These pieces soon passed out of favour, possible because their lightness and comparative fragility meant that they were not substantial enough to withstand daily use. These plain and hollow-stemmed glasses are pleasing, particularly the drawn trumpet tear-stemmed glasses of 1745-50, which are among the most numerous of all eighteenth-century English glasses. Similarly, some of the lightly engraved round funnel and ogee bowls have a certain charm, while a few hollow-knopped sweetmeats and goblets hark back to an earlier era.

It seems that, in a further attempt to reduce weight, glass-makers also tried to reduce the level of lead in their metal, and some ultra-light glasses of between 1745 and 1750 do show much lower levels of lead and an inclusion of some soda glass in the melt. The earlier soda tradition in fact persisted in Britain alongside lead glass through-

The type of English wine-glass of which this is an example, dating from 1730, has been given the name 'Kit-Cat glass' after two examples that are shown in a painting by Sir Godfrey Kneller portraying two members of the Whig group known as the Kit-Cat Club. Height: 17cm (6¾ in)

pockets into a molten glass rod held in a cylindrical mould, and then elongating and twisting the pattern made by the air by drawing and rotating the still-molten glass until it assumed the length and breadth needed for a drinking-glass stem. The concept was not discovered by English glass-makers, but they updated an earlier *façon-de-Venise* tradition. Some interesting pieces exist, in which a typical row of air beads held in the knop of a Newcastle-style light baluster spirals gracefully down the stem, showing a transitional stage in the development of the style before its full possibilities were realized.

The air-twist style was taken to the Low Countries and Scandinavia, where similar stemmed glasses were fashioned. The earliest air-twists were simple corkscrews which gradually became more and more elaborate, with

out the century, and so it is not surprising that there was a partial reversion to the lighter metal. The extremely light, drawn flutes and hollow stem glasses show a green fluorescence under ultra-violet light (indicative of soda) which is completely missing from pre-Excise types of glass. The need for lightness in English glass seems to have continued into the 1760s and 1770s, since mixed lead/soda glassware continued to be made, some of it with attractive twist stems so composed.

The baroque curved stem features from which the English glasses of the first forty years of the century derived their style and novelty thus gave way in the mid-century to plain and hollow forms. After the 1750s the baroque influences had disappeared and been replaced by the beginnings of a rococo style. Whether these changes to less bulky designs were influenced by the Excise Act of 1745 or simply by changing tastes, the results were splendid. After 1750, glass was ornamented by means of internal stem features instead of the external curves of the earlier glasses. Twist-stems became the fashion, particularly air-twists.

An air-twist stem is one in which is embedded one or several twisted columns of air, in an arrangement such as a corkscrew, cable or multiple spiral. It was made by indenting air

double series (combinations of inner and outer spirals) being made by 1760. Most of these were of plain, unknopped form, but some simple knopping was sometimes combined with twists, in which they spiral through the knops (though the knopping never approached the grandeur or weight of earlier knopped styles). Generally, air-twist glasses were tall-stemmed, with relatively small bowls and plain feet. The retention of the tall stem was sustained by the continuing fashion for drinking glasses being rested upside-down in water-filled, double-lipped coolers or 'rinsers' on the table. The long stem and easily grasped foot were vital if accidents with these wet glasses were to be avoided. Most types of table-glass were made with air-twists. They included gins, drams, cordials and ratafias, all small-capacity pieces intended for strong liqueurs and spirits; wines, ciders, meads and ales with medium-capacity bowls, those for ale being tall and funnel shaped; and other pieces such as goblets, sweetmeats and candlesticks, but these are rare. Air-twists were often engraved, in the English rather than the Dutch style, with political, commemorative and convivial motifs.

The largest group of twist-stem glasses—the so-called cotton-twists—has stems with opaque white glass embedded in them instead of spirals of air. Cotton-twists are sometimes also known as opaque-twists and enamel-twists (but this latter name is chemically incorrect). They date from the early 1760s to 1790 or so; thus they followed closely on the introduction of air-twists. It is thought that all major English producers made such glasses, and it is difficult to decide individual provenance, except perhaps in the case of glasses with horizontally ribbed bowls called Lynn glasses, traditionally believed

A group of English air-twist glasses with engraved bowls, c. 1750-60. On some—for example, far left and far right—the decoration is of barley and hops, which suggests that these were ale glasses.

to have been made exclusively at the King's Lynn factory. Most cotton-twists are well made from good-quality metal, although there are some mixed soda/lead specimens among the later types, and some pure soda examples from the North of England (for example Sunderland) and the Continent. The great majority of cotton-twist glasses were made in three pieces, the bowl and foot being separate gathers welded to the ends of the precut stem. In this they differ from many air-twists in which bowl and stem were drawn in one piece, although three-piece air-twists are also common.

Although, as with air-twists, the English did not invent the style but merely updated an earlier Venetian practice, the English cotton-twists developed a style of their own which went well beyond *latticinio*. There are over 300 distinct cotton-twist arrangements, and it seems that the enterprising glasshouses tried every spatial configuration of opaque rods, tubes, ribbons, tapes and bands in an attempt to perpetuate novelty. They were highly successful in this, and

astonishing numbers of these glasses have survived, considering the drinking habits of the day. Notable among them are the cotton-twist cordials, which are tall slender glasses topped with minute bowls, intended for the strongest of fruit liqueurs which were drunk either with tea or after dinner by the ladies, who would have 'withdrawn' to leave their gentlemen to drink port or brandy. Cotton-twist wine-glasses abound, and there are a good number of ales, many engraved with hops and barley on their tall, round funnel bowls. Goblets are less common and sweetmeats are rare. Most stems are unknopped, but a few have small, simple knops similar to those found on air-twists.

As well as engraving, two other decorative techniques, gilding and enamelling, were applied to cotton-twists. Gilding was done on cotton-twist wine- and ale-glasses, the latter having hop and barley designs picked out in this medium. English gilding is of variable quality and sometimes lacks the permanence of Continental work. Both London and Bristol are known to

A group of English cotton-twist (opaque-twist) glasses, c. 1760-75. Many of these wine and cordial glasses have survived, demonstrating great variety in the arrangement of the threads of opaque white glass embedded in the stem.

have been active gilding centres. The second technique, enamelling, appeared in the 1760s and was almost exclusively carried out by the Beilby family of Newcastle. Using both white and coloured enamels, William and Mary Beilby produced brilliant pictorial and armorial work on the bowls of wine-glasses and goblets, mainly those with cotton-twist stems. They depicted floral subjects, landscapes and gardens in rococo style, and several of their designs, including a full royal armorial and many baronial heraldic displays, are signed by William Beilby and may be regarded as the finest decorated cotton-twists. The Beilbys also worked on decanters and glasses with other stem forms.

Several other types of twisted stem developed from the same rococo trend. They include incised-twists, which at first sight look like air-twists but have their decoration on the exterior of the stem, in the form of spiralled ribbing. These are rare glasses, probably dating from 1750-55, and it is thought that they originated as cheaper northern copies of

air-twists. Another rare type is the mixed-twist, produced by combining one or more air-twists and one or more cotton-twists in one stem, usually with one component spiralling round the other. Mixed-twists presumably date from after 1760, since nothing in their style suggests that they came before cotton-twists or that they are an earlier transitional variant. A third type of twist, the colour-twist, has at least one coloured spiral thread. As the glass-makers found they could opacify glass to make white cotton-twists,

they soon realized that the addition of colouring oxides gave coloured twists. The most usual colours are red, blue, green and brown, and violet and yellow are among the rarest. Coloured spirals are usually found combined with cotton-twists, rarely with air-twists, and more rarely still on their own or combined with both air- and cotton-twists. They are thought to date from about 1770 onwards, when buyers would have been accustomed to the earlier forms of twists, and ready for something new. It seems unlikely that every glasshouse made them, as they are now even less numerous than any of the other types. It may be that they were not popular: British taste in glass throughout the eighteenth century was for crystal clarity rather than colour, and it was not until after 1780 that coloured glass began to be favoured. By then the golden age of English cut glass had begun.

William and Mary Beilby of Newcastle-upon-Tyne were responsible for some of the finest decoration of English cotton-twist glass. These enamelled and gilt goblets, dating from c. 1765-70, are signed 'Beilby Inv.^t & pinx.^t', and they are decorated with the arms, crest and motto of the earls of Pembroke and Montgomery. They were probably made for Henry, the tenth earl (b. 1734). Height: 22.3cm (8¹³/₁₆in) (Corning Museum of Glass, Corning, New York)

A group of English colour-twist glasses, c. 1760. The relative rarity of such glasses possibly reflects a preference in British taste throughout the eighteenth century for clear glass.
Heights: 10.5-19.7cm (4¹/₈-7³/₄ in)

The Netherlands

When Spanish dominion was finally removed from the Low Countries in 1706, the Netherlands comprised most of the lands now called Holland and Belgium. Both these regions had long-standing glass traditions: Altarists had settled at Liège, Muranese glass-makers at Amsterdam and Rotterdam and Rhenish glass-workers at Middelburg and Brussels, and had already established fine reputations for their work in potash-lime derivatives of *Waldglas* by the end of the seventeenth century.

Liège seems to have been the first glass-making centre to react positively to the new English style, and there are references to it being made from 1680. Whether output was English in metal as well as style is open to debate; there is evidence to suggest that the Netherlands quickly adopted the new lead glass too, but no proof. Certainly there was healthy trade contact between the two countries, which must have led to competition and the 'poaching' of successful techniques and designs. Just as it is doubtful that all the better engraved 'English' glasses of the late seventeenth century to be found in Britain are British in origin, so it is doubtful that lead glasses engraved by the Dutch in the first half of the eighteenth century are all Dutch-made.

Glass-making in the Netherlands had an unbroken history from the mid-sixteenth to the last decades of the eighteenth century. During this period styles changed several times, from *façon de Venise*, which flourished until the early years of the eighteenth century when a distinctly Germanic influence came to prominence, to a Newcastle variant of the English style, which was in vogue by 1735, especially with engravers. Later, as the number of imported light balusters declined, Dutch factories took up production themselves. After 1750, therefore, the finer, later light balusters and facet-stemmed glasses used by the great Dutch engravers such as Jacob Sang (d. 1783) were often made in the Netherlands. Later still, the English twist-stem style was adopted and copied, and the copies were even exported back to England.

In the first few years of the eighteenth century, the final development of sixteenth- and seventeenth-century Venetian styles occurred at Liège, Middelburg and Amsterdam. These grand, baroque-style glasses were lavishly decorated, even frilly. Liège produced elaborate winged goblets in the Venetian style until 1715 or later. Colours were used extensively to disguise the otherwise greyish metal, and pale blue winged appendages, trails and spiral bands were typical. Red, yellow and green were also used, in the form of applied ornamental prunts, spots, gadroons and threads. Interior twists are also to be found in stems containing colour as well as white elements. *Latticinio* and gadrooned elements survive in early eighteenth-century Netherlands glass, whereas they seem to have been superseded late in the previous century in England. These late flowerings of the Venetian influence were executed mainly in soda glass, although some traces of lead and even potash can be found. It seems that every possible addition was made to the stems of these goblets, while bowls were often engraved with diamond-point in the same manner as the earlier Dutch *Roemers* of the mid-seventeenth century, and feet were usually wide and conical with narrow folds. Many so-called seventeenth-century Venetian wing-glasses are in fact likely to be of eighteenth-century Low Countries origin.

The German *Roemer* style of drinking glass remained popular in the Low Countries well into the first quarter of the eighteenth century. The greenish metal from which it was made was presumably deliberately tinted to conform to tradition, as the new metals would have been too pure on their own, although the green is usually yellower and darker than that of earlier *Roemers*. Shapes varied little, but whereas the earlier *Roemer* feet were built up from a molten glass trail wound round a conical wooden former, later examples sometimes had blown feet to which external ornamentation was applied, a form of construction that was to become the rule by the second half of the century. Calligraphic and diamond-scratched pictorial engraving appears on a few of the bowls.

By 1710, the impact of the English style was fully felt by the glasshouses of Holland and Belgium. Faced with the possibility of losing their profitable local sales to the more robust English imports, they responded by imitation, and produced a range of baluster-stemmed glasses. They were not exact copies of the English product, however: they still had only soda glass to work with, and so the thick-walled and bulbous-stemmed English style was beyond their capabilities. Therefore they contrived a lighter, taller, hollow-knopped version, with a wide-spreading, narrow-folded Venetian-style foot, supporting a tall, elegant stem with several well-formed hollow knops and topped by a thinly blown, delicate yet capacious bowl. Glasses and goblets more than 25cm (10in) high have survived, demonstrating that thin soda glass was not necessarily ephemeral.

By 1730 the Newcastle style was predominant in the Low Countries, and Dutch glasshouses were faced with increased imports from England. By now some at least had mastered

English lead glass techniques; indeed, it is known that English glass-makers were working in Holland, and it is now thought that the Dutch began to copy the Newcastle styles, although this was not always believed to be the case. In fact, one of the longest-running and deeply felt controversies concerning eighteenth-century European glass centres round this style in the Netherlands. Until the influential work of E. Barrington Haynes *et al.* after the Second World War, it was generally held that the majority of light lead balusters of the period 1725-50 originated in Holland, but Barrington Haynes ascribed the majority of such glasses to Newcastle. However, by the early 1960s Amsterdam antique experts were able to point to conclusive archaeological evidence that lead glass and, in fact, light balusters were made in Middelburg, Ghent, Liège and 's Hertogenbosch

A Roemer of Dutch or Rhenish manufacture dating from the third quarter of the seventeenth century. The junction of the bowl and the narrow waist, which is decorated with eight raspberry prunts, is marked by a simple milled ring and the glass stands on a spreading spiral foot.
Height: 16cm (6¼in)

during the period in question. Today, therefore, it is generally accepted that there are both Newcastle and Dutch examples, all of good workmanship and with both carrying fine engraving, and so they cannot always with certainty be told apart. The styles of light Dutch balusters accurately mirror those of Newcastle, with their slightly flared bowls of wine-goblet size, multi-knopped air-beaded stems and thin conical feet. They remained the natural choice of engravers and in vogue until the advent of twist-stem glasses in the 1760s.

Holland quickly followed England in the reinvention of air-twists, and produced examples from 1750 onwards. Light, air-beaded balusters were still popular and composite-stem glasses were made which contained both air-beaded knops and air-twist sections. These hybrid designs were followed by air-twists proper in the English pattern.

Later, in around 1765, cotton-twists replaced the air-twists to keep pace with the changes of fashion in England. Good-quality Dutch cotton-twists were made, but there was also extensive production of an inferior variety. This was a series of mixed lead and soda glasses with soda predominating. These usually had bell or ovoid bowls and were much lighter and less clear than the better products. Most are thought to have been made in the Liège factories after 1770. Red and white colour-twists also appear to have been made in the same factories, and these are found engraved with Jacobite motifs, which has suggested to some experts that all these glasses are really of English origin. Other, rarer colour-twists also exist, some of which, for example, the blue and yellow and the red and green, are of better quality.

Whatever the fashions coming from abroad, diamond-point engraving continued to be popular in the Netherlands as it had been since the second half of the previous century, but new styles were adopted. Whereas the seventeenth-century workers produced their calligraphic and pictorial designs by scratching lines with a mounted diamond splinter, the eighteenth-century workers usually created their imagery from variations of light and shade derived from closely packed minute dots. These dots, or pits, in the surface of the glass were made by gently tapping a diamond stylus on the glass, in a technique known as stippling. The outstanding Dutch diamond-point engravers were Frans Greenwood (1680-1761), who worked at Dordrecht from 1720 to 1755, and David Wolff (1732-98), who was active from 1774 until the era of faceted stems and was notable for combining stippling with diamond line engraving. Several signed pieces by other artists also survive.

The softness of lead glass, English or Dutch, was found to be ideal for the delicate diamond-point treatment. Neither the German potash-lime glass nor Venetian *cristallo* could be worked with such ease, as they took a fire polish in the annealing lehrs that made their surfaces hard and brittle. (A little stippling line was, nonetheless, successfully carried out on *cristallo* glasses.) Diamond-point work reached a peak during the eighteenth century, and the perfection of fine detail on the bowls of light balusters is particularly apparent as the glasses are lifted slowly into angled light. The picture or design appears at a specific angle because every indentation has been struck at that angle, irrespective of the curvature of the bowl.

Dutch wheel engraving also reached a peak during the eighteenth century, when form and finish rivalled the best work from Bohemia and Saxony. Dutch wheel engravers maintained their strong connections with the German schools from which they had stemmed in the late seventeenth century, and even Jacob Sang, the greatest Dutch exponent, advertised his wares as 'Saxon artist glass engravings'. Much wheel-engraved work is on light baluster lead glass and is essentially commemorative in style. Births, weddings, treaties, and trade and political adventures form the mainstay of Dutch wheel engraving in general and Sang's work in particular. Sang worked on earlier glasses as well as on current production, and there are gadrooned lead goblets of the early 1700s which are engraved by his hand, presumably after 1737, the earliest of his dated pieces. He is known to have continued his trade until at least 1753. There were many other wheel engravers in the Low Countries during this period, but surprisingly few glasses are signed although the quality of the work is generally extremely high.

Spain

With the decline of Venetian influence in the late seventeenth century, Spanish glass-makers began to look elsewhere for inspiration. They turned to the German Lands, to England, the former enemy, and to the Netherlands, the former colony, and Spanish glass of the early eighteenth century shows the influence of all these countries. The resulting interplay of techniques led to four definable styles arising from all four major Spanish glasshouses in the hundred years from 1680, and these styles are among the most interesting and yet neglected of the whole century's output.

The last Venetian-style glasshouse in Spain was founded in Madrid in 1680 by Diendonne Lambottle of Namur, and it produced *cristallo* and *latticinio* wares before absorbing Flemish, English and Bohemian influences. The cosmopolitan background to the production of Spanish glass is best reflected in the governors of La Granja de San Ildefonso, the royal glasshouse near Segovia. This factory was established in 1728 by a Catalan glass-worker called Ventura Sit, who in 1740 relinquished control of all but the plate-glass business to a Frenchman, Dionisio Silvert, who in turn handed over to a Swede called Laurence Eder in 1750. Eder departed (with his father who worked in Sit's plate department) in 1764 in favour of Sigismund Brun, a German. Even so, it says a great deal for the strength of Spanish art that throughout the eighteenth century the basic glass forms followed native tradition, as they had done during the previous 200 years when Venetian influence was at its height. Thus forms of

glassware unique to Spain, such as the *porrón* and *cántir* (types of a narrow-spouted handleless flask from which wine is poured directly into one's mouth), and *almorrata* (a type of rose-water sprinkler) were decorated (but not changed) by a combination of Venetian, German, Netherlandish and English influences. The result was executed in various soda metals.

Since the Middle Ages, Spain had been Europe's principal source of the glass-making alkali called barilla, used as a source of soda. It was the ash made by burning a plant called *Salicornia herbacea* (glasswort), a low-growing salt-marsh herb. In the Alicante region, a sub-species called *Salicornia natri* (*natrium* is the Latin word for soda) was the basis for the Castile soap industry as well as the glass industry of Europe. Since the twelfth century it had been exported to Venice, and by the sixteenth century

An eighteenth-century Catalonian porrón, *a type of drinking vessel still manufactured in Spain. This example has a trefoil mouth and is decorated with opaque white threads on the neck. Height: 24.5 cm (9⅝ in) (Victoria and Albert Museum, London)*

it was being exported to Verzelini's factory in England, where it grew with difficulty, and in the eighteenth century prizes were being offered for its successful cultivation there. (It also grows in Egypt where it is known as roquetta.) Soda glass was thus the basis of the Spanish industry, but its chemical treatment did not remain unchanged, and it is possible to differentiate between different types of Spanish glass on the basis of chemical tint as much as style.

Normally, barilla-based glass was green,

because of the iron contamination of the local silica sands. Throughout the sixteenth and seventeenth centuries, this green colouration had been acceptable to most levels of Spanish society, but in the eighteenth century it was relegated to utilitarian levels. Even so, the unaltered green barilla-based Spanish glass of this period can be attractive. It was used to produce the everyday wares of the average household, such as lamps, beakers, jugs, *tazze*, and *porrón*. Though an imperfect medium, green barilla has an undeni-

An eighteenth-century Catalonian milk-glass jug decorated with enamelling and gilt in imitation of oriental porcelain.
Height: 24.8cm (9¾in)
(Victoria and Albert Museum, London)

able charm, for it represents a basic artistic achievement in a glass form which was struggling for survival, the last use of what was a style unchanged since medieval times. Particularly pleasing is the *porrón*, designed to keep wine free from insects during long hot days in the field, and to eliminate the necessity for drinking glasses. While their basic shape remained unchanged, the applied decoration varied, depending on in which of the three factories they were produced. Catalonia used stringing and ribbing as decorations, while the Andalusian *porrón* is covered with pincer-worked trails and the Castilian type is plainer, almost undecorated.

Some time during the first half of the century a deliberate attempt was made by Spanish glasshouses to alter the basic barilla colour by adding tinting oxides. A pleasing amber was produced by adding more iron and a blue-green by the addition of cobalt. The amount added must have been small, since the aim was to tint rather than to colour. Several Andalusian examples have two different tints in the same piece. At the same time, opaque white *lattimo* stripes were reintroduced into the designs, and there are pale tinted *porrón*, *cántir* (which may be highlighted), beakers and lamps with these Venetian-style additions from Catalonia, La Granja de San Ildefonso and Andalusia. The *cántir*, an upright flask with a central ring handle and two spouts—a wide one for filling and a narrow *porrón*-style one for pouring—had a bulbous bowl which was ideal for simple *lattimo* striping, combed *lattimo* and even *filigrana*. A separate and more rudimentary series of tinted barilla ware has stringing and pincer work in glass of the same colour as the body, similar to designs used on green barilla.

The glass-makers next added manganese as a clarifying agent, but it seems that only Castile and La Granja de San Ildefonso ever came close to producing a colourless soda glass; the other houses seemed satisfied with their existing metals. Castile produced ice-glass standing bowls and *tazze* in the Venetian style, and also ring-beakers (reminiscent of those of sixteenth-century Germany) and handled jugs with neck rings, similar to English and French eighteenth-century styles. La Granja, on the other hand, copied Bohemia and Silesia, and produced faceted travelling bottles, gilded decanters and simple beakers that at first glance look like *Zwischengoldglas*. They also produced beakers with candy-like pink and white *latticinio* bands in clarified barilla which is often difficult to distinguish from potash-lime in colour, but it is much lighter since it had to be more thinly blown. The engraving, though charming, never approached German standards for the same

reason; the wall thickness and depth of engraving had to be kept thin.

Towards the end of the century the Spanish glass industry, having spent many years clarifying its base metal, began deliberately to colour it. Opaque white glass, or milk glass, pieces with simple polychrome floral enamels and rich ruby, green and blue body-stained pieces began to be made. La Granja produced some excellent white-on-blue flasks, bells and vases which could be mistaken for Bristol blue glass of the same period and some mottled white on brownish-green that looks like Nailsea glassware of this type. This factory's milk glass was also of a high standard and carried shallow gilded engraving similar to that used on clarified metal. Some of the more elaborate pieces rival Bohemian work. The body-stained pieces in red and green are also interesting: some are similar to German or English pieces in the same metals, while others are a deliberate reversion to earlier Spanish forms. Typical of these are hanging ring-lamps and the *almorratas*, multi-spouted rose-water sprinklers which seem to have been made by most, if not all, the factories.

Thus native styles during the eighteenth century predominated in Spain despite foreign influences, and its basic metal, though much improved in texture and colour, seems still to have been preferred coloured. La Granja de San Ildefonso is the exception which, catering for royal and foreign dignitary tastes, often opted for a copy of Bohemian rock crystal.

Scandinavia, Russia and France

Scandinavia was less influenced by Venice than other countries, although the first Scandinavian factory, the Kungsholm Works at Stockholm, had been founded (in 1676) by a Muranese, Giacomo Bernadini Scapitta. Scapitta produced tall, thinly blown goblets in the Venetian style for royal patrons, sometimes with a purely local stem variant of twinned back-to-back initials of the monarch moulded into the stem. The use of monograms, engraved on bowls and gilded, was subsequently to be widespread on much Swedish, Norwegian and Russian glass, and seems to have originated in Germany. The German influence was certainly greater than the Venetian: for example, Christoph Elsterman, a Saxon engraver, worked in Stockholm from 1698 to 1715, and the metal used was at first based on the German potash-lime.

A second Swedish factory opened at Scania in about 1700. Skånska glass was usually more utilitarian than that from Kungsholm, although it too was engraved and gilded in the German style. Kosta Works opened in 1742 and also made German-style cut and engraved glass, as well as chandeliers in the English manner.

Norway's first glassworks, Nøstetangen, near Drammen, opened in 1741 and produced table-glass and chandeliers in the English style. German potash glass was used there until about 1748, when English lead glass appeared, presumably introduced by English glass-makers. (It is known that at least two English glass-makers, James Keith and William Brown, were tempted away from Newcastle in the mid-1750s.) Two other Norwegian factories,

operating at Hurdals Verk and Hadelands, also used lead glass. So successful was the new metal that all the Swedish factories were also converted to its use. In the mid-century the Norwegian factories produced ranges of air- and cotton-twist glasses based on English styles but with a distinctive yet elusive individuality. They are of greyer glass and usually have larger bowls than the English equivalents. The bowls often carry heraldic engraving which is more Germanic than English or Dutch, since, while the glass-blowers were English, the engravers were usually German, and included Heinrich Gottlieb Köhler who was brought from Silesia via Copenhagen to Nøstetangen. In 1760 a royal decree stopped imports to Norway and granted Nøstetangen a monopoly, but this exclusivity was short lived as Friedrick V, the factory's patron, died in 1766 and the factory declined thereafter, closing down in 1777. During its final period the Venetian influence returned, and became evident in the gadrooned and trailed work to be seen on decanter-bottles and lid finials produced there.

Russia had close ties with Scandinavia in the seventeenth and eighteenth centuries, and it seems to have been from Scandinavia that glass technology came to Russia. Glassware itself, as distinct from knowledge of its manufacture, was imported to Russia throughout the seventeenth and eighteenth centuries from the German Lands, and many *Pokale* engraved with czarist motifs were made in Saxon and Bohemian houses. The Russians had made many previous attempts to start their own glass industry, but it was not until 1634, when a Swede, Julius Koiet, was granted a licence for a works near Moscow, that they had any real success. Other glass-works—at Izmailovskii, Jamburg and Zhabino, all near Moscow—were founded, and several smaller works were later established near St Petersburg, one of which became the capital's imperial glassworks, producing items for the Winter Palace from 1743. Russian-made glass tended to follow German styles, and engraved monogrammed *Pokale* and enamelled beakers are among the few pieces of the period with authenticated Russian provenance.

In France, the Altarist heritage of forest glass or, more particularly, *verre de fougère* (fern or bracken glass) continued well into the early eighteenth century at centres such as Nevers, Rouen, Orléans and Nantes. As would be expected, this potash glass was pressed into service to simulate both Venetian and German styles but, not surprisingly, the results were often far from ideal. France did not, however, rely on the imitative approach for long. Cast crystal glass had been developed into mirror glass by Bernard Perrot in 1695, and the French

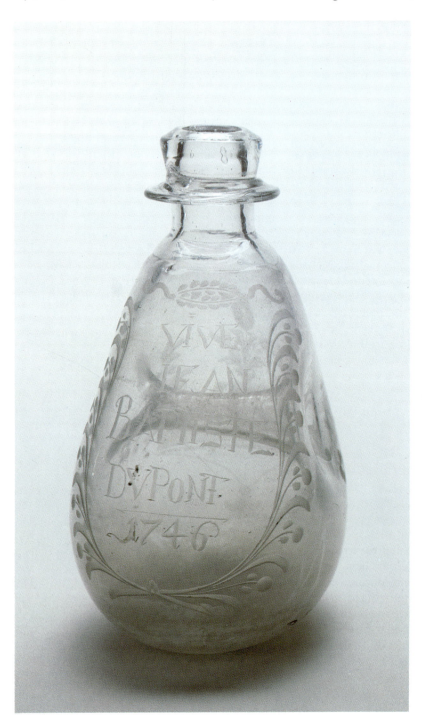

A gourd-shaped bottle with engraved decoration—a flowered heart flanked by two birds and the inscription 'Vive Jean Baptiste Dupont 1746'—probably made in the east of France.
Height: 16cm (6¼in)
(Musée des Arts Décoratifs, Paris)

mirror industry gained prominence throughout much of north-western Europe, securing the market lead in the early eighteenth century. The fashions in decorative tableware were also noted by French craftsmen, and good examples of ruby and other coloured glass survive, along with a French version of milk glass, or *Milchglas*, dating from the mid-century. Later still, perhaps as late as the 1780s, the French industry began using lead crystal, but to imply that the French merely copied the *verre d'Angleterre* may well be incorrect, as it seems that the St-Louis factory in Lorraine reinvented the product in 1781. Elaborately cut pieces became the bulk of the output, and show the clarity that was to characterize all glass subsequently produced at the great French glasshouses of St-Louis, Baccarat and Clichy.

China

Before the seventeenth century, glass in China had been regarded in an entirely different way from glass in Europe. The beads, amulets and funeral ornaments produced in ancient China show that glass was treated as a semi-precious stone, to be chiselled, carved and polished as a gem; and glass was cast but not blown. Towards the end of the seventeenth century, however, China was exposed to the European concept of blown glass. A group of Jesuit missionaries apparently traded their knowledge of Venetian glass for the opportunity to interest Emperor K'ang Hsi (1662-1722) in their religion. Whether the Emperor was influenced by their religion may be doubted, but he was immediately impressed by the glass they produced, and ordered a factory to be set up within the palace boundaries in Peking. Surviving examples of this first Chinese blown glass are remarkably Venetian in style, having wrythen bowls with stringing and simple *latticinio* inlay. These surviving pieces also show the crisselling which seems to have bedevilled every introduction of a new metal everywhere in the world. The troublesome alkali in Chinese glass seems to be barium which, though chemically similar to sodium, is much heavier and may have confused the Jesuits as to the quantities needed.

Once started, the Chinese industry was quick to develop, and although some other blown European styles followed they were not simply copies but distinctively Chinese in character, since they always applied Chinese artistic tradition to the European techniques. The Chinese produced miniature thick-walled blown bottles in a variety of rich colours, with cameo and intaglio cutting applied using lapidary techniques. Snuff bottles were the most typical

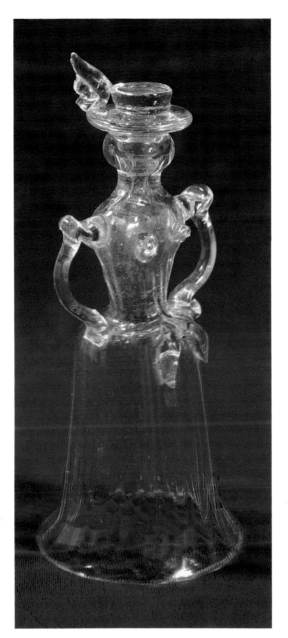

An early eighteenth-century glass in the shape of a lady, made in Normandy, France. (Musée des Beaux-Arts, Rouen)

of the output, but flasks, bowls and vases were also made. Throughout the eighteenth century the Peking glass industry continued to grow. Among the most remarkable of its products were polychrome enamelled pieces and cameo-cut overlay vases depicting flowers, birds and figures, usually with a dense white body resembling porcelain and bright, vibrantly coloured overlays, one of the most popular colours being imperial yellow. Both transparent and opaque colours were used and so was 'snow-flake' glass which had air bubbles. Interior painting on small, clear glass bottles was used to demonstrate the skill and patience of the artist. It was Chinese cut overlay glass that most impressed Emile Gallé when he visited the South Kensington Museum (now the Victoria and Albert Museum) in 1872; his work shows the influence of the Chinese technique.

CHAPTER SIX

THE LATE EIGHTEENTH CENTURY

This pair of English cut and wrought candlesticks features eight-angled Silesian stems turned upside-down and sandwiched between globular knops enclosing air bubbles.
Height: 25.75cm (12³/₄in)
(Corning Museum of Glass, Corning, New York)

Throughout the many centuries that glass has been worked, no decision has been reached as to which of its two characteristics, its plastic or glyptic nature, is the more important. Should it be considered a ductile material, to be moulded and manipulated in its hot state, or is it a substitute for crystal, to be treated as a stone and cut accordingly? Almost all glass-workers from Roman times onwards have treated glass as a plastic, the more so since the art of blowing it was discovered. The art of Venetian glass was founded on this belief and never forsook it, a fact that was a major contribution to Venice's decline in the eighteenth century as the world's major glass-making centre.

It was not until the second half of the eighteenth century that the great division in the art of glass-working became obvious, and glass began to be used successfully as a substitute for crystal and cut accordingly. Before this, although the geometrical cutting of glass was well known, it was applied to only a tiny proportion of the world's glass output. The use of the cutting-wheel had been discontinued almost completely from Roman times until it was revived in the seventeenth century in Bohemia, where it met with no great success. It was almost totally unused in Venice throughout the greatest era of glass production the world has ever known. For Venetian glass-makers, glass was a ductile material, to be manipulated and moulded—even cast—in dozens of different ways. They coloured it in many hues; inserted patterns of white and coloured rods in it; embellished it internally and externally with gold; decorated its surface with applications of other glass, moulded, tooled and tinted to form myriad fantasies; and when it was cooling or cold, they painted it with enamels (closely

related to glass chemically) and refired it to render the enamels permanent.

These were the ways in which the Venetian craftsman always worked in his Renaissance and baroque designs; but as the eighteenth century progressed, the exuberant movement of these styles descended into misapplied rococo grotesqueries, which look as though, consciously or unconsciously, they are frenzied attempts to attract attention and compete with the English-inspired cut glass that was flooding Europe. It was to be more than a century before Venice recovered and again became an innovator and major force in glass design and manufacture, while still retaining reproductions of the days of its greatness.

For now the great age of cut glass had come. Glass had been sculpted by the artist-carvers before, by the cameo-cutters and *diatretarii* of Rome and the high-relief engravers of late-seventeenth-century Silesia. It had, however, seldom been worked by artisans cutting standard geometric patterns to the outlines given them by artist-designers. The neo-classical ideas of the eighteenth century were, paradoxically, best expressed in cut crystal (as the glass of the day is often known), not in the plastic forms of truly classical art glass. And as well as geometric patterns, certain stereotyped designs, sometimes cut, sometimes merely engraved, began to appear—urns, swags, paterae (segmented circles), bucranae (ox-skulls), formalized floral designs and so on—taking their inspiration from the architecture and decorative arts of the time. Many of these forms were based on the ideas of the Adam brothers, the Scottish architects who exerted such enormous influence on late eighteenth-century taste, with their neo-classical designs ranging from architecture to ceramics.

They and their followers were responsible for building many great houses of the day, and for embellishing the interiors of many more with the plasterwork which is most readily recognized as their work today. Josiah Wedgwood followed in ceramics the elegant neo-classical designs that Robert Adam had derived from his studies in Italy, and contemporary glass-makers also developed innovatory styles of cutting appropriate to this new artistic ethic. Although the flowing arms and spherical body of an Adam-period glass chandelier may still convey something of the idea of glass as a ductile material, it is the exquisite facet-cutting, revealing the deep translucence and light-refraction of the material itself, that catches the eye. Glass as a glyptic substance had for the first time become fully acceptable to all civilized taste; it was to remain so for the next 100 years or more, and will always retain its protagonists.

It is strange indeed that this great burgeoning of cut glass did not occur until the late eighteenth century since, once launched on the international market, it never afterwards lost its appeal. Why mass production was delayed for so long remains a mystery, since the technology for cutting was present from very early times, and its application apparently depended little on the quality of the actual metal currently being produced. While English lead crystal was the finest glass for cutting that had so far been discovered, other metals of a suitable nature had long been available. In prehistory, glass manufacture, the enthralling and mysterious transmutation of common sand into gemstone, must have inspired the lapidaries to cut it as soon as—if not before—the early manipulators formed their little coloured vessels around sand cores. Indeed, glass was being cut in the Middle East early in the last millennium BC, and these early efforts were truly glyptic, being cold cutting from blocks of glass, in the techniques used for rock crystal.

Why development along these lines did not continue is hard to decide, since it would obviously soon have led to the cut glass with which we are familiar today, where the vessel or other piece is first shaped by blowing, moulding or otherwise working, prior to cutting. Indeed, by the end of the pre-Christian millennium the Romans had developed methods of wheel-cutting glass whose basic form had often been previously determined by other methods; and cutting and faceting in ways comparable to those of eighteenth-century Europe were practised in Persia in the fifth century, and several centuries later in Egypt. But apart from these instances and other notable exceptions dealt with elsewhere in this book, there is a vast and inexplicable gap in the production of cut glass—for Syrian,

Spanish, Venetian and other Renaissance Italian and German glass-makers were entirely governed by the idea of glass as a plastic medium, and showed little or no interest in glass-cutting. However, the necessary technical knowledge and skill required for cutting were present in many countries, and the power requirements for mass production were not great. After all, a Dutch diamond-cutter required only his wife or apprentice to power his wheel for far more arduous and tedious work, and the cameo glass-cutters of Rome, the *diatretarii* of Alexandria, the mysterious makers of the Hedwig beakers, and the seventeenth- and early eighteenth-century high-relief engravers of Cassel and Hermsdorf did not lack power sources—whether hand or water—for their extraordinarily highly skilled work.

By the second half of the eighteenth century English and Irish glass-cutters had developed the necessary skills for their less demanding geometric cutting—not that their work was easy, or their equipment sophisticated. As we know from contemporary accounts and illustrations, as well as from an intriguing working model, eighteenth-century Irish glass-cutters worked on a pedal-driven wheel, operated by the cutter with one foot while standing on the other—and, if the evidence of the model is to be believed, sometimes smoking a clay pipe upside down at the same time. When we remember that the piece of glass upon which he worked—a large and extremely heavy bowl or decanter, for example—was held between him and the edge of the vertically revolving wheel, so that he was always working on the side away from him, upon which the pattern of the work was further obscured by a continuous trickle of muddy water, it seems a near miracle that any precision of cutting whatsoever could be achieved. It is also noteworthy that the greater part of the cutting was done by eye alone, since the designer would have drawn on the blank piece of glass to be cut no more than a small area indicating the designs he wished the cutter to employ. This practice continued after the far more efficient power source of steam had been developed and applied to glass-cutting, and increasingly intricate work demanded of the cutters - though at least they could now sit down to display their skills.

At last had come a period when design sustained, fashion demanded and taste approved a treatment of glass in its glyptic role, as a crystalline material to be cut as a gemstone, but in a manner no stone could support: for nowhere would one find a stone in such size or quantity; in hollow, predetermined, standardized shape; in virtually flawless body, to make the myriad pieces that were now available in cut glass. And

English drinking glasses of about 1770 having faceted stems and wheel-engraved designs appropriate to their function: the glass in the centre, engraved with hops and barley, is for ale; the other two, decorated with flowers, grapes and vine leaves, are wine glasses.
Height of ale glass: 18.7cm (7³/₈in)
Height of wine glasses: 14.6cm (5³/₄in)
(Victoria and Albert Museum, London)

the British Isles had created a virtual monopoly. The unsurpassed brilliance of the British cutters' work was made possible by the susceptibility of English lead crystal to cutting and polishing, as well as its delicate and charmingly variable tints, since the glass responded much more readily to the wheel than did the lightweight and hard contemporary Continental metals. Such was the success of the British cut-glass industry, especially in Ireland, that by the end of the eighteenth century large-scale imitation was being undertaken at major foreign glass centres such as Liège, where Irish patterns in particular were produced on such a vast scale and were so successful in their deception that many pieces still appear today in overseas fine art auctions and other antique sales, where they are almost always catalogued as 'Waterford'. This has assisted in many misconceptions and legends that have grown around genuine Waterford glass, principally that of the famous Waterford 'blue tint', often faithfully reproduced in the copies, but by no means always present in the genuine article.

Great efforts, sometimes successful, were made to lure English and Irish glass-makers to Continental and American glass centres to instruct in and practise the arts of glass. From Bristol in 1770 glass-workers went to work for Henry Stiegel at his second American glasshouse at Manheim, Pa., and the English *émigré* engraver Lazarus Isaac long worked for him. In 1774, when Stiegel's glassworks closed, Isaac set up business as an engraver on his own. From Newcastle James Keith went to Norway, there to found and profoundly influence the glass industry until his retirement in 1787. Mayer Oppenheimer, although a German by birth, learnt his glass-cutting in Birmingham, and in 1784 was granted the right to make English-style cut glass in Normandy, and many French glasshouses commenced using the English metal and importing English workers to make glass '*à la façon d'Angleterre*'. The above named are examples of the few whose names are known to us. There were many other anonymous emigrations of British glass-workers, individually or *en masse*: artisans, chemists, designers, cutters, managers, all following the universal traditions of the wandering glass-makers. Of course, the late-eighteenth-century fashion for cut glass was not entirely limited to the designs or methods developed in Britain, though the inspiration may have come from there: at the same time fine and original cut-glass industries were founded without British help, in France, the German states, the Low Countries and Bohemia. The thinly blown *cristallo* of Venice, however, was not a suitable vehicle for cutting, even if glass-workers there could have become conditioned to the idea; and the hard potash metal produced in most other Continental glasshouses was more suitable for fine engraving than any other surface treatment. Their attempts at glass-cutting—whether of indigenous design or imitative of British styles—are shallow, and bite the glass little deeper than the engraver's wheel. The Continental glasshouses·that were most successful in the production of cut glass had gone over to metals the same as, or very close to, English lead crystal, even when they had not imported British workers or embraced their styles.

The British Style of Cutting

English design in cutting based on the diamond shape apparently began with the faceting of the stems of drinking glasses with hollow diamonds, a fashion developed in the mid-eighteenth century. Prior to this, English cutting seems to have consisted merely of flat-polishing, bevelling and flat-cutting on the shoulders of cruet bottles, square bottles for travelling-boxes and the like, in the shallow Bohemian manner.

The common contention that the extensive faceting of drinking glasses was connected with the current taxation of glass by weight—reducing taxation by reducing the weight of the glass—is readily disproved by simple comparison with slightly earlier and contemporary types. The styles immediately preceding and overlapping facet glasses (enamel-twists, air-twists, hollow-stems, balustroids and so on) are usually more thinly blown and lighter than facets, which required a fairly substantial thickness to allow the cutter to exercise his art without danger of breakage. In any case, the amount of metal removed during the cutting of a facet-stemmed glass is only a small proportion of the weight of the glass. The fashion clearly originated in a conscious desire to treat glass in this manner, on a large scale, and with totally different design principles in mind from what had gone before. And although Silesian glasses of the early eighteenth century have flat-faceted stems, diamonds on the shoulders and scallop-cut feet, and many Bohemian glasses of the same period have decorative flattened areas and rudimentary diamonds, English hollow facets are the commencement of a unique fashion, and by the last quarter of the eighteenth century drinking glasses decorated with them had superseded all other English stem designs.

Below: These prismatic cut-glass pieces are part of a large glass service, of the sort that would have been in common use throughout Britain after the mid-eighteenth century.
Height of ewer: 22.4cm (8¹³/₁₆in)
(Wadsworth Atheneum, Hartford, Connecticut)

The age of cutting had truly begun. Cut table-glass became common usage in Britain, and very large services of matching glassware were to be found on every table of quality. Indeed, even the clubs and the better inns and taverns also provided cut glass for the use of their patrons. The British developed a flourishing export trade to the Americas, Spain, Portugal, and even to Turkey and India, in which last two countries bell-shaped, diamond-cut hookah-bases of British manufacture found a ready market—one which Bohemian glass-makers took over at a somewhat later date.

Considerable change appeared in the basic

became shorter, eventually almost rudimentary, being simply decorated with a central blade or ball knop, often uncut but occasionally faceted, and with little other variation for forty or fifty years. The increasingly elaborate cutting of the period is largely confined to the bowls of the glasses (although it is occasionally even found on the undersides of the feet), and also appears on the by now bulbous-shaped bodies (called 'Prussian') of matching decanters and claret-jugs, on finger-bowls and wine-glass rinsers, water-jugs, cream-jugs, tumblers, water-glasses (for mouth-rinsing between courses), stands, plates and centrepieces, jellies and sweetmeats,

Right: The increasingly elaborate diamond-cutting of the late Georgian period appeared on bulbous decanters like these, called 'Prussian'-bodied, and also on jugs, bowls, tumblers and glasses of all types. Height of central decanter: 23cm (9in) (National Museum of Ireland, Dublin)

drinking-glass shapes as time went on. Facet glasses had followed roughly the lines of their immediate predecessors, so that the cup, the bell, the round funnel and the ogee remained the standard bowl patterns. The outline of the stems is also straightforward and derivative, being usually quite plain with the occasional addition of a central or shoulder knop. More elaborate knopping is rare, with a few versions showing the stem designs to be found earlier in typical Newcastle glasses. The only real difference is that where faceting appears, the tears that the earlier stems would have contained are usually absent; they were probably omitted as being unnecessary, since their object—the refraction of light—is more efficiently achieved by the facets themselves.

Later eighteenth-century drinking vessels in cut glass are markedly different. Their stems

and all the other pieces that make up a fine late-Georgian cut-glass service.

There are instances of services and individual glasses of earlier date—chiefly English, but also from other European sources—being later faceted, presumably to bring them into fashion, in the same way that Victorian silversmiths 'embellished' (and of course ruined) fine plain Georgian silver with the ornate chasing and embossing of the day. In the twentieth century plain-stemmed glasses of the early eighteenth century, usually those of drawn-trumpet shape, were likewise 'embellished' with shallow cutting on the bowls, in a vaguely Irish design. One can only assume that this was a misguided attempt to increase their value, since it does nothing for their appearance, and merely furnishes the protagonists of 'pure' plasticity in glass with a strong argument against cutting.

Lustres, Lights and Chandeliers

Luminaria—that is, light-fittings—made wholly or almost wholly of cut glass were virtually a British monopoly during the late eighteenth and early nineteenth centuries, not to be seriously challenged until the French Empire-period development of cut glass, mainly at Baccarat. Before this, French, Dutch and German chandeliers, wall sconces and so on tended to be basically of metal—ormolu, brass or even silver. Porcelain was also freely used, especially in Germany. These preferred materials are often of the highest quality, and if glass appears at all, it is merely in the form of pendant lustre drops cut to imitate the rock crystal which they used for choice on their more expensive productions. But in a British chandelier or other light-fitting the only metal parts are the connections holding arms, spires and so on to the main bodies, the pins which hold the string of lustrous cut drops and prisms together, and the loose-fitting metal sconces which fit inside and protect the delicate glass nozzles from the flames of burnt-down candles. In other words, the metal is usually functional, rarely decorative. And when at last, in the nineteenth century, decorative gilt metalwork was attempted, its quality never approached that of French ormolu.

Of course, Venice continued to contribute its often vast floral chandeliers and brackets, still made in the seventeenth-century tradition; but these continued to be formed entirely by blowing, moulding and tooling the glass in its hot, ductile state. Cutting, except of the most basic type such as bevelling mirror edges, remained foreign to the Venetian method. Although the French excelled throughout the century in the production of superb mirrors, they apparently saw no reason to enlarge their glass industry to the creation of cut glass on any large scale, and so it was left to the British to design and make the finest chandeliers and lights the world has known.

So far, we have referred to the English, or (when including Ireland) British glass industry. In time, however, there was to grow up a native Irish glass industry which, although it had its roots in England whence came its original workers, its raw materials and many of its designs, was to develop its own national idiom, style and certain unique shapes and cut features. So desirable was its production to become that almost any heavily cut piece of glass of the period is liable to be called 'Irish'.

By the mid-eighteenth century, the British chandelier had arrived at a recognizable form;

Above: Late-eighteenth-century Irish cut glass is well represented by this splendid chandelier with its sweeping, notched arms, swags of drops, all-over-cut bodies and drip-pans and nozzles cut into vandyke points. (Cecil Higgins Museum, Bedford)

Right: Hung with elaborately cut drops, this is one of a pair of English or Irish cut-glass candelabra dating from about 1765. Height: 61cm (24in)

Far right: Light-fittings such as chandeliers made entirely or almost entirely of cut glass were virtually a British monopoly during the late eighteenth century. Large numbers of such chandeliers are seen in all their glory in an original setting, the Assembly Rooms at Bath.

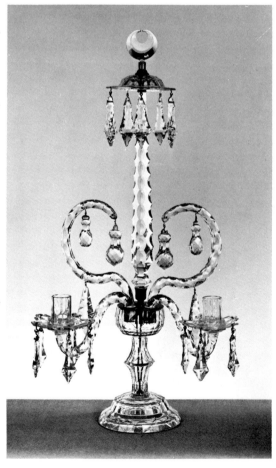

but it was the Adam period of after 1760 which saw the finest productions, many of which were from the Irish factories. The most important of these factories, both in quality and quantity of production, was the Penrose glasshouse at Waterford, established in 1783. The sweeping, notched arms, the spires, canopies and finials, the swags of glittering drops, the great spherical all-over-cut bodies, and the pans and nozzles cut into 'Vandyke' points, that go to make up an Adam Waterford chandelier surely form the glass-cutter's most magnificent production. Many museums and major public and private buildings still house splendid examples. Candelabra (branched table lights) of very Irish style match the splendour of the chandeliers. The bodies of these are frequently moulded, with square feet showing the well-known 'lemon-squeezer' depression beneath. Other forms have glass arms, serpents and spires supported on porcelain, coloured-glass or cut-glass drums or cubes, mounted in gilt metal. The beads with which these lights are dressed can also be coloured on occasion—blue, green, lemon, opaque white and blue opaline are known colours—but these are sparsely introduced in combination with clear-glass beads. Wall brackets in the same styles are also occasionally found. Table centrepieces are another rarity in this tradition. Instead of candle-sconces, they may have sweetmeat-dishes at the ends of their elegant S-shaped arms. A particularly charming and peculiarly Irish conceit is an oval mirror (there are still a few extant, signed by the Dublin maker Ayckbown), the frame set with flat-cut coloured and gilded beads, silver-leaf backed for added brilliance. Suspended from a hook on top of the frame is a chandelier which is found on close inspection to have been cut in half vertically, while visually the complete chandelier is formed by the reflection of the half-chandelier in the mirror. These pieces perfectly epitomize the charm of Irish Adam glass. The oval mirrors themselves, with beaded edges in white, blue or green glass, occur without the chandeliers and are also a uniquely Irish design.

By Regency days Adam designs had given way to chandeliers whose bodies were long, closely packed, pendant streams of drops, hanging from a canopy and held in shape by a metal frame. From this shining waterfall of glass protruded short gilt-metal arms carrying pans and nozzles for the candles, above which sometimes hung little shades or canopies (called tassels) decked with short drops, the bottoms of the chandeliers being finished with concentric circles of lustre drops. Table lights had become smaller, often designed to carry a single candle, and their cutting and dressing came, as usual, to match that

of the chandeliers. These remained large and still very imposing, but already hinted at the fussiness of the worst design elements to come in the nineteenth century. These chandeliers are not specifically Irish in design, although it is likely that a good number were made in Ireland. The contemporary styles with the strongest Irish flavour are the so-called 'dish' lights. As the name suggests, they are simply very large, shallow cut-glass dishes, suspended from the ceiling by brass or gilt-metal chains and mounted to carry candles or sometimes oil-lamps. Table lights, too, at this time were coming to be made with cut-glass fonts for oil, and with metal wick-carriers. Several patents were taken out for lamps of this sort, but all still retained a great deal of the candle-carrying shape of their progenitors. The day of the oil-lamp as the commonest source of light had not quite yet arrived, and the candle

Right: Dish lights, shallow cut-glass ormolu-mounted dishes inside which lights were placed, are an Irish design of the Regency period. Height: 109cm (43in)

Below: Another Irish style was an oval mirror with a half-chandelier hung in front of it. The frame of this one is embellished with a double row of faceted pieces of glass. (National Museum of Ireland, Dublin)

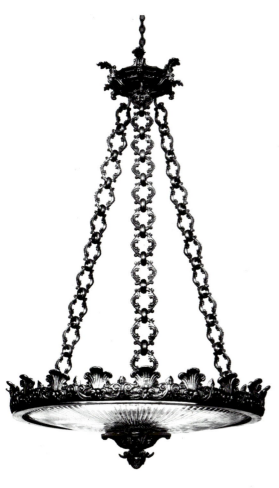

base, with a plain, unringed neck and flat-faceted spire stopper, the body of the decanter itself being seldom if ever cut, but often engraved with fruiting vines and/or a pseudo wine-label (imitating a familiar silver shape) naming the contents. This style was followed by the mallet, whose shape closely resembles that of a sculptor's mallet, the neck corresponding to the handle, and the body much wider at the base than at the shoulder. Mallets sometimes carry a little cutting on neck and base, and less commonly still stars on the body, or all-over faceting. Both decanter types date from the earliest days of faceting, and appear in coloured as well as clear glass, in blue, green or white, colours associated with Bristol, where many were made. They might be decorated locally, but often carry gilt decoration in the manner of James Giles (1718-80), the London porcelain decorator,

Left: This blue glass cruet with spire stopper and gilding was probably decorated in the London workshop of James Giles between about 1765 and 1770. (Victoria and Albert Museum, London)

was still the main inspiration for light-fittings.

As well as the more ornate and expensive candle-carriers, there was considerable demand for glass candlesticks and tapersticks. Throughout the eighteenth century, the predominant and more or less standard candlestick type had a moulded 'Silesian' stem, a feature that persisted into the time of faceting and throughout the period of drinking glasses with air-twist and cotton-twist stems (both of which stem types are rare on candlesticks). Indeed, in the early days of faceting, cutting was combined with moulding on candlesticks; but this quickly gave way to full faceting of stems, feet and nozzles in styles closely related to those of drinking glasses, while standard silver shapes were attempted more rarely. By the last quarter of the century, glass-candlestick makers, in common with the makers of all other British glass, had at last completely succumbed to the charm of cutting.

Other Table Glass and its Decoration

One of the commonest pieces of Georgian glass is the decanter. Its shape varies surprisingly little throughout the period. The shoulder decanter of the mid-century is wider at the shoulder than the

most of whose work spanned the Adam period, which was a strong influence on it. The coloured decanters whose decoration is the work of his studio are closely related to the scent bottles of the same time, which are almost always in coloured glass, faceted all over, and decorated with diaper (dotted diamond) gilding; the well-known dishevelled birds (which also appear on decanters); inscriptions as on Chelsea porcelain toys ('Gage de mon amour', 'Je pense à Vous', 'Fidèle en Amitié' and others of a rather *franglais* nature); pastoral scenes in coloured enamels and so on. Sometimes these bottles were charmingly encased in gold, silver-gilt, silver or pinchbeck cage-work boxes, or in shagreen cases.

Other decorators were working busily on coloured glass at this time. Although he did not sign anything, Michael Edkins (1734-1811) kept careful records of his work on opaque white and coloured glass, which was mainly the enamelling of flowers, birds, insects and chinoiseries. The best-known pieces attributed to him (admittedly on scant evidence) are white caddy bottles enamelled with the names GREEN and BOHEA, and decorated with flowers and a goldfinch, always a popular bird with glass decorators. Much of his work was probably done for the Bristol Temple Street Glassworks belonging to Lazarus Jacobs (d. 1796). Lazarus's son Isaac was a gilder who worked first for his father and then at the Non-Such Flint Glass Manufactory, also in Bristol, in the late eighteenth and early nineteenth centuries. He chiefly used the Greek fret or key pattern and pseudo-crests (a stag's head erased) to decorate blue and amethyst fingerbowls, plates and decanters. Unlike his contemporaries he sometimes signed his work.

The labels occurring on early decanters are an interesting reflection of the drinking habits and the drinks of the day. The range is astonishing, and encompasses the products of the brewery and apple-press as well as wines, spirits and liqueurs. Champagne, ale and cider seem to have been decanted with equal frequency and a fine disregard for their condition. Wines could have had little sparkle and beers no head in those days.

Over a fairly short period, the Indian club (rather rare) and the taper (much commoner) decanter shapes took over, and with them the practice of engraving labels ceased, though a few of these two shapes carry rudimentary ones, or just the name of the wine or spirit alone, without

any cartouche. Labelling continued on small coloured decanters, which were taper, barrel or square shaped, and fitted inside boxes or frames of silver, Sheffield plate or papier mâché. These decanters normally bear only the name of spirits—Rum, Brandy, Hollands, Shrub (and later, when they became socially acceptable, Gin and, very rarely, Whisky)—gilt, or occasionally engraved, within a cartouche of greater or lesser elaboration.

As the eighteenth century ended, labelling and engraved or gilt decoration of decanters virtually ceased, and was superseded by the then highly fashionable heavy cutting. The shape of the

Above: The gilder Isaac Jacobs often used the Greek key pattern and a stag's-head pseudo-crest on his work, as on this signed blue-tinted dish. Diameter: 18cm (7³/₄ in)

Left: An enamelled and gilded scent bottle cut all over with facets (c. 1765) having a glass stopper under its gold screw-cap.

decanter had by this time been roughly standardized to the bulbous 'Prussian' outline familiar today. The motifs used to decorate the body were usually loosely based on the diamond, with the exception of narrow vertical flutes which encircled the base of most, and flat flutes which they carried on their shoulders.

An exception to the heavy-cut style was found in the standard Irish decanter, made in vast quantities for export to the Americas, the West Indies, Portugal and elsewhere. The decanters of Cork, Belfast, Dublin and Waterford were all blown into a shallow open mould to give a standard base size and to imprint the vertical

flutes which were produced by cutting on their English counterparts. The purpose of these flutes, cut or moulded, is said to have been to obscure the cloudy and unsightly dregs that settled in the wine at the bottom of the decanter, in spite of the fact that the act of decanting was supposed to be designed to remove such dregs, as were the strainer-fitted silver wine-funnels of the day. Whatever their purpose, basal flutes are almost always present on a late eighteenth-century British decanter. The Irish also used their moulds to impress in the glass the factory name, for example, Penrose Waterford, Cork Glass Co., Waterloo Co. Cork and B. Edwards

Belfast, C.M. & Co. (for Charles Mulvaney); or the name of a factor, such as Francis Collins or Armstrong Ormonde Quay. This practice is not recorded anywhere since Roman *vitrarii* impressed their trademarks in precisely the same manner. However, only a few Irish moulds bore a mark, and even with these the decanter base often cleared the bottom of the mould, and was left unmarked. The majority of Irish mould-blown decanters, therefore, carry no mark. Unfortunately in the present century someone has been making large quantities of mould-blown copies with what would appear to be the original Cork Glass Co. moulds. These have been sufficiently realistic as to deceive a wide public, including leading salerooms, but this mark is the only spurious one yet noted.

Decanters were not the only form of table-glass to assume a characteristically Irish shape. As well as Hibernian-style luminaria, and parallel with their development, came a whole range of bowls of very idiosyncratic design. Among them are canoe bowls, which are pointed

Above: The Irish decanter was an exception to the fashionable heavy-cut style of the late eighteenth century, and, like these examples from the Cork glasshouses, was blown into a standard-size mould imprinted with vertical flutes round the base.

Left: This shouldered decanter with spire stopper, dating from about 1765, is engraved with a rare label for 'champaign' (sic).
Height: 28.5cm (11¼in)

demi-ovoid or canoe-shaped bowls of considerable capacity with vandyke-cut edges (that is, edges cut into points reminiscent of an inverted Van Dyck beard), having knopped or plain stems resting on moulded feet, either square or oval petal-moulded. There were also round and oval bowls of similar style, with the rims deeply turned over (the famous Irish turnover bowls), on the same feet and stems; kettledrum bowls, similarly footed, with capacious double-ogee bowls; lidded urns to decorate mantlepieces; butter-floats with lids and under-dishes; revolving 'lazy-Susan' stands for sweetmeat-, jelly-, syllabub- and custard-glasses, all cut to match; and subtle variants of all of these. The really notable contribution of the Irish industry to cut-glass design lay in such original and non-derivative shapes.

Before these Irish developments, British cut glass had owed much of its inspiration to silver designs. Silver fashions exerted a strong influence on glass, tableware in particular, which often slavishly followed the standard silver patterns as closely as possible. Irish designers broke with this tradition, and their turnover and canoe bowls, square 'lemon-squeezer' feet and spiky vandyke edges owe no debt to the silversmith: they are the original expression of a new artistic spirit.

A characteristically Irish shape of the late eighteenth century is the canoe-shaped bowl with vandyke-cut edges. The cutting on this example, a fruit or salad bowl on a moulded foot (c. 1790), probably represents the high point of the technique.
Diameter: 38.5cm (15³/₁₆in)
(Corning Museum of Glass, Corning, New York)

Cut Glass Elsewhere

Although the great French glass factories at Baccarat and St-Louis were founded in the 1760s, it was not until the following century, with the Empire period, that they began to challenge effectively the pre-eminence of British cut glass. The metal which they developed was by this time as pure as any ever made, and their cutters' wheels bit it deeply in characteristically French designs. During the eighteenth century France strongly favoured ormolu (gilded bronze) decoration, for glass and also for furniture which was heavily ormolu-mounted, for porcelain, home-produced and imported, fantastically set in gilt metal, and for light-fittings, fire-irons and other domestic objects. The larger French glass pieces carry far more gilt metal in their design than would ever be found in the equivalent British pieces. Luminaria such as chandeliers, wall-brackets and lustres *à la façon d'Angleterre* would be heavily embellished with ormolu, and so would other commonly manufactured pieces such as clock-cases, the manufacture of which in glass is an almost entirely French idea. Indeed, the French glass-makers of this era espoused the concept of glass as a hardstone substitute with even more enthusiasm than their British counterparts.

Other almost wholly French conceptions are caskets with ornate gilt-metal mounts, locks and keys; mounted urns, vases and decorative columns in imitation of rock crystal; and candlesticks and girandoles. Smaller table pieces such as decanters, wine-glasses, finger-bowls and plates were not usually mounted and were more closely related in shape and style to British designs. The cutting, however, though deep and solid, was more limited in its inspiration and stereotyped in its motifs. A great deal of French cutting is based on the vertical pillar, from which are derived fans, sunbursts, peacock-feather designs, notching of the pillars themselves, checkers and other variants whose Gallic origins are easily recognized. This was not one of the great periods for engraving in France: it was not until the early nineteenth century that there was any hint of the supremely fine work that was to come, with glass-engravers such as Charpentier (fl.1813-19) who, with his wife, worked at the Baccarat-owned Vonèche factory in Belgium.

The United States of America had, towards the end of the eighteenth century, exhibited an enormous appetite for imported glass, especially from Ireland, even though its native glass industry was well established. It is difficult to separate its own production from that of Europe, and especially Ireland, for the use of the mould—open, two-part or three-part—came to characterize American glass of the late eighteenth century, and Irish glass was often similarly produced.

From their beginnings in the seventeenth century as producers of no more than crude bottles and trade beads, American glass manufacturers developed and refined their products, and by the mid-eighteenth century the industry was firmly rooted. The method by which it was successfully founded was that of luring German glass-makers to America with the promise of free passage and a share of the profits of the new enterprise. From the original New Jersey factories workers spread throughout the eastern states of America, as had been the way of glass-workers everywhere from earliest times. Meanwhile others were still arriving from Europe, notably Henry Stiegel (1729-85) who, arriving from Germany in 1750, had founded a glasshouse in the 1760s to produce bottle glass, and a further, more important one later, for which he imported German, Venetian and English craftsmen. His metal was mainly 'glass of lead', and it was he who introduced engraving to American glass. Stiegel glass is also found with well-documented and recognizable patterns produced by blowing into a metal mould. The influx of glass-workers continued throughout this period, still principally from Germany. In

1784 John Amelung of Bremen founded the New Bremen Glass Works in Maryland, where a great deal of glass moulded in the Irish manner was produced. Some fine engraving (for which, indeed, the factory is famous) was also done there, and a few inscribed and dated pieces exist. Cut glass in America at this date was not very widely made, and it is very difficult to distinguish it from European imports. In general, American glass-makers chose to become masters of moulding, thus treating glass as a ductile material, though paradoxically the patterns they produced copied cut-glass diamond, step, pillar and flute designs.

By the end of the eighteenth century a successful cut-glass industry had been established in Spain at La Granja de San Ildefonso near Segovia, a glasshouse royally owned from the mid-century until some time before its closure in

In France, opaque white glass imitating porcelain was in fashion during the eighteenth century, and is decorated with enamels and gilt, like this carafe and beaker.
(Museum of Decorative Arts, Prague)

the nineteenth century. Many of the workers there were foreigners, specifically imported. Nonetheless very characteristic native styles were developed, of which cutting was only one aspect. Their work bore no resemblance to British cutting of the time, owing its origins more to the wheel-engraver, the motifs being formed by shallow cuts of identical width, semicircular in section and with rounded ends. Such cuts, formed with a large, blunt wheel, obviously limited the designer and cutter (frequently the same person) to patterns which easily become recognizable. The vessel shapes to which this decoration is applied are also limited in range, the commonest being rectangular bottles made to carry wines and spirits in fitted wooden boxes, as well as cruet- and perfume-bottles, one- or two-handled lidded drinking vessels, and flattened circular-bodied ewers with

long necks and hinged pewter lids. Small bowls, dishes, plates and beakers also occur. The cutting in all these is usually polished but sometimes left in the rough and gilded; this appears to have been a cold process, as the gilding is impermanent and often rubbed or absent.

Glass-Engraving in England and Holland

The other field of glass endeavour in which the English and Irish showed originality, though not, perhaps, great talent, was glass-engraving. But what British engraving of the late eighteenth century might lack in quality, it made up for in documentary and other interests. Nowhere else and at no other time were glasses used to carry such a variety of sentiments—personal, political, moral, and even (in the case of privateer glasses) piratical.

Until the advent of the cotton-twist stem in about 1760, Jacobite glasses (described in chapter 5) were still abundant, but although a few cotton-twist and facet-stem glasses are engraved with the English rose and bud (or buds), it was by this time well on the way to becoming merely a decorative device rather than a symbol of the Jacobite cause. By the end of the century Dutch, Scandinavian, Spanish and other glasses were being similarly decorated, although it is hardly likely that all or any of their makers had Jacobite sympathies, or were exporting the glasses to Jacobite supporters living in exile overseas. One curiosity appearing on later plain-stem and air-twist Jacobite glasses is the 'empty-bud' engraving. On these rather scarce glasses the rose and bud appear as usual, but now the bud itself is hollow. No rational explanation has ever been offered as to why this should be, the commonest irrational one being that it signifies the decay of the Jacobite movement; but surely no organization, however much in disarray, would wish to celebrate its own impending demise. Many other explanations have been offered, none convincing.

There are plenty of other superficially strange examples of engraving which on closer examination present no great puzzle. For example, the figures '45', engraved sometimes alone and sometimes in conjunction with the words 'Wilkes and Liberty', refer to the forty-fifth issue of the *North Briton*, a political paper edited by John Wilkes (1725-97) whose publication attacking statements in a speech by George III brought him fame and popularity with the masses. The loyalist glasses of His Majesty's Friends, those courtiers closest to the King, were attempts to counteract Wilkes' popularity, and

An engraved, covered beaker of colourless lead crystal made in 1788 at the New Bremen Glass Works in Maryland for the wife of its founder John Amelung of Bremen, whose factory is famous for its engraved pieces.
Height: 30.1cm (11⅞in) (Corning Museum of Glass, Corning, New York)

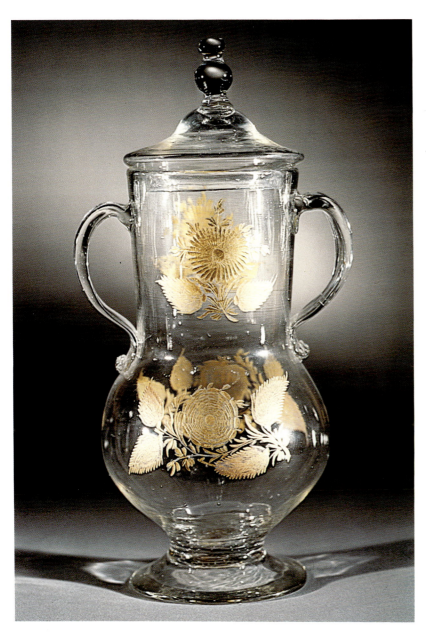

of the many specific events commemorated, none captured the engravers' (and presumably the public's) imagination more than the opening of the Sunderland Bridge in 1796, an event probably celebrated on glass more often than any other. Military glasses, though not common, also occur. They range from ordinary regimental references to toasts to the yeomanry, especially Irish volunteer regiments, where possibly the social aspects such as the consumption of alcohol were more important than any military aspirations. Nelson's funeral in 1805 was a popular subject, too, and glasses showing his funeral carriage are comparatively common. 'Peace and Plenty' glasses date from after the time of Waterloo.

There are, of course, glasses from all nations commemorating events of high importance such as coronations, marriages, births and deaths of

Above: A covered jar with fine shallow-cut and gilded flowers, made at the royal Spanish glass-house of La Granja de San Ildefonso in 1775. Height: 33.6cm (13¼in) (Pilkington Glass Museum, St Helens, Merseyside)

Right: A rare Jacobite glass, engraved with roses and an oak leaf. The inscription reads 'Reddas Incolumem' ('Return unharmed'). Height: 16.5cm (6½in) (Pilkington Glass Museum, St Helens, Merseyside)

especially his support for the American colonists, with inscriptions like 'The Friends of His Majesty's American Loyalists'. Glasses engraved 'Success to ....' and '........ Forever' are frequently political, having been commissioned by parliamentary candidates as gifts for their electors. (A liberal supply of liquor would also have been provided on polling day with which to drink the candidate's health and success, but the number of glasses required for this purpose was not great, since the franchise was then very limited.) Glass-engraving was also used to lobby against unpopular government measures and taxation. The phrase 'No Excise' on glasses engraved with apples and sometimes the word 'Cyder' reflects a successful attempt to deflect taxation from home-produced cider. Glasses with rose, thistle and shamrock were engraved in support of the Act of Union, while

royalty and other important personages; and also battles, peace treaties and other alliances. Trading and industrial glasses are common to both British and Dutch engraving. Both also engraved privateer glasses lauding the enterprises of the 'merchant venturers'' ships, their commanders also being sometimes named. But political lobbying, electioneering, popular causes, demands for advancement or punishment ('Swing, swing, great Admiral Byng') and other slogans of the kind are largely peculiar to English glass and furnish important social documents which are not available to many other nations. British engraving on glass is largely the work of artisans, not of great artist-engravers as in Holland and Germany, and so none of their names are known.

By the mid-eighteenth century, supremacy in the art of engraving on drinking glasses had, with some notable exceptions which shall be mentioned later, passed from the great German centres to the Netherlands. By the 1750s men such as Jacob Sang (d. 1783) had already

established successful commercial workshops in Amsterdam and elsewhere in Holland. Sang's origins and date of birth are unknown, but he may well have been a German, probably coming from Weimar, where the glass-engraving Sang family appears to have originated. Earlier, in the 1730s, an older relation, Andreas Sang, possibly Jacob's father, was an engraver of glass to the Duke of Saxe-Weimar; and a contemporary, perhaps a brother of Jacob's, named Johann Heinrich Sang, was Court Engraver at Brunswick from about 1745 to 1755. The fact that there were such officials shows the importance to which glass-engraving had risen in the eyes of the European courts.

To add still further confusion to Sang family matters, a certain Simon Jacob Sang was also established in Amsterdam in the 1750s, and advertising his skills as a glass-engraver. Some

Above: Simon Jacob Sang, a glass-engraver working in Amsterdam in the mid-eighteenth century, used glasses made in Newcastle for his work. Height: 23.7cm (9³/₈in)

Left: This rare English wine-glass was engraved in Holland by Jacob Sang, and is inscribed on the foot: 'Jacob Sang, inv= et fec= Amsterdam, 1759'. Height: 17.8cm (7³/₈in) (Pilkington Glass Museum, St Helens, Merseyside)

would have it that Jacob and S.J. Sang are the same man. However, both signed their work on occasion, Jacob quite frequently, and the 'S.J. Sang' diamond-point signature bears little resemblance to the flowing 'Jac. Sang fec. Amstelodam 17..' with which semicircular signature Jacob embellished the feet of the fine Newcastle glasses which he had engraved; nor does the quality or style of the engraving of S.J. Sang equal that of Jacob, though it remains fine work of the period.

In Holland, this was the age of the great artist-stipplers, who used the diamond-point to create their pictures in dots rather than lines (though sometimes both techniques were used together), producing filmy, ethereal pictures. Many of these stipple-engravers were either gifted and prosperous amateurs who engraved as a hobby, or artists in other fields who became fascinated by the potential of glass. One of the earliest and most esteemed of the amateurs was Frans Greenwood (1680-1761), a Dutchman of English extraction, who exquisitely copied the prints of his day on glass (usually light balusters imported from Newcastle), altering and adapting them to his chosen medium. Many of his pieces are signed and dated, as had become common practice with stipplers, in contrast to many other eighteenth-century glass-engravers. Greenwood was to become the inspiration (and perhaps tutor) for the stippling work of a very able Dutch painter, Aert Schouman (1710-92), who also usually chose to work on Newcastle balusters, signing his work, which is of the highest order. Both of these great engravers were pure stipplers and used no line.

Another painter and follower of Greenwood's was David Wolff (1732-98). He is the best known of all, and stippled glasses in general are, when not signed or otherwise attributable, referred to in Holland as 'Wolff glasses'. Wolff started as a line engraver and allowed stippling to creep gradually into his work. Since some of his work is both dated and signed, one can see that the earlier the engraving the more line he used, the earliest examples having no stippling at all. Much of his work is original in concept, rather than taken from popular prints, as was the case with many of his contemporaries. This was the period of the French Revolution, and a feeling of freedom was in the air, in Holland as elsewhere in Europe. Wolff appears to have espoused the cause with enthusiasm and many of his glasses (again frequently the Newcastle balusters so favoured by other stipplers, but later English facet- and composite-stems) have freedom as their motif and *'Aurea Libertas'* or similar as their inscription. Cages with open doors, birds in flight, liberty caps carried on lances and female

figures symbolic of revolution are common designs, all coupled with attendant putti and lions, and all with a strongly neo-classical flavour. Wolff was obviously a commercial engraver, and armorial, marriage, guild and other commemorative glasses by him still exist. It is remarkable that an artist who must have depended on the patronage of a rich and powerful aristocracy (he sometimes portrayed them and their Prince and Princess of Orange) could find a ready market for his revolutionary work. One wonders to whom he sold them; it was surely not to the solid Dutch burghers whose overseas enterprises in the East Indies and home land-drainage schemes had made them fortunes—or did they craftily hedge their bets and pay lip-service at least to some form of mild socialism? Other leading stipple engravers were not so controversial. Van den Blijk (1736-1814), Hoolart (working in the 1770s), Schürmann (1730-83), Adams (working on both sides of 1800) and others confined themselves to more conventional subjects, and almost always

Below: David Wolff (1732-1798) is the best-known of the Dutch stipple-engravers. This wine-glass by him (c. 1795) is stippled in diamond point with an allegory of liberty. Height: 14.6cm (5¾in) (Toledo Museum of Art, Toledo, Ohio)

favoured English glasses for their work.

Stippling was a uniquely Dutch technique, but its exponents were greatly outnumbered by the wheel-engravers, possibly because many did not have the artistic ability to use the diamond-point for their often naïve but charming efforts. Unfortunately it was not usual for wheel-engravers to sign their work, so that far less is known about them than their fellow artists of the diamond. Although there were many of exceptional talent, few except Jacob Sang have left us their names. Christian Schroeder is known to have worked at Delft and The Hague in the mid-century, engraving on mirrors and sometimes signing 'C.S. Delft' or C. Schroeder Delft' and the date. He can readily be confused with Christoffel Schröder, working at Delft at much the same time. Wilhelm Robart, who engraved at The Hague, occasionally initialled his glasses,

and there are others who have signed individual pieces; but they were exceptions, even though one would have thought that an artist would have proudly signed any of the superb wheel-engraved glasses, which carry all the stippler's subjects as well as wishes for the success of ships (similar but superior to the English privateer glasses), trading ventures, agriculture and industries, sport and pastimes, and commemorations of every conceivable social and commercial occasion. Such glasses can still be seen in some profusion; they represent the high point of the Dutch tradition of engraving on glass.

An important group of Dutch engraved glasses bears the letters VOC (for *Vereenigde Oostindische Compagnie,* 'United East India Company') with in some cases a ship (an East Indiaman) and the arms of the company or other

These Dutch wheel-engraved goblets are part of an important group of glasses bearing the letters VOC, the initials of the United East India Company which traded with the Dutch colonies there. Height of covered goblet: 33cm (13in) (Rijksmuseum, Amsterdam)

appropriate motif. These glasses have been copiously reproduced, not to say faked, since their value is high among collectors today, and this is especially so in Holland and South Africa.

Another interesting group is that of glasses sent as gifts, usually given by men to women, to commemorate special occasions or to carry amorous messages. Thus a fine glass engraved with a cock and hen and the words '*De Inclinatie*' spoke for itself (and the giver) when presented to a young lady; '*Hansie in de Kelder*' glasses, showing a putto in a cellar, were sent to congratulate pregnant women or announce a pregnancy; and '*Kraam Vrouw en de Kindje*' glasses wished well to the recently confined mother and newborn baby. Such glasses are found with inscriptions only in the Dutch language.

One unique Dutch artist of the late eighteenth century was Zeuner (we know only his surname for certain, though 'Jonas' has been given as his first name), who in about 1790 developed a technique related to German *Zwischengold* glasses (which had gold leaf between layers of glass) and French mirror decoration. In this technique, known as *verre églomisé*, Zeuner used his special skills in applying gold and silver leaf to flat plates of glass and scratching an illustration through the leaf from behind. He occasionally used colour for heightened effect, as had the Bohemian and Silesian *Zwischengold* workers of half a century or more earlier. Zeuner specialized in large scenes taken from prints, and his work is usually signed. Some of his scenes are English, which has given rise to the theory that he visited England. However, there does not appear to be any other evidence of such a visit, and he could quite easily have acquired the prints from which he took these views without ever having left Holland.

In the eighteenth century Dutch artistic endeavour in the medium of glass lay more in the field of decoration than of manufacture. Native Dutch glass is German in inspiration, but rarely so skilled in execution, and often appears rather ponderous. Perhaps for this reason, the Dutch appear to have partially adopted English lead metal and English styles for their late-eighteenth-century drinking glasses. But the finest work of their engravers—wheel, line or stipple—is almost always found on imported English glasses. For their cut-glass industry, which was emerging at the end of the eighteenth century, they appear to have depended on anonymous English glass-workers or at least on English ideas and English-type metal, for the resemblance to the styles produced in England is very strong.

Glasses similar to English types, often with engraved and gilded bowls, were produced in Norway during the second half of the eighteenth century. The deep, round funnel bowl of this wine glass from the Nøste-tangen glassworks is set on a stem with two air-twist ribbons, on a plain, conical foot, and is engraved with the interwoven initials D.A.S. and K.N.D.
Height: 17.5cm (6 15/16in)

The Rest of the World

By the 1770s, if not earlier, English lead glass had reached Scandinavia, apparently introduced by an Englishman, James Keith. Norwegian glassworks at Nøstetangen had been founded in 1741, as had the great Hurdals Verk factory which took over Nøstetangen at about the time of Keith's arrival—a time when a certain von Storm held the Norwegian and Danish monopolies for the manufacture of glass. In consequence presumably of Keith's activities, Norwegian and Danish glass of the late eighteenth century bears a strong resemblance to the British (especially to that of Newcastle from where Keith had come), so the usual bowl shapes and stem formations are found. There are certain general differences, however. The metal, though lead, is often darker in colour than the English type, and the bowls of the glasses tend to be bigger and are often engraved. We know of some of the engravers who worked in Scandinavia at this time. Heinrich Köhler, a German, worked in

Denmark and Norway with the major glass-houses (he was at Nøstetangen from 1757 till 1770) and eventually set up on his own. Villas Winter is another name known to us as that of an engraver who worked at Nøstetangen. Little cut glass was produced at this date, apart from glasses with stems faceted in the English manner.

Although the most notable Swedish glass is modern, it is worth remembering that it springs from a long tradition. The Kosta glassworks were founded in the mid-eighteenth century and Kungsholm almost a century earlier. But the glass of the late eighteenth century was German-inspired, and since a great deal of glass was imported from the German states at this time, and numerous Silesian and Bohemian craftsmen emigrated to Sweden, it is difficult to differentiate between the native product and the foreign, as is so often the case with the early glass

industry, because of the wandering habits of its work-force.

In Bohemia and the other great central European glass centres, production in the second half of the eighteenth century was somewhat in the doldrums artistically, possibly because of the steady drain of talented craftsmen and designers overseas to the Americas, Spain, Portugal, Scandinavia and elsewhere. Of course, many able men remained, men such as Friedrich Egermann (1777-1864), who had already embarked on his life's work in glass. Although his finest achievements belong to the nineteenth century, he was already enamelling glass at Blottendorf before 1800. At this time, too, Johann Josef Mildner (1763-1808) revived and elaborated the *Zwischengold* process, painting exquisite miniature portraits and applying them to his cylindrical beakers. Enamelling was also widely used, but this had largely degenerated into crude (though often naïvely attractive) colouring used on spirit-bottles and the like. Some light cutting for export was successfully undertaken, and an attempt was made to compete with the British market in hookah-bases for the East. Bohemian versions of these are globular or bottle-shaped vessels, frequently on square bases and in coloured glass, sometimes using two-layer overlay, decorated with garish enamels and some light cutting. (Heavier pieces of much higher quality, asymmetrically cut and in various shades of opaline, probably date from the early to mid-nineteenth century.)

At Warmbrunn the great Silesian engraving tradition survived, and rococo shapes and decorations were being produced well into the second half of the eighteenth century. The famous and long-lived engraver Christian Schneider, was still alive and working (he died in 1773). He had able contemporaries and followers, whose work is sometimes incorrectly attributed to Schneider, since Silesian engraving is rarely signed. The term 'Schneider glasses' has become generically descriptive in the same way that unsigned Dutch stippled glasses are referred to as 'Wolff glasses'.

Frederick the Great of Prussia took a personal interest in the glass industry, and Warmbrunn belonged to Prussia from the mid-century. But the Zechlin glasshouse of Berlin, the Prussian capital, held a monopoly in glass manufacture for the home country at this time, which evidently prevented Silesian glass from reaching the kingdom of Prussia, since there is no record of them relaxing or abandoning their ban on all glass imports. Frederick, however, continued to encourage glasshouses to open in Silesia, but he seems to have overdone it, since most failed after a short life for lack of a market for their

This flask with canted corners, made in Germany in the second half of the eighteenth century, has the rather crude but colourful enamelling used in central Europe at this time.
(Museum of Decorative Arts, Prague)

In the last few decades of the eighteenth century, the usual flow of glass-workers outward from Central Europe continued into Spain even more strongly than before; and the arrivals were as welcome as ever. Bohemian enamellers, in particular, brought their by then naïve enamelling styles with them, and many tumblers and bottles exist, in clear, opaque white and (rarely) blue glass, whose origins could not be separated between Bohemia and Spain were it not that many carry Spanish inscriptions and/or armorials. Of course it is possible that these were specially commissioned imports from Bohemia, but their volume suggests that they are Iberian-made (there are also Portuguese examples). Production of *porrón, cántir* and other typically Spanish vessels in the plastic idiom continued, with little change of form or alteration in the elaborate pincering and trailing

Above: Johann Mildner revived the Zwischengold *process for beakers on which he applied exquisite medallions, often portraits like this one of J. von Fürnberg, painted in colours on parchment in 1792.*
Height: 11.5cm (4½in)
(Museum für Kunst und Gewerbe, Hamburg)

Right: A cut and covered goblet engraved in Silesia in the 1760s by Christian Schneider, probably the most accomplished glass-engraver at Warmbrunn.
Height: 28cm (11in)
(Corning Museum of Art, Corning, New York)

high-quality and therefore expensive wares. The Silesian glass industry was in decline by the time of Frederick's death in 1786, and many Silesian glass-workers had moved to Scandinavia and to Bohemia from where, only a short time before, Frederick had been trying to tempt them. Nevertheless, the Silesian glass industry owed a debt to Frederick, which they repaid by commemorating him on many glasses carrying his portrait, and others celebrating his military victories.

One of the last decorators of glass to work at Warmbrunn was Johann Menzel (1744-1810), whose now rare glasses are held in high esteem today. These are usually a variant of *Zwischengold*, and bear miniature portraits in silhouette set on large goblets. There is often more than one portrait on each, forming couples and family groups of the ordinary middle-class people who must have been his main clients, although he also drew the famous of the day. Otherwise, the wonderful decorating work of Warmbrunn was on the wane.

although this was an age of decline for Venice, a few other glass techniques were being developed. Glass-cutting there was largely confined to mirrors and to big lustre drops in the French manner for embellishing chandeliers of gilt metal or wood, and for other light-fittings. As in France, these drops simply copied earlier rock-crystal shapes. The Venetians' finest engraved work is also found on mirrors, and also derives from an earlier age. Venetian *cristallo* was possibly too frail a material to please English, Dutch and Prussian customers, more used to their own country's much less fragile drinking vessels of lead or potash glass. Besides, monopolies and import restrictions prevented Venetian glass from reaching many of its earlier markets. There was of course a viable tourist trade, with the English in particular never missing Venice on the Grand Tour; but tourists'

Far left: A cut and engraved goblet with silhouettes of a family group in the manner of Johan Menzel, one of the last glass decorators to work at Warmbrunn, about 1790.
Height: 17.8cm (7in)
(Corning Museum of Glass, Corning, New York)

Left: Many Bohemian enamellers worked in Spain during the latter part of the eighteenth century, usually on opaque white glass like this beaker decorated with the Spanish coat of arms. (Museum of Decorative Arts, Prague)

work with which much Spanish glass was still decorated in the traditional manner. Their cut glass has already been described.

Russia also benefited from the Silesian and Bohemian glass migrations, some of which reached there via Scandinavia. The Silesian influence was strongest, and many glasses show portraits of czars and czarinas (often Catherine the Great or Elizabeth Petrovna) engraved on cut goblets of markedly Silesian type. One particular Russian glass occurs throughout the late eighteenth and nineteenth centuries. It is a goblet of the usual type, engraved with the cypher of the ruling czar (the only part of the decoration that changes) and on the other side of the bowl the royal Russian double-headed eagle engraved and black-enamelled, the rest of the engraving being gilded. This stereotypical glass was apparently made on the coronation of each new czar. As the eighteenth century drew to an end, many private glasshouses were opened in Russia, but it was not until the next century that the glass industry there really began to flourish.

Venice almost completely failed to respond to the great popular demand for cut glass that swept through Europe after 1750. In fact, the skills and also the reputation of Venice as a glass centre had sadly deteriorated. Venetian *cristallo* was not a particularly suitable metal for cutting, but

glass requirements were largely satisfied by individual lamp-workers, as can still be seen in Venice today, making their grotesques and gewgaws from glass rods softened and manipulated over a flame. Some Venetian glass manufacturers and decorators, however, were still doing original work and experimenting with new techniques.

The great Miotti family, whose name runs throughout glass history from sixteenth-century Murano to the Low Countries and England, and in Venice itself until the end of the eighteenth century, had started enamelling at this time, principally on white glass (*lattimo*). Best known

of their works are some sets of plates, decorated in monochrome with views of Venice; but they also made pieces of a less spectacular nature and of somewhat later date, as well as undecorated *trembleuse* cups and saucers (the saucer having a deep well to prevent the contents of the cup being spilled by a trembling hand), plates and other tableware in the same heavy white glass. The amount of this ware surviving suggests that their enterprise in the manufacture of *lattimo* was a modest success. Also at work in Murano in the late eighteenth century were Oswaldo and Antonio Brussa, father and son, who painted in enamels on clear glass beakers and cylindrical scent-bottles in vividly coloured but somewhat naïve style, depicting flowers and birds—the goldfinch being a favourite. Design and colours are again derived from fifteenth-and early sixteenth-century predecessors. Yet on the whole this was a time of struggle: the Venetian glass revival was yet to come.

In China, the conception of glass was that of a hardstone substitute, to be cameo-cut, often in different-coloured layers, as might be an agate or cornelian. The Chinese largely ignored its plastic possibilities. So strong is Chinese tradition that the glass they produced in the late eighteenth century varies little from that made earlier. Indeed, as with their porcelain, innovation was

probably looked on with some disfavour, as almost amounting to an insult to one's ancestors' work. The finest pieces therefore remain cameo-and relief-cut, now sometimes larger than before, but carrying the same traditional emblems and designs, and occasionally bear the reign mark for the period of the Emperor Qin Long.

Export of Chinese goods to the West was expanding hugely at this time, at the instigation of the Emperor, and Chinese glass was reaching Europe in some quantity (though it never approached the volume of porcelain exports). Commonly referred to as 'Peking glass', it is usually coloured and often opacified. Its simplest forms are small, lipped bowls with rudimentary feet, Chinese individual rice-bowls in fact. These were probably moulded initially, as they have been rather roughly all-over polished, and are usually undecorated. A large, shallow dish design, showing clear mould-marks and with a scallop-cut edge, is also quite common. Finally there are the typically Chinese snuff-bottles, which had stoppers often made of hardstones, to which are attached the characteristic little bamboo snuff-spoons. These bottles are often cameo-cut, sometimes in several coloured layers and sometimes relief-cut in glass tinted to imitate semi-precious stones—an aim often so well achieved as to deceive all but those with a knowledge of gems. The only clear-glass examples are usually internally painted with scenes and lengthy inscriptions, a decorative process so difficult that none but the Chinese would attempt it. Many modern examples of inferior quality are made in Formosa and Hong Kong, and good-quality cameo vases and other pieces are made in China in the traditional style.

CHAPTER SEVEN

THE NINETEENTH CENTURY

An ornamental birdcage, made in England c. 1880, possibly at the Richardson glasshouse in Stourbridge. The birdcage is constructed from rods of coloured glass that have been cut into lengths and then stuck together. Glass birdcages are rare and it is unlikely they ever formed part of normal production.
Height: 50.8cm (20in) (Broadfield House Glass Museum, Kingswinford)

During the nineteenth century, basic methods of glass production changed surprisingly little. More or less the same tools and processes that were in use at the beginning of the century were still being employed at its end, and not even in industrial glass did mechanization make much impact. On the other hand, from being a slightly haphazard affair with a faint air of mystery still attached to it, glass-making became much more scientifically based as the century progressed. Chemists began to be employed in the leading glasshouses, and it was not unusual for factory owners themselves to be accomplished chemists. Furnace design was improved, too, resulting not just in economies in fuel but in consistently higher temperatures and a cleaner atmosphere less likely to contaminate the glass. These scientific and technical advances gave glass-makers the confidence to experiment, and resulted in the enormous diversity of colour, shape, technique and decoration that characterizes nineteenth-century glass.

For the first quarter of the century cut glass was the dominant fashion in Europe, and the use of steam power enabled the glass-cutter to control the revolutions of his wheel with more precision than ever before, facilitating deep diamond cutting of great elaboration. It was only with the development of coloured glass in Bohemia and France that a different type of glassware began to rival the popularity of cut glass. After the Great Exhibition of 1851, while Continental glass-makers sought new directions, an original and elegant style of engraved glass was developed in England, inspired by classical antiquity and the Renaissance. This refinement of style was also extended to acid-etching. As a result, by the 1860s England was once again in the forefront of the industry, a position that was

to be maintained for the next twenty years.

Meanwhile Venice, under the leadership of Antonio Salviati, was rediscovering something of its former glory, and enamelling enjoyed a revival as a result of renewed interest in ancient Islamic glass. Stained glass also became popular again, with the revival of Gothic styles in art and architecture and the whole medieval cult to which the Pre-Raphaelites lent their talents, but on the whole the output was mediocre as there were too few craftsmen capable of making more than second-rate copies of early work. From the 1870s onwards, however, standards improved as better-quality glass was made in richer colours. The nineteenth century also marked the beginning of mass-produced glass, made by press-moulding. Pressed glass was an American invention of the 1820s, and America was to play an increasingly important role in events as the century progressed.

At its best, nineteenth-century glass is both technically and artistically brilliant. Marked by innovations which followed one another in quick succession, the glass-makers produced an enormous diversity of colours and ornamental effects during the course of the century. Improved communications led to increased exchanges of artistic ideas which resulted in a greater variety of decoration and style than ever before.

Cut Glass

Cut glass was the dominant style of glassware made in England and Ireland during the first half of the nineteenth century, and the style also had a tremendous impact on the Continent, particularly in France. Although factories at St-Louis and Le Creusot had been producing cut crystal in the

English manner since the 1780s (with the help of English cutters who had been brought there in order to instruct the French in the technique), the style became increasingly popular after the turn of the century. In 1802 the Vonèche factory on the French-Belgian border was purchased by the former manager of St-Louis, Aimé-Gabriel d'Artigues, and became an important producer of such glass. In 1819 d'Artigues also started producing cut lead crystal at Baccarat, near St-Louis in eastern France.

At this period, glass-cutting was done not only at the factories themselves but also by independent decorating establishments. The most important of these was L'Escalier de Cristal in Paris, founded in 1802, which decorated glass supplied by Vonèche with rich and intricate diamond cutting, and then embellished it with elaborate ormolu mounts. In 1819 L'Escalier created a sensation in Paris by exhibiting ornate vases, candelabra and clocks, and even crystal-glass furniture. Vonèche also supplied blanks to another important cutting establishment, Cappelman's of Brussels, which employed English cutters. This fact indicates the high esteem in which English cut glass was held. Following the foundation in 1826 of Val-St-Lambert, Belgium's most famous factory, a small team of English workers was employed there to supervise the glass-cutting department.

One unusual and complicated decorative technique used in French, English and Bohemian cut glass during this period was cameo incrustation, in which small white ceramic medallions known as sulphides were embedded within the glass. The silvery-white appearance of the sulphides combined well with the glitter of cut crystal. They were usually in the form of profile portraits, busts or figures, but other subjects included coats of arms, cyphers and landscapes. Sulphides were made from china clay and super-silicate of potash, a composition that was less fusible than glass and so would not distort, and was also capable of expansion and contraction. The technique had been tried in Bohemia in the late eighteenth century, but success was first achieved in Paris at the beginning of the nineteenth century, and the sculptor Desprez took out a five-year patent for making sulphides in 1818. In England the pioneer of cameo incrustation was Apsley Pellatt (1791-1863) of the Falcon Glassworks in London, who took out his own patent a year later. Pellatt's great flair was one of the main reasons why England kept pace with all the developments taking place on the Continent. Cameo incrustation was usually used to ornament such small items as scent-bottles and paperweights, and Pellatt claimed to extend its application to decanters, plates and chimney-ornaments.

Russian glass developed along similar lines to glass in the rest of Europe. Cut crystal was in fashion during the first two decades of the century, and then there was a shift towards coloured glass under Bohemian and French influence. There were more than 100 glassworks active in Russia at the beginning of the century, but only a few of them concentrated on good-quality tableware and decorative glass. Russia's leading factory, the Imperial Glassworks of St Petersburg, produced some of the most ambitious and artistic glass of any European country during the first half of the century, including imposing neo-classical urns, vases and ewers in both crystal and colour, with elaborate ormolu mounts, comparable to the output of the famous L'Escalier de Cristal in Paris. Like L'Escalier, the Imperial Glassworks even ventured into glass furniture, and made a blue and crystal divan for the Shah of Persia in 1828 and a crystal fountain for his successor a good twenty years before the celebrated Osler fountain appeared at the Great Exhibition. A characteristic of the cut tableware of the Russian glasshouses was its decoration with oval medallions of opaque white glass, which were enamelled and gilt with flowers, figures, inscriptions and scenes.

Cut glass also met with enthusiasm in America. By the second quarter of the nineteenth century there were half a dozen or so factories producing cut glass in Pittsburgh alone. The most important of these was Bakewell's Glasshouse, which was advertising cut glass by 1809 and employed 'excellent artists, both English and French'. The New England Glass Company of Boston, Massachusetts, was founded in 1818 to produce cut glass, and in the same year it opened a cutting shop driven by steam power and run by 'experienced European glass-cutters'. Other cut-glass firms soon opened in New York and Philadelphia. The American factories copied European models and employed European cutters, so their early cut glass is indistinguishable from what was being made in Britain and on the Continent at the same period.

For a long time, America had been Ireland's chief export market for its cut glass, and the rapid growth of the American glass industry after 1825 was one of the main causes of the decline of Ireland as a producer of cut glass. In addition, in 1825 the tax advantages the Irish glass industry had previously enjoyed were removed, and its products became subject to the same excise duties as had burdened English glass for eighty years. The Irish glass industry never recovered from these two blows: one by one, factories

closed, until by the middle of the century only the famous Waterford factory remained. Waterford put on a brave show of cut glass at the Great Exhibition, but closed that same year.

During the 1820s and 1830s the intricate relief diamond cutting so characteristic of the cut glass of the beginning of the century gave way to a broader, deeper, freer style of cutting, both in Europe and America. No doubt this was partly due to changing tastes which now favoured a broader cut; but the growing use of steam power to drive cutting-wheels (which had previously been turned by hand) also greatly facilitated the new style. The main feature of this style was broad, vertical-cut fluting which sometimes ran in a continuous line from the base to the rim of an object. The broad-cut glass of this period is most attractive: the cutting both enhanced the shapes to which it was applied and brought out the quality of the lead glass itself without dazzling the eye. The fashion was short-lived, however, and there was a resurgence of prismatic diamond cutting and glittering surfaces in the late 1840s, which culminated in the very complex cut wares, called by some the 'prickly monstrosities', of the Great Exhibition. Cut glass continued to be made throughout the nineteenth century, although it had to compete with an increasing number of other glass styles.

Above: American cut-glass cradle and pitcher, c. 1885. The last quarter of the nineteenth century witnessed a revival both in Europe and America of the flamboyant deep prismatic cutting that had been in fashion around the time of the Great Exhibition.
Length of cradle: 22.8cm (9in)
Height of pitcher: 31.5cm (12³⁄₈in)
(The Toledo Museum of Art, Toledo, Ohio)

Left: Vase on plinth, cut crystal with ormolu mounts and sulphide decoration, French, c. 1825. A fine example of the grandiose pieces in neo-classical style which were produced in France and Russia in the early nineteenth century. Two sulphides are signed 'Gallé fecit'.
Height: 101 cm (39³⁄₄in)
(Cannon Hall, Barnsley)

Bohemian Colour

Bohemia, like France, Russia and America, was greatly influenced by English cut glass, but its chief contribution to the development of glass during the nineteenth century was the introduction of a range of startling new colours and decorating techniques, which influenced every other glass-making country. Despite the English predilection for fine cut crystal, the Bohemian style was even imitated by English glass-workers during the 1830s.

At the beginning of the century, English cut glass was providing stiff competition for the Bohemian glass industry, which was also hampered by the Napoleonic Wars' disruptive effect on trade. The restoration of peace in 1815 heralded the dawn of a golden age for Bohemian glass which lasted until the middle of the

century, when the Austrian Empire, of which Bohemia was a part, was once more threatened by revolution. The art of the Empire during that peaceful interlude in central European history is in the style known as Biedermeier. This term is a nickname for what one might call a 'solid citizen', for the period was one of middle-class prosperity in which private persons, excluded from politics by the Empire's reactionary Hapsburg government in Vienna, had to content themselves with living quietly and comfortably at home. In this atmosphere all the decorative arts flourished. Because it was the product of a bourgeois society, the Biedermeier style used to be dismissed out of hand; but although its massive forms can be ungainly, coarse and lacking in imagination, at its best it displays great technical invention combined with exquisite craftsmanship.

The best examples of Biedermeier-style glass are the enamelled tumblers and beakers that were produced in Vienna and other cities. In them the thick, opaque enamelling of the previous century has given way to thin, transparent enamels, probably derived from stained-glass painting. The new enamelling style dates from about 1806; the person who claimed to have invented it was Samuel Mohn, a porcelain painter from Leipzig, who passed the skill on to his son Gottlob (1789-1825). In 1811 Gottlob moved to Vienna, where he came into contact with Anthon Kothgasser, a painter at the Royal Vienna Porcelain Manufactory, who also adopted this technique. The earliest enamelling by the Mohns and Kothgasser was done on straight-sided tumblers, but after 1814 a waisted beaker called a *Ranftbecher* became more common. The subjects depicted included views of Vienna and its palaces and churches, dramatic landscapes,

Top left: An English pattern book, from Richardson's of Stourbridge, illustrating the broad-fluted style of cutting that was in fashion in the 1830s and 1840s. (Broadfield House Glass Museum, Kingswinford)

Bottom left: An English cut-glass decanter, made by Richardson's of Stourbridge. The elaborate cutting is representative of the fashion in glass at the time of the Great Exhibition in 1851. (Broadfield House Glass Museum, Kingswinford)

allegorical figures, flowers, birds and insects, painted with great skill and precision in wonderfully delicate and naturalistic colours. Their work was highly prized, and was bought by tourists as expensive souvenirs and exchanged as gifts.

The Mohn and Kothgasser style of enamelling was copied with varying skill by other artists, notably Friedrich Egermann (1777-1864), who ran a decorating studio near Česká Lípa in northern Bohemia. Egermann, one of the most prominent Bohemian glass-makers of the first half of the century, had trained as a glass-blower and painter of ceramics and glass, and was also a knowledgeable chemist. He is best known for his invention of Lithyalin glass, a polished opaque glass marbled in strong colours to imitate agate and other semi-precious stones. He patented this glass in 1829. However, he was not the first to experiment along these lines: in southern Bohemia, Jiři, Count von Buquoy, had developed and patented an opaque black glass in 1817 and a similar dark red glass in 1819, which he called Hyalith glass. Egermann in fact used Buquoy's Hyalith as well as a dark green glass as the base colour for his Lithyalin, on which metallic oxides, stains and lustres were brushed to simulate veining and marbling before the glass was fired. In spite of his patent, Egermann's Lithyalin was soon being copied by other Bohemian factories, notably the Harrach glassworks, but the fashion for these stone glasses was short-lived, and by 1850 production had ceased.

A more lasting achievement of Egermann's was his development of yellow and ruby staining to cover clear glass. The yellow stain, which used silver chloride, was invented in 1818, and the copper-ruby stain was perfected in about 1832. The clear glass article was first cut, and the stains

were then brushed on and fixed to the surface by being fired. When left in this state the glass gave the appearance of being solid red or yellow, but staining was most frequently used in conjunction with copper-wheel engraving, which cut through the thin film of surface colour to reveal the clear glass beneath, to give the same effect as engraved flashed glass.

The Bohemian engravers were without equal in the nineteenth century. Their favourite subjects showed woodland scenes with stags, dogs and huntsmen, and they also engraved portraits, horses and even pitched battles. They considered no subject too complicated. Among

Above: Three beakers in Lithyalin glass, from the studio of Friedrich Egermann, near Česká Lípa, Bohemia, c. 1830-35. Lithyalin, stained and marbled to imitate semi-precious stones, was introduced by Egermann in about 1828.
Height: left and right, 11cm (4³⁄₈in); centre, 11.9cm (4²⁄₃in) (Museum of Decorative Arts, Prague)

Left: The technique of transparent enamelling on glass was developed by Samuel Mohn about 1806 and carried on by his son Gottlob. This beaker painted by Gottlob with a view of Rome is from his Dresden period, before he moved to Vienna in 1811. It shows the refinement of taste and exquisite workmanship that characterized the best Biedermeier glass. (Museum of Decorative Arts, Prague)

Right: Sugar-water set in uranium glass (developed by the Bohemian Josef Riedel in the 1830s) made at the Harrach glass-works, c. 1840.
Height of large decanter: 31cm (12¼in)
(Museum of Decorative Arts, Prague)

Below: Two cut and engraved goblets showing the yellow and ruby surface staining so characteristic of mid-nineteenth-century Bohemian glassware. The goblet on the right is from the workshop of Friedrich Egermann, c. 1845, and that on the left is probably the work of E. Hoffmann, c. 1840.
Height: left, 13.5cm (5⅓in).
(Museum of Decorative Arts, Prague)

these glass-engravers were Andreas Mattoni and Emmanuel Hoffman in Carlsbad (Karlovy Vary), the Pohls who worked for Count Harrach, and Karl Pfohl, August Böhm and F.A. Pelikan in the Kamenický Šenov district. Perhaps the most skilful of them was Dominik Biemann (1800-57), who spent his summers in the spa town of Franzensbad, engraving portraits of the tourists. A number of Bohemian engravers went to work in Britain, France and America; the impact they made in Britain was particularly strong.

The industrial exhibitions held in Prague in the 1820s and 1830s stimulated enthusiasm for glassware, which led to the discovery of a number of new colours, including pink, green, blue and violet. This variety of colours led to the popularity at this period of cased glass, in which two layers of different-coloured glass were used together. After the article had been annealed, parts of the outer layer were cut away to reveal the colour beneath it. The most common combinations were blue or opaque white over clear glass. In 1836 clear glass cased with two colours was introduced. France, Britain and America also produced cased glass, much of which is indistinguishable from that made in Bohemia. The most unusual new colour to appear in the 1830s was a yellow-green obtained

Two examples of Bohemian cased glass, a decanter and a vase, both dating from c. 1845. Enamelling and gilding add to the effect achieved by cutting through the outer blue layer. Bohemian cased glass was much copied in other countries so that it is often difficult to determine the origin of a piece. (Museum of Decorative Arts, Prague)

from a uranium compound; it was invented by Joseph Riedel. An opaque apple-green glass called chrysoprase also contained uranium.

In 1835 a delegation from France visited Bohemia, and took back samples of Bohemian glass for the French factories to copy. The following year the Société de l'Encouragement pour l'Industrie française began awarding prizes for successful imitations of Bohemian glass. By 1838 Georges Bontemps at Choisy-le-Roi was producing uranium glass and during the 1840s

factories such as St-Louis were using Egermann's yellow and ruby stains. However, the coloured opaline glass for which France is best known was an independent development. Opaline was a translucent milky-white glass which, by the addition of various metallic oxides, could be coloured pink, mauve, turquoise, green or several other delicate shades. The manufacture of opalines began in about 1810, the earliest examples being classical in shape and generally undecorated except for the addition of ormolu

Opaline glassware was manufactured in several countries in the nineteenth century, France producing items of particularly fine quality. This group of Bohemian opaline, dating from the first half of the century, is decorated with gilt, silver and enamels. (Museum of Decorative Arts, Prague)

mounts. In the 1830s, under Bohemian influence, polygonal shapes and stronger colours were introduced, and at the same time white opalines began to be painted in vitrified enamel colours with flowers, in imitation of porcelain.

At the first public exhibition of Russian manufactures, held in St Petersburg in 1828-9, there were signs that coloured glass was coming back into fashion. Topaz, emerald, ruby and sapphire were among the colours exhibited, along with a rosy opalescent glass that was perhaps inspired by French opalines. A speciality of the Imperial Glassworks was opaque glass in blue, green, azure, black and liver-red, which may have been influenced by the experiments of Buquoy and Egermann in Bohemia. These colours were used to ornament porcelain and furniture as well as for glass vessels, and when they were shown at the 1867 Paris Exhibition a deep red, called purpurine, was especially praised.

Not even England, the champion of clear cut crystal, could ignore the trend towards coloured glass, and as early as the 1830s cased glass was being made by the Stourbridge firm of Stevens and Williams. The greatest boost to the manufacture of coloured glass was the lifting of the excise duties on glass in 1845, exactly 100 years after they had first been imposed. It was not so much the tax itself that had damaged the industry as the regulations imposed by the Act, which had hampered manufacturers in the day-to-day running of their factories and thereby discouraged experiment. The manufacturers revelled in their new-found freedom, and

by 1849 the English glass-makers had developed a range of colours and tints to rival those of the Bohemians. French opalines also exercised a strong influence, and Richardsons of Stourbridge made exact copies of several French shapes. The English factories, however, did not produce as many colours as the French but concentrated on elegant white opaline vases with enamelled and gilt decoration or transfer-printed with classical figures.

The Great Exhibition

The Great Exhibition held at the Crystal Palace in London in 1851 displayed the finest products of all nations to the equally cosmopolitan visitors, causing much rivalry among manufacturers and heightening their desire to create attractive new products. Countries such as America, Russia and France had frequently organized exhibitions of their own manufacturers during the first half of the century, but the Great Exhibition, or the Exhibition of the Industry of All Nations as it was officially called, was the first to bring together products from all over the world. Most of Europe's leading glass manufacturers were represented as well as several from America, and the exhibition thus presented a hitherto unparalleled opportunity to examine the state of decorative glass at this halfway point in the nineteenth century. (The one exception was France, whose only representative was Clichy.)

Coloured glass and crystal, the two main types of glass produced in the nineteenth century so

French opalines inspired the manufacture of translucent white glass in England. These three items, c. 1850, are from the Richardson factory at Stourbridge. Two have transfer-printed decoration, the other enamelled flowers.
Height: left and right, 30.5cm (12in); centre, 43.8cm (17¼in)
(Broadfield House Glass Museum, Kingswinford)

far, were in evidence in equal quantities at the Great Exhibition. The Bohemian exhibitors, who included Hoffman of Prague and the Counts Harrach and Buquoy, showed some cut glass, but it was their coloured glass that attracted most attention. Hoffman, for instance, exhibited a pair of huge vases 1.2m (4ft) high in alabaster and green glass. However, Bohemia's traditional supremacy in the field of coloured glass was now receiving a serious challenge from England.

The quite spectacular range of colours shown by the English factories was evidence of the great advances in the glass industry during the brief period since the lifting of excise duties in 1845. The display by Rice Harris of Birmingham, for instance, included opal, alabaster, turquoise, amber, canary, topaz, chrysoprase, pink, blue, light and dark ruby, black, brown, green and purple; and this sort of variety was by no means exceptional.

Among other English firms to show a wide range of colours were George Bacchus and Sons, also of Birmingham, and Richardson's and David Greathead and Green of Stourbridge, and Apsley Pellatt of London. Bohemian influence showed itself not just in the colours that the English were using but also in manufacturing techniques such as casing and shapes such as the

The heroic scale of the Crystal Palace, site of the Great Exhibition in London of 1851, was matched by the crystal fountain that dominated the transept. The fountain was manufactured by the Birmingham firm of Osler, which was celebrated for its sumptuous crystal chandeliers and candelabra.
Height: 615cm (20ft)

A goblet from a set of water jug and two goblets, acid-etched with Egyptian motifs at the Northwood decorating works in Wordsley near Stourbridge, c. 1870. The design has been created using templates and by mounting the glass on a template etching machine, which worked out the spacing of the repeating pattern. By the end of the nineteenth century acid-etching had become one of the most popular forms of glass decorations.
(Broadfield House Glass Museum, Kingswinford)

Richardson's and Lloyd and Summerfield of Birmingham, and Diercx of Antwerp, for example, the results were less successful. Shapes tended to be submerged under the decoration and the objects inevitably became heavy and uncomfortable to hold. It was this type of glass that was later to incur the wrath of Ruskin and his followers, who favoured simply blown glass in the Venetian style (see page 183).

The Great Exhibition was an overwhelming success with the public. During the five months it was open it was visited by 6 million people, or 43,000 people daily. From then on, large, international exhibitions became an established part of Victorian life and were staged at frequent intervals in London, Paris, Vienna and other major cities in the second half of the century. The exhibitions inspired the creation of some excellent pieces of glass, which might not otherwise have been made; but unfortunately they also occasionally encouraged the pursuit of tasteless ostentation and novelty purely for novelty's sake.

Although these faults were evident in the glass at the Great Exhibition, the competitive spirit generated among manufacturers by this international event inspired an atmosphere of creativity and invention, the like of which has seldom been seen before or since in the decorative arts.

scalloped rim. In fact, so dependent was England on Bohemia at this time that it is sometimes difficult to distinguish between the glass produced by these two countries.

Crystal, however, was still popular. The *Art Journal* claimed in 1851 not only that English crystal was superior to that of any other country but also that it was in crystal that glass displayed 'its highest sphere of usefulness and beauty'. The main objective of the English manufacturers was to bring out the light-refracting qualities of their lead glass by means of deep prismatic cutting and produce an object that sparkled with a diamond-like brilliance.

Chandeliers showed off the refractive beauty of English lead glass to its best advantage, and some sumptuous examples were exhibited by Apsley Pellatt and Oslers of Birmingham. However, the most magnificent specimen of cut glass in the exhibition was the enormous crystal fountain made by Oslers. It was more than 6m (20ft) high, and stood at the focal point of the Crystal Palace at the crossing of the main nave and transept. The fountain was destroyed when the Crystal Palace was burned down in 1936, and all that remains are a few fragments of glass in Birmingham Art Gallery.

When the same deep prismatic cutting was applied to ordinary tableware, as it was by

Engraving and Acid-Etching

Amid the welter of cut and coloured glass at the Great Exhibition, the London retailer J.G. Green showed a water-jug of classical shape engraved with classical ornament. At the next major international exhibition in London, eleven years later, this type of glass was dominating the English stands at the expense of elaborate cutting and exotic colours. The classical style of engraving, one of the most original and attractive of the nineteenth century, dominated the luxury end of the British glass market for thirty years, and was adopted in France and Bohemia as well.

The government-sponsored schools of design, which were first established in the 1840s, played an important part in the development of classical engraved glass. Through books such as Owen Jones's *Grammar of Ornament* (1856) and R.N. Wornum's *Analysis of Ornament* (1860) students learned about different historical styles of ornament, but classical art was given the greatest emphasis. Jugs, decanters and vases were based on Greek forms (considered to be the most perfect), and engraved with figures taken from Greek vases or the Elgin Marbles, and with formal decorative motifs such as the Greek key, festoons and the Vitruvian scroll. At the London International Exhibition of 1862 Apsley Pellatt showed some glass in which formal motifs were simplified into a pattern of engraved and frosted parallel lines and bands. This style was particularly admired by the *Art Journal*, especially as it brought a type of glass that was normally expensive within popular reach. Almost as frequent as classical ornament were fanciful Renaissance motifs such as grotesques, masks and arabesques.

The classical style of engraving was one of the most brilliant and inventive areas of Victorian design. Although shapes and decoration were based on those of antiquity, the style that resulted was in fact totally original. From an aesthetic point of view it was among the best glass produced in the whole of the nineteenth century. The shapes, particularly those of water-jugs and claret-decanters, were exquisite and they were matched by engraving of the highest quality.

Classical engraving might never have flowered in Britain had it not been for the arrival of a number of highly skilled Bohemian engravers in the middle of the century. Until then there had been little scope for engravers because of the popularity of cut glass. Most of the Bohemians who settled in London, including Paul Oppitz and Franz Eisert, worked for retailers such as Copeland, Dobson and Pearce, and J.G. Green, who had blanks made to order by Thomas Webb of Stourbridge and other leading manufacturers. At the London International Exhibition in 1862 and the Paris Exposition Universelle in 1867, when classical engraving was at the peak of its popularity, these London retailers displayed the majority of the engraved glass. The other main centre where Bohemians were employed was Edinburgh, where an engraving workshop was set up by J.H.B. Millar in the late 1850s. Millar

One of the greatest exponents of glass engraving in the nineteenth century was the Bohemian August Böhm, whose travels in England and America encouraged the growth of engraving in these countries. This vase, executed at Meistersdorf in 1840, is one of his outstanding works. The engraving, based on a painting by Lebrun in the Louvre, depicts the Battle of the River Granicus in 334 BC, at which Alexander the Great, although heavily outnumbered, defeated King Darius of Persia. The reverse bears an inscription in French. Height: 58.4 cm (23 in) (On loan to Broadfield House Glass Museum, Kingswinford)

An English wheel-engraved colourless glass jug, said to have been bought from W.P. & G. Phillips and Pearce, London glass merchants, about 1869. The quality of Victorian wheel-engraved glass, in which classical and Renaissance motifs frequently featured, was of a very high order.
(Victoria and Albert Museum, London)

obtained his blanks from John Ford's Holyrood Glassworks. By 1866 he had thirty engravers working for him. Several of the Bohemian engravers moved from place to place. Wilhelm Pohl, for instance, was in Edinburgh in 1858, in Warrington in 1863 and in Manchester ten years later. August Böhm, the most famous of the Bohemians in Britain, was based in London but seems also to have worked in Stourbridge and Manchester. Later he went to America.

It was not long before other countries began to copy the English style. In 1863 Val-St-Lambert in Belgium was reported to be looking for a first-rate artist to engrave heraldic and Greek designs, and the *Art Journal* in its report of the 1867 Paris Exhibition announced that French firms were no longer engraving animals and forest scenes but had turned to historic and formal subjects. In fact, the Clichy factory had already exhibited some excellent examples of Renaissance-style engraved glass at the 1862 London Exhibition. Even Bohemia was forced to give up its beloved forest scenes and adopt a style of engraving which Bohemians themselves, working abroad, had helped to create. The greatest exponent of the classical style in Bohemia was Ludwig Lobmeyr, a glass merchant and prominent figure in Viennese artistic circles, who inspired many of the

advances made in Bohemian glass during the second half of the century. Lobmeyr was closely connected with the Museum and School of Industrial Arts in Vienna, which provided the same firm grounding in classical and Renaissance art as the schools of design in England.

The most significant new decorating technique to be introduced during the Victorian period was acid-etching. Originally it was intended to be just a cheap, mechanical alternative to copper-wheel engraving, but as the process was improved and refined it became an attractive and important form of decoration in its own right, with its own distinct character. The idea of using acid to eat into the surface of glass dates back to the end of the seventeenth century, but the technique was seldom practised until the discovery of hydrofluoric acid by the Swede Carl Wilhelm Scheele in about 1770. In the early nineteenth century acid-etching was confined chiefly to flat glass, and the decoration was produced by the fumes from the acid when it was heated rather than by the acid itself. It was not until the introduction of acid-proof containers made from gutta-percha, a type of rubber, in the 1840s, that glass began to be decorated by immersion in acid-baths.

Acid-etching began to be considered seriously as a way of ornamenting tableware and decorative glass only in the 1850s. A patent was taken out in London in 1853 by Emmanuel Barthélemy, Tony Petitjean and Jean-Pierre Bourquin for etching through cased glass. In 1857 a similar patent was issued to Benjamin Richardson of Stourbridge, who had been experimenting with etching for several years.

The basic technique was to coat the glass surface inside and out with an acid-resistant wax and then draw the design through the wax on to the glass with a sharp point. This could be done either freehand or using templates. The article was then immersed in a bath of hydrofluoric acid, which ate into the glass and created a deep line where the wax had been removed, while the rest of the surface remained untouched. At first the outlines were filled in with copper-wheel engraving, but in about 1860 the French discovered that a matt surface could be produced by using a weakened form of hydrofluoric acid known as 'white acid'. This was a major breakthrough; it enabled the engraving-wheel to be dispensed with and speeded up the whole process. Different tones could be produced depending on the strength of the acid: the more it was weakened, by adding alkali, the whiter was the finish. Perhaps the best illustration of the varied effects that could be achieved is to be seen in English pub windows of the period.

The man responsible for making acid-etching

a commercial success in England was John Northwood, a former employee of Benjamin Richardson. In 1861 Northwood established an acid-etching workshop in Wordsley near Stourbridge with a small team of highly skilled artists who decorated blanks purchased from the local factories. A number of Northwood's decorators were students at the Stourbridge School of Art, where teaching of the various historical styles of ornament was reflected in the designs that the workshop produced. The classical style predominated, as it had in engraving, but decorative motifs from Egyptian and Islamic art were also used. Formal designs were drawn on the glass with the assistance of templates, and Northwood invented a template-etching machine in 1862; but naturalistic designs such as flowers and butterflies were done freehand, often by women.

Etched glass was exhibited by a number of firms at the 1867 Exposition Universelle, an indication of the increasing importance that was now being attached to the technique. Copeland, a London glass retailer, showed a service in Greek style which may have originated from the Northwood workshop, and Greek-style etching was also shown by Messrs Cifuentes of Spain. Baccarat and St-Louis were the chief exhibitors of etched glass among the French. Baccarat's display included a punch-bowl and glasses on a plateau in crystal glass cased with blue, in which three different tints of blue were obtained by etching the colour to different depths.

The etched glass so far described was often as elaborate and expensive as the engraved glass it was meant to replace. It was only with the development of etching and pantograph machines, which inscribed simple geometrical patterns such as interlocking circles and the Greek key on to the glass, that etching achieved its original aim of providing a cheaper alternative to copper-wheel engraving. Large quantities of this type of glass were produced at the end of the nineteenth century by Holmegaard of Denmark, Val-St-Lambert in Belgium, Stuart and Sons of Stourbridge and many other factories, and machine-etched patterns became as common a form of decoration on large services of glass tableware as cutting and engraving.

The Venetian Revival

During the nineteenth century there was a resurgence of glass-making in Venice and also a revival of interest in the Venetian style in other countries. Yet the 'new' glass, both in Italy and generally elsewhere, was no more than a revival of earlier Venetian styles. In its reproduction of the shapes and decorative techniques of the past it is interesting historically and technically, but

shows little originality. However, one or two factories, notably Whitefriars in London, did delve below the decorative surface of the Venetian style and produced glass which, while obviously influenced by Venice, also showed great inventiveness.

One of the first glass-makers to take an interest in the old Venetian techniques was Georges Bontemps at his factory in Choisy-le-Roi. Bontemps showed examples of *latticinio* glass in Paris in 1838, and the following year *latticinio* was also being made by Count Harrach at his glassworks in northern Bohemia. In England it was, not surprisingly, that great inventor Apsley Pellatt who first attempted to reproduce some of the old Venetian techniques. One type of glass that Pellatt showed at the Great Exhibition was Venetian crackle glass, which was produced by a combination of plunging the hot ball of glass into cold water and chilling and reheating the glass as it was blown. Cappelman's of Brussels also exhibited Venetian-style glass at the Great Exhibition, and Belgian and French

In the second quarter of the nineteenth century there was a revival of interest in Venetian styles of glass-making in a number of centres. This jug, made in France, probably at Clichy, about 1850, employs the traditional Venetian technique of latticinio, *in which coloured canes in a prearranged pattern are picked up on a gather of glass and incorporated in the finished piece. Height: 8.3cm (3¼in) (Broadfield House Glass Museum, Kingswinford)*

glass-makers were instrumental in introducing Venetian techniques to other countries such as Finland.

The revival of the Venetian *latticinio* technique was one of the factors behind that most curious of Victorian inventions, the glass paperweight. It is not known who invented the paperweight, but the earliest surviving dated weights were made at St-Louis in France and by Pietro Bigaglia in Venice in 1845. It was France, however, that became the centre of paperweight manufacture, and the finest weights were made by the three French factories of St-Louis, Baccarat and Clichy between about 1845 and 1860. Apart from France the most important centre for paperweights was America, where production began in the 1850s, receiving a great boost a few years later with the arrival from France of two former employees of St-Louis and Baccarat, Nicholas Lutz and François Pierre. Pierre joined the New England Glass Company and Lutz worked for the Boston and Sandwich Glass Company, where in the 1880s not only paperweights were made but also large quantities of *latticinio* glass.

The two main methods of decoration used in paperweights were *millefiori* and lampworking. Prompted by the boom in paperweights, several Venetian firms devoted themselves to the production of *millefiori* canes for the home market and for export. Weights decorated with birds, insects, flowers and other such motifs required the skills of the lampworker, and often both techniques were used in the same weight.

The work of glass-makers in paperweight production was just one aspect of the revival of the glass industry in Venice, which was due mainly to the efforts of Antonio Salviati (1816-1900). A lawyer by training, Salviati became involved with glass when he formed a partnership in 1859 with Lorenzo Radi, who had been experimenting for a number of years with some of the Venetian techniques such as marbled and veined glass imitating hardstones. Salviati's glass was first seen at the London International Exhibition of 1862, but it was at the 1867 exhibition in Paris that he had his greatest success. His display included mosaic glass and chandeliers, but what attracted most attention

A group of mid-nineteenth-century American and European paperweights. The production of these highly decorative objects began shortly before 1850, initially the result of a renewed interest in Venetian techniques of glass-making. Factories in a number of countries engaged in production; Baccarat, Clichy and Saint-Louis in France and the New England Glass Company in America made some of the finest examples. (The Toledo Museum of Art, Toledo, Ohio)

The revival of the glass industry in Venice itself owed much to the efforts of Antonio Salviati. These six pieces of Salviati glass, dating from c. 1870-75, give some idea of the range of his output, which included reproductions of antique Venetian glass from the sixteenth and seventeenth centuries. Salviati was also enormously successful in popularizing the Venetian style abroad, particularly in Britain. Heights: 5.5-42.5cm (2⅛-16⅝in) (Nottingham Castle Museum)

were his reproductions of the antique Venetian glass 'with which the Queen of the Adriatic once supplied the world'—vases, bottles, and goblets and *tazze* with elaborate serpent and winged stems. The quality of Salviati glass is very mixed, however: it can be excellent, but often the colours are crude and the workmanship poor.

Besides leading the revival in Venice, Salviati played an important part in making the Venetian style popular in America and all over Europe, particularly in Britain. The company which he formed in 1866 was funded with British capital, and in 1868 he opened a showroom at 30 St James's Street in London. His glass was praised by the Director of the Royal Academy Sir Charles Eastlake in the influential book *Hints on Household Taste* (1868), and this seal of approval may be one reason why a number of museums, including Edinburgh, Glasgow, Nottingham and South Kensington, began to acquire examples of Salviati glass. The South Kensington Museum was also acquiring antique Venetian glass, and the magnificent Felix Slade collection of antique Venetian glass was put on show at the British Museum in 1868. Museums exercised a powerful influence on the development of style and taste in the late nineteenth century. Not only were they visited by vast numbers of people, far more than today, but their collections were used

by manufacturers and employees as a source of inspiration for their own designs. For example, Alexander Jenkinson's factory in Edinburgh, which produced some fine *latticinio* wares in the 1870s, is known to have made use of the Venetian glass collections at the Edinburgh Museum of Science and Art.

The two most interesting champions of Venetian glass were John Ruskin and William Morris. Venetian glass was for them a philosophy, not just a decorative style. They felt it represented the only legitimate approach to the manufacture of glass and that unless there was a return to the principles which had governed Venetian glass in its heyday in the sixteenth and seventeenth centuries, nothing beautiful could ever be produced. In his book *The Stones of Venice* (1853), Ruskin stated that one of the chief characteristics of glass was its ductility and that it was essential to reveal this quality in any vessel. This led him to make his much-quoted judgment that 'All cut glass is barbarous, for cutting conceals its ductility and confuses it with crystal', but this comment seems to have had little effect on the glass-cutters themselves. Morris also attacked the makers of cut glass, and criticized the working methods in the British glass industry, which demanded that each glass should be identical. He believed that this stifled

Thinly blown glassware in the Venetian style, manufactured in the late nineteenth century by Whitefriars Glass Works, a London factory. The ductile quality of these pieces would have satisfied those, such as John Ruskin and William Morris, who were highly critical of the contemporary taste for cut glass. Heights: 5.7–19.1cm (2¼–7½in) (City of Manchester Art Galleries)

the creativity of the glass-maker. Even that sacred cow of the British industry, the purity of its crystal, came under attack: Morris felt that it was better to have a tint, slight specks and streaks in glass, 'for these things make the form visible'.

Among the glass that came closest to realizing Ruskin and Morris's ideals was a group of thinly blown Venetian-style jugs, decanters, goblets and *tazze* in tinted opalescent glass made by Whitefriars from the 1870s onwards. Pleasingly original as these interpretations of the Venetian style were, even they looked dated alongside an extraordinary set of tableware in clear blown glass designed by Philip Webb in about 1861 for Morris's company, Morris, Marshall and Faulkner, and made by Whitefriars. The design has a simplicity and timeless quality that is outstanding amid all the historically based glass of the Victorian period. It is no coincidence that the form of the tumbler in the set can still be seen today in Britain in the standard straight pint beer-glass. Whitefriars was not alone in producing glass of such revolutionary simplicity. In 1856 Ludwig Lobmeyr had designed an astonishingly 'modern' service of table-glass that anticipates twentieth-century functionalism.

As the popularity of engraving, etching and the Venetian style increased, cut glass became correspondingly less popular in the years following the Great Exhibition, and by the time of the 1878 Paris exhibition the old system of spiky cutting had been almost abandoned in Europe. At that very moment, however, a revival of heavily cut glass was under way in America, which was to spread to Europe, particularly

Bohemia, in the following decade. This 'brilliant cutting', as the late nineteenth-century style of cut glass was known, was even more complex than the cutting shown at the Great Exhibition: the entire surface of a piece would be smothered with deep prismatic cutting, and the use of the curved mitre cut added to the rich effect. The 'Russian Pattern', patented by the Corning cutting firm of T.G. Hawkes in 1882, 'shone with the brilliancy of ten thousand closely set jewels', and this represented the ideal. At the Paris exhibition of 1889 Hawkes won a gold medal for his cut and engraved glass, and in 1905, when the industry was at its peak, there were 490 glass-cutters at Corning.

Eastern Influences

Glass, like all the applied arts, came under the influence of oriental art, particularly that of Japan, during the second half of the nineteenth century. Japan had been closed to the West since the early eighteenth century but trading links were re-established following Commodore Perry's successful expedition in 1854, and soon large quantities of bronzes, ivories, ceramics, prints and lacquer-work were being imported into Europe. The display of Japanese art at the 1862 London International Exhibition created a sensation, and books such as *Le Japon Illustré*, published in 1870 with an English edition in 1874, helped to increase the popularity of the Japanese style.

At first Japanese art was seen by glass manufacturers simply as an exciting new source of decorative motifs, and engraved or enamelled storks, bamboo and plum-blossom began to appear on glass. Gradually, however, a more serious approach was adopted. The famous English pressed-glass firm of Sowerby's, inspired by old Japanese carved ivory, patented an ivory-coloured glass, Queen's Ivory Ware, in 1879. In 1887 Thomas Webb of Stourbridge patented an ivory cameo, one of the most ingenious types of glass made in the nineteenth century. In some examples almost every known

decorating technique was combined—acid-etching, engraving, staining, enamelling, gilding and marquetry—resulting in a glass that is very similar to the work of Émile Gallé in terms of its richness and complexity of effect.

The most original and interesting response to oriental art was the creation of a new style of engraved glass called 'rock crystal', which was inspired by the oriental carving of natural rock crystal (quartz), jade and other hardstones. In 'rock crystal' the decoration was engraved deeply into the glass and then polished so that it blended in tone with the glass surface. This was in complete contrast to the shallow, matt class-

ical and Renaissance engraving of the 1860s. Engraving was usually combined with deep cutting so that the glass bore a close resemblance to a carving from a piece of natural rock crystal.

The 'rock-crystal' style originated in France and England in the late 1870s, and rock-crystal engraving was exhibited by Baccarat, Pantin and L'Escalier de Cristal for the first time at the 1878 Paris exhibition. The leading exponents of rock-crystal in England were the Stourbridge firms of Thomas Webb and Stevens and Williams, where the finest engraving was done by immigrant Bohemian artists, outstanding among whom were Frederick Kny, William Fritsche and Joseph Keller. Typical motifs included chrysanthemums, trailing blossom, fish, exotic birds and dragons. The heyday of the style in England was the 1880s. In the following decade there was a fall in demand for all types of luxury glass, and by 1914 production had virtually ceased. In 1886 the most celebrated example of English rock crystal, the William Fritsche ewer, was purchased by a New York

Left: Ewer engraved in 1886 in the 'rock-crystal' style by William Fritsche, a Bohemian who worked in England for the Stourbridge firm of Thomas Webb.
Height: 38.5cm (15⅛in) (Corning Museum of Glass, Corning, New York)

Below: Vase made by Lobmeyr of Vienna in the 1870s, the decoration inspired by Islamic glass of the thirteenth and fourteenth centuries.
Height: 16.5cm (6½in) (Nottingham Castle Museum)

A group of enamelled glassware in Islamic style produced by the Imperial Glassworks at St Petersburg and exhibited at the International Exhibition of 1862 in London.

jeweller; this stimulated the manufacture of rock crystal in America.

Islamic art also provided European glassmakers with decorative motifs for etching and engraving, but it was the ancient tradition of Islamic glass-enamelling that had the greatest influence. A Frenchman, Phillippe-Joseph Brocard, led a revival of this art. He was inspired by the famous Syrian mosque lamps of the fourteenth century, and began experimenting in the 1860s to see if he could rediscover the technique that had been used to make them. He experienced several difficulties, particularly in getting the thick opaque colours to adhere to the glass and in discovering an enamel composition that would melt at a sufficiently low temperature for the glass itself not to distort; but eventually he managed to master the technique and his enamelled glass won a first prize at the 1878 Paris exhibition. He made copies of Syrian mosque lamps as well as original bowls, vases and ewers. One of Brocard's admirers at the exhibition was the young Emile Gallé, whose own enamelled glass owed a great debt to Brocard.

The Viennese glasshouse of Lobmeyr also exhibited some excellent enamelling in the Islamic manner at Paris in 1878. Most Bohemian firms, however, drew inspiration from their own enamelling tradition, reviving traditional shapes like the *Roemer* and *Humpen* in rough green *Waldglas* (forest glass), decorated in brightly coloured enamels with shields, coats of arms, figures, dates and other motifs that had been popular in the seventeenth century.

Russian glass of the second half of the century, which exhibited a great variety of styles in both crystal and coloured glass, also showed the influence of Islamic art. Typical characteristics were thick enamelling, jewelling and gilding in the Islamic style, and the Imperial Glassworks had exhibited and won a prize for this type of glass as early as 1862 at the London International Exhibition, where it was described as having a certain Asiatic richness 'closer to the old Arabic gilt and enamelled glass than any before'. After this, no further developments of any significance took place in Russia until the advent of Art Nouveau at the end of the century.

Cameo Glass

Of the many contributions made by Britain to nineteenth-century glass-making the most remarkable was the revival in Stourbridge of the 'lost art' of cameo glass. Cameo was a form of cased glass, its characteristic feature being a thick outer layer of white glass which was carved away to leave a design in relief against a dark background. It had been made by the Romans in the first century AD but with the collapse of the Roman Empire the technique had been lost. The most important surviving example of Roman cameo glass, and the piece that inspired the revival, was the Portland Vase, bearing white figures on a dark blue background. The vase came to Britain in 1783, was purchased by the Duke of Portland in 1786 and immediately borrowed by Josiah Wedgwood to make his jasperware versions. An attempt to copy the vase in the original glass material was made in 1818, but was unsuccessful. The reliefs on the Portland Vase were used in printed form to decorate white opaline glass, and a version in crystal glass cased with blue was engraved by the Bohemian Franz Zach. Interest became even keener when Benjamin Richardson, a leading Stourbridge manufacturer, offered a prize of £1000 to the first person to produce an exact replica.

The dream of reproducing the Portland Vase was finally realized by two men, Philip Pargeter (1826-1906), the owner of the Red House Glassworks in Stourbridge where the blank was made, and John Northwood (1836-1902), who executed the carving. Although cased glass had been made since the 1830s, the manufacture of a cameo blank presented particular problems. Not only did the white outer layer have to be of uniform thickness, but the white glass and the dark blue undercolour had to have the same coefficient of expansion and contraction to prevent the glass from cracking during the annealing process. (So difficult was the latter operation that when, later, Richardson's decided to make their own reproduction of the Portland Vase in 1878, only three out of the forty blanks prepared survived annealing.) The procedure was to make an open cup shape from the white glass and drop a gather of blue glass inside the cup. The two layers were then welded together by rolling on the marver and the ball of glass was blown to shape.

As no records survived of how the original Portland Vase had been carved, Northwood had to devise his own methods. He began by drawing the design on the white glass in pencil and painting it over in a black acid-resistant varnish. The vase was then immersed in a bath of hydrofluoric and sulphuric acid which ate away the white glass down to the blue undercolour, leaving the areas protected by the varnish unaffected and causing them to stand out in rough relief. To chip away the white glass and put in the detail Northwood used simple hand-tools in the form of hardened steel points set in wooden holders, combined with an occasional touch of the engraving-wheel. Shortly before the carving was completed, the vase cracked, and several days after the crack appeared the vase broke into two pieces. Northwood was not dismayed, however; he and his assistant Edwin Grice stuck the vase together again and the remaining decoration was finished. The Portland Vase, which occupied Northwood on and off for three years between 1874 and 1876, is one of the finest achievements in the history of glass-making.

Northwood's triumph with the Portland Vase turned him into something of a celebrity, and not unnaturally the other Stourbridge factories were keen to emulate his success. The firm of Hodgetts, Richardson & Co. brought over from France a medallist and gem-engraver named Alphonse Lechevrel who during a two-year stay (1877-78) managed to complete six cameo vases carved with subjects taken from classical mythology. These were exhibited at the 1878 Paris exhibition along with a second copy of the Portland Vase carved by a gifted young artist named Joseph Locke, who had been trained by Lechevrel. Northwood himself undertook two more commissions for Pargeter, but his last major cameo work, the Pegasus Vase, was commissioned by Thomas Wilkes Webb who was anxious to make a name for himself in cameo glass. In spite of being incomplete, this vase was awarded a gold medal at the 1878 exhibition.

The most brilliant of the cameo sculptors was George Woodall (1850-1925). Woodall began his

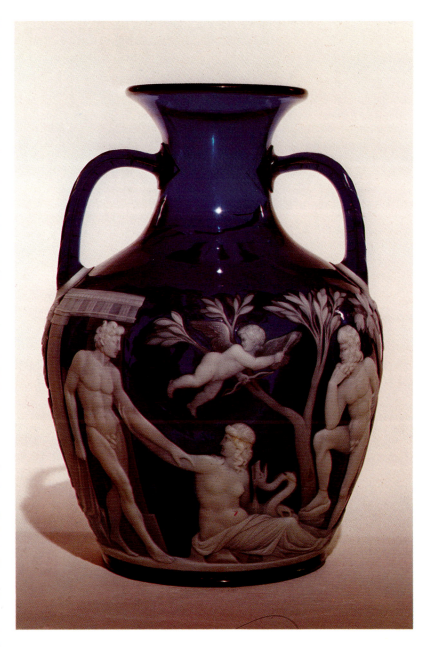

From the moment the Portland Vase, a masterpiece of Roman cameo glass, entered Britain in the 1780s it proved a challenge to potters and glass-makers alike. John Northwood's successful reproduction (shown here) was commissioned by Philip Pargeter of the Red House Glassworks in Stourbridge in 1873 and completed in 1876. (The British Museum, London)

A group of English cameo glass vases. 'The Origin of Painting' (left) by George Woodall, who worked for Thomas Webb's, dates from c. 1900. The other two vases are examples of the cheaper commercial cameo introduced in the 1880s, the centre vase by Richardson's, the other, a better-quality piece, designed by William Northwood and carved by Joshua Hodgetts at Stevens and Williams in 1887.
Heights: left, 22.9cm (9in); centre, 17.8cm (7in); right 30.5cm (12in) (Broadfield House Glass Museum, Kingswinford)

career at John Northwood's etching workshop in about 1862, and while there attended Stourbridge School of Art, passing exams in model and freehand drawing. He joined Thomas Webb's in about 1874 as a glass-engraver, and started cameo-carving around six years later. Woodall continued the classical figurative tradition established by Northwood and Lechevrel, drawing on the works of Canova and Flaxman for some of his designs. Books on Greek, Roman and Chinese ornament by Tatham, Owen Jones and others, which are still at Thomas Webb's, provided him with designs for his more stylized pieces. Woodall's skill as a cameo sculptor was quite extraordinary: using nothing more than the simple hand-tools devised by Northwood and the copper engraving-wheel to thin down the white glass, he achieved astonishing detail and perspective effects.

By about 1880 the demand for cameo glass was so great that the Stourbridge firms were forced to develop a new type of cameo that was less expensive and time-consuming to produce than the individually sculpted pieces by Northwood, Lechevrel and others. Pieces became smaller, the white outer casing was made thinner so that the removal of the surplus white glass by acid took less time, and much greater use was made of the engraving-wheel, as opposed to hand-tools, to carve the design. New bright background colours were introduced, and flowers and foliage replaced classical figurative designs.

The name given to this type of cameo was 'commercial cameo'; but despite the less than appealing sound of such a title the quality of decoration on such pieces was still exceptionally high and the designs have a freshness and spontaneity that the more academic pieces sometimes lack. Large quantities of this commercial cameo were produced between 1880 and 1890 by Thomas Webb's, Stevens and Williams and Richardson's. Webb's alone had seventy engravers working on it. In the 1890s, with the drop in demand for luxury glass, production was slowly phased out. However, there was still a market for Woodall's unique

Queen Victoria's Golden Jubilee commemorative window, Great Malvern Priory, Worcestershire, 1887.

vases and plaques, particularly in America.

The revival of cameo glass was almost exclusively an English phenomenon. A little cameo work was produced in Venice and by the American firm of Gillinder and Sons, but it was crude in comparison to the Stourbridge products. A number of Bohemian firms imitated the cameo effect by painting and firing a thick bluish-white enamel on to a dark-coloured glass. The ultimate debasement of cameo was the popular mass-produced 'Mary Gregory' glass.

Stained Glass

The nineteenth century witnessed a complete revolution in the approach to stained glass. During the first half of the century, artists continued to view it simply as a surface on which they could paint a picture, using glossy opaque enamels which were fired to flux them and make them adhere to the glass. In fact, their subjects were often copied from famous religious paintings of the past by Raphael, Guido Reni and others. These early nineteenth-century glass artists were immensely proud of their enamelled windows and the naturalistic effects they were able to achieve. They felt their technique was far superior to that used during the Middle Ages, particularly since it avoided the use of leading to join up small pieces of coloured glass. An extreme example of this pictorial approach was a window shown by the St Helens Glass Company at the Great Exhibition, which depicted 'St Michael casting out the great red dragon' and consisted of one single sheet of glass 3m by 1.5m (9ft by 5ft), 'whereby the dark stiff lines of lead and metal that disfigure the ordinary pictures are avoided'.

The more academic, archaeological study of Gothic architecture initiated by Pugin in the mid-nineteenth century led to a gradual reawakening of interest in medieval stained glass. Men such as Charles Winston and John Ruskin began to discuss the principles which should govern stained glass design, and the whole pictorial approach was called into question. Winston felt that the chief function of a window was to admit light, but for all the light an enamelled window let in it might as well have been a mural. In Ruskin's view colour and transparency were the chief glories of glass, giving the material its spiritual character, but all these qualities were sacrificed when glass was enamelled. Transparent glass should therefore be restored to its rightful position, and leading used to separate the colours and emphasize the design, as it had been in the Middle Ages. Actual painting on glass should be confined to outlines and shadows, and it had to be bold and dramatic to compete with the lead work and stand out from a distance. Winston, besides being an influential writer on stained glass, carried out research at the Whitefriars Glassworks in London and succeeded in developing most of the colours that had been used in the medieval period.

Ruskin and Winston's stained-glass aesthetic gradually won acceptance. Reviewing the 1862 London International Exhibition, the *Art Journal* noted the general improvement that had taken place since the Great Exhibition as firms began to abandon the pictorial approach in favour of a 'flatter, more legitimate style of treatment'. A number of firms produced highly competent stained glass in the second half of the nineteenth century, but the figure who stood out above all the rest was William Morris. Part of the reason for his success lies in the fact that whereas most commercial stained glass was designed by unknown craftsmen, Morris used the leading artists of his day, particularly Burne-Jones, but also Ford Madox Brown, Rosetti, and others.

This gives his glass a freshness and originality of conception which the commercial work often lacks, and makes it a genuine expression of his own age rather than a meaningless copy of a past style. So convinced was Morris of the modernity of his glass that he refused to supply windows for medieval churches, since they would be out of harmony with the buildings. (His rivals felt no such compunction.) Morris designed little stained glass himself; his role was to interpret the designs of others, select the colours of the glass and supervise the execution of the window, using the best available craftsmen. Much of his firm's finest glass was produced in the 1860s and 1870s. After Morris's death in 1896, the stained glass made by the company lost its vitality, and there was an unfortunate tendency to reproduce earlier designs in an over-pictorial manner, with mediocre results.

An English flower stand with three hanging baskets, c. 1880. This example of a household ornament that was popular in the late nineteenth century is probably from Richardson's factory at Stourbridge. The ruby threading on the baskets and leaves has been applied by machine. Height: 63.5cm (25in) (Broadfield House Glass Museum, Kingswinford)

New Technology

With the important exception of press-moulding, the basic methods of producing tableware and decorative glass changed remarkably little during the nineteenth century. The few innovations that were made were concerned with streamlining existing decorative techniques rather than with introducing anything fundamentally new. For example, in the late nineteenth century a threading machine was invented which laid a trail of molten glass round the body of a vessel with perfect regularity, an operation that had previously been done by hand, with less precision. Similarly, in the 1880s the traditional method of polishing cut glass using wheels and fine abrasives began to be replaced by acid-polishing, in which the article was immersed for a few seconds in a mixture of hydrofluoric and sulphuric acid.

Even in mass-production areas such as flat glass for windows and bottle-making, mechanization made surprisingly little impact. It was not until the 1880s that a semi-automatic bottle-making machine was invented, while the process of making flat glass that was employed at the end of the century had been in use for at least three hundred years. This was the cylinder method, in which cylinders of glass were blown, slit along their length and then flattened out into a sheet in a kiln. The other traditional type of flat glass made by blowing, the even older crown glass, died out only in the 1860s. Crown glass (see Chapter 2) was formed by blowing a globe, opening it up and spinning it so that it stretched into a disc. The third main type of flat glass in the nineteenth century was cast plate, for which molten glass was poured on to a large metal plate, flattened with a roller and, when cold, ground and polished—a technique which had been introduced in France in the late seventeenth century. Once again the process did not change fundamentally during the Victorian period, though the size of the plates increased.

The glass tax in Britain had weighed far more heavily on flat glass than it had done on decorative glass and tableware. In the case of cylinder sheet, for example, it had added as much as 300 per cent to the basic cost of production. The industry therefore received a huge boost in 1845 when the excise duties on glass were finally lifted, and another in 1851 with the abolition of window tax (the reason why many older houses in Britain have blanked-off windows). The liberating effect that the removal of excise duties had is perfectly illustrated in the supreme example of the use of glass in architecture, the Crystal Palace, built in 1851 to house the Great Exhibition. The production of the glass was a

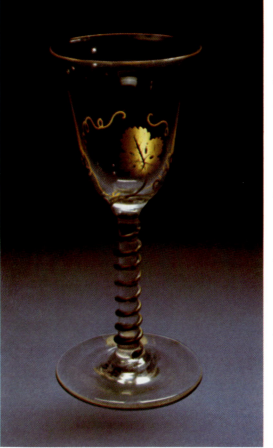

Above: Glass manufacturing in England benefited enormously from the lifting of the excise duty on glass in 1845 and from the abolition of the window tax in 1851. The Crystal Palace, which was built in 1851 to house the Great Exhibition, was the perfect expression of the new confidence in glass as an important element in architecture.

Left: The tendril wineglass was part of the range produced by Felix Summerley's Art Manufactures, a venture established in 1847 with the aim of improving the standard of manufactured goods in England by commissioning established artists to provide designs. This glass was designed by Richard Redgrave and made by Richardson's, c. 1848.

American pressed glass, the footed bowl with cover dating from c. 1880, the other items from c. 1830 to 1845. Press-moulding, which was invented in America in the 1820s, made possible the mass production of cheap glassware.
Heights: 8.6–28.9 cm (3⅜ in–11⅜ in)
(The Toledo Museum of Art, Toledo, Ohio)

just short of red heat. If they were too hot the glass would stick to them; if they were too cold the surface of the glass would be wrinkled and not clear. It was the job of one boy to keep the moulds at the correct heat.

The most important part of the whole pressed-glass process was the brass or iron mould in which the glass was formed. The largest factories had their own mould-making departments, while others used the services of independent mould-makers such as James Stevens of Birmingham. Moulds were highly prized and records show that outdated moulds, rather than being thrown away, were often sold by one factory to another, which makes the identification of pressed glass difficult.

A number of people were experimenting with pressed glass in America in the 1820s, including Benjamin Bakewell and John Robinson in Pittsburgh and Deming Jarves of the Boston and Sandwich Glass Company. At first the technique was used to make solid items such as door-knobs, but after about 1830 plates, salts, stemmed bowls called comports and tumblers began to appear in pressed glass. One of the most characteristic American products was a miniature plate less than 10 cm (4 in) in diameter called a 'cup plate', which was apparently used to hold the teacup while one drank from the saucer. In much early American pressed glass the decoration was set against a background of closely stippled dots which helped to disguise any surface blemishes that might occur during the pressing. This was known as the 'lacy style'.

As pressing techniques improved, the need for a stippled background became less vital, and by about 1850 the style had almost died out. The Americans manufactured a vast array of pressed glass in the second half of the century in all sorts of styles, shapes and colours. One of the most distinctive types was Carnival glass, which had a lurid orange or green iridescent surface, in imitation of expensive blown Tiffany glass (see Chapter 8), and was produced by spraying metallic powders on clear pressed glass. It was manufactured in Ohio and West Virginia from the last years of the nineteenth century until well into the present one.

The first European factories to make pressed glass were Val-St-Lambert, Baccarat and St-Louis in about 1830. Most of their early glass was strongly influenced by the American lacy style, but they did introduce one or two new effects, including a black and an opaque brick-red glass similar to Bohemian Hyalith and Lithyalin, with relief ornament in the Gothic style. France and America influenced the development of pressed-glass manufacture in Bohemia and Scandinavia. In 1835 Johann Meyr introduced pressed glass at

remarkable feat in itself. The glazing contract was won by Chance Bros of Smethwick near Birmingham, who, using the traditional blown cylinder method, managed to produce almost 300,000 panes of glass, each measuring 124 cm by 25 cm (49 in by 10 in) in only six months. Work continued night and day, and thirty extra blowers were hired from Lyons so that the job could be completed in time.

The one major break with traditional manufacturing methods was press-moulding which was developed in America in the 1820s and spread to Europe in the following decade. Press-moulding was a mechanical technique in which a measured amount of molten glass was dropped into a metal mould and pressed against its sides with a metal plunger, the mould forming the outer surface of the glass, the plunger the inside. Press-moulding caused a revolution in glass-making. It made mass production of glassware possible for the first time, bringing glass within the price range of a whole class of people who before had been unable to afford it.

In the 1840s a pressed-glass team comprised three men and two or three boys. The gathering and pressing of the glass was done by two of the men. The article was then removed from the mould, put on the end of a pontil-iron and taken to the furnace to be reheated by one of the boys. He then handed the glass to the third workman, who smoothed the rough edges and seam-marks before giving it to the second boy to take to the annealing tunnel. The process, however, was not quite as straightforward as it sounds. Gathering the correct amount of glass to drop into the mould required practice. If too little or too much glass were used the article would be spoiled. It was also important that the moulds were kept at the right temperature,

the Adolfov glassworks in Bohemia in an attempt to stem the flood of French and American imports, while Lobmeyr began production about the same time, using French workmen and machinery. Pressed glass was adopted with great enthusiasm in Scandinavia. The Swedish factory of Reijmyre was the first to acquire a pressing-machine, in 1836, and the Kosta glassworks followed suit four years later. Pressed glass was introduced in Finland in 1851, in Norway in 1857, and in Denmark in 1875.

The cross-currents and influences in Continental pressed glass form a vast, complex subject which has hardly begun to be investigated. The development of pressed glass in England was straightforward by comparison. The earliest centres of pressed-glass manufacture were Birmingham and Stourbridge; but in the second half of the nineteenth century the emphasis shifted to Manchester and, above all, to the north-east. The lacy style of decoration never won the popularity it had on the Continent, and most early pressed glass was made to imitate cut-glass patterns. It was not until the 1860s that pressed glass began to show some originality in design. In Manchester, Derbyshire Brothers and Molineaux and Webb began to produce some attractive tableware decorated with bold formal designs set against a frosted background. In the 1870s the same two firms made some unusual paperweights in the shape of lions, dogs, sphinxes and figures such as Punch and Judy in clear, frosted and coloured glass. Most of the designs were inspired by Staffordshire pottery, though the celebrated lion paperweight in 1874

by John Derbyshire was based on the lion by Landseer at the foot of Nelson's Column. The north-eastern factories, the most important of which were Sowerby's and Davidson's of Gateshead and Greener's of Sunderland, were noted for their coloured pressed glass. Sowerby's was the most adventurous firm and produced the widest range of colours including white opal, turquoise, gold and jet black. Davidson's speciality was his transparent blue pearline glass, patented in 1889, which shaded to an opaque blue when the glass was reheated at the furnace mouth. All three factories produced marbled wares, the most distinctive being a streaky purple-and-white glass, called slag glass because the waste slag from ironworks was used as the colouring agent.

Working Methods and Conditions

Glass-makers in the nineteenth century worked around the furnace in small teams called chairs. British practice was to have four or five chairs operating at the one time, each making different articles. A typical chair comprised four people, who were, in order of seniority, the workman or gaffer, the servitor, the foot-maker and the taker-in. In the manufacture of a wine-glass the initial shaping of the glass was done by the servitor. He then handed over to the gaffer, who, seated in the glass-maker's chair, formed the stem and foot from pieces of glass brought to him by the foot-maker, and then finished the bowl

English pressed glass, c. 1880-1900. Left: butter dish and cover by Davidson's of Gateshead in slag glass (slag from smelting works is said to have been used as the colouring agent). Right: sugar-bowl in Davidson's pearline glass. Centre: flower holder in the form of a pike, possibly by Molineaux Webb of Manchester.
Height of butter dish: 8.9cm (3½in)
Height of sugar-bowl: 12.7cm (5in)
Length of fish: 17.8cm (7in)
(Broadfield House Glass Museum, Kingswinford)

after the glass had been transferred to the pontil-rod and the blowpipe had been cracked off. The completed article was then taken to the annealing-chamber by the junior member of the team, the taker-in. In France the system was slightly different. There were normally between eight and ten people to a chair, three of them men and the rest boys. One advantage of this system was that the manufacturing operation was less rushed and the boys had time to observe and learn the skills of the trade. It also made the unit cost of production slightly cheaper than in England because, although the wage-bill was higher, this was more than offset by the greater quantity of glass that could be made.

Children were frequently used as a source of cheap labour in glass-making, as they were in every industry, and it was not uncommon in the first half of the nineteenth century to find boys of only eight years old working full-time in glasshouses. Legislation improved their position only very slowly. The apprenticeship system was used more in Britain and America than in France. For example, in Birmingham in the 1860s one in five glass-makers was an apprentice, while the proportion in France at the same time was only one in twenty. An apprenticeship lasted seven years. A boy began as a taker-in, after three or four years progressed to being a foot-maker, and so on. Engravers also went through an apprenticeship.

In the mid-nineteenth century the work-force in British factories was generally divided into two sets, which worked alternate six-hour shifts day and night from early on Monday to midday on Friday, amounting to a forty-eight or fifty-four hour week. At first the French followed the same pattern, but later in the nineteenth century they abandoned night-work and replaced it by one long shift of twelve hours with two breaks for meals. French glass-makers were paid by the day, whereas the English were on a complicated piecework system. The management in consultation with the unions agreed on the total number of each article that a chair could reasonably be expected to produce in a six-hour period or 'move', and fixed a rate of pay for each job. If a chair, through its own hard work, managed to make double the agreed number in the six hours it was paid double the rate and so on. The evidence about pay in the glass industry is slightly confusing, but generally speaking, the gaffer received twice as much as the foot-maker, with the servitor getting an intermediate amount.

According to British glass-makers who had the opportunity of travelling abroad, working conditions on the Continent were superior to those at home. Not only were British glass-

houses hot and dark, but the coal-fired furnaces made the atmosphere dirty, smoky and sulphurous. On the Continent greater use was made of gas-firing, which avoided the introduction of coal into the glasshouse itself so that the atmosphere was much cleaner. The trials and tribulations of the glass-makers, however, were as nothing compared with the dangers that surrounded the glass-cutters in their cutting shops. In the nineteenth century cut glass was polished by means of small wood, cork and brush wheels fed with fine abrasive powders such as rottenstone and putty powder, the latter being a mixture of lead and tin oxides. These powders were highly noxious and, because ventilation was inadequate, they were continually being inhaled, particularly by the boys whose job it was to feed them onto the polishing-wheels. The consequences, according to the Wordsley and Stourbridge glass-cutters, were 'Dropped Hands, Cholic and almost innumerable diseases'. In the 1890s acid-polishing began to replace polishing by wheels, but since there

In the late nineteenth century glass-makers, particularly in America, created unusual new colour effects by employing a type of heat-sensitive glass that would change colour when reheated at the furnace mouth. This jug is an example of Amberina, which was patented by Joseph Locke of the New England Glass Company in 1883. The amber glass contains a small amount of gold which causes the part that is reheated to strike a rich ruby red.
Height: 19.1cm (7½in)
(Broadfield House Glass Museum, Kingswinford)

was still no proper ventilation, and no protective clothing, the acid was also a hazard.

The improvement of wages and conditions were two of the aims of the glass-makers' union, the National Flint Glass Makers' Society, founded in 1844. The employers objected to the restrictions which the union imposed and tried to suppress the movement by refusing to take on union men. Matters finally came to a head in 1858 when, as a result of strikes in two Stourbridge factories, the manufacturers in Birmingham, Dudley and Stourbridge banded together to form their own association and closed down their factories in an attempt to force the union to abandon some of its more damaging rules. The lockout lasted four months, caused great hardship to the glass-makers and their families, and led to the permanent closure of several factories. It ended in a technical victory for the employers, but during the rest of the nineteenth century the union became stronger.

The Final Years

During the last years of the nineteenth century there was an increasing emphasis on new ways of using colour, and American, English and Bohemian manufacturers vied with each other to see who could produce the most spectacular ornamental effects in coloured glass. Novelty was all-important, and manufacturers were under pressure to keep pace with the latest developments. As soon as one firm introduced a new idea it was quickly seized upon by the rest.

Of all the many different types of glass that were produced, one of the most interesting was heat-sensitive glass which shaded to another colour when one portion of the article, usually the rim, was reheated at the furnace mouth. The first shaded glass, Amberina, was patented by Joseph Locke of the New England Glass Company, Cambridge, Massachusetts, in 1883. It was a transparent amber glass containing gold in solution, which caused the part that was reheated to develop a rich ruby colour. Amberina is most effective when it is transparent, but Locke also introduced an opaque version called 'plated Amberina' in which the amber glass was given an opal lining. The inventor of Amberina was the same Joseph Locke who had worked for Hodgetts, Richardson and Company in Stourbridge and had produced the cameo copy of the Portland Vase in 1878. He sailed to America in 1882, intending to join the Boston and Sandwich Glass Company, but when he landed representatives from the New England Glass Company reached him first and he signed for them. Locke was a most inventive glass-maker and was constantly

Left: Pomona glass cream pitcher, New England Glass Company, 1885-88. The Pomona decoration of pale blue and amber stains against a stippled acid-etched background was highly innovative but not a commercial success. Height: 9.5cm (3¾in) (The Toledo Museum of Art, Toledo, Ohio)

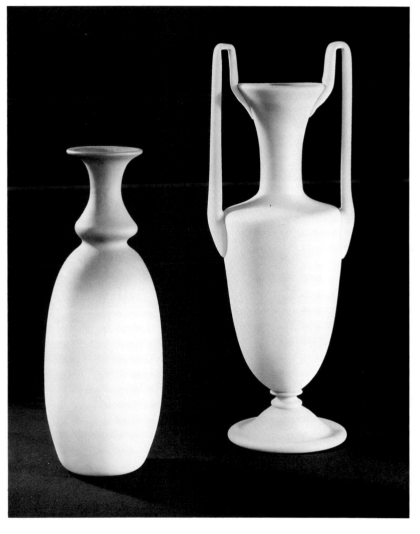

striving after new effects, which sometimes worked and sometimes did not. His most adventurous glass was Pomona, introduced in 1885, which was decorated with pale blue and amber stains against a stippled, acid-etched background. Pomona was not a popular success; Locke thought that this was because it was in advance of its time, and in its stylization it does indeed anticipate French cameo of the 1920s.

A similar glass to Amberina was Peach Blow, which shaded from yellow (at the base of the

Above: Peach Blow (left) and Burmese ware (right) were two further kinds of shaded glass that relied on the principle of reheating to create their effect. Both date from c. 1885. Heights: 28.6cm (11¼in) and 37.9cm (14⅞in) (The Toledo Museum of Art, Toledo, Ohio)

Furnace-applied decoration was a technique exploited in the late nineteenth century to produce elaborately ornamented glass. John Northwood, the English designer of these two pieces—which date from the mid-1880s and were made by Stevens and Williams, Brierley Hill— invented special tamping tools and pincers so that the decoration could be formed and applied with great precision. The vase (left) is an example of the Japanese-style decoration known as matsu-no-ke. *The blue satin-finished bowl (right), decorated with acanthus leaves, has a crimped rim that is very typical of late Victorian glass. Northwood, in fact, patented a crimping machine in 1884 that was an improvement on existing methods.*
Heights: 12.7cm (5in)
10.2cm (4in)
(Broadfield House Glass Museum, Kingswinford)

object) to a deep red (at the top). Peach Blow was inspired by the 'peach-bloom' glaze on a Chinese porcelain vase which attracted attention in 1886 when it was sold from the estate of Mrs Pierrepont Morgan for $18,000. Hobbs, Brock-unier and Company of Wheeling, West Virginia, made some impressive facsimiles of the Morgan vase in their Peach Blow and used the colour successfully on other oriental shapes.

The best-known shaded glass is Burmese, which was patented by Frederick Shirley of the Mount Washington Glass Company, New Bedford, Massachusetts, in 1885. The rights to manufacture Burmese in England were acquired by Thomas Webb and Sons of Stourbridge in 1886, who renamed the glass 'Queen's Burmese' after some examples were presented to Queen Victoria. Burmese was an opaque pale green or yellow glass which shaded to salmon pink on reheating. Various decorative wares were made in this type of glass between 1885 and 1900, either with a glossy surface or a matt finish, the latter achieved by acid-etching or sand blasting. Some Webb's Burmese is decorated with fine enamelled and gilded figural scenes, leaves, flowers and animals.

A matt, silky finish was one of the features of a popular type of late-nineteenth-century glass variously known as 'mother-of-pearl', 'pearl-satin ware' or simply 'satin glass'. The most interesting point about satin glass, however, was the decoration, which consisted of pockets of air trapped between the two layers of glass from which the item was formed. The inner layer of glass, normally a white opal, was blown into a mould, which created indentations in the surface of the glass. It was then cased in glass of another colour, thus trapping the air in pockets between the layers to form regular patterns. Any number of different air patterns could be produced, but the commonest were a herringbone pattern and diamond quilting. America, England and Bohemia all manufactured very similar satin glass.

Molten glass has been applied to vessels as a form of ornamentation since glass-making began, but seldom has this decorating technique been more popular than it was in the last twenty years of the nineteenth century, particularly in Stourbridge. The development of threading machines in the 1870s enabled fine threads of glass to be wound round the body of a vessel with new speed and precision. Threading could be used on its own or combined with other techniques. At Stevens and Williams, for instance, simple floral patterns were engraved with the intaglio wheel through fine crystal threading. Another striking effect created by Stevens and Williams was 'tapestry', in which the glass, after being threaded, was enamelled and gilded. The threading broke up the evenness of the decoration, giving the impression of the weave of a tapestry.

Unfortunately not all forms of applied ornament were as subdued as threading. All sorts of naturalistic designs were applied to glass, including acanthus leaves, fish, reptiles, flowers and even life-size strawberries and other fruits. One of the most elaborate designs was matsu-no-ke, registered by Stevens and Williams in 1884, which consisted of Japanese-style rustic branches dotted with daisy-like flowers, which twisted round the article to which they were applied, and also formed a stem or a foot.

Matsu-no-ke was designed by John Northwood, who between 1882 and 1902 was Artistic Director at Stevens and Williams. During this period the firm developed several other unusual effects including metal deposit, whereby a film of metal such as copper was deposited by means of an electric current on glass that had first been painted with a metallic flux, and silveria, in which silver foil was embedded between two layers of clear glass. Silveria was invented by Northwood in conjunction with his son, but perhaps his greatest success was 'moss agate', which he introduced in the late 1880s. Moss agate consisted of an inner layer of soda glass which was cased in lead glass and then rolled in powdered glass of different colours to simulate the markings of natural moss agate. The glass was then cased again with lead crystal and after it had been shaped water was poured into the interior

which caused a crackle effect in the soda-glass lining. In Paris, Rousseau and Léveillé were also experimenting with internal colouring and crackle effects at this time. Stevens and Williams' moss agate comes at the end of a long tradition of glass imitating semi-precious stone, but it was one of the most successful.

Northwood's most gifted colleague at Stevens and Williams was Frederick Carder (1863-1963), the son of a Brierley Hill potter, who joined the firm in 1881 as designer in charge of shapes and applied decorations. Carder played a part in many of the new varieties of glass being developed at Stevens and Williams, including moss agate, and might have been the man to lead British glass into the exciting new areas being explored by Gallé in France and Tiffany in America. Unfortunately, on the death of John Northwood in 1902, Carder failed to obtain the position of Artistic Director at Stevens and Williams. In disappointment he emigrated to America, where he was able to give free rein to his inventive genius.

Moss agate was one of the original and exciting types of glass produced in England in the late nineteenth century. It has a modern appearance, not unlike today's studio glass. Unfortunately, rather than heralding the start of an exciting new era, moss agate marked the close of a chapter in the history of English glass.
Height: 13.3cm (5¼in)
(Broadfield House Glass Museum, Kingswinford)

CHAPTER EIGHT

ART NOUVEAU GLASS

Tiffany eighteen-light pond-lily lamp with Favrile glass shades and bronze lily-pad base, c. 1900. The design of this lamp won a gold medal at the 1902 Turin World Fair; variations of it include a floor model and smaller table lamps with fewer shades.

Glass lent itself well to the concept of Art Nouveau, an international style of decoration that matured steadily through the 1890s, reaching its peak at the turn of the century, and continuing to be fashionable until the end of the following decade. Its sources were the artistic ideals preached by William Morris, the oriental flavour of the Aesthetic Movement, and the mysticism of the Pre-Raphaelite and symbolist painters. There were two main decorative styles in Art Nouveau, and both of them were expressed in glass. The one most commonly associated with the movement, and developed in France and Belgium, drew its inspiration from nature, and created a decorative idiom by exaggerating the curvilinear shapes of plant forms, with stems and tendrils twisting almost beyond recognition in labyrinthine patterns. These distortions were meant to express the emotional force of nature. The second style, 'the linear two-dimensional and symbolic conception of Art Nouveau', reached the apex of restrained geometric elegance in the work of the Glasgow School led by Charles Rennie Mackintosh and, where glass was concerned, more particularly in the work of the Vienna Secession movement as seen in the artefacts produced for the 'Secession' exhibitions by the Wiener Werkstätte.

The best glass of the Art Nouveau period was exhibited at national and international industrial fairs, where master craftsmen displayed their finest wares in the hope of attracting a wider audience. The most famous fairs celebrating the turn of the century were the Universal Exhibition in Paris in 1900 and the major International Exhibitions at St-Louis and Turin in 1901. There were also smaller annual 'arts and crafts' exhibitions in Europe, England and America. The work shown at these was publicized in a rash of art and decorative arts journals that were brought out towards the end of the century, the most comprehensive being *Studio* magazine in England, *Art et Décoration* in France, and *Deutsch Kunst und Dekoration* in Germany.

Cameo glass in double and triple layers was the most popular type of glass during the Art Nouveau period. The freedom and depth of expression achieved in this medium by Emile Gallé are remarkable by any standards: Gallé was without doubt the most outstanding glass artist of this period, perhaps even the greatest of all time. His artistry inspired many others to work in the same medium, particularly in the glass-producing area around Nancy, where he had his own workshops. Elsewhere, notably in Austria and America, iridescent glass was very fashionable. German glass of this period is best known for the quality and imagination of its enamelled decoration. Two other important innovations belong to this period: in America, Louis Comfort Tiffany adapted stained-glass techniques to create his famous leaded-glass lamps; and in France the *pâte-de-verre* process (in which ground glass was worked as a paste and fired like an enamel) was refined—by Daum, Décorchemont and Argy-Rousseau—to create jewel-like vases and sculptures. The combination of new techniques and a new decorative language, at the turn of the century, brought about major changes in the glass industry and in glass artistry. During the Art Nouveau period the long-established traditions of stuffy Victorian design were finally broken, and the birth of a truly modern movement, full of vitality and originality, heralded the arrival of the twentieth century.

Emile Gallé in his studio: a portrait by his artist-friend Victor Prouvé, 1892. Gallé, shown working on a cameo vase, is surrounded by botanical specimens, the main source of his inspiration. (Musée de l'Ecole de Nancy)

Emile Gallé

Emile Gallé (1846-1904) was born in Nancy and, apart from a few years abroad during his student days, spent his whole life there. His father owned a glass and faience factory in Nancy, the capital of the former Duchy of Lorraine, where there had been a strong tradition of fine glass-making since the sixteenth century, and which, during the Art Nouveau period, enjoyed world-wide fame for its industrial achievements. Since his childhood, Gallé had been fascinated to the point of obsession by the plant and insect world, not only in the richness and detail of design in nature but in its symbolical and emotional force. Gallé studied philosophy and botany in Weimar from 1862 till 1866, and after working for a time in the glass industry at the firm of Burgun, Schwerer & Co. in Meisenthal (the only German factory to

produce cameo glass in the Art Nouveau style) and at Saint-Clément, he set up his own glass workshop in Nancy and joined forces with his father, who stepped down as head of the family business in 1874.

Emile Gallé's personal philosophy was carved into the doors at the entrance to the factory: 'Ma racine est au fond des bois' ('My roots lie in the heart of the woods'). His outlook on life can best be described as that of a 'poet-industrialist', who believed that poetry could find expression through industry. From the first, Gallé's vases were enormously successful, and his well-run factory, which had about 300 employees at the height of its production, catered for the growing demand among collectors, museums and the retail trade. Gallé opened several of his own retail outlets, including 'L'Escalier de Cristal', at 12 rue Richier in Paris during the 1880s, and a shop on South Molton Street in London, opened shortly before his death in 1904. His work was also exhibited at the Paris gallery of interior decoration 'La Maison de l'Art Nouveau' (owned by art dealer Siegfried Bing) from the time it opened in 1896. Gallé reached his widest audiences at the exhibitions held by 'L'Union Centrale de L'Art Décoratif', (particularly in 1878 when he first showed his work there, and also in 1884 and 1889), and the high point of his career was his success at the 1900 Paris Universal Exhibition. The Gallé factory produced faience as well as glass in its early days, and went on to make exquisite pieces of carved and inlaid furniture from Gallé's own designs.

Gallé's main interest, however, was as a poet and technician in glass. He often incorporated poetic quotations into his designs, and began befriending poets early in his career (the poet Victor Prouvé was a lifelong friend and associate). Gallé was much moved by the symbolist poets and his vases bear quotations from Poe, Baudelaire, Mallarmé and Maeterlinck. Later in Gallé's life, Robert de Montesquiou became a close personal friend.

At the beginning of his career Gallé looked to enamelled glass either in the medieval or the Islamic style for inspiration. He was influenced by two contemporary and highly regarded glassworkers, Philippe-Joseph Brocard (fl. 1867-90) and Eugène Rousseau (1827-91). Rousseau experimented with colour and technique, in particular the artistic effects of internal crackling as a decorative device. (One of his pupils, Ernest Leveillé, became his associate and successor during the 1880s.) But these artists did not develop their style, whereas Gallé's style changed and evolved throughout a career spanning nearly forty years. His taste also leaned in his early work towards rococo design which surrounded him at its most elegant and elaborate in the architecture of his native Nancy. The early pieces used transparent glass with rich polychrome enamelling, and from the very first designs incorporating plants and insects were used. Later on, perhaps after a visit to London in 1872 when he saw oriental artefacts at the Victoria and Albert Museum and learnt about decoration in the aesthetic taste, he was much taken with Chinese and Japanese styles, and even devised an almost illegible vertical signature in tremulous distorted characters resembling Japanese ornament. There were also some straight borrowings, as in a series of scent bottles with stoppers.

Gallé's most important innovation, though, came with the introduction of his technique of cameo decoration. The influence for this was again oriental: the idea was derived directly from Chinese cased-glass vases of the Ch'ien Lung period. The cameo technique is basically one where an object is built up of two or more layers of differently coloured glass fused together, and after being moulded or blown a pattern is painted in outline on the body of the glass; the painted areas are then covered with an acid-resistant bitumen (Bitumen of Judaea) and the vases dipped several times (according to the varying depths of cutting required) in acid baths. The acid eats into those areas not protected by the bitumen, exposing the colours of the layers beneath. The vases are finished by being polished on large emery wheels. Using this medium, Gallé developed his own unmistakable style and, by extending these already known techniques of cameo glass, created complex technical innovations. These included mould-blown 'blowout' vases with two and three layers of glass, the *marqueterie de verre* technique whereby, in a process based on wooden marquetry, shaped and coloured lumps of glass were pressed into the heated body of the glass and then carved and finished when the glass was cold, and also techniques of applied glass, where three-dimensional sculptural glass objects or shapes were applied to the body of the glass while it was still hot. By the 1890s all influences had become incorporated into a deeply original style which has led to Emile Gallé being described as pre-eminent in this field, and his name to being almost synonymous with Art Nouveau.

At the factory the work was clearly divided into the simplest industrial pieces of cameo glass, the more complicated limited editions, and the very complex *pièces uniques*. All designs were executed by Gallé in his atelier on the premises, and carried out with varying degrees of skill by his work-force. The industrial pieces were

Perfume bottle with carved and applied decoration, by Emile Gallé, the form and ornament of Chinese inspiration. This is a fine example of an 'artistic' as opposed to an industrial Gallé piece.

decorated with flowers and insects in the Art Nouveau manner and, generally speaking, the more complex their colouring, techniques and design, the greater is their interest to the collector and connoisseur. The more complicated refinements of hand-carving, fire-polishing, or *martelé* effects varied in quality according to the refinement and skill of the individual craftsman doing the work.

The most outstanding pieces are naturally those which Gallé worked himself. His own craftsmanship was confined to pieces in which he alone could express himself artistically and indulge in technical showmanship. Many of these are examples of the Art Nouveau style at its most luxuriant. From the 1880s onwards, Gallé had experimented with colouring, veining and other internal effects such as inclusions of metal foil. His colouring effects, covering a wide range

of subtle tonings, were achieved as a result of experiments with various oxides.

Among the more remarkable of Gallé's pieces are those in which the conception has a surrealist feeling well in advance of its time. This is seen in a series of vases with applied decoration, where the applications look like melting wax. Sometimes the designs are floral in inspiration, as in the series of *Roses de France* vases, but in many instances the decoration is in the form of abstract drippings with only the vaguest figurative connections. They have a strong emotional presence, and sometimes a forceful ugly quality anticipating the melting flesh of a Francis Bacon painting.

There are also examples of surrealist sculptural creations, including a hand dripping in seaweed and with shell-like encrustations, and one of his most famous pieces, the mushroom lamp, *Les Coprins*, in which three giant mushrooms made of glass (in some places five layers deep) are set in a wrought-iron base to form an electric lamp, the caps acting as lamp-shades beneath which weak electric light bulbs give the whole an almost sinister internal glow. Imagery such as this completely changed the aesthetics of glass within a single decade, and created a fashion and considerable demand for Gallé's highly original style.

Daum Frères and the École de Nancy

Gallé's ideas seemed like prophetic teachings to many other glass-makers, who felt compelled to follow his lead. His work thus served as the chief inspiration for European Art Nouveau glass artists. Among those who used his idiom, by far the most successful were the Daum brothers, whose factory was at Nancy, where it is still run today by the Daum family. The company was founded in 1870 by Jean Daum, an exile from Alsace after the Franco-Prussian war. He started by manufacturing utilitarian glass such as window-panes and watch-glass, but the company did not prosper under the direction of its founder. At Jean Daum's death in 1885 two of his six children, Auguste (1853-1909) and Antonin (1864-1930) took over, and under their direction the company's fortunes flourished.

Artistic production began in 1890, and Art Nouveau glass in the manner of Gallé was made by the brothers until 1925. Of the two, Antonin was the artist. Less of a poet at heart than Gallé, he studied nature for its visual rather than its spiritual beauty. For him the magic lay primarily in colour, and in capturing the exact shade of a poppy or a sunflower. Symbolism was fashionable, but the symbolism of Daum glass is traditional, a symbolism based on logic rather than poetry: for example, a cameo lamp is decorated with bats flying away at the approach of light. Antonin Daum, writing of the principles of the company in 1903, spoke of their 'study of living things, love of truth, a return to intellectualism, to poetic feeling in decoration, to logical principles of design and decoration'.

Early Daum art glass had mainly heraldic decoration such as rampant lions or the cross of Lorraine. The decoration was finely painted in enamels highlighted with sporadic gilding. Before 1890, objects were mainly utilitarian, and included jugs, scent bottles and ring-holders. Then, as the influence of Art Nouveau design grew stronger, shapes became more organic and the decorative idiom came from the 'language of flowers'. The first showing of artistic Daum glass was at Chicago in 1893, and the first major prize was awarded at the 1900 Paris Exhibition. Until then, only small technical differences and a slightly different treatment of subject-matter had distinguished Gallé from Daum. For instance,

Daum made more use of the *martelé* technique for background to decoration, in the belief that this multi-faceted surface gave more life to the body of the vase as the light hit it. It was not until the first decade of the twentieth century, however, that Daum glass developed a strong identity of its own.

Towards 1900 there were several important developments. The most important one, and the one which made Daum stand out from other kinds of glass, was a mottled effect achieved by rolling the hot glass in coloured powdered glass; the powders adhered to the body of the glass and melted again in the heat of contact, providing a new layer of glass. This technique was used both for the body of the glass, providing a rich background to cameo decoration, and, particularly effectively, for the modelling of detailed sculptural applied decoration such as insects,

Right: A sculptural vase decorated with gourds, executed in the Daum factory in 1910. The remarkable life-like quality has been achieved by using pâte-de-verre *in combination with blown glass.*
Height: 53cm (20 15/16 in)

Below: Two goblets by Daum with acid-etched and enamelled decoration of the cross of Lorraine and rampant lions, c. 1893. The heraldic decoration precedes the better-known Art Noveau floral decoration. The cross of Lorraine was often used as part of the Daum signature.
Heights: 11 and 15cm (4 3/8 and 6in)

shells and buds, or clusters of fruit. In a few instances it could reproduce an almost surreal and lifelike texture, as in some of the glass gourds made by Daum.

Another speciality, particularly suited to landscape decoration, was a process called *intercalaire* whereby there was decoration between the layers of the glass as well as on the surface. This device was used to reproduce the effect of a snowscape or heavy rain, giving the decoration remarkable depth and perspective. There were thirty-eight vases of this type shown at the 1900 Exhibition. The process was complicated and hazardous, because the fact that

there were two layers of cameo decoration meant that the first had to be covered with a glass skin which had to act as the surface for the second layer of decoration.

Daum's further experiments with vitrified powders led to two important discoveries. The first was seen in a series of opaque vases known as *céramique de jade*. By rolling the glass in a carefully controlled pattern of coloured glass powders, the opaque surface resembled a complicated ceramic glaze, whose decoration was abstract in imitation of precious minerals such as jade or amber. The effect was heightened by the inclusion of gold foil which shattered into

Three Daum vases, made using the intercalaire *technique, 1900-03. In this technique, which created a remarkable depth of perspective, atmospheric effects, for instance mist or rain, were achieved by carving on an intermediate layer of glass that was then reheated and covered with another layer of glass, which was itself treated with etching or carving. Heights: 23, 20.4 and 30cm (9, 8 and 12 in)*

Dish with lizard poised ready to spring, executed in pâte-de-verre *by Almeric Walter for the Daum factory, 1912.* Pâte-de-verre *was well suited to convey the scaly quality of fish and reptiles, which were popular subjects among sculptors in this medium. Diameter: 25 cm (9⁷/₈ in).*

small particles when the glass was blown. These strange experimental pieces are rare and highly prized, but more remarkable for their technical achievement than for their beauty. The second discovery was more far-reaching, providing a glass substance known as *pâte-de-verre*, from which sculpture could be moulded with immense subtlety of colouring and with detail remarkable for its definition. Antonin Daum called *pâte-de-verre* 'the greatest discovery of our time in art glass, never hinted at in glass-making of any previous period, and a discovery France can be proud of'.

The *pâte-de-verre* process is a progression from transparent enamels. Powdered glass, flux and colouring agents are fused and fired in a mould, to produce sculptured and unusual colour effects. It was actually known in ancient Egypt, and revived by Henri Cros (1840-1907), who experimented with pastes containing powdered glass in the course of his work at the Sèvres porcelain factory; and George Despret (1862-1952) also worked in this medium. The first Daum *pâte-de-verre* sculptures and vases date from 1906, when Almeric Walter joined the firm after his studies at the Ecole de Sèvres. He did the designs and collaborated with the glass technician H. Bergé at Daum; the pieces worked by this team usually bear both their signatures. The sculptures were made in sectional moulds. At first, small classical sculptures were produced, copies of Tanagra figures in a single colour. As confidence grew, their modelling became bolder and more original, and the best pieces are the small jewel-like animal sculptures, with animals nestling in their natural habitat, and vases encrusted with naturalistic subjects. Flat pieces of *pâte-de-verre* were also made, in the first place as small panels intended to

fit in wooden trays, then as larger panels for *vitrines* (glass cases), cupboards and screens, and eventually this medium was used for church windows. Jacques Gruber made a name for himself with his designs for *pâte-de-verre* panels.

Daum has produced *pâte-de-verre* pieces continuously since 1906, with styles changing according to fashion. During the Art Nouveau period there were others working in *pâte-de-verre*, including Argy Rousseau and François Décorchemont, who both excelled in the medium. Décorchemont came to it after having already achieved considerable success as a potter and painter. He started working in glass only in 1904, at his own factory.

The glass produced around Nancy became known as Ecole de Nancy. Apart from Gallé and Daum, there were a number of smaller firms such as d'Argental, Delatte and Legras, working to meet the growing demand for cameo glass in the Art Nouveau style. Because they were imitators rather than originators, their work is less interesting, though it is often as accomplished. The Müller Brothers, for example (both of whom had their training under Emile Gallé), turned out some exquisite pieces of art glass at their factories in the nearby centres of Lunéville and Croismaire.

The new spirit in glass spread beyond France, and was expressed in a distinctive style by the Moser glassworks at Karlsbad, Bohemia, which reacted eagerly to the ideas introduced by Gallé. Founded in 1857 by Ludwig Moser, the company specialized during the Art Nouveau period in the very deep cutting of curvilinear floral designs, sometimes heightened with gilding. This was done either on a clear, heavy crystal body or sometimes on glass with an amethyst or pale green tint. The Ecole de Nancy influence was also felt in Belgium, where the leading company was Val-St-Lambert at Seraing-sur-Meuse. This was a large concern, recorded in 1894 as having 4500 employees, and making decorative glass of all sorts. It first exhibited pieces in the Art Nouveau style in 1897 at the Brussels World Fair. The chief designer at Val-St-Lambert for nearly forty years (1888-1926) was Léon Ledru, who had studied at the Ecole des Beaux-Arts in Paris; he worked in a variety of styles, but during this period before the First World War he copied the Ecole de Nancy. The Müller brothers worked at Val-St-Lambert in 1906 and 1907 before setting up their own glass company, and are reputed to have made around 400 pieces during their term of employment there. However, the most original work to come from Val-St-Lambert was a series of vases with abstract decoration created by the Belgian architect-designer Henry van der Velde, who in 1895 had played a part in the design of the influential Paris gallery 'La Maison de l'Art Nouveau'.

Tiffany and his Followers

There was one other major development during the Art Nouveau period, and that was in iridescent glass. The great innovator was the American glass designer Louis Comfort Tiffany (1848-1933), whose work was first seen by Europeans at exhibitions in the last years of the nineteenth century, and widely copied both in Europe and in America. He was the son of a New York jeweller whose firm, Tiffany & Co., was founded in 1837, and the Tiffanys could trace their ancestry back to 1660 when Squire Humphrey Tiffany settled in Massachusetts Bay Colony. Much to his parents' surprise, Louis Tiffany became absorbed by the study of art. He studied informally under the landscape painter George Inness, and after only a year had a painting chosen for exhibition at the National Academy of Design, in 1867. The following year he went to Paris to continue his studies under Léon Bailly, doing mainly exotic landscapes and genre paintings in the fashionable Near Eastern styles. He continued to work as a painter but found that his interests were becoming wider,

Left: Iridescent lustre vase with peacock-feather decoration, Tiffany Studios, c. 1900. (Manchester City Art Gallery)

Below: A group of pâte-de-verre objects by Argy Rousseau and Almeric Walter. In the Art Nouveau period a number of artists used pâte-de-verre to make small sculptural pieces and vases with relief decoration, the medium allowing remarkably subtle gradations of colour. Diameter of large plate: 28.2cm (11⅛ in) Diameter of small dish: 15.5cm (6⅛ in) Heights: 21-31cm (8¼–12¼ in)

and chose the whole field of the decorative arts as his profession, remarking that there was 'more in it than painting pictures'.

After his return to New York in 1879, he formed a partnership with two other associates and formed a company, Louis C. Tiffany and Associated Artists, which created a style that became known for its 'unborrowed, individual look'. The company designed interiors with an exotic and colourful atmosphere that drew heavily from unrelated styles, partly oriental, partly medieval, with hanging lamps in mosque-style and stained-glass windows. Tiffany's most prestigious job was the redecoration of the White House in 1883, and this and many other lavish commissions from millionaire clients allowed him to indulge his interests. Gradually these came to be more and more focused on the manufacture of glass for decorative purposes, and after various abortive attempts he started his own glass company at Corona, Long Island, in 1893.

Although the name Tiffany is now synonymous with glass, the man himself was by no means solely responsible for the reputation that accompanies his name. He was a moderately successful painter and an adventurous experimenter in glass chemistry, but his enormous success was due to his ability, as an inspired ruler of a business empire, to surround himself with outstanding talent and use it to full advantage. As 'director of productions' he did not believe in promoting other individual talents, but preferred to give himself star billing, even though a great measure of his success was directly due to his team of talented craftsmen and designers. There were three main areas of glass-making in which the company excelled: stained glass, Favrile glass, and leaded glass.

Where stained glass was concerned, Tiffany's main preoccupation was with technique. His own designs were either purely geometric or landscape subjects related to his work as a painter, but he was equally happy to translate designs by other artists into glass, using his own method of making stained glass, as in the case of the series of windows executed by Tiffany after designs by the Nabi painters and installed at Bing's 'La Maison de l'Art Nouveau' in 1895. Tiffany had been struck by the poor quality of contemporary stained glass, and made the following observation:

> The glass used for claret bottles and preserve jars was richer, finer and had a more beautiful quality in colour than any glass I could buy. So I set to puzzling out this curious matter and found that the glass from which bottles are made contained the oxides of iron and other impurities which are left in the sand when melted.

He conducted endless experiments with combinations of metal oxides to achieve every possible colour gradation, aiming to outdo the brilliant colour effects of medieval stained glass. To achieve additional depth in what was essentially a very flat medium, he introduced jewel-like lumps of glass in brilliant colours, and wrinkled glass that would catch the light. The fabric of Tiffany windows, made up of flat, wrinkled, bulging or concave pieces of glass, is richer than any stained glass that went before it, and used a technique akin to a jeweller's art of setting stones within a solid framework. An article in *The American Arts Review* in 1881 stated:

> He has carried the use of pure mosaic farther, perhaps, than it has ever been carried before. Mr Tiffany has shown that many of the most beautiful passages of landscape can be better represented in glass than in paint. Effects of rippled or quiet water, sunset and moonlit clouds, mysterious involutions of distant hills and woods, are given with a force and suggestiveness impossible in any other material.

Tiffany wanted to eliminate brushwork from his windows, and in an article written in 1917 for *Harper's Bazaar* commented:

> I could not make an inspiring window with paint. By the aid of studies in chemistry and through years of experiments I have found means to avoid the use of paints, etching or burning, or otherwise treating the surface of the glass so that now it is possible to produce figures in glass of which even the fleshtones are not superficially treated, built up of what I call 'genuine glass' because there are no tricks of the glassmaker needed to express flesh.

Tiffany conducted his experiments at the Heidt Glasshouse in Brooklyn. John La Farge, the other outstanding stained-glass artist of the period, was also working there at the time. At first they exchanged ideas and discoveries, but eventually became fierce rivals. In 1880 Tiffany had attempted to set up his own glass studios, employing a Venetian master-blower who had worked previously at Salviati of Murano. But after two disastrous fires, he went back to the Heidt Glasshouse and did not start his own furnace till he opened the studio at Corona, Long Island, in 1893. Before this date Tiffany was occupied principally with stained glass and any other decorative glass that could be used in his interior-design projects, such as glass tiles and jewel-like light-fixtures, either flat, round or faceted, which were incorporated into light-fittings, where the wonders of recently invented electricity could create brilliant sparkling effects as the light bounced off a variety of different glass surfaces.

When Tiffany set up his own glasshouse at Corona, he employed an Englishman, Arthur Nash, who had previously worked for one of the leading British pioneers of modern glass, Thomas Webb of Stourbridge. Nash supervised the building of the factory at Corona and was to spend the rest of his working life there. His influence on the development of iridescent glass, later called Favrile glass, cannot be overestimated.

The name 'Favrile' was adopted for the hand-blown art glass pieces which Tiffany started making when the factory at Corona was established. The name is taken from the word *fabrile*, meaning hand-made or hand-crafted. Its iridescent surface was produced by being treated while hot with metallic salts which were absorbed into the glass, creating a metallic lustre. Tiffany had long been obsessed by iridescence; as early as 1880 he had taken out a patent for making decorative iridescent glass. It was not a new discovery; during the second half of the

View of Oyster Bay, stained glass window from the Tiffany Studios, commissioned for the William Skinner House in New York, c. 1905. (The Morse Gallery of Art, Winter Park, Florida)

nineteenth century, a number of European glass manufacturers had registered patents for their own particular forms of iridescence. Tiffany was, however, exceptionally inventive in his application of this technique as an artistic device, achieving dazzling colour effects.

The discoveries Tiffany had made in his stained-glass experiments, combined with the talents of Arthur Nash, resulted in some beautiful pieces. Tiffany shipped the first results to Bing in Paris, and Bing's reaction was one of amazement that it was still possible to create something new from glass, even after so many previous achievements. The partnership between Nash and Tiffany was a most creative one, and Nash became in a sense Tiffany's 'blowing-arm', using his glass-blowing skills to turn Tiffany's chemical discoveries into decorative art. A visitor to the studio in the late 1890s commented on the '5000 colours and varieties' kept in the stock room. The various kinds of iridescence came to have special names such as 'lava' glass, 'nacreous' ware and 'cypriot' glass. These particular varieties depended on their decoration for 'studied' accidental effects—but other forms of decoration demanded a high degree of control, particularly where the decoration depicted a specific kind of flower. In some such vases a technique traditionally associated with the

Left: 'Cypriot' vase by Louis Comfort Tiffany, c. 1892. Several names were used by Tiffany & Co. to describe the special iridescent effects inspired by the nacreous surface of ancient glass that has been naturally oxidized. Height: 14cm (5½in)

Below: A group of fine Tiffany flower-form vases in Favrile glass, c. 1900. These always bear the engraved initials of Louis Comfort Tiffany as well as a model number and, sometimes, the original printed paper label.
Heights: 29.4-40.2cm (11½in–15¹⁵⁄₁₆in)

manufacture of paperweights was employed.

The basic technique used in Favrile glass was to charge the hot ball of iridescent glass at certain pre-arranged points with small quantities of glass of different colours. In this operation was hidden the germ of the intended ornamentation. The ball was then returned to the furnace before being subjected once more to similar treatment, the process sometimes being repeated as many as twenty times. When all the different glasses had been combined and manipulated in different ways to create the finished article, the motifs introduced into the original ball of molten glass could be seen to have grown with the vase itself, but in different proportions. The kaleidoscopic effects that could be achieved by this method were endless. Some vases were also cut and ground, and some etched, but these carefully controlled techniques form the essential qualities of Tiffany Favrile glass. Shapes were either traditional vase shapes, sometimes with an 'organic' twist in line with current fashion, or Tiffany swan-neck vases which were copies of Persian rose-water sprinklers, or flower-form vases like the jack-in-the-pulpit vase (named after an American flower) which Arthur Nash had probably brought over from Stourbridge.

Tiffany lamps, that is, the standard models which used the stained-glass techniques, first appeared towards the turn of the century. Before this date specially commissioned chandeliers and other light-fittings had been made, notably for the new Lyceum Theatre in New York, the first theatre wholly to use electricity. The table lamps which became a standard production at Tiffany had a bronze base supporting a leaded shade. There were large hanging shades as well as table lamps and floor lamps. They were hardly useful as sources of light, providing a jewel-like glow rather than practical illumination. The bases ranged from simple neo-classical columns to elaborate sculptural fantasies in the form of tree-trunks, lily pads or other suitable subjects that related to the decorated shades. The shades were sometimes purely geometrical, but more often had floral decoration or depicted exotic creatures that seemed strange and magical, glowing in the half-light provided by the dim bulbs inside. Among the most successful models were the dragon-fly lamp (designed by Clara Driscoll), exhibited at the Paris Exhibition of 1900, and the wisteria lamp of 1904 (by Mrs Curtis Freschel). Other successful models included the ivy, the pansy, the daffodil and the geranium. There were also non-representational shades such as those with 'linen-fold' glass panels, and turtle-back lamps, in which lumps of green-blue iridescent glass suggestive of the form after which they were named were mounted in

bronze. The leaded-glass shades came in various sizes, and there were colour variations within each pattern. One of the most famous Tiffany lamps was the lily-cluster model with 'morning-glory' shades in iridescent gold glass. This was designed by Tiffany himself and won a grand prize at the Turin Exhibition of 1902. The original design was made to hold eighteen bulbs, one inside each of the shades, but the model was adapted so that the cluster could be composed of anything from three to twenty shades. The lamps

were immensely popular and a regular feature of American interior design during the first quarter of the century; the genuine ones are rare and highly prized items today.

Not surprisingly, Tiffany had many imitators; one company could not cope alone with the huge demand either for the new leaded lamps or for iridescent glass. Firms like Handel and Duffner & Kimberley designed their own leaded shades, but they were never as varied or as rich in glass content as Tiffany's. The earliest American imitator of the iridescent ware was Martin Bach, who had been among Tiffany's glass-workers at Corona in 1894. He set up his own plant, known

Tiffany dragon-fly lamp, the original model dating from c. 1900. The leaded glass shade, which combines flat stained glass with jewel-like polished 'pebbles', is supported by a gilt bronze base. This lamp, as other models, was produced in various sizes and colour combinations and with different sculptural bases.

Right: Iridescent glass lamp with gilded metal mounts, by Loetz, c. 1900. The iridescent glassware of this German firm, inspired directly by the output of the Tiffany Studios, was of high quality despite being produced in large quantities.

Below: Vase in iridescent lustre glass with iridescent blue decoration, manufactured by the American Quezal Art Glass and Decorating Company, c. 1915. The signature 'Quezal' is etched on the base. Height: 18.5cm (7¼in) (Pilkington Glass Museum, St Helens)

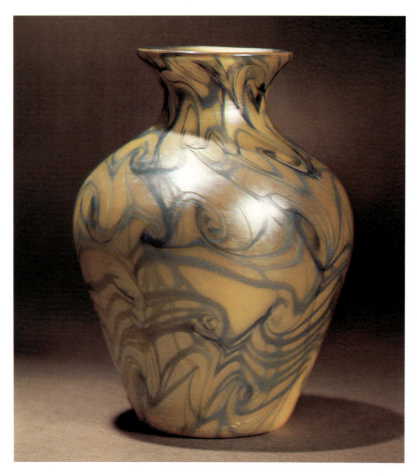

as Quezal Art Glass & Decorating Co., in 1901. Another imitator was Victor Durand, but the most successful iridescent glass apart from Tiffany's was that made by an Englishman working in the United States, Frederic Carder, at the Steuben Glassworks. He developed and began producing, in 1904, a type of cut glass known as Aurene glass, which was usually either iridescent gold or brilliant blue. Tiffany was so incensed by Carder's imitation that he initiated law proceedings against him in 1913, though the matter was settled out of court in the following year.

Tiffany glass was not only widely copied in America; in Europe, particularly in Germany, iridescent art glass was in great demand, and the Loetz glass company, which actually called some of its early iridescent ware 'gläser à la Tiffany' made no secret of the source of its artistic inspiration. Johann Loetz started his company in Klostermühle in 1840, and after his death it was taken over by his widow and became known as 'Johann Loetz Witwe' (*Witwe* = widow). It was Loetz's grandson, Max Ritter von Spaun, who headed the firm during the Art Nouveau period, until his death in 1909. He was appointed artistic director in 1879, and iridescent glassware started to appear at the end of the 1880s. While von Spaun did nothing to hide his debt to Tiffany, the main difference in his approach was that he wished to cater for popular taste and produce artistic pieces that were affordable by all. Two separate patents for iridizing processes were taken out by Loetz in the mid-1890s, by which time Loetz glass had won praise at World Fairs. It was awarded prizes at the Chicago Fair in 1893 and at the Paris World Fair in 1900. After Von Spaun's death many of the designs were executed by the Czech designer Maria Kirschner.

All Loetz glass is of the highest quality; it was made in vast quantities in an infinite variety of colours and shapes. The decoration is hardly ever representational, but depends entirely on the abstract designs created as a result of complex technical formulas. In the best Loetz pieces the colour combinations are exquisite, with intense blues, greens and pinks heightened with silver and gold iridescence. The shapes range from the simplest containers to the contorted, organic shapes of Art Nouveau. Some of the earlier pieces are direct imitations of Tiffany shapes such as the Persian rose-sprinkler and the tulip-form vase. Many names were patented for the different types of abstract decoration, and sometimes, as in the case of 'Papillonglas' and 'Octopusglas', suggested the type of decoration implied by the abstract designs in the glass. More often, the names suggested romanticism, as with 'Orpheus Glas', 'Isis Glas' and 'Phänomenglas'.

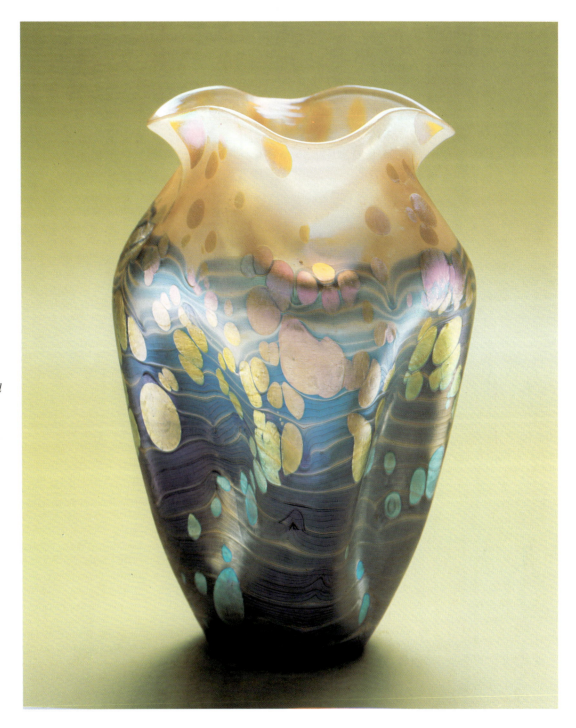

Loetz glass vase in iridescent colours, c. 1900. The iridescent wares produced by the Loetz factory found a ready market in America as well as in Europe.
Height: 18.7cm (7⅜in)

Each separate variety was made according to a special formula, sticking to a particular colour range or a particular range of metallic oxides. Loetz glass is very often unsigned, and a signed piece is not necessarily artistically superior to an unsigned piece. But the silky surface and the intensity of colour, which no other European glass of this type managed to achieve, made it easily identifiable. It is conceivable that a piece of Loetz could pass for Tiffany, but Tiffany pieces are hardly ever unsigned.

There were at least two other German glass companies making iridescent art glass in the style of Tiffany—Pallme König & Habel and Wilhelm Kralik Söhne—but the quality of the glass is not comparable to Loetz. Pallme König & Habel of Steinschönau made iridescent glass that is easily identifiable by the relief net of trailed glass threads used as a decorative device, and by curious forms that are purposely misshapen.

Other Developments in Germany and Bohemia

Apart from this fashion for iridescent glass, there was a strong tradition of enamelled decoration on glass in Germany. The enamelling was usually

black highlighted with other colours, particularly gold. The enamelling was done a little while after the craze for Art Nouveau had died down at the end of the first decade of the twentieth century. One of the best-known enamellers of this period was Karl Massanetz, whose beautiful lace-like patterns are painstakingly applied to the surface of the glass in fine black enamel. The enamellers learnt their art at the various state schools specializing in glass. Two of the most famous of these opened during the 1880s: Fachschule Steinschönau, where Massenetz first studied, was founded in 1880 in the town of that name in northern Bohemia, and Fachschule Haida was founded in 1882. These schools had three-year courses during which all the theoretical and practical knowledge of drawing on glass was taught. The designs of students and professors were produced and retailed by local glass factories, Johan Oertel & Co. at Haida and Friedrich Pietsch at Steinschönau. One other school, founded later in 1904, was Fachschule Zwiesel, which also produced excellent pieces, and flourished under the directorship of Bruno Mauder from 1910 onwards.

One of the most individual glass-workers in Germany during the Art Nouveau period was Karl Koepping (1848-1914) who was both a teacher and a glass artist of remarkable virtuosity. Koepping's iridescent lamp-blown goblets in the form of flowers are paper-thin, fragile ornaments conceived purely as decoration, never intended for use. Their long stems imitate the winding shape of tendrils, and their bowls imitate the shape of a particular bud, often a tulip; sometimes a long thin leaf is applied to the stem. Koepping also made simpler vessels intended as liqueur glasses, although again it is difficult to believe that they were ever meant to be used. The shimmering metallic effect of oxidization adds to the jewel-like quality of these pieces. For a time in the 1890s, Koepping worked in Berlin in close collaboration with the master glass-blower Friedrich Zitzmann, but the collaboration did not work, since Koepping demanded that Zitzmann do nothing more than execute his designs.

Most German and Austrian glass factories gave over a significant part of their production to manufacturing drinking glasses. Throughout its history of glass-making, Germany, like Venice, has had a strong tradition of making fine drinking vessels. During the Art Nouveau period good drinking glasses were produced by Theresienthal & Josephinenhütte but some of the finest (and ones that could actually be used) were produced by the Rheinische Glashütten in Köln Ehrenfeld. They are usually made of thin, pale green glass overlaid with another colour,

either wine-red, indigo-blue or honey-yellow; the overlay is meticulously carved into delicate petal shapes which spread around the goblet from the top of the stem.

The Secessionists

At the turn of the century the Vienna Secession movement broke away, as the name suggests, from the tradition of organic Art Nouveau with a more geometric approach to decoration. The Secessionists were a group of young Viennese artists and architect-designers who felt it was time to rethink the 'spaghetti' Art Nouveau style. They held their first exhibition in 1898, and in 1903 an association of workshops, the 'Wiener Werkstätte', was formed, where artists and craftsmen in different fields of decoration could work side by side, producing artefacts that

Above: Iridescent vase with trailed threading, typical of the glass made at Gebrüder Pallme König & Habel in Bohemia around the turn of the century. (Museum of Decorative Arts, Prague)

Left: Three vases with enamelled decoration and gilding, executed at Steinschönau, c. 1915. This kind of glass has become known as 'Fachschule Glas', as it was executed after designs by students of technical schools.

Right: Two wine-glasses designed by Otto Prutscher (one of the designers of the Wiener Werkstätte) for Meyrs Neffe, 1909. This geometric cameo cut was a new development of a traditional Bohemian cut-glass technique. Heights: 21 and 20.8cm (8¼ and 8⅛ in)

Below: Glass bowl and cover with enamelled design, by Josef Hoffman, c. 1905. Hoffman, primarily an architect, was one of the key figures of the Vienna Secession.

would complement one another and harmonize to form a clean, clear-cut, unified style. In the modern outlook of this Viennese avant-garde, ornament evolved out of functionalism, and gratuitous decoration was frowned upon. Many of the glass-artists involved produced simple geometric shapes, often without ornament of any kind, and their designs were executed by a variety of Austrian and German glasshouses, particularly the Austrian firm of J. & L. Lobmeyr. Josef Hoffmann, who with Koloman Moser was a co-director of the Wiener Werkstätte, executed many glass designs for Lobmeyr, and their simple, functional shapes and lack of ornament must have looked startlingly modern to people who were still essentially Victorians. The Loetz factory also executed some Hoffmann designs which were in striking contrast to their more familiar iridescent ware. (Kolo Moser also designed for Loetz.) In Wiener Werkstätte pieces, shapes were often designed by one hand and any decoration by another. For instance, many of Hoffmann's pieces were decorated by Dagobert Peche. Strangely, the decoration sometimes echoed the Biedermeyer style of around 1820-40, but this combination of a strictly modern shape with romantic decoration could be very effective. The strictest geometric designs were those of Otto Prutscher, whose elegant drinking glasses, executed by the firm of Meyr's Neffe, were usually in clear glass overlaid with a brilliant colour which was then cameo-cut in strong geometric patterns.

The Arts and Crafts Movement and Christopher Dresser

The various trends that led to Art Nouveau design all sprang from a desire to break with the heaviness of Victorian styles. By the time Gallé began his work, this break had already been made by a generation of designers who looked back to Medievalism or who drew their inspiration from the decorative arts of the Middle and Far East. Most historical accounts of the Art Nouveau period cite William Morris (1834-96) as the great innovator. As part of the Pre-Raphaelite brotherhood (founded in 1848) and creator of the Arts and Crafts Movement, his thinking brought about fundamental changes in the principles of decorative design. Both he and Ruskin applied their thinking to every branch of the decorative arts, and Ruskin in particular had very precise theories about glass, criticizing the early

Silver and glass centre-piece, with hallmarks for 1903, designed by Harry Powell for James Powell & Sons of Whitefriars, the English firm for which he was chief designer during the late Victorian period. The design of this piece shows the influence of the English Arts and Crafts Movement and of Art Nouveau.

Victorian preference for cut glass, which, according to another critic in the 1870s, looked more like 'a massive lump of misshapen material better suited to the purpose of braining a burglar than decorating a table'. Ruskin felt that the two chief characteristics of glass were 'its ductility when heated and its transparency when cold, both nearly perfect... All work in glass is bad which does not, with loud voice, proclaim one or other of these great qualities'. Furthermore, as part of his belief that the process of working the

material should not destroy the special qualities of glass he felt that no glass-worker should ever spend more than an hour in making any vessel.

One glass manufacturer in particular, James Powell & Sons of Whitefriars, responded to this impassioned plea for change, and during the late 1850s and 1860s the pioneers of the Arts and Crafts Movement developed a personal friendship with the Whitefriars glass-makers. In 1859 the company was chosen by William Morris to execute glass designs commissioned from the architect and artist Philip Webb for Morris's own home, the Red House, which Webb had designed. When the firm of Morris, Marshall & Faulkner & Co. was founded in 1861 to produce all kinds of decorative objects, Powell glass to Webb's designs and to those of another Arts and Crafts architect, T.G. Jackson, was sold exclusively by them. The revolutionary change, to the Victorian eye, lay in the simplicity of their designs, which had a puritanical tendency towards functionalism and away from ornament. The Arts and Crafts Movement believed above all in honesty both of design and of manufacture, in a move away from industrialization and towards hand-worked craftsmanship. Where glass was concerned this meant that the skill of the blower should be clearly visible in the finished object. There was a definite change towards blown and worked shapes in the

Venetian manner, partly because of the appearance in London of the Venetian glass firm of Salviati, which opened a showroom on Regent Street in 1868.

Powell was quick to respond to these new fashions in glass, and by the 1870s was using many of the traditional Venetian decorative devices such as pincering, moulded fluting, ribbing, filigree and festooning. The fashion for aestheticism also led to the use of Egyptian shapes such as the elegant 'folded' lotus-flower vase.

In 1875 Harry Powell took over as art director and principal designer at Whitefriars, guiding the company's designs sensitively through aestheticism and Arts and Crafts towards Art Nouveau. Although its critics would say that it owed too much to Venice, Powell glass has special qualities which distinguish it from Venetian glass.

Three large stained-glass windows designed by Edward Burne-Jones for Morris & Co., c. 1870. The Burne-Jones Pre-Raphaelite figures stand out against a typically Morris background.

It is subtle in colouring, usually with a pale olive-green tint but sometimes also honey-yellow or pale aquamarine. The green glass often has enamel streaks. During the 1880s and 1890s there was a fashion for finely engraved plant motifs, and towards the end of the century the shapes became more influenced by fully fledged Art Nouveau design, and Powell designed pieces combining metal and glass, achieving a delicate balance between the two. The designs of some of these pieces are closely related to designs by C.R. Ashbee for the Guild of Handicrafts, which was at the centre of the Arts and Crafts movement; the Guild always used the Powell glassworks when a piece included glass, and the Regent Street firm of Liberty & Co. also used Powell for their combined metal and glass pieces designed by Archibald Knox and others. Throughout this period there was also a stained-glass studio at Powell, begun in 1845. It was used by many Pre-Raphaelite artists, notably Edward Burne-Jones, for the execution of their stained-glass designs.

Christopher Dresser (1834-1904) worked in many fields of applied art, and his designs predate those of all who are considered truly Art Nouveau designers. His meticulous study of linear detail in all plant forms broke down the established principles of Victorian design, giving a new freedom of line to the whole of the next generation of artists. His study of plant forms provided the basis for most of his designs, giving them a freshness and originality which makes them look modern even today. Historically Dresser came before Gallé, but his spirit puts him in the avant-garde in a way that Gallé could never be. His ideas of stripping design to bare essentials look far ahead towards the most progressive ideas that were to be developed in the twentieth century.

Dresser's glass designs date from the mid-1880s to the mid-1890s and were executed by James Couper & Sons of Glasgow (who at a later date also executed the designs of the Glaswegian architect-designer George Walton). The glass was known as Clutha Glass; 'Clutha' is the archaic nickname for the River Clyde which flows through Glasgow; the name is intended to evoke the bubbles and fluidity that are characteristic of this type of glass. It often also has white striations and metal foil inclusions which add richness and variety. The Dresser shapes are either original designs inspired by the geometry of the plant world and sometimes direct copies of pre-Colombian, Roman or middle-Eastern shapes which he admired for their clarity of line. A good example of this is the Dresser design based on a seventeenth-century water-sprinkler which Dresser had seen in the

Victoria and Albert Museum. Dresser had two main principles of design: first, that the material should be worked in a manner most befitting its nature; and second, that one must always consider the vessel's purpose when evolving a design. His ideas pointed the way for the designers of Art Nouveau and far beyond. Of his approach to working glass he said:

Let a portion of molten glass be gathered upon the end of a metal pipe and blown into a bubble while the pipe drops vertically from the mouth of the operator, and a flask is formed such as is used for the conveyance of olive oil; and what vessel could be more beautiful than such a flask?... If a material is worked in its most simple and befitting manner, the results obtained are more beautiful than those which are arrived at by any roundabout method of production.

Three 'Clutha' vases designed by Christopher Dresser for J. Couper & Sons, Glasgow, c. 1890-95. 'Clutha' is a reference to an archaic name for the River Clyde that runs through Glasgow. In the economy of his designs, based in many cases on plant forms, Dresser was much in advance of his time.

CHAPTER NINE

GLASS BETWEEN THE WARS

Dish of pâte-de-cristal *by François-Emile Décor-chemont, c. 1920. The design of this piece marks a transition from the forms of Décorchemont's Art Nouveau phase to the more characteristic simple and massive forms he produced in the 1920s and 1930s.*

The turn of the century had marked a high point of creativity in glass. Works of art in glass of unprecedented technical complexity and virtuosity, notably from the workshops of Emile Gallé and Louis Comfort Tiffany, had consolidated the concept of glass as a medium of artistic expression. After the First World War manufacturers and artisans continued this tradition, and during the 1920s and 1930s they experimented with a wide variety of new styles and techniques.

Within this tradition an increasing distinction emerged between the fine object in glass as luxury domestic decoration and the work of art in glass, in which the artist chose glass as an expressive medium, as potentially rich as oil on canvas. The distinction was between the well-designed, expensive, industrially produced luxury multiple and the individually wrought studio creation. This divergence is clearly visible between the productions of René Lalique (1860-1945), a talented designer and successful entrepreneur, and of Maurice Marinot (1882-1960), an artist who abandoned the easel for the furnace, to create vessels which capture his artistic vision.

In the 1920s French decorative artists led the world at every level from cabinet-making to jewellery design, combining a sophisticated inventiveness with the ability to execute designs to the highest possible standards. In glass as in other media the French demonstrated the widest range of skills and devised some of the most stylish forms and decorations, defining and promoting the styles which made France the centre of the fashionable world. In 1925 the Exposition Internationale des Arts Décoratifs et Industriels Modernes, held in Paris, displayed the French nation's supremacy in the applied arts. The name of the exhibition was a source of the term 'Art Deco', used to describe the style that developed at this time.

As well as the host of new talents that emerged in France between the wars, there survived a number of artists and factories with established reputations. In certain instances, such as the creations of the Daum factory and of François Décorchemont, changing times brought new styles and ideas and continued success, while in others reluctance or inability to evolve led to gradual eclipse. The story of glass in France was, above all, however, one of variety and accomplishment.

In the United States, where Tiffany had made so dramatic an impact at the turn of the century, there was little innovation in the production of fine glass objects, the Tiffany style remaining the strongest influence in a declining market. Much of the glass produced in central Europe was equally conservative. The lustre wares which had come into vogue in the Art Nouveau period, especially in Austria, were still being made, and the traditional skills of cutting, engraving and enamelling associated with Austrian and Bohemian manufacturers remained in demand and, under such stylistic influences as that exerted by the decorative designers of the Wiener Werkstätte, found charming and fashionable new decorative repertoires. British glass factories failed to have any real impact in this period, and only two artists, Keith Murray and Clyne Farquharson, distinguished themselves, and in turn brought credit to the glassworks for which they acted as designers.

During this time Scandinavian and Italian factories and workshops emerged as sources of new styles and ideologies, destined to be the most influential forces in the years immediately after the Second World War. The Swedish factories of Orrefors and Kosta, and several of the glassworks of Murano, perhaps most notably the Venini works, laid the foundations of a post-war renaissance.

The role of glass in the context of decorative objects was, however, rather overshadowed by its new and exciting one as a major ingredient of the International Modernist style. Built on theories of functionalism, truth to materials and the alignment of art and industry, and with major precursors as far back as William Paxton, Modernism crystallized in the 1920s, inspiring a new spirit in architecture and design appropriate to the Machine Age. Glass and steel were the key

ingredients in a design ethic which ranked function above all and which, without abandoning stylishness, rejected the traditional view of decoration as an end in itself.

Glass was used dramatically and emphatically in architecture, in interior design, and in the design of furniture and light-fittings. Modernism was first established in Germany and France, in the Bauhaus and in the loose-knit group which included Le Corbusier and which in 1930 was to form the Union des Artistes Modernes. To the Modernists glass meant light, space and optimism. The style found international popularity and, in the United States, where steel-reinforced

Glass bottle and stopper by Maurice Marinot, c. 1925. Marinot, many of whose creations in glass were stoppered bottles and covered jars, has used internal chemical effects and surface enamelling in working this piece. Height: 26.7cm (10½in)

buildings were tentatively being pushed skywards, the futuristic dream of glass towers
reaching up into the sky was to become a reality
with the arrival from Germany of the revolutionary architect Mies van der Rohe (1886-1969), a
former director of the Bauhaus.

New Ventures in France

René Lalique and Maurice Marinot, in their
respective and complementary fields, were the
giants of their era, and comparison of their
oeuvre forms a fruitful basis for the study of glass
between the wars. Both were French. They were
the leading talents in their field, in a country rich
in talent.

Maurice Marinot's glass is the fruit of a
passionate encounter between a fiery artistic
spirit and a fiery and mercurial medium in which
he saw a magically expressive potential. In his
glass vessels, all but the very earliest wrought
entirely by his own efforts, he captured a
powerful abstract poetry of light, colour, texture
and form. In that his achievement represents the
individual triumph of the artist-craftsman in
pursuit of artistic rather than decorative or
functional ends, Marinot's career might be
regarded as the major precursor of the
contemporary Studio Glass movement which
had its specific beginnings in the 1960s.

Marinot, born at Troyes, studied painting at
the École des Beaux-Arts in Paris. In 1905 he
was one of a group to exhibit characteristically
fierce-coloured paintings at the Salon
d'Automne and so acquire the label 'Les Fauves'
('the wild beasts'). Marinot's contemporaries in
the Fauve group included Henri Matisse, André
Derain and Kees Van Dongen. Marinot
continued to exhibit at the Salons until 1913, and,
indeed, to paint throughout his life; but a visit in
1911 to the small glassworks of the brothers
Viard at Bar-sur-Seine was to change the course
of his career.

Seduced by the beauty of the molten metal,
Marinot's first idea was to use glass as his canvas,
and he designed forms for vases and bottles
which were made up by the Viard brothers and
then decorated by Marinot with boldly stylized
flowers and figures in bright enamels. Several of
these early pieces were exhibited at the Salon
d'Automne in 1912 as part of an exhibit
conceived by André Mare. In the following year
Adrien Hébrard, the celebrated bronze-founder
and art dealer, became his exclusive agent,
exhibiting Marinot's glass in his rue Royale
gallery.

Marinot soon determined to learn the skills of
glass-making so as to be able to execute his
designs personally, and the Viards put a bench

*Left: Design for glass
bottle and stopper by
Maurice Marinot,
c. 1925.*

*Below: Bottle and stopper
by Maurice Marinot,
c. 1925. Internal chemical
effects have been incorporated in the deeply cut
green glass.
(Victoria and Albert
Museum, London)*

and tools at his disposal. Marinot's first-hand encounters with the medium soon encouraged a progression from painting decoration on glass to incorporating the decoration within the glass itself. Abandoning enamels in the very early 1920s, he turned his attention to working within the mass, exploring furnace and cold techniques. From using glass almost as a canvas on which to apply a design, he made the important step forward of exploiting its intrinsic sculptural and other qualities of colour, texture and effect. His early enamelled works fall into the category of decorative Art Deco, though executed with a distinctive Fauve gusto. His second phase, after he had abandoned enamels, led to the production of works significant in the history of glass, and in which he created a dynamic and potent abstract art form.

Marinot's reputation as one of France's foremost artist-craftsmen flourished. He was the subject of numerous articles and references in the art press, and the significance of his work was widely recognized by his contemporaries. He exhibited regularly at Hébrard's gallery, and in 1925 enjoyed wide acclaim for his exhibits in the Paris Exposition Internationale. Examples of his glass were included in various exhibition pavilions, notably the Pavillon d'un Ambassadeur, and in the Museum of Contemporary Art designed by Sue et Mare. In the same year he exhibited for the first time in New York.

Marinot's creations fall into certain broad categories. After his initial attempts at enamelling, his vessels were always heavy-walled, the thick glass incorporating internal effects or having a deeply etched decoration. The internal effects ranged from minutely disciplined flights of air bubbles, often with a smoky tint, through streaks of usually muted colour, to his 'sandwich' effects with a layer of colour, speckled and often involving spirals, between inner and outer layers of clear glass. The etched pieces were very deeply acid-cut with aggressive, usually abstract geometric motifs, the acid texturing contrasting with the smooth raised areas to emphasize the effects of light. Certain pieces would be worked at the furnace, with heavy applications of molten glass emphasizing the form. A few pieces were modelled into or applied with formalized mask features. Most of his creations are bottles with distinctive spherical stoppers, and jars with covers; he also made some vases.

The Viard Glassworks closed in 1937. Marinot retired for health reasons, and his distinguished career in glass came to an end. He continued to paint until his death in 1960.

Marinot's vigorous and novel approach inevitably inspired others. Several artists estab-

Heavy glass vase by André Thuret, c. 1925. Thuret, a follower of Maurice Marinot, has used internal chemical effects in this thick-walled creation. Height: 28.5cm (11¼in)

lished their reputations working in the Marinot style, and certain factories enjoyed commercial success with decorative interpretations and derivations of the ideas first explored by him. The most distinguished of his followers were Henri Navarre, André Thuret and Georges Dumoulin. Navarre and Thuret both first experimented with glass in the early 1920s, making heavy-walled clear- or smoky-glass vessels with internal effects, Navarre's usually with a sombre palette, Thuret's more adventurous in colour. Navarre would further decorate his creations with heavy applications, pressed on or wrapped around the body; Thuret would pinch the semi-molten glass into undulating shapes. Dumoulin, a painter and ceramist, made a series of handsome vessels with internal colour and bubble effects and surface applications. The Daum factory produced the best decorative interpretations of Marinot's techniques.

Even more than Daum, René Lalique had the greatest commercial success of all manufacturers of decorative glassware between the wars, and the reputation he established as the world leader in luxury glassware has persisted under the guidance of his descendants. The Lalique showrooms in Paris' prestigious rue Royale still testify to a career which evolved almost by chance.

Lalique started as a designer of jewellery in the Art Nouveau style, and was esteemed as France's most inventive, technically brilliant and innovative jeweller: he won the Légion d'honneur. Then the direction of his interests changed. A distinctive feature of his jewellery was his use of precious and non-precious materials in juxtaposition, and of every type of enamel. No doubt his use of vitreous enamels and of cut glass in his jewellery led to a fascination with glass itself and encouraged his first experiments. In 1902 he set up a small glass workshop with a staff of four, experimenting with the creation of sculptural glass vases cast by the *cire perdue* ('lost wax') method. A wax model was made and encased to form a mould, then the wax was melted and poured away. The mould was filled with glass. Since the mould had to be broken to release the glass and the wax model was also destroyed, each cast was unique. These early casts are now highly prized by collectors.

In 1907 Lalique was commissioned by the perfumer René Coty to design decorative glass bottles for his perfumes. His first designs were manufactured by Legras & Cie, but he soon equipped himself to manufacture his designs himself. In 1909 he bought more extensive premises and started series production. His interest in the creation of the exquisite jewels on

which he had built his reputation gradually waned, and by the outbreak of the First World War he no longer made them. The new direction of his career was consolidated in 1918 when he bought a large factory at Wingen-sur-Moder. After a career making unique, hand-crafted jewels for a tiny but wealthy market, Lalique's determination was now to bring a combination of good design and quality series production to a wider, though still a luxury, market.

Lalique's venture was a great success throughout the 1920s. Major public and private commissions were given him and there was considerable acclaim for his exhibits at the Paris exhibition of 1925. Among his commissions were orders for decorative glass fittings for the luxury liners *Paris* in 1920, and *Île de France* in 1927. In the mid-1930s he was among the leading craftsmen and decorators who made the new liner *Normandie* into a magnificent floating showcase for the applied arts of France. He also designed the glass fountains for the Rond-Point des Champs-Élysées; and Jacques Doucet, the

Glass vase, an early experimental piece by René Lalique, made by the cire-perdue *method, c. 1905-10. Lalique drew on his experience as a jeweller in his application of the* cire-perdue *technique to the creation of sculptural glass vases.*
Height: 12cm (4³⁄₄ in)

1945, his name internationally renowned.

The success of the Lalique venture naturally inspired a number of imitators. Foremost among these was Marius-Ernest Sabino, whose glass-works produced vases and decorative objects in a blue-white opalescent glass similar to Lalique's. Other imitators included André Hunebelle, Paul d'Avesn and the foundry of Etling, whose name is to be found on moulded glass vessels and figures.

The Lalique style found a wide market. By contrast, the 1920s and 1930s were years of decline for many of the glass-workshops in and around Nancy which had made the town an important glass-making centre at the beginning of the century. A notable exception to this decline was the Daum factory, where new techniques and new styles which kept up with changing tastes and fashions ensured its

couturier and a notable patron of the arts, commissioned from him a set of doors with cast panels of naked athletes for his new villa at Neuilly.

Lalique's glass was made in moulds, either by blowing or by pouring the liquid metal. He managed to produce vessels with moulded decorations in exceptionally high relief and with crisply rendered detail. The base glass which he used was of several distinct types. The most characteristic Lalique glass is either colourless, incorporating contrasts of translucent and semi-opaque areas, or opalescent milky white, the milkiness acquiring shades of blue as the piece is turned in the light. Surface staining in the shallows was used to emphasize the decoration in certain designs; others were produced in a variety of strong colours, notably brilliant blue, amber and deep reds, emerald green and, more rarely, black.

The product range was enormous and, in addition to a seemingly limitless variety of vases, included tableware, dressing-table items, jewellery, car mascots, clock-cases, sculptures (including a series of stylized Madonnas and the celebrated 'Suzanne au Bain'), lamps of every description from small table lamps to massive chandeliers, and even decorative glass furniture and architectural fittings. Lalique's decorative repertoire included animal, insect and floral and plant motifs; human, usually female, figures; and exotic mythical beings such as sirens, chimeras and firebirds. The elegant stylization and sophisticated draughtsmanship he had shown in his jewellery was just as evident as he subtly adapted these themes and motifs to the now-fashionable Art Deco idiom.

Lalique worked until 1939, when the Second World War stopped production. He died in

Far left: The interior design of the liner Nor-mandie, which made its maiden voyage in 1935, was a magnificent oppor-tunity to demonstrate the quality of the applied arts in France. The glass panelling and light fittings of the Grand Dining-room were de-signed by René Lalique.

Left: Double doors com-posed of moulded glass panels designed by René Lalique, c. 1920. Similar panels were used by Lalique as early as 1902 in the doors to his own premises.

Right: Pâte de verre figure of a dancing maiden by G. Argy-Rousseau, c.1925.

Right: Two Daum vases of clear glass with vivid coloured bands which have been decorated with a cut floral decoration Heights: 25 and 30cm (9⅞ and 11⅞ in)

Below: Massive Daum glass vase with internal effects and deep etched decoration, c. 1925. Height: 36cm (14⅛ in)

continuing success. Reopened in 1919 under the artistic guidance of Paul Daum, the factory produced ranges of crisply cut cameo vases in an Art Deco style, using bright colour and formalized floral motifs. Its most exciting products were the wide range of vases and lamps deeply etched and roughly textured in a style inspired by Marinot. These pieces, often in colourless glass or in bright blue, yellow or green, incorporated bold geometric motifs; and their impact was all the the greater because they were often very large.

The Gallé workshops, which had inspired other local artists and studios, had lost their inspiration with the death of Emile Gallé in 1904. They continued production after the First World War, and survived until the early 1930s, but the mainstay of their output was a vast quantity of inferior acid-etched cameo-glass vases and lamps which found their way into many homes as wedding gifts. These carried on in a rather uninteresting way the naturalistic decorative themes introduced in previous decades but now increasingly unfashionable. Novel exceptions included 'blow-out' vases decorated with elephants (in which the decoration was in the mould itself, then further emphasized by acid etching), and large vases decorated with polar bears or seagulls. André Delatte set up a workshop in Nancy in 1921, producing cameo glassware derivative of Gallé, and the name Richard is found on similar late pieces.

The firm of Müller Frères at Lunéville near Nancy reopened in 1919, and was successful in the manufacture of mottled-glass light-fittings and moulded vessels with geometric decorations. Jacques Gruber, a founder member of the École de Nancy who had created extraordinary organic sculpted furniture, earned a reputation in the 1920s for his stylish Art Deco leaded glass, which was incorporated into many buildings including the Pavillon d'un Ambassadeur at the Paris exhibition of 1925. Gruber's designs for leaded glass included abstract geometric motifs and stylized figurative subjects such as sporting characters. He did much to free stained glass from its traditional almost exclusive use in churches, and to bring it into domestic and other contexts.

The techniques of *pâte-de verre* (ground glass worked as a paste and fired), which had been revived in the late ninteenth century by Henri Cros, had by the 1920s been developed to allow the relatively large-scale manufacture of high-quality items. Three artists distinguished themselves in this material, each with a quite distinctive approach. Almeric Walter and François-Emile Décorchemont had both experimented well before the war, Décorchemont as early as 1902. Walter had first exhibited in 1903, and Argy-Rousseau showed his first pieces in 1914.

The Walter workshops produced a wide range of decorative objects, some of them also functional, including vases, dishes, pots with covers, book-ends, pendants, statuettes and paperweights. The medium was opaque and colours were dense, usually ranging broadly through greens and blue-greens, ambers and ochres. The most popular decorative themes were insect and animal subjects. Pieces would usually bear the monogram or full name of the sculptor responsible for the piece as well as that of Walter. The foremost of these sculptors was Henri Bergé.

François-Émile Décorchemont had made fine Art Nouveau pieces, at first in a light and delicate *pâte-d'émail* (enamel paste), then in a heavier, more robust *pâte-de-verre*. Through the 1920s he worked in this heavier medium, achieving a difficult combination of massiveness and extreme clarity in pieces, usually vases or bowls, distinguished by their simple shapes and minimal decoration. Décorchemont was the purist among the three artists to work in *pâte-de-verre* in the 1920s and 1930s; he exhibited in the gallery of Georges Rouard and earned the widest critical

'Elephant' vase, manufactured in the Gallé Glassworks, 1920s. The acid-etched decoration of this piece of double-overlay cameo glass has been enhanced by the further relief effect achieved by mould blowing.
Height: 38cm (15in)

acclaim of any of them. His use of colour was as disciplined as that of his form and decoration: most pieces are virtually monochromatic, with streaks of a single colour, often a rich blue, green, tortoiseshell-brown or amethyst, caught in a sea of colourless translucence. In the 1930s he turned his attention to stained-glass windows.

Gabriel Argy-Rousseau in 1921 set up a partnership, Les Pâtes-de-Verre d'Argy-Rousseau, and started manufacture of a wide range of decorative wares. He worked in a thin-walled *pâte-de-verre* and developed a high-grade material of considerable clarity comparable to that evolved by Décorchemont. The material, which has a crystal-like ring when struck, is known as *pâte-de-cristal*. Argy-Rousseau worked successfully throughout the 1920s on the series production in reusable piece-moulds of vases, pots with covers, lamps, pendants,

Pâte-de-cristal bowl by François-Emile Décorchemont, c. 1925-30. Décorchemont had previously produced Art Nouveau pieces in a delicate pâte-d'émail, *and used a heavier medium in the 1920s and 1930s to make pieces of massive and disciplined form and subtle colouring.*

ashtrays, bowls and decorative sculptures and plaques. His colour range included splendid rich purples and mauves, and his decorative themes embraced naturalistic plant and animal subjects, human figures and abstract or highly formalized motifs. Argy-Rousseau's fanciful creations found less favour during the 1930s, though he continued to exhibit until 1952.

These were only a few of a host of fine glass-makers in France. A number of people working in enamelled glass created wares that

perfectly expressed the Art Deco style. The retail firm of Delvaux, with premises in the rue Royale, sold charming enamelled pieces manufactured in the firms's own workshops, the most characteristic being decorated with stylized floral bouquets. The two most inventive enamellists were both closely associated with another highly regarded retail gallery, that of Georges Rouard in the avenue de L'Opéra. Marcel Goupy, artistic director of the firm, designed and supervised production of enamelled wares from 1918 until 1936. He would enamel abstract or figurative designs on clear glass vessels, sometimes with internal colour effects which served as a counterpoint to the surface enamels. Stylized hunters were a favourite theme. Auguste-Claude Heiligenstein worked for four years under Goupy, learning the skills of enamelling, then under his own name in association with various workshops, notably Legras-Pantin with which he worked until 1935. His elaborately decorated vases reflect the Art Deco revival of classical themes. Georges Chevalier designed enamelled wares for Baccarat.

Other manufacturers favoured colouring their glass in the mass. The most prolific was the firm established in 1913 at Épinay-sur-Seine by the brothers Ernest and Charles Schneider, whose wares bear a sometimes bewildering variety of signatures. The cameo or engraved marks 'Le Verre Français', 'Schneider' and 'Charder', or the factory mark of a piece of *millefiori* cane embedded in the surface, are to be found on lamps and vases. Usually large and colourful, these pieces employ techniques including internal bubbles and, most characteristically, mottled internal colour effects. The 'Le Verre Français' mark is found on boldly decorative cameo vases and lamps in two layers of mottled glass etched with broad, formalized designs in contrasting polished and rough textures. The signature 'Degué' is found on mottled glass similar to that of the Schneider works, often in decorative light-fixtures.

One facet of Art Deco was the fashion for geometric patterns with motifs derived from Cubism, and these were adapted to glass by a number of designers, most notably of course by Maurice Marinot. Others evolved a more decorative interpretation, among them Jean Luce, Aristide Colotte and anonymous artists in the Legras workshops. Among the interesting but less well-known talents to emerge in France in the 1920s were the Spanish-born Jean Sala, who experimented with rough-textured blown glass, and who was responsible for a series of free-blown glass fish; and the designer Edouard Cazaux, who created a series of glass vessels with moulded friezes of stylized figures.

The Glass of Other European Countries

During the 1920s and 1930s Scandinavian, and particularly Swedish, glass-designers developed what had been an insignificant industry into a major international influence. This dramatic emergence of the Swedes and their Scandinavian neighbours came through their application of functionalist, Modernist theories to industry and manufacture. While other nations were fighting the First World War the Swedish Society of Industrial Design, Svenska Slöjdföreningen, dating from 1845, engaged in a serious and successful endeavour to apply high design standards to mass-produced wares. The liberal intellectual climate which governed industrial design inspired a freshness and vitality which characterized glass production as it did the other applied arts.

The centre of this new creativity was the glass factory of Orrefors. The factory, originally an iron-foundry, had since 1898 manufactured simple domestic glassware. In 1913 Johan Ekman took it over with the idea of developing new ranges of decorative glass. He took on two designers, Simon Gate in 1916 and Edward Hald in 1917, both of whom brough tremendous new energy and inspiration to Orrefors. They were painters, Gate trained in a classical tradition, Hald a pupil of Matisse, and neither had any previous experience in glass; but they at once understood the potential of the medium and developed a fine repertoire of techniques in collaboration with a team of able craftsmen headed by Knut Bergquist, master glass-blower with Orrefors since 1914.

The two most notable techniques developed by Gate and Hald were Graal and Ariel. Graal glass, developed from the cameo techniques of Gallé, involved further furnace work after the cameo cutting and a final clear casing. These stages combined to give a fluidity to the decoration trapped within the walls of the glass, and this was felt to express better the liquid nature of the medium than did the static quality of Gallé's cameo work. Ariel glass, developed in about 1930, was also a type of cased glass in

Left: 'Pearl Fisherman', engraved glass from Orrefors Glasbruk, Sweden, designed by Vicke Lindstrand, 1934. Lindstrand was designer at Orrefors from 1928 to 1941.

Below: Art Deco glass bottle and stopper manufactured for and retailed by the firm of Delvaux, Paris, c. 1920-25. Height: 28.5cm (11in)

Right: Glass amphora designed by Napoleone Martinuzzi and manufactured by Venini of Murano, 1928-30. Height: 35cm (13¾in)

Far right: Polychrome overlay glass lamp with lightly etched cameo decoration, Czechoslovakia, 1920s. Height: 38cm (15in)

Below: Vase of Graal glass designed by Vicke Lindstrand. In this technique cameo cutting is followed by further furnace work and a final clear casing.

which a pattern was sandblasted on to the body of a vase, making channels and pockets in which air would be trapped by a second casing of clear glass. The effect could be further emphasized with inlays of colour. Ariel was used to considerable effect not only by Hald but also by Vicke Lindstrand, designer with Orrefors between 1928 and 1941, and by Edvin Ohrström.

Orrefors produced fine engraved work in the 1920s in a charming, light and fanciful vein with neo-classical figures and delicate traceries. After 1930 these gave way to simple, bold and dynamic designs including stylized nudes and a series of swimming figures, with deeper engraving on a heavier glass base.

The pattern established by Orrefors of enlisting professional designers to raise the standards of industrial and workshop production was followed in other Swedish and Scandinavian glassworks. The Swedish Kosta factory produced a distinguished range of cut-glass vases designed by Elis Bergh, and designers Sven Ericson, Ewald Dahlskog and Sven Erik Skawonius each made a valuable contribution to the factory's growing reputation. Edvard Strömberg, variously attached to Kosta in 1917 and 1918, to Orrefors until 1928, subsequently to Eda and then working independently from 1933, produced a distinguished range of glass vessels of finely proportioned and restrained forms in subtle tints.

In Norway designer Sverre Pettersen was employed in 1928 by the Hadelands factory. He created designs for simple tableware as well as for engraved and, later, sandblasted decorations in a modern vein. In Denmark the beginning of a new era was marked for the Holmegaard glassworks by the arrival in 1925 of Jacob Bang as resident designer. In Finland perhaps the most worthy application of functionalist ideas to glass production was the range of amoeboid-section vessels designed in 1938 by architect Alvar Aalto for the Karhula-Iittala glassworks.

In the years between the wars certain Italian glassworks, too, were laying the foundation for a renaissance of Italian and, particularly, of Venetian glass with which they would dominate the industry after the Second World War. This Italian revival was inspired above all by two men, Paolo Venini and Ercole Barovier.

In 1921 Venini entered into partnership with Giacomo Cappellin, setting up in Murano a company under the name 'Vetri Soffiati Muranesi Cappellin-Venini e C'. At first Venini concentrated on reinterpreting traditional Venetian forms, making delicate thin-walled vessels, often with applied scrolling handles, knopped stems and broad circular bases, and in lightly tinted glass. In 1925, however, he set up his own

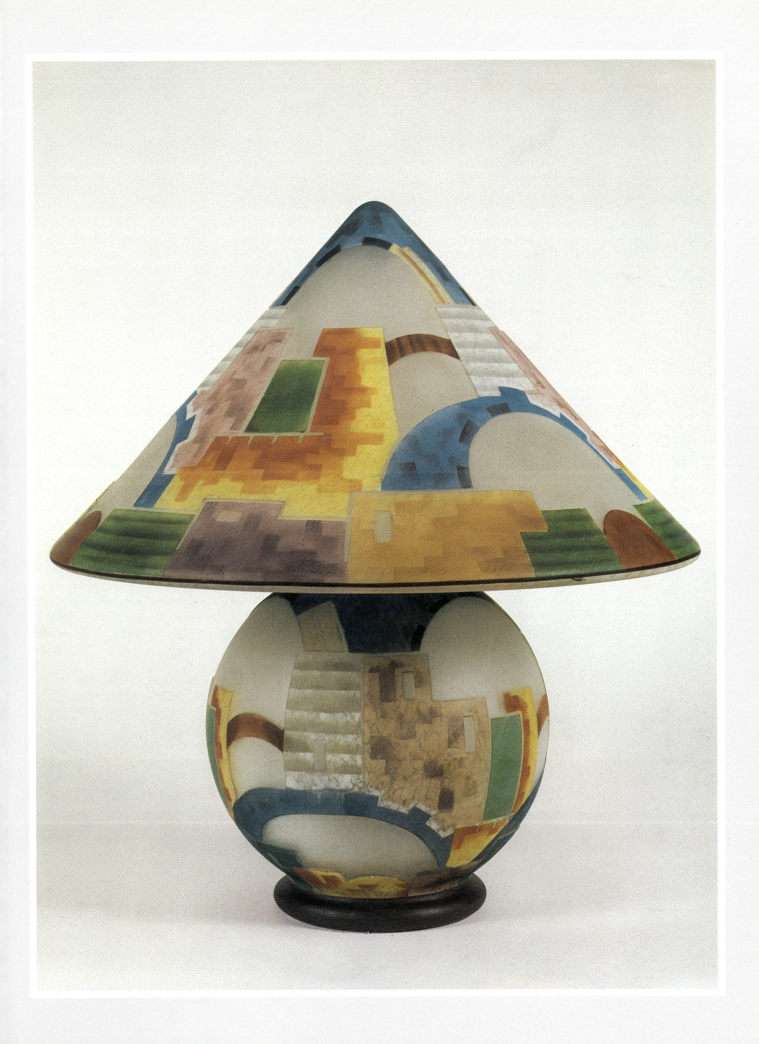

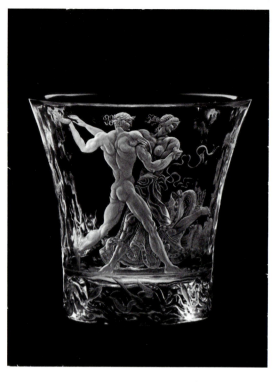

'The Dance', massive glass vase, partly cut and hand polished and with copper-wheel engraved decoration, designed by the Hungarian glass-artist Jaroslav Horejc, 1924.

Cut glass bowl and cover manufactured by Koloman Moser of Karls-bad for the Wiener Werkstätte, c. 1920.

company and his work took a new direction. The forms remained simple but were now influenced by functionalism and Modernism. Venini experimented increasingly with surface textures and internal colour effects. One of his chief designers was Napoleone Martinuzzi who created exuberant sculptural pieces including trees and giant cacti.

Also at Murano was Ercole Barovier, born into a family with a long tradition of glass-making. He distinguished himself by his lively experiments in texture and colour, generally applied to simple, fluid forms. Typical of his effects are *vetro gemmato*, introduced in 1936, glass with a haphazardly pitted surface;

and *vetro rugiada*, introduced in 1940, glass with a surface texture giving the impression of a fine covering of dew-drops. The most prominent Italian designer of engraved decorations for glass was Guido Balsamo-Stella, who treated classical subjects in an Art Deco style. His work was of particularly fine quality.

In Vienna, the avant-garde artists and designers of the turn of the century had given a tremendous boost to all the applied arts. Under the leadership of Josef Hoffmann the city became an internationally important centre of progressive thought and endeavour in architecture and design. After the First World War the earlier crisp, functionalist approach had been largely superseded by a more decorative style. Themes ranged from disciplined scroll-work to whimsical figurative motifs.

The Wiener Werkstätte (see page 215) had their own glass-decorating workshops where technically straightforward pieces could be executed. The two designers whose work best captures the spirit of the Werkstätte in these years were Michael Powolny and Dagobert Peche. Powolny taught at the Vienna School of Arts and Crafts from 1909 until 1941, and is known as a designer of both ceramics and glass. His glass was usually of simple form, enamelled with scattered motifs or disciplined abstract friezes and panels. Dagobert Peche, a member of the Werkstätte from 1915 until his death in 1923, was perhaps the most whimsical of the Vienna group, and worked in every area of decorative design. His most characteristic glass is enamelled with freely placed floral, figurative or graphic motifs on simple forms. Other Wiener Werkstätte designers of note included Mathilde Flögl, Hilda Jesser, Otto Prutscher, Vally Wieselthier and Eduard Josef-Wimmer.

In Germany, Wilhelm von Eiff (1890-1943) was one of the finest glass-engravers of the twentieth century. His work ranged from classical-style pieces to bold, Modernist designs. In 1921 he worked with the noted Viennese engraver Stephen Rath. From 1922 onwards he taught cutting and engraving techniques in Stuttgart, influencing a generation of pupils.

In 1921 the German firm of Württembergische Metallwarenfabrik (WMF), primarily a manufacturer of metalware, started producing a range of art glass under its director Hugo Debach, and later under Karl Wiedmann. The first type of glass they produced, Ikora-Kristall, had an internal decoration of air-bubbles and colour. In 1925 WMF began to manufacture Myra-Kristall, plain forms with rich, iridescent surfaces, no doubt inspired by Tiffany and Loetz glass but somewhat less subtle.

In Belgium, the leading glassworks of

Val-St-Lambert reopened after the First World War and, in the years leading up to the Paris 1925 Exposition Internationale, to which Val-St-Lambert contributed a major display, prepared a dramatic new series of vases using decorative themes and techniques in the Art Deco idiom. The 1920s were successful years and brought several designers and craftsmen to prominence, among them Charles Graffart, master engraver, Modeste Denoël, Felix Matagne and Joseph Simon. The firm survived the recession of the 1930s and the Second World War, though only with difficulty.

The Royal Dutch Glassworks of Leerdam under the directorship of Christiaan Lebeau set up their Unica Studio in 1922-23 to produce one-off pieces. The studio's best-known designer was Andreas Dirk Copier (b. 1901), who made heavy crystal vases and blown glass. Both his art glass and his tableware designs helped Leerdam to win an international reputation, and he is still working today.

British and American Conservatism and Innovation

At a time when French artisans were devising so many novel techniques and styles of glass production, the British glass industry was suffering from a deep-rooted conservatism. The clear and brilliant lead crystal which had been the basic metal of the industry for centuries was still virtually the only glass in production; there was hardly any interest in colour or in the many skills perfected in Continental or American glass-works. The industry was geared towards the production of classic tableware, and traditional cutting was, with few exceptions, the only style of decoration. The establishment in 1915 of a Department of Glass Technology at the University of Sheffield, and in 1916 of the Society of Glass Technology, led to improvements in the quality of the lead crystal used by the industry but did nothing to inspire a fresh aesthetic approach.

The most notable exception to the conservative leanings of the British glass industry was the work of architect and designer Keith Murray. In 1925 Murray visited the Paris Exposition Internationale, which made him realize the extent to which British glass was in the doldrums. His feeling was strengthened by the Swedish Exhibition in London in 1931; but now he was active himself. In 1932 he saw his first designs put into effect at the Whitefriars works, and in the same year he entered what was to be a fruitful seven-year partnership with the firm of

Glass vase with cut decoration, designed by the British glass-artist Clyne Farquharson and manufactured by John Walsh, 1939. (Victoria and Albert Museum, London)

Stevens and Williams. Murray's designs for Stevens and Williams represent a happy alliance of art and industry, and are characterized by the architect's eye for balance and proportion and an elegant restraint in the flat-cut or engraved decoration. He designed undecorated tableware, and decorative vases and other vessels distinguished by the disciplined, well-laid-out decoration, usually of abstract geometric motifs, simple repeat patterns or flat-cut faceting. One attractive series of vases was engraved with a motif of cacti. He impressed on British manufacturers that the artist could make an important contribution to the industry.

Clyne Farquharson was a professional glass designer with a similar spirit. For the Birmingham firm of John Walsh he conceived an elegant series of vases with cut decoration of formalized leaves and stems. A Stourbridge firm, Stuart &

Sons, commissioned designs for glass from a number of prominent artists with varying degrees of success. Graham Sutherland, Paul Nash and Eric Ravilious produced designs for cut decoration which showed these artists' obvious sympathy with the medium. The sobriety of their work was also to be found in the designs of William Wilson for James Powell & Sons. Between them, these designers pioneered a style which combined vitality and dignity in a traditional medium.

A more colourful exception was the Monart range of vessels produced by J. Moncrieff of Perth. These had swirls of internal colouring and bubbles, and were closer in style to pieces by Schneider than to anything else produced in the United Kingdom.

In the United States, too, the glass industry was in decline. There was a continued, though decreasing, commercial exploitation of the skills first evolved by Louis Comfort Tiffany in the 1890s, as the changing tastes of the 1920s and 1930s cast into disfavour the decorative leaded lamps and richly coloured glass which had been so popular with the previous generation. Tiffany's Corona glass factory had already been taken over by A. Douglas Nash in 1919 after financial difficulties. Tiffany himself died in 1933; it was the end of an era. Soon Tiffany Studios went bankrupt and closed. The firm of Quezal was closed down in 1925; Handel & Co. survived until 1936. Between 1924 and his death in 1931 Victor Durand, working with Martin Bach Jnr, son of Quezal's founder, was successful in making and selling lustre glassware, and added new techniques to the Quezal range; but the venture died with him.

The one sign of hope for the future in an otherwise declining area was the successful launching in 1933 of the restyled Steuben Glass, Inc., a division of the Corning Glass Works, with architect John Monteith Gates as director of design and Sidney Waugh as designer. They worked in high-grade crystal glass, and their simple, strong, blown forms were enhanced with fine engraving. It was a bold step, in the midst of the Depression, to abandon the coloured and lustre wares which had been the mainstay of production since the Art Nouveau era; but Steuben succeeded. The venture depended as much on clever marketing as on the quality of production. Gates designed the retail outlets as exclusive shops within leading stores, and had the brilliant idea of commissioning designs for engraving from a number of internationally prominent artists. A collection of twenty-seven designs by artists including Henri Matisse, Jean Cocteau, Georgia O'Keefe, Marie Laurencin, Pavel Tchelitchev and Eric Gill was launched in

1940. It was a commercially shrewd move, bringing on the firm the reflected glory of these distinguished artists. Further collaborations followed after the war.

Glass and Modernism

Modernism has been the most powerful single influence on twentieth-century design. Its aesthetic espouses industry, the machine, mechanized production methods, functional materials and concepts. Modernism had its nineteenth-century precursors, its early twentieth-century pioneers; but in the 1920s the movement gathered speed and strength to emerge as a distinctive new style. The International Style, as it is also labelled, largely rejected ornamentation. Purity of form and surface, clarity of concept and construction were its ideals. The use together of two materials, steel and glass, became the most succinct expression of the ideal, not only in large-scale architectural schemes, notably the skyscrapers which were to become the major statements of faith of the Modernists, but also in interior design and furnishings.

The first impetus came from the avant-garde architects and designers of Germany whose teachings after 1919, in the newly formed Bauhaus, were to become the gospel of the International Modernist movement. In the new architecture born in early twentieth-century Germany, glass played a vital part, functionally and symbolically.

The Modernist ethic found followers elsewhere in Europe and in the United States. It was not long before the characteristic features of Modernism were incorporated into a new design language, to be exploited by designers whose primary concern was style and stylishness as an end in itself. In this context glass became less a symbol of the Modernist mode of thought than a symbol of modernity, of up-to-the-minute chic. Mirror-glass-faced cocktail cabinets, frosted-glass panelling or flooring, crisply cut and enamelled 'Modernist' glass liqueur services and even glass-panelled chairs were the fashionable world's reinterpretation of the idealists' visions. The medium itself was the subject of increasing experiment. Mixes with greater strength and resistance were sought, so that the potential uses of glass could be extended to include such innovations as heat-resistant oven- and tableware.

The first director of the Bauhaus was Walter Gropius, an architect who had been a pupil of Peter Behrens, design director of the giant German industrial concern AEG. In his design for AEG's turbine factory (1909), Behrens had

used glass walls in a way that was to influence not only Gropius but also two other architects who at various times worked under him: Mies van der Rohe and Le Corbusier. When Gropius left Behrens in 1911 he designed a glass-walled building of his own, a factory (for the footwear firm Fagus) in which glass continued right to the corners of the building, giving an extraordinary effect of lightness.

The Staatliches Bauhaus (of which 'State Architectural Institution' is a literal but utterly inadequate translation) was set up at Weimar in 1919, combining the former schools of Fine Art and of Arts and Crafts in an endeavour, in the words of the school's manifesto, to 'create a new guild of craftsmen…[to] create the new building of the future, which will embrace architecture and sculpture and painting and which will rise one day towards heaven from the hands of a million workers like the crystal symbol of a new faith'. In that same year Mies van der Rohe, who was to become director of the Bauhaus in 1930, conceived a personal interpretation of the 'crystal skyscraper' in an extraordinary project for a glass skyscraper. From 1920 to 1921 he worked on a model for an even more surprising glass skyscraper in which the structural elements were taken back from the walls to the interior, giving an unprecedented visual lightness to curving walls of glass towering up through thirty floors.

From 1923 one workshop, under Josef Albers, pursued the craft of architectural stained glass. Albers's own designs, on strict horizontal and vertical grids, call to mind the graphic works of the de Stijl group whose best-known member was the painter Mondrian. In 1925 the Bauhaus moved to Dessau, where new buildings by Gropius, with workshops and accommodation,

Above: Model factory, Cologne, designed by Gropius and Meyer, 1914. In the early twentieth century glass was of vital importance, symbolically as well as functionally, for the avant-garde architects of Germany.

Top left: Engraved urn made by Steuben Glass, glass design by John M. Gates, engraved design by Marie Laurencin, 1938. It is in the style established during the 1930s and 1940s by Gates, who became the leading designer at Steuben in 1933. The tapestry-like decoration has been engraved by copper wheel. Height: 27.9cm (11in)

Bottom left: Iridescent glass vase made under the 'Durand' trademark by the Vineland Flint Glassworks, Vineland, New Jersey, 1920s. Height: 15.25cm (6in)

were opened in 1926. They incorporated the now characteristic walls and corners of glass.

Perhaps the most successful application of Bauhaus principles to industrial design in glass was in the work of Wilhelm Wagenfeld, a Bauhaus student from 1922 to 1925. In the early 1930s he designed a range of heat-resistant glass cooking pots for the Schott & Gen. Glassworks. He became art director to the Vereinigte Lausitzer Glassworks in 1935 and was responsible for a range of undecorated, functionalist clear glass tableware for mass production. In contexts as diverse as skyscrapers and kitchenware the Bauhaus gave glass a specifically twentieth-century character.

The practical implementation of Modernist ideals witnessed at the Bauhaus had its strongest contemporary counterpart elsewhere in the French 'L'Esprit Nouveau' group. *L'Esprit*

Nouveau was the title given to their journal, first published in 1920, by Amadée Ozenfant and Le Corbusier, passionate advocates of a new spirit in architecture in which light, clarity and practicality were the basis of a socialistic dream of the city of the future. The journal ran for twenty-eight issues, until 1924, in which year Le Corbusier and Ozenfant, in partnership with Pierre Jeanneret, presented their radical 'Pavillon de l'Esprit Nouveau' at the Paris Exposition Internationale. This pavilion was in effect a display dwelling, constructed of standardized elements on a grid scheme and incorporating the dramatic wall of glass which, filling the interior with light, was already a characteristic of the new architecture. In the same exhibition, where René Lalique's elaborately decorative glass struck a more traditional note, another revolutionary statement was made by architect Robert Mallet-Stevens with his Modernist design for a Pavillon du Tourisme, a building of rigidly austere geometric construction, bathed in light from a flat ceiling of glass and geometric leaded-glass friezes by Louis Barillet. Mallet-Stevens pursued his interest in the architectural possibilities of leaded glass in a series of dramatic glass walls leaded in strictly horizontal-vertical geometric grid patterns, comparable to the work of Albers.

The formation in 1930 of the Union des Artistes Modernes as an exhibition society gave an identity to French Modernist designers, prominent among whom were founder members René Herbst, Francis Jourdain and Robert Mallet-Stevens. Glass was used extensively by the artists of the UAM in a surprising variety of contexts, ranging from architectural uses, sometimes dramatic in their novelty, to the use of glass in interior design, furniture and other domestic objects. Several artists of the group collaborated on the interior fittings of the Indian palace of the Maharajah of Indore. The palace, built and fitted between 1930 and 1933, was a spectacular monument to Modernism at its most stylish, and prominent amongst the furnishings were such creations as the Maharani's green glass bed and glass dressing-table by Louis Sognot and Charlotte Alix.

Numerous designers and decorators were inspired by the UAM, and the late 1920s and early 1930s saw a spate of furniture, object and interior designs incorporating glass. Designer Pierre Legrain created an angular glass piano in the late 1920s, the workings clearly visible through the clear glass casing. In 1933 the magazine *L'Illustration* published photographs of the refurbished apartment of Suzanne Talbot, in which decorator Paul Ruard set the luxurious furniture, designed by Eileen Gray in the early 1920s, in a stark Modernist setting of frosted glass, using panels for the walls and large square tiles for the floor.

The single most remarkable design exercise in the use of glass, however, was surely the Maison de Verre created by Pierre Chareau between 1928 and 1931. Chareau, a founder member of the UAM, distilled his entire philosophy into this revolutionary design for a Parisian doctor's town house, incorporating surgery and dwelling. The scheme, remarkable in its use of exposed steel structure, industrial components such as rubber flooring and perforated sheet metal, comes to life through the designer's imaginative use of glass. Wired glass was used for internal partitioning, but the most dramatic concept was Chareau's use of slim, square, glass bricks for almost entire elevations. The glass bricks were textured to allow privacy while filling rooms with light, and Chareau designed them with a curvature which would fill the rooms at night with a diffused light from outside projectors. Chareau's Maison de Verre is a functionalist living- and working-space conceived in the purest Modernist-Industrial aesthetic, and stands as a distinguished landmark in the history of a new architecture in which function and light, steel and glass were the prime elements.

The Modernist style found followers throughout Europe. In many countries there could be found the distinctive architecture of the movement, characterized by undecorated white block façades, plain tubular metal balustrading, flat roofs and the unbiquitous expanses of metal-framed windows, often sweeping round curved corners. In Britain the style is best expressed in such architectural works as Eric Mendelsohn and Serge Chermayeff's elegant De la Warr Pavilion at Bexhill-on-Sea (1933-36), Wells Coates's Embassy Court Flats in Brighton (1935) with their horizontals of window-glass sweeping round the south-east corner, and the London *Daily Express* building by Ellis and Clarke (1929-32), faced in Black Vitrolite glass, again with the glass sweeping round a curved corner. Other British architects of note who worked in the Modernist style included Raymond McGrath, Oliver Hill, Brian O'Rorke, Erno Goldfinger and the team of Lubetkin and Tecton. All at various times

showed a boldness in the use of glass in keeping with the spirit of the Modern Movement.

The British designers, however, differed from their European contemporaries in the ways in which they used glass in interior contexts. Although glass facings were never widely adopted for interior domestic use, the material was widely and effectively used in such settings as hotel foyers. Oliver Bernard's stylish back-lit glass panelling for the entrance to the Strand Palace Hotel, built between 1929 and 1930, is a fine example of a distinctively British use of glass, and Oliver Milne's schemes for the redecoration of public areas of Claridge's Hotel in 1930 made great use of mirror-glass panelling. Oliver Hill incorporated large glass panels bearing bold, simple figurative composition by Eric Gill in his interior schemes and, for the Gayfere House in London, used mirror-glass

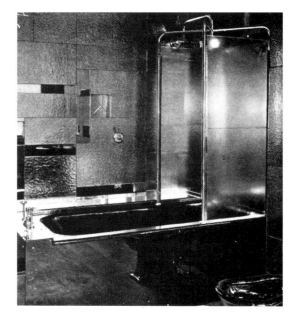

Top left: Glass bathroom designed by the British artist Paul Nash and executed by James Clark & Sons, 1932. This bathroom, which Clark featured in advertisements for their services, was designed for Tilly Losch, wife of the art patron Edward James.

Bottom left: 'Futurama', model city of the future, designed by the American Norman Bel Geddes and shown at the New York World Fair in 1939. The emphasis on glass as a major building material anticipates the architecture of the post-war period.

panelling on walls and ceilings. For the glass-making firm of Pilkington Brothers Hill designed an extraordinary all-glass dressing-room which was shown at the Dorland Hall Exhibition of 1933. It had textured glass walls and a glass-tile floor, and the dressing-table, stool, day-bed and table were all of clear glass.

Perhaps the most remarkable exercise in glass in interior design was the glass bathroom designed in 1932 by Paul Nash for Tilly Losch, wife of eccentric art patron Edward James, and executed by James Clark & Son. This room used glass of various textures and colours, a deep metallic purple contrasting with areas of peach and colourless mirror glass, and demonstrated Nash's inventiveness in exploiting newly developed types of glass. At a more popular level, mirror glass, often tinted pink, peach or blue, was widely used in facing occasional tables and the ubiquitous cocktail-cabinets of the period.

During the late 1930s, several prominent Modernists left their native Germany, fleeing an increasingly repressive society for the freedom of the United States. Foremost amongst them was Mies van der Rohe, who was eventually to build there the steel-and-glass skyscrapers of which he had dreamed in Europe. Van der Rohe, Gropius and eventually, after a period spent in Britain, their former colleague at the Bauhaus, Marcel Breuer, brought a new purism to American architecture, which through the 1930s had been dominated by the often eccentric work of the 'Streamlined Moderne' school.

Frank Lloyd Wright (1869-1959) stands as a curiously isolated figure in the early evolutionary stages of the Modern Movement in America. His work includes notable designs for stained-glass windows, dating from the early years of the century. Counterpointing clear glass with disciplined geometric motifs in coloured glass, Wright's stylish and restrained exercises anticipated by a quarter of a century the work on somewhat similar lines of Albers and Mallet-Stevens in Europe.

In the late 1920s and 1930s various American designers used glass in conjunction with steel, and created Modernist furniture in the fashionable idiom, adding the peculiarly American feature of 'streamlining', sweeping aerodynamic forms which were a mere stylistic curiosity on static objects. Donald Deskey, Gilbert Rohde, Paul Frankl, Walter Dorwin Teague and Raymond Loewy were prominent among these designers who used mirror glass extensively in interior schemes, in many instances as a ground for murals, panelling or screens with etched or painted decorations. Typical motifs might range from abstract geometric designs to such fashionable subjects as skyscrapers or jazz bands.

It was, however, above all through Modernist architecture rather than in modish furnishings that glass played so important a role, in America as in Europe. Walls of glass and sweeping glass corners became a feature of the urban landscape.

Although it was Bauhaus *émigré*, Mies van der Rohe, who was the dominant influence on the skylines of American cities with his purist steel-and-glass blocks, America had its own visionaries, one of the most inventive of whom was Norman Bel Geddes. In 1939 at the New York World's Fair, he presented his Futurama, a model city of the future. It was a Modernist urban dream in which lofty tower blocks stretched skywards, their steel skeletons symbolically sheathed in glass, and it anticipated much of the architecture of the post-war years, and its preoccupation with glass as a major building material.

The De la Warr Pavilion, Bexhill-on-Sea, England, the work of the architects Eric Mendelsohn and Serge Chermayeff, completed 1935. This leisure centre, an elegant expression of the Modernist style in which glass and metal play a major role, was intended to suggest to future generations ways of using their free time.

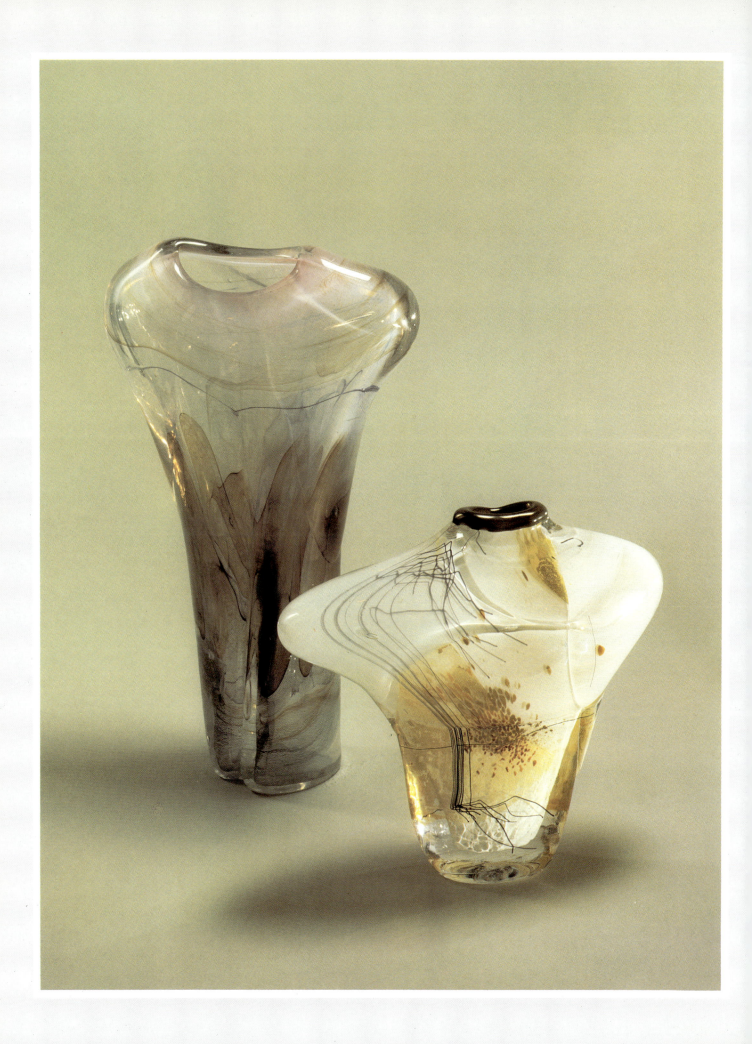

CHAPTER TEN

GLASS SINCE 1945

Two vases by Sam Herman. During the late 1960s the American-born Sam Herman was a leading figure among glass-artists in Britain and in the next decade his students from the Royal College of Art, London, formed the core of British glass-artists.

The period since the end of the Second World War has been one not only of great technological progress in the glass industry, but also of fundamental changes of attitude in both the art and the craft of glass-making. Modern glass is a much improved substance, and the modern glass-worker has cast aside some of the long-established traditions of this ancient craft. He may be an expert technician dealing with the complexities of electronic equipment, or a fully fledged artist who believes in using glass as a medium for self-expression. New technology and new attitudes have allowed widespread experiment, which in turn has led to a new freedom of approach. Such freedom tends to cause stylistic disarray, and it is perhaps still too soon to sort out the good from the bad, because there is if anything an excess of choice. But this period is already emerging as one of the very richest in artistic and technological invention, and one that has created new boundaries for the glass enthusiast.

Technological and Artistic Developments

At the end of the Second World War, the glass industry continued much as before in providing for household and industrial needs. With the extensive rebuilding of Europe in post-war years the demand for architectural glass was very great. Skyscraper architecture, since its beginnings in the first decades of the century, had given added importance to the role of glass in building: the early skyscrapers incorporated great amounts of glass simply because they needed so many windows. But since then the use of glass in architecture has progressed far beyond func-

tionalism. With major advances in shaping and manufacturing technology, sheet glass can now be used to form almost all the outer skin of a building, and its variety of tints and lustres and seemingly magical reflective qualities have transformed the appearance of modern cities. An all-glass exterior picks up reflections of entire buildings, bending or stretching them with the changing play of light. These reflections provide one of the great new visual delights of our time. All-glass exteriors, as in the Solow Building in New York, with its sensational curving base (built by Skidmore, Owings & Merrill in 1974) or the Tolmers Square Building with its shimmering iridescent exterior in London (built by Renton, Howard Wood, Levin Partnership in 1982), make the most dramatic use of glass in architecture.

It is largely due to an invention at the British firm of Pilkington Brothers that glass has become such a versatile building material. At Pilkingtons the revolutionary 'float' process was invented; this automated method of production combines what was previously a series of separate operations into one continuous procedure, in which glass emerges from the furnace on to giant rollers and then literally floats on molten tin in a controlled atmosphere, enabling it to take on a flawlessly smooth surface without any distorting impurities. In the next stage of the process the glass passes along more rollers into annealing lehrs where it is cooled slowly to relieve internal stresses. This simple but brilliant procedure enables large areas of sheet glass to be made in a range of thicknesses, replacing both traditional plate glass, previously the only way of making large sheets but laborious because of the casting, grinding and polishing involved, and the early twentieth-century method of making

smaller sheets of thinner window glass by vertical drawing with a set of rollers above a bath of molten glass. Other architectural glass includes wired, ribbed and patterned glass and cast-glass blocks laid in mortar like bricks, which were popular in the 1960s for external and internal walls. Glass fibre is another much-used modern material, for example, formed into blankets for insulation and soundproofing, and combined with plastics and sometimes with concrete in composite materials for boat and car bodies and other mouldings.

Because of its combination of versatility and beauty, glass plays an important part in almost every branch of modern industry. At present there are more than 500 different kinds of glass being made and used commercially in the United Kingdom alone. During the improved economy of the 1950s and 1960s greater funds for research programmes became available which eventually led to the discovery of important new materials and major breakthroughs in mass-production methods. There has been particular interest in new varieties of high-silica glass for withstanding very severe heat-shocks, and among the spectacular applications for this range of heat-resistant glasses are nose-cones for missiles, and windows and antenna shields for space vehicles. The material used in missile nose-cones is 'glass ceramic'. It was discovered by accident in 1957: a sample of photosensitive glass, which contains chemicals causing it to darken when exposed to light, was irradiated, then heated far above its usual developing temperature because of a fault in the furnace. Instead of melting, it turned into an opaque, strong material, the first of the glass ceramics.

Today every stage of glass manufacture has become mechanized and continuous. The manufacture of household glass has been revolutionized by computer control, so that in the United States glass-container production has doubled between 1949 and 1963, reaching a figure of 25,000 million containers a year. The total annual production of hand-made bottles in Britain in 1700 was 3 million; now, with round-the-clock working, the figure is in the region of 14 million per day. A modern machine can produce over 100,000 glass vessels a day. The overall result is a greater variety of household glass than there has ever been. With so many techniques in use and with so many types of improved glass now available, the competition among designers is tremendous. Every firm is striving to introduce something new, which can make even the choosing of a simple item of domestic glass quite difficult. Hard glass can be blown more thinly than ever before; there is brilliant glass soft enough to withstand elaborate

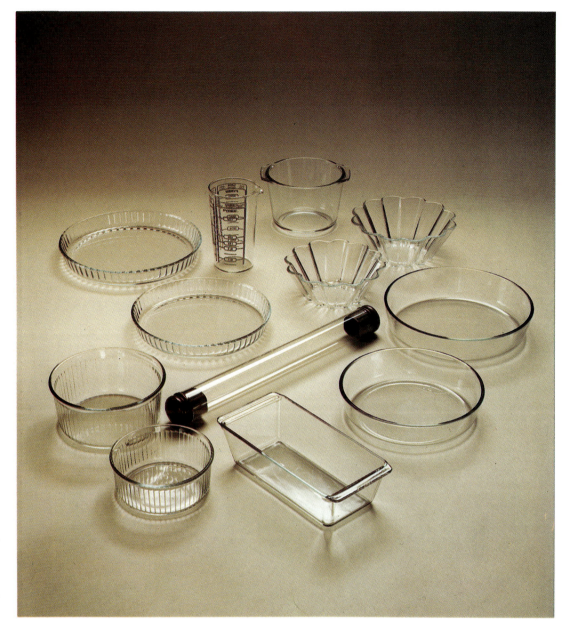

surface cutting; and lead glass has achieved an even higher degree of purity. New technical developments, for all their appearance of soullessness, have helped rather than hindered the production of beautiful objects such as the colourful Venini decanters of the 1950s and 1960s and the prize-winning 'Papyrus' series of drinking glasses designed in 1976 for Rosenthal. Modern lighting, particularly since the invention of dimmer switches, brings out the best in glass. Murano glass companies, Venini and Salviati in particular, have continued the Venetian tradition of making elaborate chandeliers (though in contemporary styles) as well as developing a newer tendency for decorative glass ceilings with concealed lighting. Sources of light have also been much improved, for example by the invention of miniature tungsten-halogen bulbs. One other outstanding improvement in domes-

tic glass has been ovenware made of glass ceramic which can be taken straight from the refrigerator to the top of a red-hot burner.

Until the mid-1960s artistic glass was made almost exclusively in studio departments attached to the major glassworks. This was an area where prestige played a greater part than profit, firms considering it important because of the notice it attracted at the many trade fairs where there were coveted prizes to be won in this field. The most important of these were the World Fairs and the Milan Triennale Fairs. For Czechoslovakia, particularly, these fairs meant a great deal, as they were the only means the Czechs had of drawing attention in the West to the pioneering spirit of their glass industry. They also provided a rare opportunity for designers to create really large-scale works which could show the sculptural qualities of glass in interior design.

One such example was a panel entitled 'Ice Pack' by Timo Sarpaneva, measuring 9.6m by 4.4m (31ft 6in by 14ft 6in), for the Finnish Pavilion at Expo '67.

Except in Britain, most of the major glassworks had a studio department, where glass was produced by a team of workers, in which each member had a clearly defined role. Except in rare cases (such as that of Nils Landberg, who was a master blower at Orrefors), glass was designed on paper and executed by a team of expert craftsmen. The oldest traditions of glass-making continued in this environment. In most countries the designer's work was confined to the drawing-board. More often than not, designs were executed by artists hardly connected at all with the glass industry. For example, at Steuben Glass Inc. in the United States two important collections of glass since 1945 have been their 'British Artists in Crystal' series (1954) and the 'Asian Artists in Crystal' series (1956). In the second of these, Asian artists prepared the drawings, while American designers created the shapes of the glass and American artisans interpreted the drawings in crystal.

In the Scandinavian countries, however, designers worked in closer contact with craftsmen. Indeed, many of them, like Ingeborg Lundin and Sven Palmqvist, were themselves trained as glass-workers and employed full-time by the Scandinavian glass factories. The Scandinavian craftsmen-designers of the 1950s brought about great changes in studio glass production that heralded the beginnings of the Studio Glass movement of the 1960s.

Above: Red-wine, white-wine and champagne glasses in the 'Papyrus' series, designed by Michael Boehm for Rosenthal Studio Line, 1976. The yellow-green stems and bases have been applied by hand to the colourless blown-glass bowls.
Heights: 20.3, 24.3 and 18.5cm (8, 9⅝ and 7¼in)

Since the 1960s art glass has moved away from an industrial environment. Both glass technology and glass artistry are now taught at university level, whereas before that time there were virtually no university courses. Glass-artisans learned their trade in the industry, and the designers and artists mostly came to glass by a circuitous route, usually involving a fine-art or design course of some sort. Now there are well over 100 glass-making departments in American colleges and universities alone. In Britain the Royal College of Art introduced a glass-making department under the American glass-artist Sam Herman in 1967, and there are now at least four more excellent glass courses at degree level in the country.

The prizes to be won are no longer so much those at industrial fairs, but those attached to museum exhibitions. Many major museums have contemporary art-glass collections, and this fact alone, combined with a strong university involvement, gives modern glass-artists a new status. A more intellectual attitude has been taken towards their art, and in a very short time glass has become accepted as a serious art-form. The twenty years during which these changes have occurred are spanned by the two most significant museum glass shows of the period. The first of these, 'Glass 1959, A Special Exhibition of International Contemporary Glass', was held in New York at the Corning Museum of Glass in 1959. The second, in 1979 and also at Corning, was called 'New Glass—A Worldwide Survey'. Glass 1959 was the first of the major museum shows, and one of the most important single events in shaping the future of modern glass. The differences between the two occasions show clearly how directions have

Right: 'Freedom and the Spirit', two crystal prisms designed and engraved by the English artist Laurence Whistler for Steuben Glass, New York, 1977. This celebration of Anglo-American friendship depicts in one prism the gothic spire of Salisbury Cathedral and in the other the torch in the hand of the Statue of Liberty, the World Trade Center and the United Nations Headquarters. Height: 38.1cm (15in)

Left: 'Ice Pack', detail of a monumental glass sculpture designed by Timo Sarpaneva and executed by Iittala for the Finnish Pavilion at Expo '67 in Montreal. Dimensions: 9.6 by 4.4m (31ft 6in by 14ft 6in)

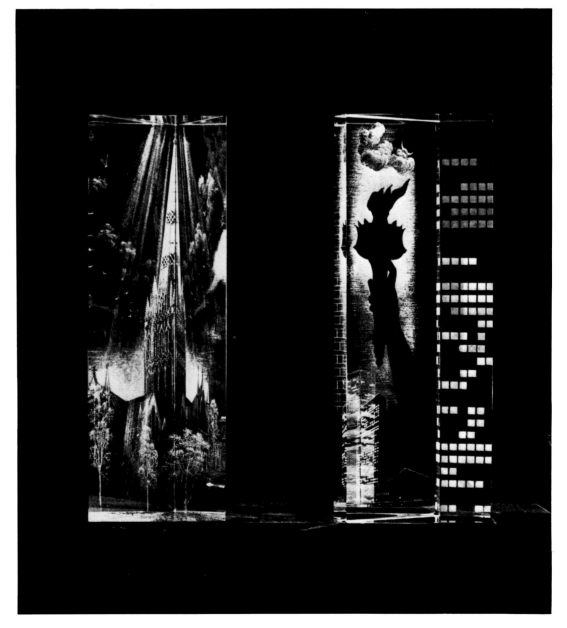

changed. In 1959 2000 slides were submitted for consideration compared with 6000 in 1979. In the catalogue of 1959 Edgar Kaufmann said:

I am no friend to extravagant compositions in glass. As sculpture or as a field for the graven image, in the sense of the fine arts, glass seems woefully forced. Twentieth-century glass seems to me nobly represented in the Pyrex dish...

By contrast, Thomas Buechner wrote in the 1979 catalogue:

This exhibition is about a profound change that is taking place in the history of glass. After thirty-five centuries of utilitarian use, glass has become the amorphous substance from which functionless art is made. Suddenly glass has become a medium of the Fine Arts, a material in which to conceive and create often directly, for purely aesthetic purposes.

Industrial Studio Glass

Until geographical frontiers lost their relevance with the spread of the International Studio Glass movement in the early 1960s, there were distinct national styles. Countries were competing with one another at World Fairs in a nationalistic spirit. More recently the art of the individual has been all-important, and it is much less easy to identify a newer piece of glass by its national characteristics. Significantly, perhaps, the 1959 Corning catalogue is divided up by nationality, whereas the 1979 catalogue is simply in alphabetical order.

Apart from these two fairs, there were the World Fairs in Belgium in 1958, in Brazil in 1965, in Mexico in 1966 and in Canada in 1967. The prizes awarded at these fairs, and the Grand Prix at the Milan Triennale exhibitions, counted for a great deal at the time, and serve as a useful guide even now. The fairs also serve as landmarks because they were used for unveiling new ideas, in the hope that they would thereby win the maximum acclaim.

During this period Scandinavian (particularly Swedish) design dominated the field. The Italians, above all colourists, were innovative and very active; but the sheer volume produced by the Scandinavians, who were the most inventive in terms of technique, gave them the edge. In Czechoslovakia there was also a flourishing glass industry, but it developed in comparative isolation; in some aspects, such as glass sculpture, it was far ahead of its time, but the Czech industry was mainly preoccupied with

Above: Studio pieces dating from the 1950s and 1960s designed at the Swedish Orrefors glass-works. The piece on the left is by the master blower Nils Landberg and the two other pieces in the foreground are by Ingeborg Lundin, a blue and clear glass Ariel piece and a clear vase with large splashes of pink.

Right: Heavy glass vase with a controlled pattern of air bubbles, designed by the Finnish artist Gunnel Nyman for the Notsjö Glassworks, Nuutajärvi.

reforming itself in a new political climate.

In Scandinavia glass has been one of the most important industrial exports of the twentieth century. The Swedish glass industry is located mainly in the south-eastern region of Småland, where, within a 50-km (30-mile) radius there are about forty glassworks. The oldest of them is Kosta, established in 1742, which produced some excellent designs in the 1950s. Their chief designer at this period was Vicke Lindstrand, who had worked previously for Orrefors. His designs include a variety of different techniques including prismatic cutting, subtly shaded *latticinio* (with a preference for blues and greens) and some fine engraving; but his most original work is in some of the delicately controlled abstract shapes he created, often with swirling linear designs in bright colours. One of his simplest and most successful designs was the 'Dark Magic' series, where a single streak of colour sweeps or spirals elegantly through a clear glass shape.

Scandinavian designers were able to achieve such variety because they had access to highly trained craftsmen specializing in the different skills of the glass trade. While an individual glass-worker rarely masters more than a couple of skills—the master blower seldom also becomes a master engraver, for example—in Sweden a strong tradition of team-work developed in the factory-studio environment. It takes time for collaboration to produce results, and it is a special characteristic of the Swedish glass industry that it developed a successful studio tradition. The precedent was set in the 1920s and 1930s at Orrefors, where Simon Gate and Edward Hald worked for twenty years as heads of a design team. Other factories followed suit, and by the 1950s a pattern of patient collaboration between artists and craftsmen had established itself in the Swedish glass industry.

Since 1945 a new generation of excellent designers has been working at Orrefors. Individual artists have developed recognizable styles, and many of them have continued to develop the Ariel and Graal techniques of trapping air in patterns within the glass, using sandblasting and cutting respectively, for which Orrefors won such renown during the 1920s and 1930s (see Chapter 9). Ingeborg Lundin has produced fine Ariel models with images of animals or strong geometric patterns. Edvin Öhrström has a preference for semi-abstract Modernist images. The greatest technical innovator at Orrefors has been Sven Palmqvist, who joined Orrefors in 1936 and helped to develop the Kraka technique, in which a network design punctuated with air-bubbles sits between layers of glass; and Ravenna glass, developed

during the 1940s, which has been described as one of the finest creations of the modern art of glass. The bright, mosaic-like patterns of Ravenna glass are achieved by brilliantly coloured inlaid patterns surrounded by narrow channels of trapped air, which have been sprinkled with brightly coloured sand. The most spectacular example of this technique is a free-standing glass wall entitled 'Light and Dark', composed of 200 blocks of Ravenna glass, at the Union Internationale des Télécommunications in Geneva. The most renowned glass-blower at Orrefors is Nils Landberg, whose elongated blown shapes are in finely shaded pastel colours that merge imperceptibly into one another. More recently, Gunnar Cyrén has created some delightful glass for Orrefors, particularly the brightly coloured series of 'Pop Glasses', started during the early 1960s.

Studio glass is still made at Orrefors, although it is now difficult to tie down a more independent generation of glass-artists. Many of the other Swedish glassworks had studio departments, with designers who developed a house style. At Flygfors Paul Kedelv designed some strong, asymmetric shapes, midway between vessel and sculpture, that are typical of the 1950s. Many of them are illustrated in the 1950s *Studio Yearbooks*, which are an excellent guide to contemporary taste. The Flygfors pieces complement the distorted lines of the furniture that was then fashionable. Bengt Edenfalk at Skrufs designed heavy-walled vases with bubble patterns. At Boda Erik Hoglund, the chief designer, is best known for a series of eccentric decanters, some in humanoid shapes, others with crudely stamped applications like wax seals. At Åfors Ernest Gordon (born in England in 1926) has turned out some of the simplest and most

'Light and Dark', a free-standing glass screen composed of blocks of Ravenna glass, designed by Sven Palmqvist and executed at the Swedish Orrefors glassworks. This remarkable example of a technique developed during the 1940s stands in the Union Internationale des Télécommunications in Geneva.

elegant of Swedish designs, and crystal from Strömberghyttan is easily recognizable because of its distinctive blue-grey tint. All Swedish glass in fact, whether domestic ware or studio glass, is of outstanding quality. The main difference between the glass made in Sweden before and after the war is its colour: before the war it was mostly clear with engraved decoration, but from the 1950s onwards it followed the Italian fashion for colour.

In Denmark, the two main glassworks are Kastrup & Holmegaards, where Per Lütken and Michael Bang are chief designers. Per Lütken, who joined Holmegaards in 1942 (the two factories merged in 1954) has tried his hand at many styles, but his best work is characterized by clearly defined shapes in a variety of colours, usually smoky grey or smoky blue, and sometimes sage green. Function is the core of Lütken's design; his vases need flowers and his bowls are intended for use. There is a feeling of lightness and clarity of thought in all his work, and his designs capture the essentially liquid qualities of glass. Michael Bang's father Jacob (d. 1965) also worked for Holmegaards, making simple but vigorous blown glassware.

Norwegian and Danish glass have many similarities. Their design is much more closely related to function than that of Swedish glass. Perhaps this is because these countries have less of a studio tradition, and are more concerned with commercialism. In Norway the Hadelands glass factory in Oslo, founded in 1762, is responsible for the best of Norwegian glass design. Willy Johannsen became art director there in 1947, heading a team of designers, Severin Bjørby, Haakon Bjørklid and Arne Jon Jutrem, all of whom were born in the 1920s.

Right: A group of two-colour vases designed by Timo Sarpaneva for the Finnish glassworks Karhula Iittala. Sarpaneva, who has had experience of working in other media, including metal and wood, developed a number of ingenious methods for making moulds, for instance using carved wood and ice.

Below: Vase by the Finnish designer Tapio Wirkkala for Karhula Iittala. Wirkkala has achieved recognition as a graphic artist and as a designer in media other than glass, including ceramics, silver and wood. His glass designs have won him numerous prizes (for example, at the Milan Triennale Fairs) and he has executed designs in various media for Rosenthal.

The Finnish glass industry has some of the most outstanding artists of this period, notably Tapio Wirkkala and Timo Sarpaneva, who work for one of the leading Finnish glassworks, Karhula Iittala, an amalgamation of two separate firms which joined during the 1940s. Wirkkala has been with the firm since 1947 and Sarpaneva since 1950. Both of them are versatile designers who do not devote their energies exclusively to glass: Sarpaneva has also designed fabrics, ceramics and even candles; Wirkkala is among other things a sculptor, an outstanding wood-carver and a silversmith. Both of them have won the Grand Prix at Milan Triennales and an impressive list of important prizes elsewhere. Each has remarkable originality, Wirkkala for his imaginative technical innovations, notably his carved wooden moulds into which the glass is blown, thus taking on the texture of the wood. Vases, bowls and drinking glasses have been designed with this 'tree-bark' texture, many of them still in production today, thirty years after they were designed. Sarpaneva's shapes are stark and uncompromising, with colours sharply separated, as in his series of small spheres divided exactly in half with a coloured top and a clear base. Wirkkala is more organic, with shape and texture often reminiscent of the Finnish landscape. His massive, textured vases look as if

Top: A group of glass pieces dating from the late 1950s or the early 1960s produced by the Italian firm Venini. The bright palette is typical of Italian glass of the period.

Above: The clean form of this piece by Kaj Franck is typical of much post-war Finnish glassware.

they are carved out of ice, and his series of heavy crystal shapes with deeply engraved vertical lines look like eccentric plant-forms.

Of the many other leading Finnish glass-artists Kaj Franck is probably the most prolific. His works have strong, clear-cut shapes and are always pleasing to handle. These three artists have been largely responsible for the high praise that is accorded to Finnish functional glassware. Others who have made valuable contributions include Oiva Toikka, Helena Tynell and Nanny

Stil. A studio glass movement also existed in Finland, with a limited range of unique pieces being made in factory studios. When Finnish glass first began to attract notice in the 1940s, this was thanks in large part to the designer Gunnel Nyman, who died in 1949 at the sadly premature age of thirty-nine. She evolved a personal style that was later widely copied, with heavy, clear, ground shapes decorated internally with intricate all-over, symmetrical patterns of tiny bubbles.

Italian glass has a very different appeal, based on spontaneity, freshness and an elusive elegance. Italian shapes depend on hot techniques such as blowing, almost to the exclusion of the cold techniques of cutting and engraving. The city of Venice remains at the heart of the Italian glass industry, with a long history of glass-blowing unparalleled anywhere else in the world. The art of the Venetian glass-blower dominates Italian glass-artistry, and essentially all new techniques and new designs, whether free-blown or mould-blown, revolve around this particular skill. Post-war Italian glass can be distinguished by its bold palette of bright colouring, in which vibrant primary colours are fearlessly juxtaposed. A good example is the series of vases designed in the early 1950s by Paolo Venini, called 'Canne', in which vases

'Vortice' (Vortex), glass sculpture by the Italian glass artist Livio Seguso, 1978. Seguso, who had previously worked for nearly ten years at Salviati, has had his own studio at Murano since 1969. He uses hot-glass techniques exclusively. Dimensions: 42 by 45cm (16¹/₂ by 17³/₄ in)

of free-blown glass are made from pairs of alternately coloured canes welded together. Italian shapes of this time had an easy asymmetry and a looseness of form reminiscent of folded fabric: in fact one of the most popular shapes was that of the 'folded-handkerchief' vases first made by Venini in the 1940s and later copied by other firms, notably Fontana Arte.

The firm of Venini, founded in 1921 by Paolo Venini, a Milanese lawyer, attracted top designers from all over the world. His enthusiasm and love of glass gave the company a special importance, for it was Venini's originality of style and unerring taste that brought about the renaissance of Italian glass artistry in the twentieth century. From 1949 onwards Venini was assisted by his wife, Ginette Ginous, who worked as a colour consultant and whose influence brought about a very noticeable change with the bright palette that characterizes Venini glass of the post-war period. When the factory reopened after the war, work started on projects from a design group headed by the brilliant architect and designer Gio Ponti. At the first Triennale of Milan after the war in 1947, the theme was 'Shapes for Utility'. With characteristic wit Venini presented a group of non-functional glass pieces: an umbrella, a pair of gloves, a revolver, a woman's hat and purse and a walking-stick. In the same year Fulvio Bianconi began his long career with Venini, designing a series of witty caricature-like figures based on characters from the *Commedia dell'Arte*. They were made of opaque milky glass, sometimes with black decoration, sometimes with brightly applied colour. Bianconi also designed a series of obelisks, introduced the 'handkerchief' shapes, and worked on a series of 'Zanfirico' techniques in which filigree designs are incorporated into the glass. Zanfirico was a natural development of the ancient art of *latticinio*, updated into a modern idiom. Bianconi and Venini together also developed the many variations of *vetro pezzato* and *vetro tessuto* ('patched glass' and 'woven glass'), a series of complicated designs on glass which were among the most original concepts in glass of the post-war years, and confined to the Venetian glass-makers of the 1950s and 1960s. The famous 'Morandi' bottles (named after the Italian painter Morandi, one of whose favourite subjects was groups of bottles), also date from this period, although some of them are still in current production; they are brightly coloured, with loose vertical or horizontal bands and pointed, tear-shaped or spherical stoppers.

Throughout the 1950s and 1960s Venini was winning prizes and adding to its fame. Artists

In the 1950s Italian glass-makers were fascinated by the idea of patchwork designs in glass. This patchwork vase is from the Barovier firm, where Dino Martens, one of the best known of those who experimented with patchwork techniques, was one of the designers.

and designers from all over the world visited the factory, many of them staying to do designs, including Tapio Wirkkala, and during the late 1960s the first wave of American studio glass-artists, including Dale Chihuly and Richard Marquis. In 1976 the firm was revitalized by a new collaboration with Laura de Santillana, the granddaughter of Paolo Venini, whose plate 'Numeri' of free-cast glass with numbers from 0 to 9 inlaid in a mosaic pattern won an award at the 1979 Corning exhibition.

Undoubtedly Venini dominated the Italian glass scene, but other firms such as Barovier, Salviati, Seguso Vetri d'Arte and Fratelli Toso joined in the revival. Their individual contribution was not on the same scale, but between them they could boast considerable talent. The Venetian glass firms have always had a complicated and interwoven history of family feuds and reconciliations, so it is easier to deal with the outstanding individual artists than with the firms themselves. Flavio Poli at Seguso Vetri d'Arte designed massive vases in impressive sculptural shapes. Ercole Barovier had his own subtly shaded versions of patchwork vases, much quieter in colour than Venini's even though they are sometimes heightened with gold. He has been succeeded by his son Angelo Barovier. At Salviati Luciano Gaspari was chief

*Top left: 'Meteor, Flower and Bird', by the Czech artists Jaroslava Brych-tová and Stanislav Libenský for the lobby of the new Corning Museum of Glass, Corning, New York, opened 1980.
Height: 305cm (120in)*

*Bottom left: 'Space', glass sculpture by the Czech artist Pavel Hlava, 1980.
Height: 40cm (15¾in)*

Below: Two examples of Czech glass from the 1950s, by Jiří Harcuba (left) and by Ladislav Oliva (right).

designer, with a preference for heavy-walled vessels in a variety of colours. Ermano Toso designed a series of long-necked decanters with dramatically shaped stoppers for Fratelli Toso. Dino Martens at Aureliano Toso evolved a complicated technique in which the body of the glass was made up of a patchwork of varying multicoloured *latticinio* designs. Venetian glass-designers were totally committed to colour: to them it was not a mere decorative feature, it was the point of departure, the unashamed basis for design and technique.

In Czechoslovakia the glass industry was nationalized in 1948. In the interests of modernization and mechanization, the smaller enterprises were amalgamated to form larger units, and in 1952 the Central Art Centre for Glass and Fine Ceramics was formed in Prague. This was an independent body, but under the auspices of the Ministry of Light Industry. The new government was anxious to develop and continue the tradition of Bohemian glass. The Bohemians had a reputation for excellence in all branches of the industry, and were equally adept at turning out functional and decorative glass, and at all the hot and cold techniques.

The reorganized industry had difficulty in absorbing the large numbers of skilled glass-workers, and was able to produce only a fraction of the designs of almost 100 glass-artists. Nonetheless, the Prague School of Applied Arts was very active, and it was realized that the new generation of glass-workers would have to broaden the scope of the glass industry if there were to be full employment. New decorative techniques were researched. The most successful innovation of these years was a new concept of enamelled decoration developed by Stanislav Libenský at the Prague School; when he left for the Železný Brod Glassworks he continued to work on this technique, among others. Many of the contemporary studio glass-artists who are famous in Czechoslovakia today, such as Pavel Hlava, Adolf Matura and Jiří Harcuba, also trained at the Prague School.

More by chance than intention, many of the seeds for the International Studio Glass movement were sown during the 1950s in Czechoslovakia. Perhaps because of the excess of professionally trained glass-artists in Czecho-slovakia, there was a move by some away from industrial design towards studio glass, but where possible, artists tried not to sever their links with industry but rather to find industrial outlets for their ideas. This has led to the production of large-scale architectural works, made possible by financial support from the government.

Little Czech glass was seen in western Europe until 1957, when the decision was made to exhibit at the Milan Triennale. In 1958 Czech glass was on show again at Expo in Brussels; for this occasion René Roubíček created a glass collage described as 'a large object of blown and flat coloured elements', which was awarded the Grand Prix. There was a good representation in the 1959 Corning show, and by the time the Milan Triennale came around again in 1960 the excellence of modern Czech glass was in no doubt. A critic wrote of Czech glass exhibited in 1960 that it was 'industry raised to the level of Art'.

It is still not easy to see modern Czech glass outside Czechoslovakia although there have been a number of travelling exhibitions. There is, however, very little in permanent collections in the West. The enthusiasm which greeted Czech glass at the fairs was a tremendous boost to the industry, and particularly to the export of glass

for domestic use. In the West, Czech drinking glasses, especially those designed by Věra Lišková, became very popular; Lišková is a freelance artist who has gone on to specialize in figural and abstract sculptures shaped free-hand over an oxy-acetylene flame. During the 1950s and 1960s Ladislav Oliva worked on new techniques of sandblasting and cutting with an assured feeling for modern abstract design. Stanislav Libenský is one of the best-known artists, both for the work he has done on his own and for the architectural and sculptural glass he and his wife Jaroslava Brychtová have designed together.

The success of the Czech glass industry has allowed numerous glass-artists to enjoy a long and successful career: among the older generation born during the 1920s (apart from those already mentioned) the work of Václav Cigler,

Anton Drobník, Jan Kotík, Jaroslav Horejc, Břetislav Novák Senior and Ludvíka Smrčková, was among the most important done during the two decades after the war. Most of these artists, each developing his personal skills, were also teachers either at the Schools of Glass-making at Kamenický Šenov, Nový Bor and Železný Brod, or otherwise at the Academy of Applied Arts in Prague.

Until the Second World War the French had been the undisputed leaders of the modern movement in glass. Even though its leading protagonists, Daum and Lalique, continued to dominate the French industry, their style was more traditional than the concepts being developed in Czechoslovakia, Italy and Scandinavia. Marc Lalique, the son of René Lalique, took over the company after his father's death; although he has been responsible for a range of new designs, the company has not found a modern identity and tends to hark back to the glory of its founder. Daum has been more adventurous, first under the directorship of Michel Daum and, since about 1945, under Jacques Daum, both of whom are members of the dynasty which has owned and run the company since 1875. Going against the trend in post-war years, Daum drained its palette of colour and experimented with what was for them a new material, clear heavy crystal. It was a look that was at once heavy because of its solid mass and light because of the limpid clarity of the crystal. It met with praise and approval in French journals such as *Mobilier et Décoration*, but its popularity was short-lived. The shapes were semi-abstract, more often than not leaning towards the figurative. They are remarkable in their own way, but hampered by a certain clumsiness. The modern experiments in *pâte-de-*

verre (midway between glass and enamel) have been more successful. In 1968 Jacques Daum started a limited edition series of *pâte-de-verre* sculptures; leading painters and sculptors were commissioned to do designs, notably Salvador Dali, whose soft clocks are particularly successful in this translucent substance which suggests a semi-liquid consistency.

Elsewhere in Europe glass companies shared the competitive mood of post-war years, and other glass to be seen at World Fairs included the products of Belgium, where the style remained derivative. The largest manufacturers, Val-St-Lambert, produced table and industrial glass, with some good designs by Charles Graffart who joined the firm in 1906 and became director of design in 1942 until 1958.

Dutch glass, on the other hand, continued to be avant-garde. Andreas Copier, born in 1901, and who had joined the Leerdam Glassworks as an apprentice in 1914, remains the greatest glass-artist and craftsman in Holland. Working as a factory employee, he has never attracted as much attention as some other artists of equal skill, but he has been producing outstanding unique pieces at Leerdam ever since the 'Unica' series of such pieces was begun in the early 1920s. Copier, now in his eighties, is still working and has been consistently inventive throughout his career. It was to him that some early pioneers of the American Studio Glass movement, including Marvin Lipofsky and Harvey Littleton, turned for inspiration when they came to look and learn at Leerdam in the late 1960s. In the post-war years Copier has developed several new techniques, including enamelled decoration between layers of colourless glass, and the vacuum technique, in which air is sucked out of the vessel to make dents and depressions in its shape. He was one of the first to experiment with non-functional free-blown shapes as early as 1958. Under his directorship other talent has also blossomed, notably that of Floris Meydam and Willem Heesen as artists, and Sybren Valkema, one of the outstanding technicians (and teachers) of post-war years. Floris Meydam, born in 1919, started designing Unica pieces in 1935, and since the early 1950s has worked on abstract forms, mostly in clear crystal; they are free-blown and then cut by techniques normally used for optical glass. Willem Heesen did not begin making pieces for the Unica series until the 1960s. Before this he was working on standard production lines at Leerdam. Max Verboeket, working for Kristalunie, Maastricht, is perhaps the only prominent Dutch artist working for a firm other than Leerdam.

In Germany, glass manufacturers—with a few notable exceptions—have been concerned mainly

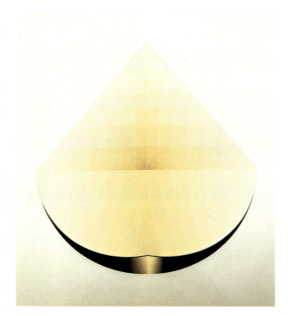

Far left top: Bowl (limited edition of twenty) by the Czech husband-and-wife team of Stanislav Libenský and Jaroslava Brychtová, c. 1950.

Far left bottom: Carved glass vase with figurative design in high relief by René Roubíček, c. 1950.

Left: 'Signal Cosmique' by Jan Zoritchak, 1981. (Musée des Arts Décoratifs, Paris)

Below: Vase by the Dutch glass-maker Andreas Copier.

with industrial needs. At Gralglas good designs were put into production under the supervision of Theodor Baumann and Josef Stadler. At Jenau Glaswerk Schott & Gen., Mainz, the designs of Heinz Loeffelhardt for tableware in heat-resistant glass continued the tradition established by Wilhelm Wagenfeld before the Second World War. Hanns Model of Stuttgart, who had been a pupil of Wilhelm von Eiff until he opened his own workshop in 1933, maintained his established reputation as a designer and cutter. There were other companies such as Richard Süssmuth & Albin Schaedel, and smaller studio workshops like those of Nora Ortlieb and Marianne Schoder. The ceramic firm Rosenthal-Porzellan started a glassworks in 1950, since when they have pursued a policy of buying good design from all over the world and putting it into production at reasonable prices under their own label. But there was no real excitement in German glass design until the 1960s, with the first European response to the American Studio Glass movement.

In Britain, apart from a few isolated individuals there was very little activity in artistic glass in the immediate post-war years. Among glass-engravers, Laurence Whistler, who had begun his work in 1935, continued to do his exquisite 'Applied Pictures' in a neo-classical style. The other outstanding engraver of post-war years is the New Zealand-born artist John Hutton, whose most famous works are the engraved glass screen in Coventry Cathedral, a screen for Guildford Cathedral and the Tolstoy panel for the National Library of Ottawa. He also engraved a series of massive vases for Whitefriars Glassworks. In Scotland the Juniper Workshop was established in 1956 by Helen Turner, who was associated with the Glass Design Department of the Edinburgh College of Art until the 1960s; this was perhaps the only place in Britain where artistic experiment was encouraged. Ronald Renton and Val Rossi have also been chief designers there; Val Rossi is particularly interested in sculptural aspects of glass. There was a small studio-glass department at Wedgwood, and out of it came a series of good pieces designed by Ronald Stennett-Wilson, who also designed for King's Lynn Glass Ltd. James Powell & Sons (Whitefriars Glass) and Clyne Farquharson turned out some moderately interesting designs, and the Stourbridge works continued to produce fine crystal stemware, but on the whole the scene was a drab one.

In the United States there were few developments outside the research programmes on glass technology and glass chemistry. A few small studios were in existence where artists worked in the 'craft tradition'. Maurice Heaton, born in

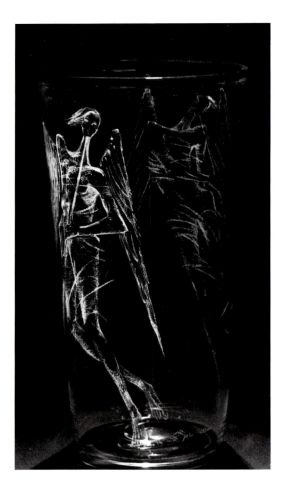

Left: Massive glass vase with etched design of trumpeting angels, by John Hutton for Webb & Co., 1950s. The work is one of a series of large etched vases executed by Hutton at the time he was working on the glass screen for the new Coventry Cathedral. The figures he etched on the vases were based on those incorporated in the design for the screen.

Below: Vase designed by Ronald Stennett-Wilson, who did designs for two English companies, the studio-glass department at Wedgwood and King's Lynn Glass Ltd.

1900, developed a personal style of enamel decoration with sgrafitto figural designs etched into the enamel. Edris Eckhardt, who trained at Cleveland Institute of Art and studied under the sculptor Archipenko, made small figures in multicoloured multiple-layer glass, and in 1953 developed a gold glass process. Several companies, including the Pilgrim Glass Corporation, the Rainbow Art Glass Co., the Viking Glass Co. and Blenko Glass, all in West Virginia, the Dearborn Glass Company in Michigan, the Glass Guild Inc. at Kew Gardens, New York, and the Erickson Glass Works in Poremen, Ohio, had good design departments.

However, as before the war, the Steuben factory at Corning, New York, remained into the 1960s the most important industrial maker of art glass in the United States. Its chief artistic work has been in a series of major pieces of engraved crystal. Many of these intricately hand-worked pieces are unique and were specially designed for museum collections, or as presents to and from heads of state, such as the Papal Cup, presented to Pope Pius XII in 1956, and the Queen's Cup presented to Queen Elizabeth II on a state visit.

There are also limited editions of less exotic pieces, including bowls, vases, candlesticks and

Interest in glass has grown in Japan during the last decade and international art glass has been shown at several important museum exhibitions. This heavy lead-crystal vase with an engraved figure of a sea-goddess is the work of a leading glass-artist, Kozo Kugami, and was designed for the Kagami Crystal Glassworks in 1980.
Height: 27cm (10⅝in)

other decorative objects, all in the flawless pure crystal made according to the formula discovered at Corning in 1932, in which all discolouration was eliminated. James Plant, in the third edition of his monograph *Steuben Glass*, published in 1971, wrote of the company's growing importance in the history of glass: 'Steuben is beginning to take its place among the world's illustrious producers of objets d'art, in the tradition of Cellini and Fabergé.'

In the Far East two Japanese glassworks make artistic glass in the western tradition. They are the Awashima Glass Company in Tokyo, founded in 1956, where the chief designer is Masakichi Awashima; and the Kagami Crystal Glass Works, also in Tokyo, whose team of designers includes Kozo Kagami, a one-time pupil of the renowned German glass-artist Wilhelm von Eiff. Most of the glass produced by

these companies is either mould-blown or pressed in clear or frosted glass. Their output demonstrates a consistently high level of technical accomplishment.

The International Studio Glass Movement

A single event marked the birth of the new art-glass movement, which is now accepted along with sculpture and painting as a mainstream art-form. Harvey Littleton, whose father was a leading glass scientist at Corning, suggested during the American Craftsmen's Council conference at Lake George in 1959, that 'glass should be a medium for the individual artist'. He could not have foreseen the full effect of his remark.

Unlike most of the other pioneers of the

'Loop', glass sculpture by the American Harvey Littleton, 1978. Littleton, who began his working life as an apprentice at the Corning Glassworks, has been one of the major forces in the Studio Glass movement.
Height: 38cm (15in)

'*Split Piece*', polychrome glass sculpture by Marvin Lipofsky, one of the pioneers of the Studio Glass movement in America. This piece, one of a series executed in Murano for Fratelli Toso during the 1970s, was made with the help of Gianni Toso.

Studio Glass movement, very few of whom had started out their careers as glass-workers, Littleton began his working life as an apprentice at the Corning glassworks in 1945, and then took an art course at Brighton School of Art in England. His deep-seated faith in the ideals outlined at Lake George led to two workshop seminars sponsored by the Toledo Museum of Art in 1962. At this time Littleton was primarily a ceramist, as were the eight students who made up the team for the first of the Toledo seminars. The workshop took place at an improvised studio in a garage on the Toledo Museum's grounds, and immediately ran into difficulties. In the true pioneering spirit, they were working almost exclusively from instinct, and their technical skill was inadequate: they could not melt the glass. Dominick Labino, at that time research vice-president of Johns-Manville Fibre Glass Corporation, came to the rescue, and with his great technical ability provided the hungry potters with molten glass; but apparently little was accomplished in the way of glass art.

There were, however, two important consequences of the experiments at Toledo. First of all Labino developed a new formula for a glass that could be melted at a temperature low enough for it to be workable in the average studio or classroom, and he also invented a new small furnace suitable for this environment, thus dispensing with elaborate and costly equipment which had previously confined glass-blowing to industrial surroundings.

In the second place, as a direct result of the findings of the seminar, Harvey Littleton managed to persuade authorities at the University of Wisconsin, where he had been teaching since 1951, to start the first university studio-glass programme in the United States. It triggered a tremendous reaction as other American universities quickly followed suit. Marvin Lipofsky, another of the Toledo pioneers, opened a department at the University of Berkeley in California. Today there are well over 100 American schools which offer courses in glass-blowing, and it is estimated that there are over 1000 artists working in glass in the United States alone.

Since 1962 the changes in attitude have been remarkable. Much has been written about the new trends in studio glass since then, and every commentator has one fundamental thing to say, which is that glass artistry no longer conforms in any way to the clear-cut principles of a bygone age before that date. Of all the arts affected by the explosive tendencies of Pop Art and 'Funk' the medium of glass has suffered the most direct hit. Glass was a virgin territory for this new

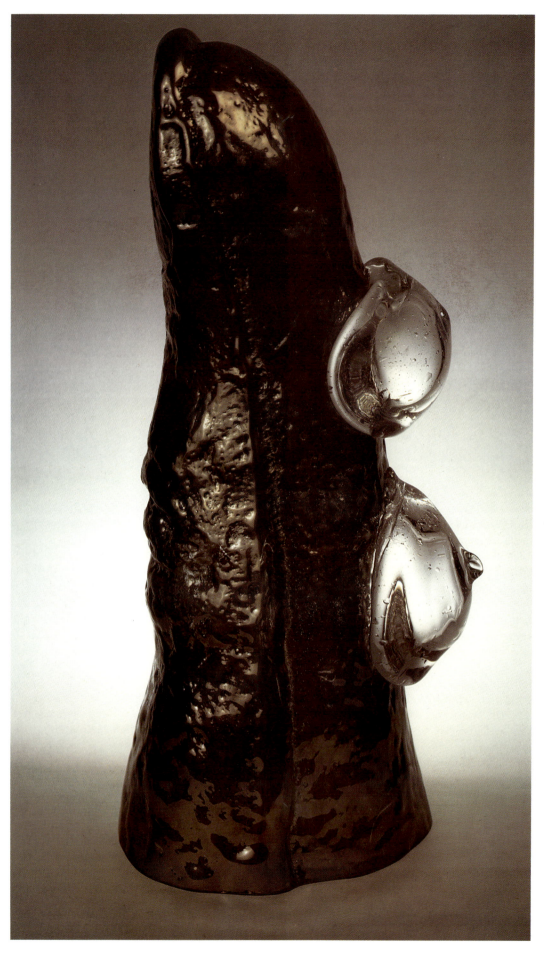

'Pop Piece', blown glass sculpture by Erwin Eisch, one of the most influential of the German glass-artists. Eisch, the first pop artist to interpret his ideas in glass, turned to this medium for sculpture after meeting the American Harvey Littleton in 1957.

generation of artists, and in this respect it had a strong appeal to those spending their formative years in the heyday of Pop culture, whose main concern was to find new subject-matter and new media in which to express it. In a previous decade it would not have occurred to those same art students to express their ideas and their fantasies in glass. Erwin Eisch, the first of the new-wave glass-artists in Europe, summed up the major changes:

> The Art Nouveau glass-artists were concerned primarily with vessel forms... but for me a vessel cannot serve as an artistic point of departure; my primary concerns are pure three-dimensional form, glass as a medium for expression, and art for its own functionless sake.

The link between a university and a museum environment is an obvious one, and it was a natural development that exhibitions of contemporary glass should begin to appear in museums. The prototype for nearly all subsequent museum events was the 1959 Corning show, and because of this particular museum's strong connections with industry, it was also an easy transition. Prospective entrants were asked to submit slides of their work, and final entries were chosen by a panel of five judges. Prizes were awarded for the best work in various categories. Over the years methods of selection have changed slightly; some museums tend to be more autocratic than others, and with changing ideals the prizes have been categorized differently. Apart from being important events in themselves, these exhibitions were important for the catalogues that were published in conjunction with them, since they form the main reference material for work carried out during the 1960s and 1970s.

The international flavour of the 1979 Corning show was significant: the atmosphere was not one of competitiveness so much as one of international co-operation. During the 1960s the Toledo Museum extended its support by holding 'Glass Nationals' in 1966, 1968 and 1970, culminating in 'American Glass Now' in 1972, jointly sponsored with the Museum of Contemporary Crafts in New York. In 1972 the Museum Bellerive in Zürich held a show entitled 'Today's Glass, Art or Craft?', which introduced the American developments in glass to Europe. The Germans were profoundly influenced by new studio glass from America, and during the 1970s a series of exhibitions was held in Germany. One of the most important was the 'Coburger Glaspreis' exhibition held in 1977, with participants from America, Europe and Asia. Perhaps the most comprehensive exhibition to date has been the 1979 Corning Show 'New

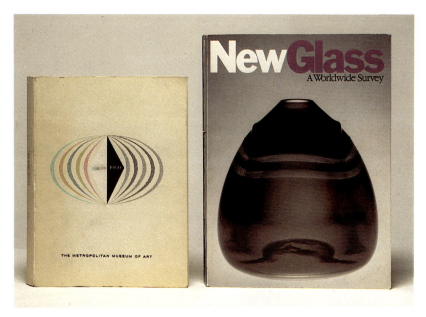

Glass - A Worldwide Survey', partly because of its impressive scale, and partly because it was a travelling exhibition, still on the road in 1982. There were also numerous exhibitions of contemporary glass held in Japan during the 1970s, and the biggest Japanese exhibition to date, entitled 'Contemporary Glass - Europe and Japan', was held at the National Museums of Modern Art in Kyoto and Tokyo in 1980.

During the last ten years commercial galleries have been opened for the promotion and sale of contemporary glass, and a collector's market is fast developing, with 'early pieces' (from the 1960s) changing hands for high prices. In the 1960s price was hardly a factor to be considered but the work of today's leading glass-artists is within the reach of only a very few. Even so, enthusiasm for modern glass continues to grow, particularly in America, Czechoslovakia, Germany and Japan, with many other countries becoming more aware of its growing importance.

One curious fact about the glass-artists of the 1960s and 1970s is that hardly any of them were originally drawn to glass. Many of them were potters, some were metal-workers, some had trained as painters and others had taken a general design course. The simple reason for this is that glass training schemes had previously not existed outside the industry. Many of the first new-wave glass-artists have become teachers as well, creating another curious situation in which most of the university courses have been planned and given by self-taught men. The students of the 1960s and 1970s have been pioneers as much as their instructors. This exciting era of experiment has given way to a new university environment with impressive facilities which are far removed from the makeshift arrangements of Harvey

The catalogues of the various exhibitions that have exposed the work of glass-artists to an international public are a major source of reference for studio glass of the last two or three decades. Two of the most significant of these exhibitions have been organized by the Corning Museum of Glass, Corning, New York. One, in 1959, served as the prototype for many subsequent exhibitions. 'New Glass - A Worldwide Survey', a travelling exhibition first shown in 1979, provided an exceptionally comprehensive view of recent developments.

Littleton and Marvin Lipofsky in the early 1960s.

Although it goes against the spirit of the International Studio Glass movement to make national divisions, this remains the most practical approach. The Americans were the pioneers and have been largely responsible for the changes that have occurred in other Western countries. Dominick Labino, who came to studio glass in 1963, appears to be emerging as the father-figure of the modern movement. He had previously spent most of his life in the industry, and holds fifty-seven United States patents and several hundred in foreign countries; and three of his developments for glass-fibre insulation were used in the Apollo spacecraft. As an artist he has experimented with the colour and texture of glass. Though his shapes are not remarkable, there is magic in the thin veils of colour in his 'Immersion' pieces, a series of solid lumps of glass, their shapes reminiscent of icebergs, with layered inclusions in a delicate range of colours. In the light of recent stylistic development his 1960s pieces now look awkward and misshapen, along with many of the other 'free-form' shapes of the beginnings of the Studio Glass movement.

Three of the other pioneers who are still working today, Marvin Lipofsky, Harvey Littleton and Dale Chihuly, also belong to the 'free-form' school of glass-makers. Lipofsky in particular liberated blown glass from the firmly established traditions of careful control. His work is entirely abstract, with lumpy, bubbly sculptural objects in bright colours that demand attention by their strong presence; their untidiness exploits to the full the spontaneity of hot glass processes. With a sure eye for ordered shapelessness and a lively feeling for colour,

'Seaform Series', Dale Chihuly, 1981. This American glass-artist, who has worked as an independent since the early 1970s, has been preoccupied for some years by the intricate arrangement of bowls within bowls. The molten glass is laced with delicately coloured threads then pressed into optical moulds and spun into delicate thin shells.

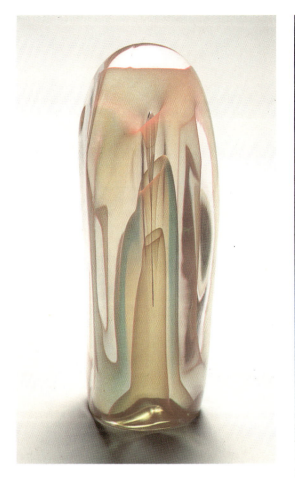

Lipofsky has created splendid 'pop art' objects. Harvey Littleton's work is more calculated. He is best known for his bent-glass-tube sculptures and his 'bowls within bowls'. In the glass-tube pieces there are virtuoso shapes (sometimes in clear glass, sometimes brightly coloured) which command the type of admiration one might feel for a virtuoso contortionist, able to discipline his limbs into positions that defy the laws of nature. The 'eye bowls', as they have come to be called, are interesting because, in the spirit of kinetic art, they form a group of movable objects. Chihuly is also interested in interrelated shapes; his forms are freer than Littleton's and do not necessarily fit into one another; but he makes groups of basket-like objects which, although separate, depend on one another for a corporate existence. He has also worked on a series of cylindrical shapes in translucent coloured glass with brilliantly coloured inlaid 'woven' patterns; these reflect his background as a weaver and are inspired by Navajo textile design.

Most of the early pioneers, including André Billeci, James Carpenter and Robert Fritz, are still working, but there is a division between those who have chosen an academic life and those who have sought to earn a living as artists. With the creation of so many university posts such a choice has been a matter of personal temperament, and those whose names are today in the forefront are the ones who have opted for publicity by working for exhibitions and gallery showings. Mark Peiser has been one of the most successful of these, developing his own personal style. He is above all a meticulous craftsman and a perfectionist with the patience and skill to work a complicated technique in which colourless glass encases intricate lampwork decoration. He revels in the complexity of his chosen technique, and his work, which is usually naturalistic with trees and flowers, is easy on the eye, and has the appeal of a precious object. Peiser is a good example of a glass-artist who took many turnings before discovering glass. He studied electrical engineering in the 1950s and music during the 1960s, coming to glass purely by chance during the course of his work as a product designer.

Of those artists who have been working since

Left: Dominick Labino has been a major figure in the Studio Glass movement in America, playing an important role in the development of a formula for glass that melts at a low temperature. This piece is typical of his use of coloured inclusions to give subtle colouring.

Above: Blue blown-glass vase from the 'Contiguous Fragment' series, by Joel Philip Myers, 1981. Height: 28.6cm (11¼ in)

'Mosaic' glass bowl by Klaus Moje, c. 1976. Moje has lived and worked in Germany for most of his life but has recently moved to Australia. His glass is traditional in conception but he is master of many techniques, including cutting, polishing and the firing of painted decoration on glass.

the 1960s, Joel Philip Myers is one whose work seems to have steadily improved, and is the result of nearly twenty years of experiment and change. He has always been an innovator, and his outstanding technical mastery has given him a facility accorded to few glass-artists. His free-form and 'pop' sculptural shapes of the 1960s have given way to a greater discipline in recent years, but whatever style he has chosen, he has brought to it a rare talent for combining technical and artistic imagination. His 'Contiguous Fragment' series, begun in 1980, combines a variety of skills. These blown black glass forms have applied glass elements, fumed, sand-blasted, and acid-etched. One can detect all sorts of influences, but nevertheless these are original works of art which cannot be compared to anything else.

Of the many younger artists working today in the United States, Tom Patti and Jon Kuhn are making a remarkable impact. Tom Patti, born in 1943, met with success early, largely because of the visual surprises resulting from his technical ideas. He works in coloured and colourless sheet glass, laminated and blown, sometimes with fine wire inclusions. A piece of his was chosen for the cover of the 1979 Corning 'New Glass' catalogue. John Kuhn, born in 1949, is again remarkable for his originality. In *American Craft* for October/November 1980, he describes the nature of his work and the way he treats the material:

> My work investigates tactile and colour values related to physical phenomena. The heavy chemical treatment of the glass, for example, produces a rocklike surface which refers to geological outcroppings. By cutting beneath this surface I expose patterns in coloured glass which

strongly suggest landscapes. The tension between interior and exterior serves as an analogy for the mind as a place of peace in the tumult of the physical world.

In Canada there is a growing glass movement closely related to its slightly older North American counterpart, with some outstanding work by artists such as Karl Schank with his brightly coloured laminated glass sculptures and the inventive techniques used to fine artistic ends by Andrew Kuntz.

The two main criteria for judging contemporary art glass are those of technical brilliance and of artistic expression. Obviously there cannot be artistry without technical skill, but in some instances the skill itself becomes artistry. In West Germany the two leading creators of art glass quite distinctly represent opposite extremes. Erwin Eisch is mainly concerned with self-expression, while Klaus Moje and Isgard Moje-Wohlgemuth are technical perfectionists, and yet they are all brilliant artists.

Erwin Eisch, born in 1927, began his professional life as a sculptor. Then, in 1957 he met Harvey Littleton and became fascinated with the idea of using glass instead of bronze for his sculptures. In 1964 he attended the glass seminar at the University of Wisconsin, and ever since then has worked out his ideas in glass at his workshop in Frauenau. Since the 1960s Eisch has been the dominant influence among German glass-artists and, more than any other single European glass-artist, he was responsible for the first beginnings of the International Studio Glass movement in Europe. He himself is basically a product of pop culture, with a strong leaning towards 'Funk'. The irreverent way in which he uses his chosen materials is full of wit and cynicism. In his work he hints at functionalism, but mainly in order to ridicule it: a teapot made in 1972 is grossly misshapen and has a spout in the shape of a female breast. His objects are usually free-blown and decorated with gilding, etching, or enamelling. Although the casualness of his pieces might suggest otherwise, there is great skill in their making; it would be easy, however, to assign their carefully thought out, lumpy, anti-functionalist shapes to sheer incompetence.

No such mistake is possible in the case of Klaus Moje. His intricately worked bowls and plates in brilliant opaque glass reminiscent of alabaster have the elegance of a mathematical formula. Whereas Eisch throws out new ideas with ease, Moje reworks the same idea over and over again, with variations here and there, but the final result remains always new and exciting. Klaus Moje and his wife Isgard Moje-

Wohlgemuth have worked for many years as a team, developing a process where the blown glass shape is ground and then painted with metallic oxides which are fired at high temperatures.

There are a great many other glass-artists working in Germany. Many techniques are used, but lamp-blown glass is something of a German speciality, with Albin Schaedel, Kurt Wallstab and Roderich Wohlgemuth its most successful exponents.

In East Germany, there is a lively group of artists who are mainly preoccupied with reviving and extending various aspects of *latticinio*. Of the other eastern bloc countries, Hungary is beginning to attract notice with a group of young artists with interesting avant-garde ideas.

Elsewhere in Europe, glass-artists work in greater isolation than in Germany or the United

Bowl by Ann Wärff, who, after designing at Kosta Boda, Sweden, for many years, is now an independent artist of worldwide renown.

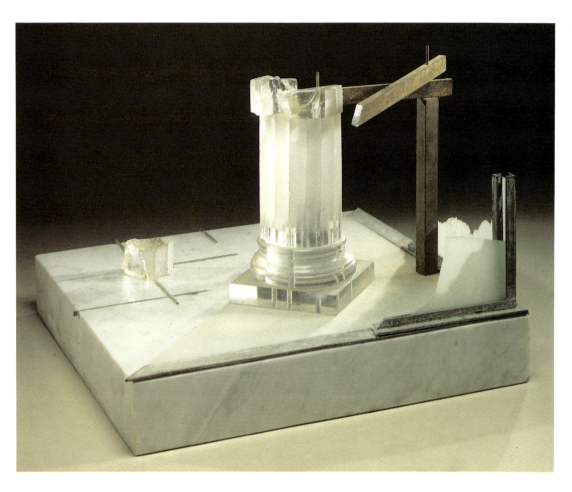

Sculpture by Clifford Rainey, one of the first British glass-artists to use glass in conjunction with other materials in sculpture

States. There are fewer university courses outside these two countries, and correspondingly fewer individual glass studios. But there are outstanding individual artists working in many countries. Ann Wärff, who previously worked for Kosta in Sweden, has now set up on her own and is considered to be one of the outstanding artists of post-war years. For a time she made up a husband-and-wife team with Goran Wärff; such teams are quite often found among glass-artists. She works mainly in cased and etched glass, using these techniques to paint dream-like scenes in pale pinks and rich blues and greens on vases and bowls. Elsewhere, there are artists whose names would appear in any full account of contemporary glass, though here space forbids giving more than their names: Paolo Martinuzzi in Venice, Durk Valkema and Bert van Loo in Holland (as well as those already mentioned earlier in the chapter), Benny Motzfeld in Norway, Oiva Toikka and Pertti Santalahti in Finland. Quite a few of the younger American artists have made their homes in Europe; Richard Meitner in Holland, Jack Ink in Austria, Darryl Hinze in Denmark, and Sam Herman, Charlie Meaker and Steven Newell in Britain.

In Britain there has been a noticeable increase in the number of glass-artists over the past decade. This is largely due to thriving glass departments, notably at West Surrey College of Art, Stourbridge College of Technology and Art, North Staffordshire Polytechnic and the Royal College of Art in London, to the sponsorship of the Crafts Council and, more recently, to Pilkington Brothers, who sponsored the Corning 'New Glass' Show at the Victoria and Albert Museum in 1981. The first wave of British glass-artists was in fact headed in the late 1960s by the American-born Sam Herman, whose pupils at the Royal College of Art formed the nucleus of British glass-artists for the following decade; these included Annette Meech, Pauline Solven, Dillon Clarke, Jane Bruce, John Cooke and Peter Aldridge. One of the difficulties for British glass-artists, not encountered in other fields, is the sheer cost of the equipment needed to set up a studio. It is usually too expensive for just one artist, and so small workshops have been set up with a handful of artists pooling their resources. One of the first of these was the Glasshouse, which opened in London during the 1970s and is still operating today.

A few British glass-artists have made international reputations for themselves, for example Clifford Rainey who was probably the first in the country to combine glass with other media in his sculptural pieces, and Stephen Procter, also a sculptor and now joint head of the thriving glass department at West Surrey College of Art. Among the youngest British glass-artists, a few are attracting much attention: for example Arlon Bayliss with his 'Proteus' series of coloured wing-like sculptures, and Colin Reid with his kiln-formed pieces.

The one country where there was no sudden change of gear in the 1960s is Czechoslovakia. There the major changes took place during the 1950s, and there has been steady growth and development ever since. The many artists who started working in the 1950s are still working today, and post-war Czechoslovakia can boast a longer history of modern art glass than any other country in the world. Some of the older artists like Pavel Hlava and Jiři Harcuba have evolved with the changing decades and still belong to the avant-garde. There are also a great many younger ones who started working during the late 1960s and 1970s; some original work has been done by Jiři Suhajek, who perhaps benefited from his years from 1968 to 1971 at the Royal College in London. František Vízner creates glass with an off-hand shape: its simple, natural appearance does not hint at the perfectionist skill involved in the making of it. Břetislav Novák Junior makes monumental sculptural objects, exploiting to the full his great talent as a glass-cutter. Glass-cutting, particularly optical cutting, has remained a Czech speciality.

While the Studio Glass movement has spread, a gap has developed between the artist and the craftsman. They are still shown together, and there is room for both, but their separate roles are becoming more clearly defined. Glass-artists are beginning to get the recognition that their creative talents deserve. The separation between art and craft can never be complete, as art must always depend on craft; but different criteria are involved when craft becomes art.

It is difficult to know how to categorize some of the work that has been done in the last two decades. Much of it was quite simply bad, with too many craftsmen passing for artists, but because of its newness there has tended to be an absence of criticism. Edgar Kaufmann, in his notes as a member for the selection committee for Corning 1959, talks of 'pieces maturing in that post-fashionable oblivion whence come the tested masterpieces that speak for their epochs'. He adds: 'It is not good to interrupt their fallow season'. Nobody much has interrupted the fallow season of 1940s and 1950s glass until now, but the time has come for it to be rediscovered and evaluated afresh, while glass made since 1968 is still enjoying approval.

Bowl in smoky blue glass made at the Škrdlovice Glassworks, Czechoslovakia, and cut by the glass-artist František Vízner, late 1970s. Vízner has made several variants of this piece in different colours. Although the forms of this artist's work suggest functional shapes, his pieces are generally non-functional. Diameter: 28.3cm (11⅛in)

GLOSSARY

abrade
To grind shallow patterns into glass with a wheel.

acid etching
See etching.

acid polishing
The process of giving cut glass a polished surface by dipping it briefly in a bath of hydrofluoric acid mixed with sulphuric acid.

air-twist
See twist.

alabastron
A small perfume flask of a type common in the Ancient World. It was usually made of pottery but sometimes of core glass.

almorrata
A type of rose-water sprinkler with numerous spouts, made in northern Spain in the sixteenth to eighteenth centuries.

Amberina
A kind of shaded amber glass, patented by Joseph Locke of the New England Glass Company, Cambridge, Massachusetts, in 1883. It contained gold in solution, which caused the part that was reheated to take on a ruby colouring.

amphora
A large jar with two loop handles for storing liquids, generally made of pottery although examples of Roman glass are known.

annealing
A process involving heating and gradual cooling of glass in an annealing oven (lehr) that toughens glass and reduces internal stresses.

baluster
A type of drinking glass, principally of English manufacture, with a baluster stem, that is, one with the swelling form characteristic of the architectural feature from which it takes its name. Variations of the baluster stem are numerous: sometimes the baluster is inverted; sometimes it is decorated with knops and tears.

balustroid
A type of baluster glass but with a lighter, more elongated stem. Balustroids are usually found on glasses made in Newcastle.

barilla
A plant of salt marshes in the Mediterranean region, gathered particularly in the vicinity of Alicante, Spain, and burned to make a soda ash formerly used instead of potash as the alkali in the making of glass.

base-ring
A ring of glass added to the base of a vessel after its body has been made.

batch
A mixture of measured raw ingredients which, when melted and fused in the melting pot, will produce glass.

blank
A glass object intended to be decorated, prior to the decoration being applied.

Blankschnitt
Literally, polished cut. A style of engraved decoration found on German potash glass, particularly Nuremberg glassware, in which the relief effect is enhanced by the polish given the ground part of the intaglio.

blowing
The process of shaping a molten mass of glass by blowing air into it through a blowpipe.

blowpipe
A metal tube used to gather a blob of molten glass and through which air is blown by the glass-maker into the glass to shape it.

bottle glass
An unrefined, naturally coloured (green or brown) glass used for making early glass bottles in England in the mid-seventeenth century.

brilliant-cut
A style of cut glass with very deep, complex and highly polished cutting, developed in the USA in the latter half of the nineteenth century.

broad glass
Sheet glass made by cutting the ends off a long bubble of blown glass, then cutting and flattening the resultant cylinder.

cage-cup (*vasa diatretum*)
A type of beaker made by the Romans in which the body is surrounded by an openwork pattern of glass attached by small glass struts.

calcedonio
Variegated opaque glassware made in Venice in the late fifteenth century, to imitate earlier Roman agate glass (which was intended to resemble the semi-precious stone).

cameo glass
Cased glass in two or more layers, the outer layer carved on a wheel to create a design in relief of one colour on another. The technique, similar to the cameo cutting of stones and shells, was known to the ancient Egyptians and Romans, and revived in the nineteenth century.

cane
A thin rod of clear or colour glass, used to make the stems of certain type of glasses or that is cut in slices and used in the manufacture of *millefiori* or mosaic glassware.

cántir or ***cántaro***
A typically Spanish (Catalonian) vessel in use from the seventeenth to the nineteenth century, shaped like a closed jug with a central ring handle and two spouts, a short one for filling and pouring and a longer, thin one through which liquid can be squirted directly into the mouth.

cased glass
Glass with two or more layers of different colours, usually having the outer layer or layers partly cut away to make a design of one colour on another. The process was known in Roman times and was popular with manufacturers in Bohemia and Britain in the nineteenth century.

cire perdue (lost wax)
A casting process adapted from metallurgy, in which a model of the object to be cast is carved in wax and then encased in a mould. The wax is then melted and poured out of the mould which is refilled with molten glass.

claw-beaker (*Rüsselbecher*)
A blue or green glass beaker of a type commonly made in Germany from the fifth to the eighth century. It tapered from a wide mouth to a small base and was decorated with two or three rows of hollow claw-like prunts.

cold-painting
The application of coloured decoration to glassware without subsequent firing.

colour-twist
See twist.

combing
Wavy or zigzag decoration achieved by applying coloured threads to the surface of a molten glass object, marvering the threads into the glass and pulling them with a special comb to form a pattern.

core-forming
A technique dating from c.1500 BC, in which a vessel is made by trailing molten glass round a shaped core of mud or clay and sand mixed with dung, the core being removed after annealing.

crisselling (crizzling)
A defect in glass consisting of a network of fine cracks. The 'disease', which leads to deterioration of the glass, is caused by a faulty balance of the ingredients in the batch. One of the most important remedies, the addition of lead oxide, was developed by George Ravenscroft in about 1676.

cristallo
A type of soda glass made with the ashes of sea plants (barilla), first developed in Venice in the fourteenth century, and which subsequently became the standard metal of the Venetian glass industry. Its softness in a molten state meant that it could easily be worked into elaborate shapes; the glass itself was suitable for diamond-point engraving but too brittle for cutting.

crown glass
Sheet glass made by blowing a bubble of glass, cutting the bubble open and then rotating it rapidly on a rod, with repeated reheating, until it formed a flat disk. The glass was then annealed and panes of the required shape cut from it. The process, which was known to the Romans, produced the 'bull's-eye' panes of medieval glass, which were from the centre of the sheet where the rod had been attached.

crystal
Colourless, transparent glass that resembles rock-crystal, natural quartz. The term is now generally applied to high-quality cut glass with a minimum lead oxide content.

cullet
Fragments of glass that are melted down with the fresh ingredients of a new batch.

cut glass
Glassware decorated with facets and grooves made by cutting into its surface with a wheel of iron or stone. The technique, which has been employed since pre-Roman times, was applied with particular success to English and Irish lead glass in the late eighteenth and nineteenth centuries.

devitrification
The process by which molten glass is cooled too slowly and thereby becomes crystalline, with a milky appearance, and no longer able to be used as glass.

diatreta
See cage-cup.

dichroic
Having the property of showing different colours when viewed by transmitted or reflected light.

églomisé
The decorative application of gold or silver leaf to a glass surface which is then engraved. It was usually applied on the reverse of an object and protected by varnish, metal foil or another layer of glass.

enamelling
Decoration in which finely powdered glass coloured with metal oxides is applied to the surface of a glass object and then fused to the glass surface by firing.

engraving
The process of cutting a design into the surface of a glass object with a sharp implement such as a needle or wheel.

etching, acid-etching
A technique in which controlled exposure of the surface of glass to hydrofluoric acid results in shiny, matt or frosted decoration of the exposed area.

façon de Venise, à la
Literally, in the Venetian style. A term used to describe high-quality glassware made throughout Europe in the sixteenth and seventeenth centuries.

Favrile glass
A type of iridescent glass in Art Nouveau style developed by Tiffany c.1892 and inspired perhaps by Roman glass with iridescence resulting from weathering.

filigree (Italian *filigrana*, 'thread-grained')
A decorative technique in which opaque white or coloured glass threads are embedded in clear metal to form a very fine network pattern.

finial
An ornamental knob surmounting a decorative glass object or vessel, most often on its cover, where it also serves as a handle.

flashing
Applying a thin layer of glass of a contrasting colour to the body of a glass object by dipping. The coating, much thinner than a casing or an overlay, may be cut to reveal the glass beneath it to form a pattern.

fluting
A pattern on cut glass consisting of either rounded or mitred parallel grooves.

flux
An alkaline substance, such as potash or soda, which is an essential glass-making ingredient added to the batch to aid the fusion of the silica, another essential ingredient.

foot-ring, foot-rim
A slightly projecting rim on the bottom of a glass object, on which the object stands

forest glass (*verre de fougère*, Waldglas)
Glass of primitive quality, generally greenish but sometimes brownish or yellowish, produced in European glasshouses in medieval and later times. Ashes of burnt wood or ferns provided the alkali content of this glass.

free-blown
Formed and shaped solely on a blowpipe.

frit
Certain preheated ingredients of glass, cooled and ground into a powder and added to the other ingredients to facilitate fusion of the batch.

gadroon
A continuous decorative pattern of short sections of ribbing, originally inspired by patterns on contemporary silverware in the late seventeenth century.

gather
The blob or mass of molten glass attached to the blowpipe or pontil before an object is formed from it.

Graal glass
A type of ornamental glass developed in Sweden in 1916. It was made by cutting and etching a pattern on coloured glass and then returning the piece to the furnace to give the design fluidity before encasing it in clear glass.

grisaille
(1) Decorative painting in shades of grey on glass, sometimes used to imitate relief sculpture;
(2) A brownish paint made from iron oxide, fused onto glass and used to define details in stained-glass windows.

grozing iron
A tool for snipping off a raw rim or edge of a piece of glass, leaving a slightly jagged edge.

Hochschnitt
Literally, high engraving. A technique of decoration on glass by wheel-engraving, the design in relief being created by cutting away the ground. The technique, which was known to the Romans, is particularly associated with Bohemian and German glass of the late seventeenth century.

Humpen
A type of tall cylindrical beaker (up to 60cm high) of forest glass, with a slightly projecting kick base or applied foot-ring, and normally bearing elaborate enamel decoration. Used for drinking beer or wine, *Humpen* were made in Germany, Silesia and Bohemia from the mid-sixteenth to the eighteenth century.

ice glass
Decorative glassware with an outer surface resembling cracked ice, produced either by plunging white-hot glass briefly into cold water and then reheating and reblowing it or by rolling the hot glass in splinters of glass before reheating it to fuse the splinters to the glass.

imbricated
Arranged so as to overlap, like fish scales.

intaglio
The technique of engraving or wheel-cutting a design below the surface of a glass object, to produce an image in relief where the background is in the highest plane. Known in German as *Tiefschnitt* (literally, deep carving), the opposite of *Hochschnitt*.

intercalaire
A process of applying two layers of decoration to a glass object, the first one covered with a glass skin which acts as the surface for the second layer.

iridescence
A rainbow-like effect on a glass surface caused by weathering.

kick
A concavity in the base of a glass vessel ranging from a slight indentation to a deep conical hollow.

knop
A decorative blob or bulge on the stem of a glass, either hollow or solid and of varying shape.

***latticinio/latticino (latte,* milk)**
Clear glass embedded with opaque white glass threads forming a filigree pattern.

***lattimo* (German *Milchglas*, 'milk glass')**
Opaque white glass, a term used to denote an object decorated with marvered bands of opaque white glass or one entirely of such glass.

lead glass
A type of soft glass containing a large amount of lead oxide, first made in about 1676 by George Ravenscroft as a remedy for crisselling, and eventually superseding the more fragile Venetian soda glass.

martelé
Literally, hammered. A decorative technique producing a multi-faceted surface, used particularly by Daum and Gallé as a background texture to a design.

marver
An iron or marble table upon which the gather is rolled into an evenly shaped mass, in a process known as 'marvering'.

metal
The substance, glass, both in its molten and cold states. The term is normally used to distinguish the fused material from the finished object.

millefiori
Literally, 'a thousand flowers'. A decorative technique dating from the first century BC in which slices of coloured glass canes, usually arranged to resemble flowers, are embedded in clear molten glass.

muffle kiln
A low-temperature kiln used for refiring glass to fix enamelling and gilding. The glass objects would be placed in a fire-clay box, or muffle, to protect them from the smoke and flames of the kiln.

nef
A table ornament in the shape of a rigged sailing ship, sometimes with a spout in the hull for its use as a ewer.

omphalos bowl
A shallow, low-rimmed bowl with an indented base, of a type made during the Iron Age.

paraison
The bubble of molten glass formed on the blowpipe after air has been blown into it.

pâte-de-verre
Literally, 'glass paste'. A mixture of crushed glass, flux and colour fused together in a mould.

pincers
A tool used for pinching the threading or other ornamentation on an object for decorative effect.

pontil
A solid metal rod used, tipped with a wad or ring of hot glass, to remove a blown object from the blowpipe in order to allow the top to be finished and any other final shaping to be done. When the glass has cooled and solidified it is knocked off the rod, leaving a rough mark, the 'pontil mark'.

Pokal
A style of engraved lidded goblet with a flared bowl, made in Germany from the late seventeenth to the mid-nineteenth century and used for drinking toasts.

porrón* or *porró
A type of drinking vessel with a narrow neck and a long tapering spout but no handle, used in Spain for drinking wine by pouring it directly into the mouth.

potash glass
A type of hard glass containing potash (potassium carbonate) derived from plant ash, and suitable for cutting and engraving.

prunt
A blob of glass applied to a glass object as a decoration, and sometimes drawn to a point or impressed with a pattern (raspberry prunt) or a mask (lion's head prunt).

puzzle glass
A glass designed so as to be as difficult as possible to drink from, for use in drinking competitions whereby spilling a drop meant refilling the glass and trying again (thus leading to great drunkenness).

Roemer
A traditional German drinking vessel with an ovoid bowl, a hollow cylindrical stem decorated with raspberry prunts and a spreading, coiled or blown foot.

Rüsselbecher
See claw-beaker.

shears
A tool used to trim a piece of glassware, for example the rim of a vessel, in the course of its manufacture.

soda glass
Glass in which the alkali is soda (sodium carbonate) rather than potash. Venetian *cristallo* is a soda glass and much soda glassware is in the *façon de Venise* style. The soda was traditionally obtained from barilla.

stippling
The technique of tapping a glass surface with a pointed implement so as to produce a pattern with tiny dots (stipples).

striking
Reheating a glass object in order to develop a colour or special effect, as when making ruby glass or Amberina.

sulphide
A medallion or cameo of opaque glass enclosed in transparent glass as, for instance, in a paperweight.

sweetmeat glass
A tall-stemmed container, used in England in the late seventeenth and early eighteenth centuries to hold crystallized fruits and other kinds of sweetmeats.

tazza
Literally, cup. A shallow ornamental cup or dish on a stemmed foot, usually used for displaying food such as fruit and sweetmeats.

thread
A thin strand of glass as used in filigree, trailed or combed decoration.

Tiefschnitt
See intaglio.

trailing
The process of laying threads of hot glass on to a glass object to form a decorative pattern.

trembleuse
A cup and saucer in which the cup fits into a projecting ring or well in the saucer, so that spillage of the contents by a shaky hand is avoided.

twist
A decorative device in the stems of eighteenth-century drinking glasses, produced by twisting a glass rod in which were embedded columns of air (air-twists) or threads of white or coloured glass (cotton-twists, colour-twists), or a mixture of the three, to give elaborate corkscrew patterns.

vari-baluster stem
A stem with balusters of varying sizes.

vetro a fili
Literally, threaded glass. A type of filigree decoration in which clear glass has a pattern in continuous uncrossing lines.

vetro a reticello
Literally, glass with a small network. A type of filigree decoration in which clear glass has a pattern of embedded threads in a diagonal, criss-crossing arrangement.

vetro a retorti
Literally, glass with twists. A type of filigree decoration in which intricately twisted threads are embedded in clear glass in parallel lines.

Waldglas
See forest glass.

Warzenbecher
A type of very heavy glass tumbler (literally, wart beaker), made of *Waldglas* and decorated with prunts, dating from the sixteenth and seventeenth centuries. They frequently bear an inscription in German on the top third of the glass.

wheel-engraving
The process of decorating glass by means of a rotating wheel which grinds a pattern or inscription into the glass surface.

wrythen
Decorated with swirling vertical ribbing to give a spiral effect.

weathering
The deterioration of glass (caused by exposure to adverse conditions) that may show in the form of iridescence or frosting.

Zwischengoldglas
Literally, gold between glass. A process used on Bohemian drinking glasses whereby engraved gold leaf applied to the outer surface of one glass was protected by being encased in another glass and sealed with resin.

BIBLIOGRAPHY

Aloi, R., *Vetri d'Oggi* (Ubrico Hoepli, 1955)
American Craft (American Craft Council, New York; bi-monthly)
Amic, Yolande, *L'Opaline française au XIXe siècle* (Librairie Gründ, Paris, 1952)
Art et Décoration: Revue Mensuelle d'Art Moderne (Librairie Centrale des Beaux-Arts, Paris, 1897 onwards)
Arts Council, *The Thirties: British Art & Design before the War*, exhibition catalogue (Arts Council, London, 1980)
Ash, Douglas (ed.), *Dictionary of British Antique Glass* (Pelham, London, 1978)
Ash, Douglas, *How to Identify English Drinking Glasses and Decanters, 1680-1830* (Bell, London, 1961)
Ashmolean Museum: *English Drinking Glasses in the Ashmolean Museum* (Ashmolean Museum, Oxford, 1977)
Auth, S. H., *Ancient Glass at the Newark Museum* (Newark Museum, New Jersey, 1976)

Bangert, Albrecht, *Glass: Art Nouveau and Art Deco* (Studio Vista, London, 1977)
Barag, D., 'Glass Pilgrim Vessels from Jerusalem', Parts I, II and III in *Journal of Glass Studies*, Vols 12 and 13 (Corning Museum of Glass, New York, 1970-71)
Barrelet, J., *La Verrerie en France de l'époque gallo-romaine à nos jours* (Paris, 1953)
Barrington-Haynes, E., *Glass Through the Ages* (Penguin Books, Harmondsworth, 1948)
Bate, Percy, *English Table Glass* (Charles Scribner's Sons, New York, 1905)
Baumgärtner, S., *Edles Altes Glas, Sammlung Heine* (Karlsruhe, 1971)
Beard, Geoffrey, *Modern Glass* (Studio Vista, 1968)
Bedford, J., *Bristol and Other Coloured Glass* (London, 1952)
Berckenhagen, E., *Berliner und Märkische Gläser* (Darmstadt, 1956)
Bernt, W., *Sprüche auf Alten* (Munich, 1928)
Billeter, E. G., *Objekte des Jugendstils* (Benteli Verlag, Berne, 1975)
Bles, Joseph, *Rare English Glasses of the Seventeenth and Eighteenth Centuries* (Houghton Mifflin Co., Boston, 1925)
Boesen, G., *Venetian Glass at Rosenborg* (Copenhagen, 1960) (English text)
Brinton, W., *European Glass* (1936)
British Museum, *Masterpieces of Glass: A Selection*, exhibition catalogue ed. by Harden, D. B. et al. (London, 1968)
Brozova, Jarmila, 'Bohemian Lithyalins and Friedrich Egermann' in *Journal of Glass Studies*, Vol. 23 (Corning Museum of Glass, New York, 1981)
Bucher, B., *Die Glassammlung des K. K. Osterreichischen Museums* (Vienna, 1888)
Buckley, Francis, *History of Old English Glass* (Dingwell-Rock, New York, 1925)
Buckley, Wilfred, *European Glass* (Ernest Benn, London, 1926)
Buckley, Wilfred, *Aert Schouman and the Glasses that He Engraved* (London, 1931)
Buckley, Wilfred, *Notes on Frans Greenwood and the Glasses that He Engraved* (Ernest Benn, London, 1930)
Buckley, Wilfred, *David Wolff and the Glasses that He Engraved* (Methuen, London, 1935)

Chambon, R., *L'Histoire de la Verrerie en Belgique du IIme siècle à nos jours* (Brussels, 1955)
Charleston, R. J., 'Glass of the High Medieval Period (12th to 15th Century)' in *Bulletin de L'Association Internationale pour L'Histoire du Verre*, No. 8, 1977-80
Charleston, R. J., 'Glass Furnaces Through the Ages' in *Journal of Glass Studies*, Vol. 20 (Corning Museum of Glass, New York, 1978)
Churchill, A., *A Coronation Exhibition of Royal, Historical, Political, and Social Glasses* (London, 1937)
Churchill, A., *Glass Notes* (London, 1940-56)
Constable – Maxwell Collection of Ancient Glass, catalogue (Sotheby, Parke, London, 1979)
Corning Museum of Glass, New York: *Glass Drinking Vessels from the Strauss Collection* (1955),
Glass 1959: A Special Exhibition of International Contemporary Glass, Czechoslovakian Glass 1350-1980,
New Glass: A Worldwide Survey,
Glass in the Ancient World: The Ray Winfield Smith Collection, a Special Exhibition (1957), and
Journal of Glass Studies
Cramp, R., 'Window Glass from the Monastic Site of Jarrow' in *Journal of Glass Studies*, Vol 17 (Corning Museum of Glass, New York, 1975)

Cramp, R., 'Decorated Window Glass and Millefiori from Monkwearmouth' in *The Antiquaries Journal*, Vol. 50 (2) (1970)
Crompton, Sidney (ed.), *English Glass* (Ward Lock, London, 1967)

Daum, Noël, *Daum – Maîtres Verriers* (Edita Denoël, Lausanne, 1980)
Davis, Derek C., *English Bottles and Decanters, 1650-1900* (World Publications, New York, 1972)
Dexel, W., *Glas, Werkstoff und Form* (Ravensburg, 1953)
Dillon, Edward, *Glass* (Methuen, London 1907)
Dreier, F. A., *Glaskunst in Hessen und Kassel* (Kassel, 1969)
Dreier, F. A., 'Glasveredelung in Venedig' in *3000 Jahre Glaskunst*, exhibition catalogue (Kunstmuseum, Lucerne, 1981)
Dudley Westropp, M., *see* Westropp

Egg, E., *Die Glasbrütten zu Hall und Innsbruck im 16 Jahrhunderts* (Innsbruck, 1962)
Eisn, G. A., assisted by Kochakji, F., *Glass*, 2 vols (New York, 1927)
Elville, E. M., *English and Irish Cut Glass 1750-1950* (Country Life, London, 1953)
Elville, E. M., *English Table Glass* (Country Life, London, 1951)
Elville, E. M., *The Collector's Dictionary of Glass* (Country Life, London, 1961)
Evison, V. I., 'Glass Cone Beakers of the "Kempston" Type' in *Journal of Glass Studies*, Vol 14 (Corning Museum of Glass, New York, 1972)
Evison, V. I., 'Germanic Glass Drinking Horns' in *Journal of Glass Studies*, Vol. 17 (Corning Museum of Glass, New York, 1975)

Fleming, J. A., *Scottish and Jacobite Glass* (Jackson Son & Co., Glasgow, 1938)
Fossing, P., *Glass Vessels before Glass-blowing* (Copenhagen, 1940)
Francis, Grant R., *Old English Drinking Glasses* (Herbert Jenkins, London, 1920)
Francis, Grant R., *Jacobite Drinking Glasses* (Harrison & Sons, London, 1925)
Frothingham, Alice W., *Spanish Glass* (Faber, London, 1964)
Frothingham, Alice W., *Barcelona Glass in Venetian Style* (Hispanic Society of America, New York, 1941)

Garner, Philippe, *Contemporary Decorative Arts from 1940 to the Present* (Facts on File Inc., New York, 1980)
Garner, Philippe, *Emile Gallé* (Academy Editions, London, 1976)
Gasparetto, A., *Il Vetro di Murano* (Venice, 1958)
Gelder, H. E. van, *Glas en Ceramiek* (Utrecht, 1955)
Glas Kunst 81 (Kassel, 1981)
Goldstein, Sidney M., Rakow, Leonard S., and Rakow, Juliette K., *Cameo Glass: Masterpieces from 2000 Years of Glassmaking* (Corning Museum of Glass, New York, 1982)
Goldstein, Sidney M., *Pre-Roman and Early Roman Glass in the Corning Museum of Glass* (Corning Museum of Glass, New York, 1979)
Grover, Ray and Lee, *Contemporary Art Glass* (Crown, New York, 1975)
Grover, Ray and Lee, *Carved and Decorated European Art Glass* (Charles E. Tuttle, Rutland, Vermont, 1970)

Han, Verena, 'The Origin and Style of Medieval Glass found in the Central Balkans' in *Journal of Glass Studies*, Vol. 17 (Corning Museum of Glass, New York, 1975)
Harden, D. B., Painter, K. S., Pinder-Wilson, R. H., and Tait, H., *Masterpieces of Glass: A Selection* (British Museum, London, 1968)
Harden, D. B., *Catalogue of Greek and Roman Glass in the British Museum: Vol. I: Core- and Rod-formed Vessels and Pendants and Mycenean Cast Objects* (British Museum, London, 1981)
Harden, D. B., 'Domestic Window Glass, Roman, Saxon, and Medieval' in *Studies in Building History*, ed. E. M. Jope (London, 1961)
Harden, D. B., 'Early Medieval Glass' in *Bulletin de l'Association Internationale pour l'Histoire du Verre*, No. 8 (Liège, 1977-80)
Harden, D. B., *Roman Glass from Karanis* (University of Michigan Press, Ann Arbor, 1936)
Harrison, M., *Victorian Stained Glass* (Barrie & Jenkins, London, 1980)
Hartshorne, A., *Old English Glasses* (Edward Arnold, London, 1897)
Heinemeyer, E., *Glas*, Katalogue des Kunstmuseums (Düsseldorf, 1966)
Hettes, K., *Venezianisches Glas aus Tschechoslowakischen Sammlung* (Prague, 1960)
Hollister, Paul, *The Encyclopedia of Glass Paperweights* (W. H. Allen, London, 1970)
Honey, William B., *Glass: A Handbook & Guide to the Victoria and Albert Museum Collection* (The Victoria and Albert Museum, London, 1946)
Hughes, George Bernard, *English Glass for the Collector* (Lutterworth, London, 1958)

Hughes, George Bernard, *English, Scottish and Irish Table Glass from the Sixteenth Century to 1820* (Batsford, London, 1956)
Hurst Vose, Ruth, *Glass* (Connoisseur Illustrated Guide Series, London, 1975)
Hurst Vose, Ruth, *Glass* (Collins Archaeology Series, London, 1980)

Isings, C., *Roman Glass from Dated Finds* (J. B. Wolters, Groningen, 1957)

Janneau, Guillaume, *Le Verre et l'Art de Marinot* (H. Floury, Paris, 1925)
Jansen, B., *Catalogus van Noord-en Zuid-nederlands Glas* (The Hague, 1962)
Jantzen, J., *Deutsches Glas aus Funf Jahrhunderten* (Düsseldorf, 1960)
Journal of Glass Studies, see Corning Museum of Glass

Kämpfer, Fritz, and Beyer, Klaus G., *Glass: A World History*, translated and revised by Edmund Launert (Studio Vista, London, 1966)
Kenyon, G. H., *The Glass Industry of the Weald (1350-1620)* (University Press, Leicester, 1967)
Kisa, A., *Das Glas im Altertume*, 3 vols (Leipzig, 1908)
Klesse, B., *Glas Kataloge des Kunstgewerbemuseums* (Cologne, 1963)
Klesse, B., *Glassammlung Helfried Krug*, Vol. I (Munich, 1965); Vol. II (Bonn, 1973)
Knittle, Rhea M., *Early American Glass* (The Century Company, New York, 1927)
Koch, Robert, *Louis C. Tiffany, Rebel in Glass* (Crown, New York, 1964)

Lalique: *Catalogue des Verreries de René Lalique* (René Lalique & Co., Paris, 1932)
Lalique, Marc and Marie-Claude, *Lalique par Lalique* (Edipop, Lausanne, 1977)
Lamm, C. J., *Das Glas von Samarra* (Berlin, 1928)
Lipp, F. C., *Bemalte Gläser* (Munich, 1974)

McKearin, George S. and Helen, *American Glass* (Crown, New York, 1948)
Mariacher, G., *Glass from Antiquity to the Renaissance*, trans. by Michael Cunningham (Hamlyn, London, 1970)
Mariacher, G., *Italian Blown Glass from Ancient Rome to Venice* (Thames & Hudson, London, 1961)
Mariacher, G., *Vetri del Cinquecento* (Milan, 1959)
Mentasti, Rosa Barovier, *Il Vetro Veneziano* (Electa, Milano, 1982)
Meyer-Hersig, E., *Der Nürnberger Glasschnitt des 17 Jahrhunderts* (Nuremberg, 1963)
Michaelova, O., *Spanish Glass in the Hermitage* (Leningrad, 1970)
Morris, B., *Victorian Table Glass and Ornaments* (Barrie & Jenkins, London, 1978)
Mosel, C., *Die Glas-Sammlung des Kestner-Museums* (Hanover, 1957)
Mostra Venezia, La, *Mille Anni di Arte del Vetro a Venezia* (Venice, 1982)
Municipal Museum of The Hague, *Old Glass* (The Hague, 1957)

Neuberg, F., *Ancient Glass* (London, 1962)
Neuwirth, Waltraud, *Das Glas des Jugendstils* (Prestel Verlag, Munich, 1973)
Newman, Harold, *An Illustrated Dictionary of Glass* (Thames & Hudson, London, 1977)
Northwood, John, II, *John Northwood – His Contribution to the Stourbridge Flint Glass Industry 1850-1902* (Mark & Moody, Stourbridge, 1958)

Oppenheim, A. Leo et al., *Glass and Glass-making in Ancient Mesopotamia* (Corning Museum of Glass, New York, 1970)

Pazaurek, G. E., *Die Gläsersammlung des Nordböhmischen Gewerbe-Museums in Reichenberg* (Leipzig, 1923)
Pazaurek, G. E., *Gläser der Empire und Biedermeierzeit* (Leipzig, 1923)
Pazaurek, G. E., *Kunstgläser der Gegenwart* (Klinkhardt & Biermann, Leipzig, 1925)
Perrot, P. N., *Three Great Centuries of Venetian Glass*, exhibition catalogue (Corning Museum of Glass, New York, 1958)
Polak, Ada, *Glass: its Makers and its Public* (Weidenfeld & Nicolson, London, 1975)
Polak, Ada, *Modern Glass* (Faber & Faber, London, 1962)
Poser, K. H., *Alte Trinkgläser in Schleswig-Holstein* (Neumünster, 1981)

Revi, Albert Christian, *Nineteenth-century Glass: Its Genesis and Development* (Thomas Nelson, Walton-on-Thames, Surrey, rev. ed. 1968)
Rosenthal, Leon, *La verrerie française depuis cinquante ans* (G. Vanoest, Paris and Brussels, 1927)
Ross, C., 'The Excise Tax and Cut Glass in England and Ireland 1800-1830' in *Journal of Glass Studies*, Vol. 24 (Corning Museum of Glass, New York, 1982)

Saldern, Axel von, *German Enamelled Glass* (Crown, New York, 1971)
Saldern, A. von, 'Glass finds at Gordion' in *Journal of Glass Studies,* Vol. I, pp. 22-49 (Corning Museum of Glass, New York, 1959)
Saldern, A. von, 'Mosaic Glass from Hasanalu, Marlik and Tell Al-Rimah' in *Journal of Glass Studies*, Vol. 8, pp. 9-25 (Corning Museum of Glass, New York, 1966)
Schlosser, I., *Das Alte Glas* (Brunswick, 1956)
Schlosser, I., *Venezianer Gläser*, exhibition catalogue (Vienna Museum of Applied Arts, 1951)
Schmidt, R., *Brandenburgische Gläser* (Berlin, 1914)
Schmidt, R., *Das Glas* (Berlin and Leipzig, 2nd ed., 1922)
Schmidt, R., *Die Gläser der Sammlung Mühsam* (Berlin, 1926)
Schmidt, R., 'Die venezianischen Emailgläser des XV and XVI Jahrhunderts', *Jahrbüch der Preussischen Kunstsammlungen*, No. 32 (1911)
Schrijver, E., *Glas en Kristal* (Bussum, 1961)
Schweiger, Werner J., *Wiener Werkstätte Kunst und Handwerk 1903-1932* (Ch. Brandstaetter, Vienna, 1928)
Shelkovnikov, B. A., 'Russian Glass from the 11th to the 17th Century' in *Journal of Glass Studies*, Vol. 8 (Corning Museum of Glass, New York, 1966)
Shelkovnikov, B. A., 'Russian Glass in the First Half of the Nineteenth Century' in *Journal of Glass Studies*, Vol. 6 (Corning Museum of Glass, New York, 1964)
Spillman, Jane S., *American and European Pressed Glass in the Corning Museum of Glass* (Corning Museum of Glass, New York, 1981)
Spillman, Jane S., and Farrar, E. S., *The Cut and Engraved Glass of Corning (1868-1940)* (Corning Museum of Glass, New York, 1977)
Stennett-Willson, R., *The Beauty of Modern Glass* (Studio Vista, London, 1958)
Stennett-Willson, R., *Modern Glass* (Studio Vista, London, 1968)
Strasser, R. von, *Masterpieces of Germanic Glass, 15th-19th Centuries* (Neenah, 1979)
Studio, The: An Illustrated Magazine of Fine & Applied Art (London, 1893 onwards)
Studio Yearbooks of Decorative Art (Studio Vista, London)

Tait, H., *The Golden Age of Venetian Glass* (exhibition catalogue) (British Museum, London, 1979)
Thorpe, W. A., *English Glass* (A. & C. Black Ltd., London, 3rd ed. 1961)
Thorpe, W. A., *A History of English and Irish Glass*, 2 vols (Hale, Cushman & Flint, Boston, 1929)
Toledo Museum of Glass, *Art in Glass* (Toledo, 1969)

Urbancova, J., 'Neo-Renaissance and Neo-Baroque Ornament on North Bohemian Engraved Glass' in *Journal of Glass Studies*, Vol. 23 (Corning Museum of Glass, New York, 1981)
Uresova, L., *Bohemian Glass* (London, 1965)

Victoria and Albert Museum, *Bohemian Glass*, exhibition catalogue (Victoria and Albert Museum, London, 1965)
Vintners, Worshipful Company of, *Drinking Vessels, Books, Documents, etc.*, exhibition catalogue (Vintners Hall, London, 1933)
Voronov, N., and Ruchuk, E., *Soviet Glass* (Aurora Art Publishers, 1973)

Wakefield, Hugh, *Nineteenth-century British Glass* (Faber, London, 1961)
Warren, Phelps, *Irish Glass* (Faber, London, 1970)
Warren, Phelps, 'Later Chinese Glass 1650-1900; in *Journal of Glass Studies*, Vol. 19 (Corning Museum of Glass, New York, 1977)
Watkins, Lura W., *American Glass and Glass-making* (Chanticleer Press, New York, 1953)
Weinberg, G. D., 'A Medieval Mystery: Byzantine Glass Production' in *Journal of Glass Studies*, Vol. 17 (Corning Museum of Glass, New York, 1975)
Weiss, G., *The Book of Glass* (Barrie & Jenkins, London, 1971)
Weiss, G., *Ullstein Gläserbuch* (Frankfurt/Berlin, 1966)
Wenzel, M., 'A Reconsideration of Bosnian Medieval Glass' in *Journal of Glass Studies*, Vol. 19 (Corning Museum of Glass, New York, 1977)
Westropp, Michael Dudley, *Irish Glass* (J. B. Lippincott Company, Philadelphia, 1920)
Whitehouse, David, 'Notes on Late Medieval Glass in Italy' in *Annales du 8ᵉ Congrès International de L'Étude Historique du Verre* (Liège, 1981)
Wills, G., *English and Irish Glass*, 16 parts (Guinness Signatures, London, 1968)
Wolfenden I. G., *English 'Rock Crystal' Glass 1878-1925*, exhibition catalogue (Dudley Art Gallery, 1976)

Young, S., *A History of the Worshipful Company of Glass Sellers of London* (London, 1913)

INDEX
Numbers in italics refer to captions of illustrations

ACKNOWLEDGMENTS

The Publishers would like to express their gratitude to Victor Arwas (Editions Graphiques, London), Lewis P. Caplan, Mrs Raymond Chambon, Noël Daum, Dr Attilia Dorigato (Museo Vetrario di Murano), Richard Gray (City Art Gallery, Manchester), Martin Kunz (Kunstmuseum, Lucerne), Martin Mortimer (Delomosne and Son Ltd.), Priscilla Price (Corning Museum of Glass, Corning, New York), Maureen Thompson, Marion Wenzel, and Pam Wood (Nottingham Castle Museum).

Museums and Art Galleries
Ars Antiqua Art Ancien S.A., Geneva, 10; Metropolitan Borough of Barnsley, 170; Bauhaus-Archiv, Berlin, 237; The Bede Monastery Museum, Jarrow Hall, 44; Bibliothèque Royale Albert Ier, Brussels, 42 top; by courtesy of Birmingham Museums and Art Gallery, Birmingham, 91; by courtesy of the Trustees of the British Museum, London, 12 top left and right, 14, 16, 19, 25 (purchased with funds bequeathed by James Rose Vallentin), 26 and 28 bottom (Felix Slade bequest), 41, 42 bottom, 43 top, 62, 76, 77 bottom, 78 top, 79, 80 top, 102 left, 104, 187; Broadfield House Glass Museum, Dudley, 168, 172, 178 bottom, 179, 181, 188, 190, 191 bottom, 193, 194, 196, 197; Cathedral Treasury, Halberstadt, 55 top; The Corning Museum of Glass, Corning, New York, 38, 54 bottom, 55 bottom, 59, 73, 89, 135, 144, 156, 158, 165 right, 166 left, 185 left, 256 top; The Corning Museum of Glass Exhibition (Catalogue) *Czechoslovakian Glass 1350-1980*, 99 top, 122 bottom, 173 top, 174 top, 256 bottom, 271 bottom; Darmstadt Museum, Darmstadt 48; Dommuseum, Chur, 68; Editions Graphiques (Victor Arwas Collection), 3 Clifford Street, London W1, 198, 210; Essener Glasgalerie, Esse-Rüttenscheid, 262; by courtesy of the Trustees of the Cecil Higgins Art Gallery and Museum of the Decorative Arts, Bedford, 150 top; courtesy of the Hispanic Society of America, New York, 87, 88; Iittala Museum of Glass, Iittala, 246 bottom; The Israel Museum, Jerusalem, 29 (Shrine of the Book); Galerie Wolfgang Ketterer, Munich, 212 top, 216 top; Khartoum Museum, Khartoum, 33 top right; Kölnisches Stadtmuseum, Cologne, 124 right; Kunstgewerbemuseum der Stadt Köln, Cologne, 83 bottom left; Kunsthistorisches Museum, Vienna, 85; Kunstmuseum, Düsseldorf, 43 bottom, 46; Kunstmuseum, Lucerne, Exhibition (Catalogue) *3000 Jahre Glaskunst*, 27, 28 top, 30, 32 top, 33 top left, 36, 58, 60, 61, 68, 100 left; City of Manchester Art Galleries, Manchester, 184, 207 top; Merseyside County Museums, 130; The Metropolitan Museum of Art, New York, 66 (Rogers Fund), 81 right (Gift of Henry G. Marquand), 208 (Collection of Morse Gallery of Art, Winter Park, Florida, by courtesy of the Charles Hosmer Morse Foundation); Municipal Museum, Prague, 86; Musée de Cluny, Paris, 82 bottom; Musée de l'Ecole de Nancy, Nancy, 200; Musée Départemental des Antiquités, Rouen, 47 top; Musée des Arts Décoratifs, Paris, 142, 259 top; Musée des Beaux-Arts et de la Céramique, Rouen, 143; Musées Nationaux, Paris, 40; Museo Civico, Locarno, 28 top; Museo del Castello Sforzesco, Milan, 70 right; Museo Provinciale D'Arte, Trento, 71; Museo Vetrario di Murano, Venice, 69, 78 bottom, 90 bottom, 120; Museos de Artes Decorativas, Barcelona (Plandiura Collection), 112; Museum Für Kunst und Gewerbe, Hamburg, 165 left; Museum of Decorative Arts, Prague, 81 left, 92, 94, 97 left, 99 top, 100 right, 121 bottom, 122 bottom, 123, 124 left, 125 bottom, 157, 164, 166 right, 173, 174, 175, 176, 202 right; National Museum of Ireland, Dublin, 149, 152; Nationalmuseum, Stockholm, 103 right; Galerie Nefer, Zurich, 32 top; Nottingham Castle Museum, Nottingham, 183, 185 right; Palazzo Rezzonico, Venice, 119 top; Pilkington Glass Museum, St Helens, 108, 159, 160 left, 212 bottom (Gift of G. McKinley, 1974); Rijksmuseum, Amsterdam, 102 right, 162; Rosenborg Castle, Copenhagen, 118; by courtesy of the Office of the Shōsō-in Treasure-house, Nara-ken, 64 bottom, 65 top; SM-Galerie, Frankfurt, 266 (Dick Busher), 268; Staatliche Museen Preussischer Kulturbesitz, Berlin, 64 top; Tokyo National Museum, Tokyo, 65 bottom; The Toledo Museum of Art, Toledo, Ohio, 11 top, 12-13 bottom, 15, Gifts of Edward Drummond Libbey 17, 18, 20, Gifts of Edward Drummond Libbey 21, 22, 23, 24, 31, 32 bottom, 33 bottom, Gifts of Edward Drummond Libbey 34, 35 right, 35 left, 37, Gifts of Edward Drummond

Libbey 52, 70 left, Gift of Florence Scott Libbey 80 bottom, Gifts of Edward Drummond Libbey 107 left, 109, 161, Gift of Mrs G. A. Morison and Dorothy-Lee Jones 171, Gift of Edward Drummond Libbey 182, Gift of Edward Drummond Libbey, Mr and Mrs Joseph S. Riegel and Mrs C. Duckworth 192, Gift of William Donovan, through Dorothy Donovan Farrell and Alexander K. Liddell and Mrs Christian Dewar 195 bottom; Treasury of St Mark's, Venice, 54 top, 56; The Victoria and Albert Museum, London, 77 top, 103 left, 111, 127 right, 139, 140, 147, 153 right, 167, 180, 223 bottom, 235; Wadsworth Atheneum, Hartford, 148-9 (Bequest of Miss Ellen A. Jarvis); reproduced by permission of the Trustees of the Wallace Collection, London, 63, 82 top, 83 bottom; Winchester City Museum, Winchester, 47 bottom; Zavičajni Muzej, Trebinje, 53.

We would like to thank the following for lending us their materials: Archivio IGDA, 158; Archivio IGDA/M. Carrieri, 8, 33 top right, 70 right; Archivio IGDA/G. Dagli Orti, 57, 110; Archivio IGDA/F. Ferruzzi, 54 top, 119 top; Archivio IGDA/C. Sappa, 50; Bavaria-Verlag, Gauting, 55 top, 237; Hans L. Benzian Collection, Switzerland, 27, 30; Fritz Biemann, Zurich, 121 top, 160 right; Bridgeman Art Library, London, 131, 132-3, 134-5; Buchecker-Collection, Lucerne, 100 left, 122 top, 125 top; Lewis P. Caplan, London, 2, 249, 251, 252 top, 255, 259 bottom; John Carson, 106, 126, 127 left, 128 top, 129, 132 left; Raymond Chambon Collection, Marcinelle, 90 top; Christie, Manson and Woods Ltd., London, 95, 96, 97 right, 98, 99 bottom, 101, 207 bottom; Cinzano (UK) Ltd., London, 137, 163; Noël Daum Collection, Paris, 204, 205, 206, 228 top; Franco Deboni Collection, Arch. Deboni, S. Croce, 84, Venice, 232 top; Delomosne and Son Ltd., London, 150, 153 left, 155; Erwin Eisch Collection, Frankenau, 264; L. Garner Collection, London, 178 top, 191 top, 200, 201, 202 left, 203, 220, 222, 223 top, 224, 225, 226, 227, 228 bottom, 229, 230, 231 right, 233, 234 bottom, 236 bottom, 238 top, 239, 240 top; Sam Herman, London, 242; Pavel Hlava, Czechoslovakia, 256 bottom; Wolfgang Hoyt/ESTO, 244; Kagami Crystal Glass Works Ltd., Tokyo, 261; Dan Klein Collection, London, 216 bottom, 217, 218, 248, 252 bottom; Kofler-Truniger Collection, Lucerne, 36; Marvin Lipofsky, Berkeley, 263; J&L Lobmeyr, Vienna, 234 top; Jeremy Marks, Woodmansterne Ltd./The National Trust, 151; Mas, Barcelona, 45 (Macaya Collection); *Masterpieces of Industrial Art and Sculpture At The International Exhibition 1862*, by J. B. Waring (plate 51), 186; Joel Philip Myers, Bloomington, 267 right; National Monuments Record, London, 241; The National Trust, Erdigg Hall, 107 right; The National Trust, Waddesdon Manor, Aylesbury, Buckinghamshire, 6; Orrefors Glasbruk, Orrefors, 231 left; private collection, Frankfurt, 58, 60, 61; private collection, London, 132-3, 134-5, 253, 260, 267 left, 269, 270; private collection, Germany, 33 top left; Rheinisches Bildarchiv, Cologne, 83 bottom left, 124 right; RIBA, London, 238 bottom, 240 bottom; Rosenthal China Ltd., London, 246 top; Scala, Florence, 56; Sig. Livio Seguso, C. L. Brussa Murano, Venice, 254; Sotheby, Parke Bernet & Co., London, 74, 77, 83 top left, 84, 105, 119 bottom, 136, 211, 232 bottom; Steuben Glass, New York, 236, 247; Maureen Thompson, Long Melford, 116, 154; Union Internationale Des Télécommunicatons, Geneva, 250; František Vízner, Czechoslovakia, 271; Wear Glassworks, Sunderland, 245.

We would also like to thank these photographers for their help:
Robert Baumann, Lucerne, 30, 33 top left, 36, 60, 61, 68, 100 left, 122 top, 125 top, 213; Milan Blecha, Prague, 215; A. C. Cooper Ltd., London, 154 right; Philip de Bay, London, 140; Cris Haigh, Barnsley, 170; Sonia Halliday, 44, 48, 49, 113, 114, 115, 189; Richard Holt, London, 126 right, 128 top, 217; Angelo Hornak, London, 77 top, 139, 168, 172 top, 177, 179, 181, 188, 190, 191 bottom, 193, 194, 196, 197, 198, 210, 219, 223 bottom, 242, 253, 265, 267 left, 269, 270; J. Koch, Lucerne, 27, 28 top, 32 top; B. Naesby, Copenhagen, 118; L. Sully-Jaulmes, 142; Rodney Todd-White & Son, London, 132 left; Paul Williams, London, front cover, 2, 106, 116, 126 left, 127 left, 129, 249; Gabriel Urbánek, Prague, 258.